Sixth SIGHAN Workshop on Chinese Language Processing

(IJCNLP 2008)

Hyderabad, India
11-12 January 2008

ISBN: 978-1-62748-365-0

Printed from e-media with permission by:

Curran Associates, Inc.
57 Morehouse Lane
Red Hook, NY 12571

Some format issues inherent in the e-media version may also appear in this print version.

Printed by Curran Associates, Inc. (2013)

For permission requests, please contact the Association for Computational Linguistics at the address below.

Association for Computational Linguistics
209 N. Eighth Street
Stroudsburg, Pennsylvania 18360

Phone: 1-570-476-8006
Fax: 1-570-476-0860

acl@aclweb.org

Additional copies of this publication are available from:

Curran Associates, Inc.
57 Morehouse Lane
Red Hook, NY 12571 USA
Phone: 845-758-0400
Fax: 845-758-2634
Email: curran@proceedings.com
Web: www.proceedings.com

Preface

Welcome to Hyderabad for the Sixth SIGHAN Workshop on Chinese Language Processing! As the workshop co-chairs, we are indeed honored to pen the first few words in the SIGHAN-6 proceedings. Over the last few years, exciting research endeavors in Chinese language processing have been pursued vigorously all over the world. We feel privileged to be able to chair the Sixth SIGHAN, particularly at this juncture in our history when the Chinese language is receiving worldwide attention which places us at an important period of growth and change.

SIGHAN-6 received 14 regular paper submissions this year, 9 of which are accepted for presentation, contributing to yet another stimulating and inspiring scientific program. We would like to thank all the authors who submitted their research work, and all the reviewers who have put an immense amount of timely and quality work into the paper review. We would also like to express our gratitude and appreciation to the chair of SIGHAN, Prof. Benjamin Tsou, who has led SIGHAN to what it is today, especially for his invaluable advice at various stages of the development of SIGHAN-6.

Our workshop also uniquely features the Fourth International Chinese Language Processing Bakeoff, which was jointly held with the First CIPS Chinese Language Processing Evaluation over the summer of 2007. In addition to the classic Chinese word segmentation and named entity recognition tasks, there is a new track on Chinese POS-tagging. The bakeoff was co-organized by SIGHAN, ChineseLDC, and the Verifying Center on Chinese Language and Character Standards of the State Language Commission of PRC, and coordinated by Dr. Guangjin Jin of the Institute of Applied Linguistics, MOE, China. Special thanks to Dr. Jin and the bakeoff organizing committee for organizing another successful bakeoff. The generous support from the benchmarking corpora providers (Academia Sinica; City University of Hong Kong; Institute of Applied Linguistics, MOE, China; Microsoft Research Asia; Peking University; Shanxi University; and University of Colorado) is greatly appreciated. Certainly the bakeoff cannot stand without the support from the 28 participating teams. We have collected 23 bakeoff system reports in this volume.

SIGHAN-6 marks its second time to co-locate with IJCNLP, the flagship conference of the Asian Federation of Natural Language Processing. The organization of our workshop will not be so smooth without all the logistic support from the IJCNLP-08 committee, particularly the Workshop Committee, the Publication Chair Dr. Jing-Shin Chang, as well as everyone in the Local Organizing Committee. To them we would like to express our heartiest gratitude.

Last but not least, thank you for your active participation. Enjoy our program, and we wish you an educational and entertainment-filled experience in Hyderabad.

Olivia Oi Yee Kwong and Haizhou Li
November 2007

Organizers

Workshop Co-Chairs:

Olivia Oi Yee Kwong, City University of Hong Kong
Haizhou Li, Institute for Infocomm Research

Bakeoff Organizing Committee:

Guangjin Jin, Institute of Applied Linguistics, MOE, PRC (Co-ordinator)
Xiao Chen, City University of Hong Kong
Yongsheng Guo, Institute of Applied Linguistics, MOE, PRC
Changning Huang, Microsoft Research Asia
Qun Liu, Chinese Academy of Sciences

Program Committee:

Keh-Jiann Chen, Academia Sinica
Minghui Dong, Institute for Infocomm Research
Jianfeng Gao, Microsoft
Chu-Ren Huang, Academia Sinica
Xuanjing Huang, Fudan University
Donghong Ji, Wuhan University
Daniel Jurafsky, Stanford University
Chunyu Kit, City University of Hong Kong
Kui-Lam Kwok, Queens College
Gina-Anne Levow, University of Chicago
Dekang Lin, Google
Qun Liu, Chinese Academy of Sciences
Qin Lu, Hong Kong Polytechnic University
Qing Ma, Ryukoku University
Jianyun Nie, University of Montreal
Hwee Tou Ng, National University of Singapore
Martha Palmer, University of Colorado
Scott Piao, University of Manchester
Richard Sproat, University of Illinois at Urbana-Champaign
Keh-Yih Su, Behavior Design Corporation
Maosong Sun, Tsinghua University
Bing Swen, Peking University
Benjamin Tsou, City University of Hong Kong
Haifeng Wang, Toshiba (China) R&D Center
Kam-Fai Wong, Chinese University of Hong Kong
Dekai Wu, Hong Kong University of Science and Technology
Yujie Zhang, National Institute of Information and Communications Technology of Japan
Jun Zhao, Chinese Academy of Sciences

Tiejun Zhao, Harbin Institute of Technology
Ming Zhou, Microsoft Research Asia
Jingbo Zhu, Northeastern University

Additional Reviewers:

Xiangyu Duan, Chinese Academy of Sciences
Wei Gao, Chinese University of Hong Kong
Shiqi Li, Harbin Institute of Technology
Nianwen Xue, University of Colorado
Yongzheng Xue, Harbin Institute of Technology

Workshop Program

Friday, 11 January 2008

09:00–09:10 Opening Remarks

Session 1: Translation and Transliteration

09:10–09:35 *An Example-based Decoder for Spoken Language Machine Translation*
Zhou-Jun Li, Wen-Han Chao and Yue-Xin Chen

09:35–10:00 *Automatic Extraction of English-Chinese Transliteration Pairs using Dynamic Window and Tokenizer*
Chengguo Jin, Seung-Hoon Na, Dong-Il Kim and Jong-Hyeok Lee

10:00–10:25 *Mining Transliterations from Web Query Results: An Incremental Approach*
Jin-Shea Kuo, Haizhou Li and Chih-Lung Lin

10:25–11:00 Break

Session 2: Information Extraction and Word Sense Disambiguation

11:00–11:25 *An Effective Hybrid Machine Learning Approach for Coreference Resolution*
Feiliang Ren and Jingbo Zhu

11:25–11:50 *Use of Event Types for Temporal Relation Identification in Chinese Text*
Yuchang Cheng, Masayuki Asahara and Yuji Matsumoto

11:50–12:15 *Chinese Word Sense Disambiguation with PageRank and HowNet*
Jinghua Wang, Jianyi Liu and Ping Zhang

12:15–14:15 Lunch

Friday, 11 January 2008 (continued)

Session 3: Word Segmentation and Parsing

14:15–14:40 *Stochastic Dependency Parsing Based on A* Admissible Search*
Bor-shen Lin

14:40–15:05 *Analyzing Chinese Synthetic Words with Tree-based Information and a Survey on Chinese Morphologically Derived Words*
Jia Lu, Masayuki Asahara and Yuji Matsumoto

15:05–15:30 *Which Performs Better on In-Vocabulary Word Segmentation: Based on Word or Character?*
Zhenxing Wang, Changning Huang and Jingbo Zhu

15:30–16:00 Break

Session 4: Bakeoff Overview and Presentations

16:00–16:20 *The Fourth International Chinese Language Processing Bakeoff: Chinese Word Segmentation, Named Entity Recognition and Chinese POS Tagging*
Guangjin Jin and Xiao Chen

16:20–16:40 *A Two-Stage Approach to Chinese Part-of-Speech Tagging*
Aitao Chen, Ya Zhang and Gordon Sun

16:40–17:00 *NOKIA Research Center Beijing Chinese Word Segmentation System for the SIGHAN Bakeoff 2007*
Jiang Li, Rile Hu, Guohua Zhang, Yuezhong Tang, Zhanjiang Song and Xia Wang

17:00–17:20 *Chinese Word Segmentation and Named Entity Recognition Based on Conditional Random Fields*
Xinnian Mao, Yuan Dong, Saike He, Sencheng Bao and Haila Wang

Saturday, 12 January 2008

Session 5: Bakeoff Presentations

09:10–09:30 *BUPT Systems in the SIGHAN Bakeoff 2007*
Ying Qin, Caixia Yuan, Jiashen Sun and Xiaojie Wang

09:30–09:50 *The Character-based CRF Segmenter of MSRA&NEU for the 4th Bakeoff*
Zhenxing Wang, Changning Huang and Jingbo Zhu

09:50–10:10 *Chinese NER Using CRFs and Logic for the Fourth SIGHAN Bakeoff*
Xiaofeng Yu, Wai Lam, Shing-Kit Chan, Yiu Kei Wu and Bo Chen

10:10–10:30 *Unsupervised Segmentation Helps Supervised Learning of Character Tagging for Word Segmentation and Named Entity Recognition*
Hai Zhao and Chunyu Kit

10:30–11:00 Break

11:00–12:30 SIGHAN Business Meeting

Table of Contents

An Example-based Decoder for Spoken Language Machine Translation

Zhou-Jun Li
National Laboratory for Parallel and Distributed Processing, Changsha, China
School of Computer Science and Engineering, Beihang University, China
lizj@buaa.edu.cn

Wen-Han Chao
National Laboratory for Parallel and Distributed Processing, Changsha, China
cwh2k@163.com

Yue-Xin Chen
National Laboratory for Parallel and Distributed Processing, Changsha, China

Abstract

In this paper, we propose an example-based decoder for a statistical machine translation (SMT) system, which is used for spoken language machine translation. In this way, it will help to solve the re-ordering problem and other problems for spoken language MT, such as lots of omissions, idioms etc. Through experiments, we show that this approach obtains improvements over the baseline on a Chinese-English spoken language translation task.

1 Introduction

The state-of-the-art statistical machine translation (SMT) model is the log-linear model (Och and Ney, 2002), which provides a framework to incorporate any useful knowledge for machine translation, such as translation model, language model etc.

In a SMT system, one important problem is the re-ordering between words and phrases, especially when the source language and target language are very different in word order, such as Chinese and English.

For the spoken language translation, the re-ordering problem will be more crucial, since the spoken language is more flexible in word order. In addition, lots of omissions and idioms make the translation more difficult.

However, there exists some "useful" features, such as, most of the spoken text is shorter than the written text and there are some fixed translation structures. For example, (你能…? / Would you please … ?), (能…?/May I…?).

We can learn these fixed structures and take them as rules, Chiang (2005) presents a method to learn these rules, and uses them in the SMT. Generally, the number of these rules will be very large. In this paper, we propose an example-based decoder in a SMT model, which will use the translation examples to keep the translation structure, i.e. constraint the reordering, and make the omitted words having the chance to be translated.

The rest of this paper is organized as follows: Since our decoder is based on the inversion transduction grammars (ITG) (Wu, 1997), we introduce the ITG in Section 2 and describe the derived SMT model. In Section 3, we design the example-based decoder. In Section 4, we test our model and compare it with the baseline system. Then, we conclude in Section 5 and Section 6.

2 The SMT model

ITG is a synchronous context-free grammar, which generates two output streams simultaneously. It consists of the following five types of rules:

$$A \xrightarrow{p} [AA] \mid \langle AA \rangle \mid c_i / e_j \mid c_i / \varepsilon \mid \varepsilon / e_j \qquad (1)$$

Where A is the non-terminal symbol, [] and <> represent the two operations which generate outputs in **straight** and **inverted** orientation respectively. c_i and e_j are terminal symbols, which represent the words in both languages, ε is the null words. The last three rules are called lexical rules. p is the probability of the rule.

In this paper, we consider the phrase-based SMT, so the c_i and e_j represent phrases in both languages, which are consecutive words. And a pair of c_i and e_j is called a phrase-pair, or a **block**.

During the process of decoding, each phrase c_i in the source sentence is translated into a target phrase e_j through lexical rules, and then rules [] or <> are used to merge two adjacent blocks into a larger block in straight or inverted orientation, until the whole source sentence is covered. In this way, we will obtain a binary branching tree, which is different from the traditional syntactical tree, since each constituent in the branching tree is not a syntactical constituent.

Thus, the model achieves a great flexibility to interpret almost arbitrary reordering during the decoding, while keeping a weak but effective constraint. Figure 1(a) gives an example to illustrate a derivation from the ITG model.

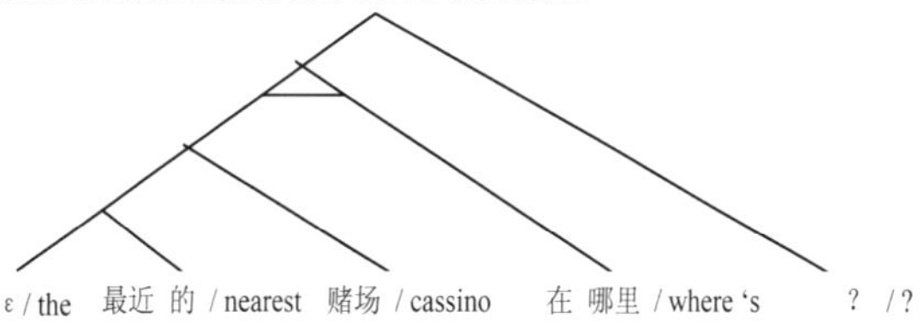

(a) An ITG tree

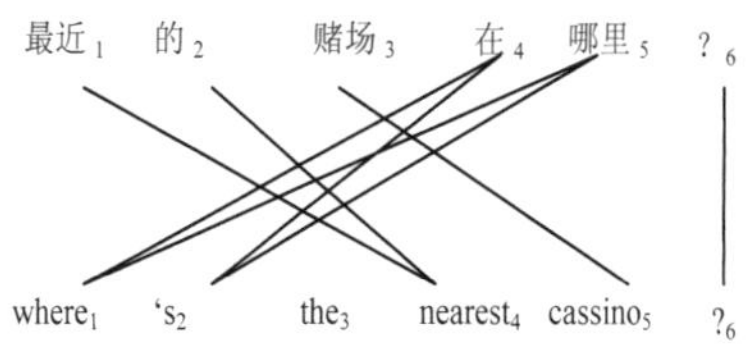

(b) A word alignment

Figure 1. (a) An ITG tree derived from the ITG where the line between the branches means an inverted orientation, otherwise a straight one, (b) A word alignment corresponds to the ITG tree in (a).

Since we regard the process of the decoding as a sequence of applications of rules in (1), i.e., the output sentence pair (*C*,*E*) will be a derivation *D* of the ITG, where *C* represents the source sentence and *E* is the target sentence.

Following Och and Ney (2002), we define the probability for each rule as:

$$\Pr(rule) = \prod_i h_i(rule)^{\lambda_i} \tag{2}$$

Where the h_i represents the feature and λ_i is the corresponding weight of the feature.

We will consider mainly the following features for rules:

- Translation Models: $P(e|c)$, $P(c|e)$, $P_{lex}(e|c)$ and $P_{lex}(c|e)$. The first two models consider the probability of phrase translation; and the latter two consider the lexical translation, i.e., the probability that the words in source (or target) phrase translate to the ones in the target (or source) phrase.
- Reordering model: $P(o|b_1,b_2)$, where o is the output orientation and b_1, b_2 are the two blocks in the rule.
- Language model: $\Delta \Pr_{lm}(e)$, which considers the increment of the language model for each rule.

And the probability for the derivation will be:

$$\Pr(D) = \prod_{r \in D} \Pr(r) \tag{3}$$

So the decoder searches the best *E** derived from the best derivation *D**, when given a source sentence *C*.

$$D^* = \mathop{\arg\max}_{c(D)=C} \Pr(D) \tag{4}$$

2.1 Building the models

In our SMT model, we use the translation models and reordering model. They will be built from the training corpus, which is a word-aligned bilingual corpus satisfying the ITG constraint.

We define the word alignment *A* for the sentence pair (*C*,*E*) in the following ways:

- A region $(i..j, s..t)$: $i..j$ represents a sequence of position index in sentence *C*, i.e. $i, i+1, ..., j$ and $s..t$ represents a sequence of position index in sentence *E*, i.e. $s, s+1, ..., t$. We also call the $i..j$ and $s..t$ are regions in monolingual sentences. The region corresponds to a phrase pair, which we called as a block. The length of the block is $\max(|j-i+1|, |t-s+1|)$.

- A link $l = (i..j, s..t)$: And each link represents the alignment between the consecutive words in both of the sentences, which position indexes are in $i..j$ and $s..t$. If one of the $i..j$ and $s..t$ is ε, i.e. an empty region, we call the link a null-align.
- A word alignment A: a set of links $A = \{l_1, l_2, ..., l_n\}$.

We can merge two links $l_1 = (i_1..j_1, s_1..t_1)$ and $l_2 = (i_2..j_2, s_2..t_2)$ to form a larger link, if the two links are adjacent in both of the sentences, i.e. $i_1..j_1$ is adjacent to $i_2..j_2$ where $i_2 = j_1 + 1$ or $i_1 = j_2 + 1$, or $i_1..j_1$ (or $i_2..j_2$) is ε, so do the $s_1..t_1$ to $s_2..t_2$. If the region $(i..j, s..t)$ can be formed by merging two adjacent links gradually, we call the region is independent, and the corresponding block is also independent.

In our system, the word alignment must satisfy the ITG constraint, i.e. the word alignment is able to form a binary branching tree. Figure 1(b) illustrates a word alignment example; the number below the word is the position index. In the example, the region (1..3, 3..5) is independent, and the block (*最近 的 赌场, the nearest cassino*) is also independent.

In order to obtain the word alignment satisfying the ITG constraint, Wu(1997) propose a DP algorithm, and we (Chao and Li, 2007) have transferred the constraint to four simple position judgment procedures in an explicit way, so that we can incorporate the ITG constraint as a feature into a log-linear word alignment model (Moore, 2005).

After obtaining the word-aligned corpus, in which each word alignment satisfy the ITG constraint, we can extract the blocks in a straightforward way. For the word alignment forms a hierarchical binary tree, we choose each constituent as a block. Each block is formed by combining one or more links, and must be independent. Considering the data sparseness, we limit the length of each block as N (here N=3~5).

We can also collect the reordering information between two blocks according to the orientation of the branches.

Thus, we will build the translation models $P(e|c)$, $P(c|e)$, $P_{lex}(e|c)$ and $P_{lex}(c|e)$, using the frequencies of the blocks, and the re-ordering model $P(o|b_1, b_2)$, $o \in \{straight, invert\}$ in the following way:

$$p(o|b_1,b_2) = \frac{\text{freq. of } (O(b_1,b_2) = o)}{\text{freq. of } cooccur(b_1,b_2)} \quad (5)$$

Considering the data sparseness, we transfer the re-ordering model in the following way:

$$p(o|b_1,b_2) = p(o|b_1,*) \bullet p(o|*,b_2) \quad (6)$$

where * represents any block, $p(o|b_1,*)$ represents the probability when $O(b_1,*) = o$, i.e., when b_1 occurs, the orientation it merges with any other block is o. So we can estimate the merging orientation through the two blocks respectively.

2.2 A Baseline Decoder

In order to evaluate the example-based decoder, we develop a CKY style decoder as a baseline (Chao et al. 2007), which will generate a derivation from the ITG in a DP way. And it is similar with the topical phrase-based SMT system, while maintaining the ITG constraint.

3 The Example-based Decoder

The SMT obtains the translation models during training, and does not need the training corpus when decoding; while the example-based machine translation system (EBMT) using the similar examples in the training corpus when decoding.

However, both of them use the same corpus; we can generate a hybrid MT, which is a SMT system while using an example-based decoder, to benefit from the advantages within the two systems.

Our example-based decoder consists of two components: retrieval of examples and decoding. Figure 2 shows the structure of the decoder.

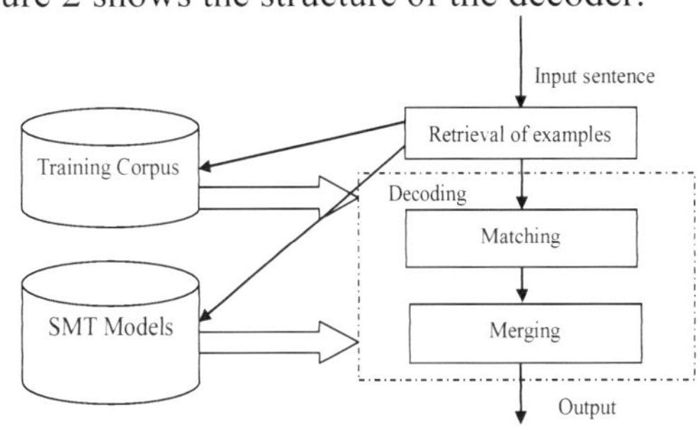

Figure 2. The structure of the example-based decoder.

3.1 Retrieval of Examples

Our training corpus is a sentence-aligned bilingual corpus. For each sentence pair (*C,E*), we obtained the word alignment *A*, satisfying the ITG constaint through the methods described in section 2. We call the triple (*C,A,E*) as an example.

So, the problem of retrieval of examples is: given the input source sentence C_0 and the training corpus, collecting a set of translation examples {(C_1, A_1, E_1) , (C_2, TA_2, E_2),....} from the corpus, where each translation example (C_i, A_i, E_i) is similar to the input sentence C_0.

The quality of the retrieval of the similar examples is very import to the hybrid MT. For the translating may run in a large-scale corpus and in a real-time way, we divide the retrieval of similar examples into two phases:

- Fast Retrieval Phase: retrieving the similar examples from the corpus quickly, and take them as candidates. The complexity should not be too high.
- Refining Phase: refining the candidates to find the most similar examples.

3.1.1 The Similarity Metric for Fast Retrieval

Given an input sentence $I = w_1 w_2 ... w_n$ and an example (*C*, *A*, *E*), we calculate the number of the matched source words between the input sentence and the source sentence *C* in the example firstly.

$$Sim_w(I, Exam) = \frac{2 * Match_w}{Len(I) + Len(C, A, E)} \quad (7)$$

where $Match_w$ is the number of the matched words and $Len(I)$ is the number of words in I, and $Len(C,A,E)$ is the number of the words in the in C.

Given an input sentence $I = w_1 w_2 ... w_n$, we obtain the relative blocks in the translation model for each word $w_i (i \in \{1,2,...n\}$. We use B^i_{k-gram} to represent the blocks, in which for each block (c,e), the source phrase c use the word w_i as the first word, and the length of c is k, i.e. the $c = w_{i..(i+k-1)}$. For each c, there may exists more than one blocks with c as the source phrase, so we will sort them by the probability and keep the best N (here set N=5) blocks. Now we represent the input sentence as:

$$\sigma(I) = \{b \mid b \in B^i_{k-gram}, 1 \le i \le n, 1 \le k \le n\} \quad (8)$$

For example, in an input sentence "我 来自 中国", $B^1_{1-gram} = \{(我, i), (我, me), (我, my), (我, Mine)\}$

Note, some B^i_{k-gram} may be empty, e.g. $B^2_{2-gram} = \phi$, since no blocks with "来自 中国" as the source phrase.

In the same way, we represent the example (C, A, E) as:

$$\varphi(C, A, E) = \{b \mid b \in B^i_{k-gram}, b \in A^*\} \quad (9)$$

where A^* represents the blocks which are links in the alignment A or can be formed by merging adjacent links independently. In order to accelerate the retrieval of similar examples, we generate the block set for the example during the training process and store them in the corpus.

Now, we can use the number of the matched blocks to measure the similarity of the input and the example:

$$Sim_b(I, Exam) = \frac{2 * Match_b}{B^I_{gram} + B^{Exam}_{gram}} \quad (10)$$

where $Match_b$ is the number of the matched blocks and B^I_{gram} is the number of B^i_{k-gram} ($B^i_{k-gram} \ne \phi$) in $\sigma(I)$, and B^{Exam}_{gram} is the number of the blocks in $\varphi(C, A, E)$.

Since each block is attached a probability, we can compute the similarity in the following way:

$$Sim_p(I, Exam) = \frac{2 * \sum_{b \in Match_b} \Pr ob(b)}{B^I_{gram} + B^{Exam}_{gram}} \quad (11)$$

So the final similarity metric for fast retrieval of the candidates is:

$$Sim_{fast}(I, Exam) = \alpha Sim_w + \beta Sim_b + \gamma Sim_p \quad (12)$$

where $0 \le \alpha, \beta, \gamma \le 1 \quad \alpha + \beta + \gamma = 1$. Here we use mean values, i.e. $\alpha = \beta = \gamma = 1/3$. During the fast retrieval phase, we first filter out the examples using the Sim_w, then calculate the Sim_{fast} for each example left, and retrieve the best *N* examples.

3.1.2 The Alignment Structure Metric

After retrieving the candidate similar examples, we refine the candidates using the word alignment structure with the example, to find the best M similar examples (here set M=10). The word alignment in the example satisfies the ITG constraint, which provides a weak structure constraint.

Given the input sentence I and an example (C,A,E), we first search the matched blocks, at this moment the order of the source phrases in the blocks must correspond with the order of the words in the input.

As Figure 3 shows, the matching divides the input and the example respectively into several regions, where some regions are matched and some un-matched. And we take each region as a whole and align them between the input and the example according to the order of the matched regions. For example, the region (1..3,3..5) in (C,A,E) is unmatched, which aligns to the region (1..1) in I. In this way, we can use a similar edit distance method to measure the similarity. We count the number of the Deletion / Insertion / Substitution operations, which take the region as the object.

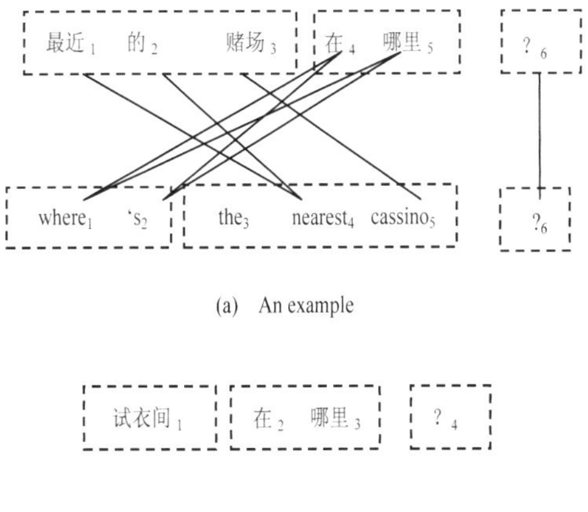

(a) An example

(b) An input

Figure 3. An input and an example. After matching, there are three regions in both sides, which are included in the line box, where the region (4..5,1..2) in the example matches the region (2..3) in the input, so do (6..6,6..6) to (4..4). And the region (1..3,3..5) in the example should be substituted to (1..1) in the input.

We set the penalty for each deletion and insertion operation as 1, while considering the unmatched region in the example may be independent or not, we set the penalty for substitution as 0.5 if the region is independent, otherwise as 1. E.g., the distance is 0.5 for substituting the region (1..3,3..5) to (1..1).

We get the metric for measuring the structure similarity of the I and (C,A,E):

$$Sim_{align}(I,Exam)=1-\frac{D+I+S}{R_{input}+R_{exmaple}} \tag{13}$$

where D, I, S are the deletion, insertion and substitution distances, respectively. And the R_{input} and $R_{exmaple}$ are the region numbers in the input and example.

In the end, we obtain the similarity metric, which considers all of the above metrics:

$$Sim_{final}(I,Exam)=\alpha' Sim_{fast}+\beta' Sim_{align} \tag{14}$$

where $0\le\alpha',\beta'\le1$ $\alpha'+\beta'=1$. Here we also use mean values $\alpha'=\beta'=1/2$.

After the two phrases, we obtain the most similar examples with the input sentence.

3.2 Decoding

After retrieving the translation examples, our goal is to use these examples to constrain the order of the output words. During the decoding, we iterate the following two steps.

3.2.1 Matching

For each translation example (C_k, A_k, E_k) consists of the constituent structure tree, we can match the input sentence with the tree as in Section 3.1.2.

After matching, we obtain a translation of the input sentence, in which some input phrases are matched to blocks in the tree, i.e. they are translated, and some phrases are un-translated. The order of the matched blocks must be the same as the input phrases. We call the translation as a translation template for the input.

If we take each un-translated phrase as a null-aligned block, the translation template will be able to form a new constituent tree. And the matched blocks in the template will restrict the translation structure.

Figure 4(a-c) illustrates the matching process, and Figure 4(c) is a translation template, in which "你 能" and "吗 ? " have been translated and "打开 你的 包" is not translated. And the translation template can be derived from the ITG as follows (here we remove the un-matched phrase):

$$\begin{aligned} & A -> [A_1 A_2] \\ & A_1 -> < A_3 A_4 > \\ & A_2 -> 吗?/? \\ & A_3 -> 你 / you \\ & A_4 -> 能 / could \end{aligned} \quad (15)$$

Since we have M (here M=10) similar examples, we will get more than one translation template for the input sentence. So we define the evaluation function f for each translation template as :

$$f(temp) = \log P(D_{trans}) + \log H(C_{untrans}) \quad (16)$$

Where $P(D_{trans})$ is the probability for the new ITG tree without the un-translated phrases, which is a derivation from the ITG, so we can calculate it using the SMT model in Section 2 (formula 3).

And the $H(C_{untrans})$ is the estimated score for the un-translated phrases. In order to obtain $H(C_{untrans})$, we estimate the score for each un-translated phrase $c_{m..n}$ in the following way:

$$H(c_{m..n}) = \max\{\max_k H(c_{m..k}) \bullet H(c_{k..n}), \max_{e^*} p(e^* \mid c_{m..n})\} \quad (17)$$

That is, using the best translation to estimate the translation score. Thus we can estimate the $H(C_{untrans})$ as:

$$H(C_{untrans}) = \prod_c H(c_{m..n}) \quad (18)$$

We call the un-translated phrases as child inputs, and try to translate them literately, i.e., decoding them using the examples. If there are no un-translated phrases in the input, the decoding is completed, and the decoder returns the translation template with the best score as the result.

3.2.2 Merging

If one child input is translated completely, i.e. no phrase is un-translated. Then, it should be merged into the parent translation template to form a new template. When merging, we must satisfy the ITG constraint, so we use the rules [] and <> to merge the child input with the adjacent blocks. Figure 4(c-f) illustrates a merging process.

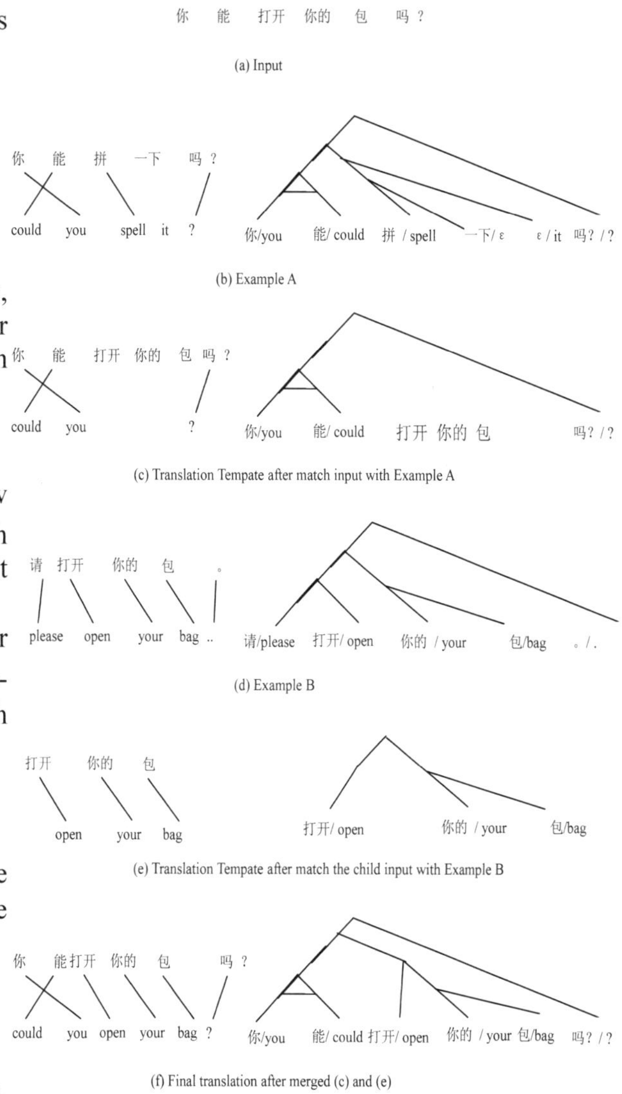

Figure 4. An example to illustrate the example-based decoding process, in which there are two translation examples.

When merging, it may modify some rules which are adjacent to the child inputs. For example, when merging Figure 4(c) and (e), we may add a new rule:

$$A_1^{'} -> [A_1 A_{child}] \quad (19)$$

A_{child} is the root non-terminal for the child input. And we should modify the rule $A -> [A_1 A_2]$ as:

$$A -> [A_1^{'} A_2] \quad (20)$$

The merged template may vary due to the following situations:

- The orientation may vary. The orientation between the new block formed from the child template and the preceding or posterior blocks may be straight or inverted.

- The position to merge may vary. We may merge the new block with either the whole preceding or posterior blocks, or only the child blocks of them respectively, i.e. we may take the preceding or posterior blocks as the whole blocks or not.

Thus, we will obtain a collection of the merged translation templates, the decoder will evaluate them using the formualte (16). If all the templates have no un-translated phrases, return the template with the best score.

3.2.3 Decoding Algorithm

The decoding algorithm is showed in Figure 5.

In line 5~8, we match the input sentence with each similar example, and generate a collection of translation templates, using the formular (16) to evaluate the templates.

In line 9~11, we verify whether the set of the templates for the input is null: If it is null, decoding the input using the normal CKY decoder, and return the translations.

In lin 12~23, we decode the un-matched phrase in each template, and merge it with the parent template, until all of the template are translated completely.

In line 24, we return the best N translations.

```
1: Function Example_Decoder(I,examples)
2: Input: Input sentence I, Similar Examples examples
3: Output: The best N tranlsations
4: Begin
5:   For each exampleA in examples Do
6:     templates = Match(exampleA,I);
7:     AddTemplate(templates,I);
8:  End {For}
9:  If templates is null then
10:    templates = CYK_Decoder(I);
11:    return templates;
12: For each templateA in templates Do
13:   If templateA is complete then
14:     AddTemplate_Complete(templateA,I);
15:   Else
16:     RemoveTemplate(templateA,I);
17:     For each untranslated phraseB in templateA do
18:       childTemplates = Example_Decoder(phraseB);
19:       For each childTemplateC in childTemplates Do
20:         templateD=MergeTemplate(templateA,childTemplateC);
21:    End{If}
22:    AddTemplate(templateD,I);
23:  End{For}
24:  return BEST_N(complete_templates);
28: End
```

Figure 5. The decoding algorithm.

4 Experiments

We carried out experiments on an open Chinese-English translation task IWSLT2007, which consisting of sentence-aligned spoken language text for traveling. There are five development set, and we take the third development set, i.e. the *IWSLT07_devset3_**, to tune the feature weights.

		Chinese	English stemmed
Train. corpus	Sentences	39,963	
	Words	351,060	377,890
	Vocabulary	11,302	7,610
Dev. Set	Sentences	506	
	Words	3,826	
Test Set	Sentences	489	
	Words	3,189	

Table 1. The statistics of the corpus

Considering the size of the training corpus is relatively small, and the words in Chinese have no morphological changes, we stemmed the words in the English sentences.

Table 1 shows the statistics for the training corpus, development set and test set.

In order to compare with the other SMT systems, we choose the Moses[1], which is an extension to the state-of-the-art SMT system Pharaoh (Koehn, 2004). We use the default tool in the Moses to train the model and tune the weights, in which the word alignment tool is Giza++ (Och and Ney 2003) and the language model tool is SRILM(Stolcke, 2002).

The test results are showed in Table2.

The first column lists the different MT systems, and the second column lists the Bleu scores (Papineni et. al, 2002) for the four decoders.

The first system is the Moses, and the second is our SMT system described in section 2, which using a CKY-style decoder. We take them as baseline systems. The third is the hybrid system but

[1] http://www.statmt.org/moses/.

only using the fast retrieval module and the fourth is the hybrid system with refined retrieval module.

Considering the result from the Moses, we think that maybe the size of the training corpus is too small, so that the word alignment obtained by Giza++ is poor.

The results show that the example-based decoder achieves an improvement over the baseline decoders.

Decoder	Bleu
Moses	22.61
SMT-CKY	28.33
Hybrid MT with fast retrieval	30.03
Hybrid MT with refined retrieval	33.05

Table 2. Test results for several systems.

5 Related works

There is some works about the hybrid machine translation. One way is to merge EBMT and SMT resources, such as Groves and Way (2005).

Another way is to implement an exmaple-based decoder, Watanabe and Sumita (2003) presents an example-based decoder, which using a information retrieval framework to retrieve the examples; and when decoding, which runs a hill-climbing algorithm to modify the translation example (C_k, E_k, A_k) to obtain an alignment (C_0, E'_k, A'_k).

6 Conclusions

In this paper, we proposed a SMT system with an example-based decoder for the spoken language machine translation. This approach will take advantage of the constituent tree within the translation examples to constrain the flexible word reordering in the spoken language, and it will also make the omitted words have the chance to be translated. Combining with the re-ordering model and the translation models in the SMT, the example-based decoder obtains an improvement over the baseline phrase-based SMT system.

In the future, we will test our method in the written text corpus. In addition, we will improve the methods to handle the morphological changes from the stemmed English words.

Acknowledgements

This work is supported by the National Science Foundation of China under Grants No. 60573057, 60473057 and 90604007.

References

Wen-Han Chao and Zhou-Jun Li.(2007). *Incorporating Constituent Structure Constraint into Discriminative Word Alignment.* MT Summit XI, Copenhagen, Denmark, September 10-14, 2007. pp.97-103.

Wen-Han Chao, Zhou-Jun Li, and Yue-Xin Chen.(2007) *An Integrated Reordering Model for Statistical Machine Translation.* In proceedings of MICAI 2007, LNAI 4827, pp. 955–965, 2007.

David Chiang. (2005). *A Hierarchical Phrase-Based Model for Statistical Machine Translation.* In Proc. of ACL 2005, pages 263–270.

Declan Groves and Andy Way: *Hybrid Example-Based SMT: the Best of Both Worlds?* In Proceedings of the ACL Workshop on Building and Using Parallel Texts, pp. 183-190(2005)

P. Koehn.(2004) Pharaoh: a beam search decoder for phrase-based statistical machine translation models. In: Proceedings of the Sixth Conference of the Association for Machine Translation in the Americas, pp. 115–124.

R. Moore. (2005). *A discriminative framework for bilingual word alignment.* In Proceedings of HLT-EMNLP, pages 81–88, Vancouver, Canada, October.

Franz Joseph Och and Hermann Ney.(2002). *Discriminative training and maximum entropy models for statistical machine translation.* In Proceedings of the 40th Annual Meeting of the ACL, pp. 295–302.

Franz Joseph Och and Hermann Ney. (2003) *A Systematic Comparison of Various Statistical Alignment Models.* Computational Linguistics 29(1), 19–52

Kishore Papineni, Salim Roukos, Todd Ward and Wei-Jing Zhu. (2002). *BLEU: a Method for Automatic Evaluation of Machine Translation.* In Proceedings of the 40th Annual Meeting of the Association fo Computational Linguistics (ACL), Philadelphia, July 2002, pp. 311-318.

A. Stolcke. (2002). *SRILM – An extensible language modeling toolkit.* In Proceedings of the International Conference on Spoken Language Processing, Denver, Colorado, 2002, pp. 901–904.

Taro Watanabe and Eiichiro Sumita. (2003). *Example-based Decoding for Statistical Machine Translation.* In Machine Translation Summit IX pp. 410-417.

Dekai Wu. (1997). *Stochastic Inversion Transduction Grammars and Bilingual Parsing of Parallel Corpora.* Computational Linguistics, 23(3):374.

Automatic Extraction of English-Chinese Transliteration Pairs using Dynamic Window and Tokenizer

Chengguo Jin
Dept. of Graduate School for Information Technology, POSTECH, Korea
chengguo@postech.ac.kr

Dong-Il Kim
Language Engineering Institute, YUST, China
dongil@ybust.edu.cn

Seung-Hoon Na
Dept. of Computer Science & Engineering
POSTECH, Korea
nsh1979@postech.ac.kr

Jong-Hyeok Lee
Dept. of Computer Science & Engineering
POSTECH, Korea
jhlee@postech.ac.kr

Abstract

Recently, many studies have been focused on extracting transliteration pairs from bilingual texts. Most of these studies are based on the statistical transliteration model. The paper discusses the limitations of previous approaches and proposes novel approaches called dynamic window and tokenizer to overcome these limitations. Experimental results show that the average rates of word and character precision are 99.0% and 99.78%, respectively.

1 Introduction

Machine transliteration is a type of translation based on phonetic similarity between two languages. Chinese Named entities including foreign person names, location names and company names, etc are usually transliterated from foreign words. The main problem of transliteration resulted from complex relations between Chinese phonetic symbols and characters. Usually, a foreign word can be transliterated into various Chinese words, and sometimes this will lead to transliteration complexity. In addition, dozens of Chinese characters correspond to each pinyin which uses the Latin alphabet to represent sounds in Standard Mandarin. In order to solve these problems, Chinese government published the "Names of the world's peoples"[12] containing 630,000 entries in 1993, which took about 40 years. However, some new foreign names still cannot be found in the dictionary. Constructing an unknown word dictionary is a difficult and time consuming job, so in this paper we propose a novel approach to automatically construct the resource by efficiently extracting transliteration pairs from bilingual texts.

Recently, much research has been conducted on machine transliteration. Machine transliteration is classified into two types. One is automatic generation of transliterated word from the source language [6]; the other one is extracting transliteration pairs from bilingual texts [2]. Generally, the generation process performs worse than the extraction process. Especially in Chinese, people do not always transliterate foreign words only by sound but also consider the meanings. For example, the word 'blog' is not transliterated into '布劳哥' (BuLaoGe) which is phonetically equivalent to the source word, but transliterated into '博客'(BoKe) which means 'a lot of guests'. In this case, it is too difficult to automatically generate correct transliteration words. Therefore, our approach is based on the method of extracting transliteration pairs from bilingual texts.

The type of extraction of transliteration pairs can also be further divided into two types. One is extracting transliteration candidates from each language respectively, and then comparing the phonetic similarities between those candidates of two languages [2, 8]. The other one is only extracting transliteration candidates from the source language, and using the candidates to extract corresponding transliteration words from the target language [1]. In Chinese, there is no space between two words and no special character set to represent foreign words such as Japanese; hence the candidate extraction is difficult and usually results in a low precision. Therefore, the method presented in [2] which extracted transliteration candidates from both English and Chinese result in a poor performance. Compared to other works, Lee[1] only extracts transliteration candidates from English, and finds equivalent Chinese transliteration words without extracting candidates from Chinese texts. The method works well, but the performance is required to be improved. In this paper we present a novel approaches to obtain a remarkable result in extracting transliteration word pairs from parallel texts.

The remainder of the paper is organized as follows: Section 2 gives an overview of statistical machine transliteration and describes proposed approaches. Section 3 describes the experimental setup and a quantitative assessment of performance of our approaches. Conclusions and future work are presented in Section 4.

2 Extraction of English-Chinese transliteration pairs

In this paper, we first extract English named entities from English-Chinese parallel texts, and select only those which are to be transliterated into Chinese. Next we extract Chinese transliteration words from corresponding Chinese texts. [Fig. 1] shows the entire process of extracting transliteration word pairs from English-Chinese parallel texts.

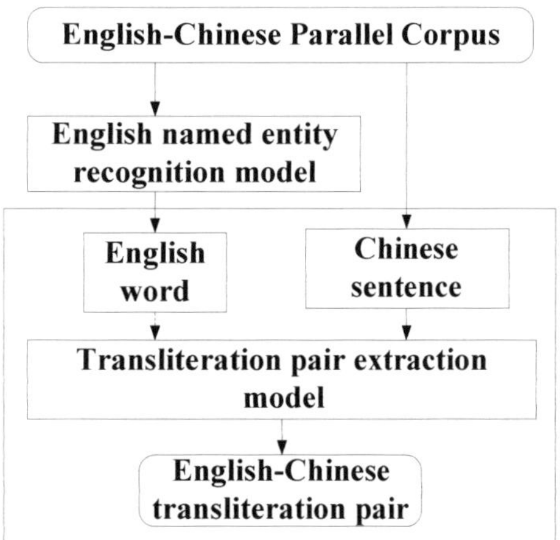

[Fig 1]. The process of extracting transliteration pairs from English-Chinese parallel corpus

2.1 Statistical machine transliteration model

Generally, the Chinese Romanization system pinyin which is used to represent the pronunciation of each Chinese character is adopted in Chinese transliteration related studies. For example, the Chinese word '克林顿' is first transformed to pinyin 'Ke Lin Dun', and we compare the phonetic similarities between 'Clinton' and 'KeLinDun'. In this paper, we assume that E is written in English, while C is written in Chinese, and TU represents transliteration units. So P(C|E), P(克林顿|Clinton) can be transformed to P(KeLinDun|Clinton). In this paper we define English TU as unigram, bigram, and trigram; Chinese TU is pinyin initial, pinyin final and the entire pinyin. With these definitions we can further write the probability, P(克林顿|Clinton), as follows:

$$P(\text{克林顿} \mid Clinton) \cong P(kelindun \mid Clinton)$$
$$\cong P(ke \mid C)P(l \mid l)P(in \mid in)P(t \mid d)P(un \mid on) \quad (1)$$

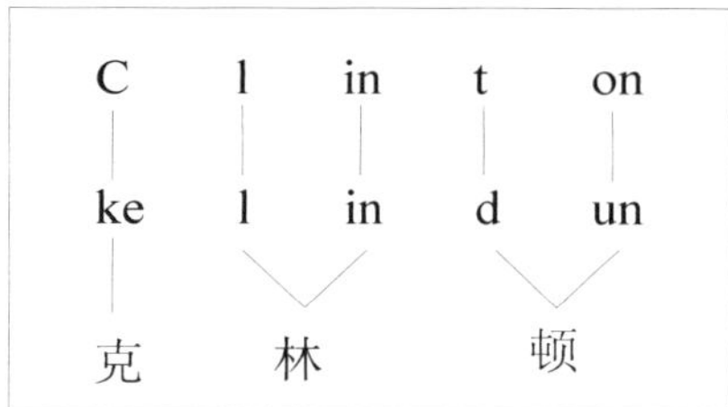

[Fig 2]. TU alignment between English and Chinese pinyin

[Fig 2] shows the possible alignment between English word 'Clinton' and Chinese word '克林顿''s pinyin 'KeLinDun'.

In [1], the authors add the match type information in Eq. (1). The match type is defined with the lengths of TUs of two languages. For example, in the case of $P(ke \mid C)$ the match type is 2-1, because the size of Chinese TU *ke* is 2 and the size of English TU *C* is 1. Match type is useful when estimating transliteration model's parameters without a pronunciation dictionary. In this paper, we use the EM algorithm to estimate transliteration model's parameters without a pronunciation dictionary, so we applied match type to our model. Add Match type(M) to Eq.(1) to formulate as follows:

$$P(C \mid E) \approx \max_M P(C \mid M, E)P(M \mid E)$$
$$\approx \max_M P(C \mid M, E)P(M) \quad (2)$$

$$\log P(C \mid E) \approx \max_M \sum_{i=1}^{N} \left(\log P(v_i \mid u_i) + \log P(m_i) \right) \quad (3)$$

where u, v are English TU and Chinese TU, respectively and m is the match type of u and v.

English Word: Clinton
Chinese Transliteration word: 克林顿(KeLinDun)
Chinese sentence:
明天克林顿将访问韩国
(Clinton will visit Korea tomorrow.)

English TU	Chinese TU	Match type	Chinese characters
	mi	[0,2]	明
	n	[0,1]	
	g	[0,1]	
	t	[0,1]	天
	i	[0,1]	
	an	[0,2]	
C	ke	[1,2]	克
li	li	[2,2]	林
n	n	[1,1]	
t	d	[1,1]	顿
on	un	[2,2]	
	ji	[0,2]	将
	an	[0,2]	
	g	[0,1]	
	f	[0,1]	访
	an	[0,2]	
	g	[0,1]	
	we	[0,2]	问
	n	[0,1]	
	h	[0,1]	韩
	an	[0,2]	
	g	[0,1]	国
	uo	[0,2]	

[Fig 3]. The alignment of the English word and the Chinese sentence containing corresponding transliteration word

[Fig 3] shows how to extract the correct Chinese transliteration "克林顿"(KeLinDun) with the given English word "Clinton" from a Chinese sentence.

2.2 Proposed methods

When the statistical machine transliteration is used to extract transliteration pairs from a parallel text, the problems arise when there is more than one Chinese character sequence that is phonetically similar to the English word. In this paper we propose novel approaches called dynamic window and tokenizer to solve the problems effectively.

2.2.1 Dynamic window method

The dynamic window approach does not find the transliteration at once, but first sets the window size range according to the English word candidates, and slides each window within the range to find the correct transliterations.

English TU	Chinese TU	Match type	Chinese characters
C	ke	[1,2]	克
li	li	[2,2]	林
n	n	[1,1]	
t	d	[1,1]	顿
on	un	[2,2]	
	Score: -4.29		
C	ke	[1,2]	克
li	li	[2,2]	林
n	n	[1,1]	
	yi	[0,2]	意
t	d	[1,1]	顿
on	un	[2,2]	
	Score: -6.94		
C		[1,0]	
li	li	[2,2]	林
n	n	[1,1]	
t	d	[1,1]	顿
on	un	[2,2]	
	Score: -7.28		

[Fig 4]. Alignment result between English word "Clinton" and correct Chinese transliteration, add a character into correct Chinese transliteration, and eliminate a character from correct Chinese transliteration.

If we know the exact Chinese transliteration's size, then we can efficiently extract Chinese transliterations by setting the window with the length of the actual Chinese transliteration word. For example, in [Fig 4] we do alignment between the English word "Clinton" and correct Chinese transliteration "克林顿"(KeLinDun), add a character into correct Chinese transliteration "克林意顿"(KeLinYiDun), and eliminate a character from correct Chinese transliteration "林顿"(LinDun) respectively. The result shows that the highest score is the alignment with correct Chinese transliteration. This is because the alignment between the English word and the correct Chinese transliteration will lead to more alignments between English TUs and Chinese TUs, which will result in highest scores among alignment with other Chinese sequences. This characteristic does not only exist between English and Chinese, but also exists between other language pairs.

However, in most circumstances, we can hardly determine the correct Chinese transliteration's length. Therefore, we analyze the distribution between English words and Chinese transliterations to predict the possible range of Chinese transliteration's length according to the English word. We present the algorithm for the dynamic window approach as follows:

Step 1: Set the range of Chinese transliteration's length according to the extracted English word candidate.

Step 2: Slide each window within the range to calculate the probability between an English word and a Chinese character sequence contained in the current window using Eq 3.

Step 3: Select the Chinese character sequence with highest score and back-track the alignment result to extract the correct transliteration word.

[Fig 5] shows the entire process of using the dynamic window approach to extract the correct transliteration word.

<table>
<tr><td>English Word</td><td colspan="2">Ziegler</td></tr>
<tr><td>Chinese Sentence</td><td colspan="2">齐格勒与意大利化学家居里奥共同获得了 1963 年诺贝尔化学奖。</td></tr>
<tr><td>English Sentence</td><td colspan="2">Ziegler and Italian Chemist Julio received the Nobel prize of 1963 together.</td></tr>
<tr><td>Extracted transliteration without using dynamic window</td><td colspan="2">家居里奥 (JiaJuLiAo)</td></tr>
<tr><td>Correct transliteration</td><td colspan="2">齐格勒 (QiGeLe)</td></tr>
<tr><td colspan="3">Steps</td></tr>
<tr><td colspan="3">1. Set Chinese transliteration's range according to English word "Ziegler" to [2, 7] (After analyzing the distribution between an English word and a Chinese transliteration word, we found that if the English word length is L, then the Chinese transliteration word is between L/3 and L.)</td></tr>
<tr><td colspan="3">2. Slide each window to find sequence with highest score.</td></tr>
<tr><td colspan="3">3 Select the Chinese character sequence with highest score and back-track the alignment result to extract a correct transliteration word.</td></tr>
<tr><td>Window size</td><td>Chinese character sequence with highest score of each window (underline the back-tracking result)</td><td>Score (normalize with window size)</td></tr>
<tr><td>2</td><td>奇格 (QiGe)</td><td>-9.327</td></tr>
<tr><td>3</td><td>齐格勒 (QiGeLe)</td><td>-6.290</td></tr>
<tr><td>4</td><td>齐格勒与 (QiGeLeYu)</td><td>-8.433</td></tr>
<tr><td>5</td><td>齐格勒与意 (QiGeLeYuYi)</td><td>-9.719</td></tr>
<tr><td>6</td><td>家居里奥共同 (JiaJuLiAoGongTong)</td><td>-10.458</td></tr>
<tr><td>7</td><td>齐格勒与意大利 (QiGeLeYuYiDaLi)</td><td>-10.721</td></tr>
</table>

[Fig 5]. Extract the correct transliteration using the dynamic window method

The dynamic window approach can effectively solve the problem shown in [Fig 5] which is the most common problem that arises from using statistical machine transliteration model to extract a transliteration from a Chinese sentence. However, it can not handle the case that a correct transliteration with correct window size can not be extracted. Moreover, when the dynamic window approach is used, the processing time will increase severely. Hence, the following approach is presented to deal with the problem as well as to improve the performance.

2.2.2 Tokenizer method

The tokenizer method is to divide a sentence with characters which have never been used in Chinese transliterations and applies the statistical transliteration model to each part to extract a correct transliteration.

There are certain characters that are frequently used for transliterating foreign words, such as "施(shi), 德(de), 勒(le), 赫(he) …". On the other hand, there are other characters, such as "是(shi), 的(de), 了(le), 和(he),…", that have never been used for Chinese transliteration, while they are phonetically equivalent with the above characters. These characters are mainly particles, copulas and non-Chinese characters etc., and always come with named entities and sometimes also cause some problems. For example, when the English word "David" is transliterated into Chinese, the last phoneme is omitted and transliterated into "大卫"(DaWei). In this case of a Chinese character such as "的"(De) which is phonetically similar with the omitted syllable 'd', the statistical transliteration model will incorrectly extract "大卫的"(DaWeiDe) as transliteration of "David". In [1], the authors deal with the problem through a post-process using some linguistic rules. Lee and Chang [1] merely eliminate the characters which have never been used in Chinese transliteration such as "的"(De) from the results. Nevertheless, the approach cannot solve the problem shows in [Fig 6], because the copula "是"(Shi) combines with the other character "者"(zhe) to form the character sequence "者是"(ZheShi) which is phonetically similar with the English word "Jacey", and is incorrectly recognized as a transliteration of "Jacey". Thus, in this case, although the copula "是"(Shi) is eliminated from the result through the post-process method presented in [1], the remaining part is not the correct transliteration. Compared with the method in [1], our tokenizer approach eliminates copula "是"(Shi) at pre-processing time and then the phonetic similarity between "Jacey" and the remaining part "者"(Zhe) becomes very low; hence our approach overcomes the problem prior to the entire process. In addition, the tokenizer approach also reduces the processing time dramatically due to separating a sentence into several parts. [Fig 6] shows the process of extracting a correct transliteration using the tokenizer method.

English Word	Jacey
Chinese Sentence	这本书的作者是佩尼娜汤姆森和杰西格雷厄姆。
English Sentence	The authors of this book are Peninah Thomson and Jacey Grahame.
Incorrectly extracted transliteration	者是(ZheShi)
Correct transliteration	杰西(JieXi)

Steps		
1. Separate the Chinese sentence with characters, "这, 的, 是, 和" (including non-Chinese characters such as punctuation, number, English characters etc.), which have never been used in Chinese transliteration as follows: 本书的作者是佩尼娜汤姆森和杰西格雷厄姆		
2. Apply statistical transliteration model to each part and select the part with highest score, and back-track the part to extract a correct transliteration.		
No.	Chinese character sequence of each part (underline the back-tracking result)	Score (normalize with window size)
1	本书 (BenShu)	-24.79
2	作者 (ZuoZhe)	-15.83
3	佩尼娜汤姆森 (PeiNiNaTangMuShen)	-16.32
4	杰西格雷厄姆 (JieXi)	-10.29

[Fig 6]. Extracting the correct transliteration using the tokenizer method.

In conclusion, the two approaches complement each other; hence using them together will lead to a better performance.

3 Experiments

In this section, we focus on the setup for the experiments and a performance evaluation of the proposed approaches to extract transliteration word pairs from parallel corpora.

3.1 Experimental setup

We use 300 parallel English-Chinese sentences containing various person names, location names, company names etc. The corpus for training consists of 860 pairs of English names and their Chinese transliterations. The performance of transliteration pair extraction was evaluated based on precision and recall rates at the word and character levels. Since we consider exactly one proper name in the source language and one transliteration in the target language at a time, the word recall rates are the same as the word precision rates. In order to demonstrate the effectiveness of our approaches, we perform the following experiments: firstly, only use STM(Statistical transliteration model) which is the baseline of our experiment; secondly, we apply the dynamic window and tokenizer method with STM respectively; thirdly, we apply these two methods together; at last, we perform experiment presented in [1] to compare with our methods.

3.2 Evaluation of dynamic window and tokenizer methods

[table 1]. The experimental results of extracting transliteration pairs using proposed methods

Methods	Word precision	Character precision	Character recall
STM (baseline)	75.33%	86.65%	91.11%
STM+DW	96.00%	98.51%	99.05%
STM+TOK	78.66%	85.24%	86.94%
STM+DW+TOK	99.00%	99.78%	99.72%
STM+CW	98.00%	98.81%	98.69%
STM+CW+TOK	99.00%	99.89%	99.61%

As shown in table 1, the baseline STM achieves a word precision rate of 75%. The STM works relatively well with short sentences, but as the length of sentences increases the performance significantly decreases. The dynamic window approach overcomes the problem effectively. If the dynamic window method is applied with STM, the model will be tolerant with the length of sentences. The dynamic window approach improves the performance of STM around 21%, and reaches the average word precision rate of 96% (STM+DW). In order to estimate the highest performance that the dynamic window approach can achieve, we apply the correct window size which can be obtained from the evaluation data set with STM. The result (STM+CW) shows around 98% word precision rate and about 23% improvement over the baseline. Therefore, dynamic window approach is remarkably efficient; it shows only 2% difference with theoretically highest performance. However, the dynamic window approach increases the processing time too much.

When using tokenizer method (STM+TOK), only about 3% is approved over the baseline. Although the result is not considerably improved, it is extremely important that the problems that the dynamic window method cannot solve are managed to be solved. Thus, when using both dynamic window and tokenizer methods with STM (STM+DW+TOK), it is found that around 3% improvement is achieved over using only the dynamic window (STM+DW), as well as word precision rates of 99%.

[table 2]. Processing time evaluation of proposed methods

Methods	Processing time
STM (baseline)	5 sec (5751 milisec)
STM+DW	2min 34sec (154893 milisec)
STM+TOK	4sec (4574 milisec)
STM+DW+TOK	32sec (32751 milisec)

Table 2 shows the evaluation of processing time of dynamic window and tokenizer methods. Using the dynamic window leads to 27 times more processing time than STM, while using the tokenizer method with the dynamic window method reduces the processing time around 5 times than the original. Hence, we have achieved a higher precision as well as less processing time by combining these two methods.

3.3 Comparing experiment

In order to compare with previous methods, we perform the experiment presented in [1]. Table 3 shows using the post-processing method presented in [1] achieves around 87% of word precision rates, and about 12% improvement over the baseline. However, our methods are 11% superior to the method in [1].

[Table 3] Comparing experiment with previous work

Methods	Word Precision	Character Precision	Character Recall
STM (baseline)	75.33%	86.65%	91.11%
STM+DW+TOK	99.00%	99.78%	99.72%
STM+[1]'s method	87.99%	90.17%	91.11%

4 Conclusions and future work

In this paper, we presented two novel approaches called dynamic window and tokenizer based on the statistical machine transliteration model. Our approaches achieved high precision without any post-processing procedures. The dynamic window approach was based on a fundamental property, which more TUs aligned between correct transliteration pairs. Also, we reasonably estimated the range of correct transliteration's length to extract transliteration pairs in high precision. The tokenizer method eliminated characters that have never been used in Chinese transliteration to separate a sentence into several parts. This resulted in a certain degree of improvement of precision and significantly reduction of processing time. These two methods are both based on common natures of all languages; thus our approaches can be readily port to other language pairs.

In this paper, we only considered the English words that are to be transliterated into Chinese. Our work is ongoing, and in near future, we will extend our works to extract transliteration pairs from large scale comparable corpora. In comparable corpora, there are many uncertainties, for example, the extracted English word may be not transliterated into Chinese or there may be no correct transliteration in Chinese texts. However, with large comparable corpora, a word will appear several times, and we can use the frequency or entropy information to extract correct transliteration pairs based on the proposed perfect algorithm.

Acknowledgement

This work was supported by the Korea Science and Engineering Foundation (KOSEF) through the Advanced Information Technology Research Center (AITrc), also in part by the BK 21 Project and MIC & IITA through IT Leading R&D Support Project in 2007.

Reference

[1] C.-J. Lee, J.S. Chang, J.-S.R. Jang, Extraction of transliteration pairs from parallel corpora using a statistical transliteration model, in: Information Sciences 176, 67-90 (2006)

[2] Richard Sproat, Tao Tao, ChengXiang Zhai, Named Entity Transliteration with Comparable Corpora, in: Proceedings of the 21st International Conference on Computational Linguistics. (2006)

[3] J.S. Lee and K.S. Choi, "English to Korean statistical transliteration for information retrieval," International Journal of Computer Processing of Oriental Languages, pp.17–37, (1998).

[4] K. Knight, J. Graehl, Machine transliteration, Computational Linguistics 24 (4), 599–612, (1998).
[5] W.-H. Lin, H.-H. Chen, Backward transliteration by learning phonetic similarity, in: CoNLL-2002, Sixth Conference on Natural Language Learning, Taipei, Taiwan, (2002).
[6] J.-H. Oh, K.-S. Choi, An English–Korean transliteration model using pronunciation and contextual rules, in: Proceedings of the 19th International Conference on Computational Linguistics (COLING), Taipei, Taiwan, pp. 758–764, (2002).
[7] C.-J. Lee, J.S. Chang, J.-S.R. Jang, A statistical approach to Chinese-to-English Backtransliteration, in: Proceedings of the 17th Pacific Asia Conference on Language, Information, and Computation (PACLIC), Singapore, pp. 310–318, (2003).
[8] Jong-Hoon Oh, Sun-Mee Bae, Key-Sun Choi, An Algorithm for extracting English-Korean Transliteration pairs using Automatic E-K Transliteration In Proceedings of Korean Information Science Socieity (Spring). (In Korean), (2004).
[9] Jong-Hoon Oh, Jin-Xia Huang, Key-Sun Choi, An Alignment Model for Extracting English-Korean Translations of Term Constituents, Journal of Korean Information Science Society, SA, 32(4), (2005)
[10] Chun-Jen Lee, Jason S. Chang, Jyh-Shing Roger Jang: Alignment of bilingual named entities in parallel corpora using statistical models and multiple knowledge sources. ACM Trans. Asian Lang. Inf. Process. 5(2): 121-145 (2006)
[11] Lee, C. J. and Chang, J. S., Acquisition of English-Chinese Transliterated Word Pairs from Parallel-Aligned Texts Using a Statistical Machine Transliteration Model, In. Proceedings of HLT-NAACL, Edmonton, Canada, pp. 96-103, (2003).
[12] Xinhua Agency, Names of the world's peoples: a comprehensive dictionary of names in Roman-Chinese (世界人名翻译大辞典), (1993)

Mining Transliterations from Web Query Results: An Incremental Approach

Jin-Shea Kuo
Chung-Hwa Telecomm. Laboratories, Taiwan
d8807302 @gmail.com

Haizhou Li
Institute for Infocomm Research, Singapore 119613
hzli@ieee.com

Chih-Lung Lin
Chung Yuan Christian University, Taiwan
linclr@gmail.com

Abstract

We study an adaptive learning framework for phonetic similarity modeling (PSM) that supports the automatic acquisition of transliterations by exploiting minimum prior knowledge about machine transliteration to mine transliterations incrementally from the live Web. We formulate an incremental learning strategy for the framework based on Bayesian theory for PSM adaptation. The idea of incremental learning is to benefit from the continuously developing history to update a static model towards the intended reality. In this way, the learning process refines the PSM incrementally while constructing a transliteration lexicon at the same time on a development corpus. We further demonstrate that the proposed learning framework is reliably effective in mining live transliterations from Web query results.

1 Introduction

Transliteration is a process of rewriting a word from one language into another by preserving its pronunciation in its original language, also known as *translation-by-sound*. It usually takes place between languages with different scripts, for example, from English to Chinese, and words, such as proper nouns, that do not have "easy" or semantic translations.

The increasing size of multilingual content on the Web has made it a live information source rich in transliterations. Research on automatic acquisition of transliteration pairs in batch mode has shown promising results (Kuo *et al.*, 2006). In dealing with the dynamic growth of the Web, it is almost impossible to collect and store all its contents in local storage. Therefore, there is a need to develop an incremental learning algorithm to mine transliterations in an on-line manner. In general, an incremental learning technique is designed for adapting a model towards a changing environment. We are interested in deducing the incremental learning method for automatically constructing an English-Chinese (*E-C*) transliteration lexicon from Web query results.

In the deduction, we start with a phonetic similarity model (PSM), which measures the phonetic similarity between words in two different scripts, and study the learning mechanism of PSM in both batch and incremental modes. The contributions of this paper include: (i) the formulation of a batch learning framework and an incremental learning framework for PSM learning; (ii) a comparative study of the batch and incremental unsupervised learning strategies.

In this paper, Section 2 briefly introduces prior work related to machine transliteration. In Section 3, we formulate the PSM and its batch and incremental learning algorithms while in Section 4, we discuss the practical issues in implementation. Section 5 provides a report on the experiments conducted and finally, we conclude in Section 6.

2 Related Work

Much of research on extraction of transliterations has been motivated by information retrieval techniques, where attempts to extracting transliteration pairs from large bodies of corpora have been made. Some have proposed extracting translations from parallel or comparable *bitexts* using co-occurrence analysis or a context-vector approach (Fung and Yee, 1998; Nie *et al.*, 1999). These methods compare the semantic similarities between source and target words without taking their phonetic similarities into account.

Another direction of research is focused on establishing the phonetic relationship between transliteration pairs. This typically involves the encoding of phoneme- or grapheme-based mapping rules using a generative model trained from a large bilingual lexicon. Suppose that *EW* and *CW* form an *E-C* transliteration pair. The phoneme-based approach (Knight & Graehl, 1998) first converts *EW* into an intermediate phonemic representation and then converts the phonemic representation into its Chinese counterpart *CW*. The grapheme-based approach, also known as *direct orthographical mapping* (Li *et al.*, 2004), which treats transliteration as a statistical machine translation problem under monotonic constraints, has also achieved promising results.

Many efforts have also been channeled to tapping the wealth of the Web for harvesting transliteration/translation pairs. These include studying the query logs (Brill *et al.*, 2001), unrelated corpora (Rapp, 1999), and comparable corpora (Sproat *et al.* 2006). To establish cross-lingual correspondence in the harvest, these algorithms usually rely on one or more statistical clues (Lam *et al.*, 2004), such as the correlation between word frequencies, and cognates of similar spelling or pronunciations. In doing so, two things are needed: first, a robust mechanism that establishes statistical relationships between bilingual words, such as a phonetic similarity model which is motivated by transliteration modeling research; and second, an effective learning framework that is able to adaptively discover new events from the Web.

In Chinese/Japanese/Korean (CJK) Web pages, translated terms are frequently accompanied by their original Latin words, with the Latin words serving as the appositives of the CJK words. In other words, the *E-C* pairs are always closely collocated. Inspired by this observation in CJK texts, some algorithms were proposed (Kuo *et al.*, 2006) to search over the close context of an English word in a Chinese predominant bilingual snippet for transliteration.

Unfortunately, many of the reported works have not taken the dynamic nature of the Web into account. In this paper, we study the learning framework of the phonetic similarity model, which adopts a transliteration modeling approach for transliteration extraction from the Web in an incremental manner.

3 Phonetic Similarity Model

Phonetic similarity model (PSM) is a probabilistic model that encodes the syllable mapping between *E-C* pairs. Let $ES = \{e_1, \ldots e_m, \ldots e_M\}$ be a sequence of English syllables derived from *EW* and $CS = \{s_1, \ldots s_n, \ldots s_N\}$ be the sequence of Chinese syllables derived from *CW*, represented by a Chinese character string $CW \to w_1, \ldots w_n, \ldots, w_N$. If each of the English syllables is drawn from a vocabulary of *X* entries, $e_m \in \{x_1, \ldots, x_I\}$, and each of the Chinese syllable from a vocabulary of *Y* entries, $s_n \in \{y_1, \ldots, y_J\}$, then the *E-C* transliteration can be considered as a generative process formulated by the noisy channel model, which recovers the input *CW* from the observed output *EW*. Applying Bayesian rule, we have Eq. (1), where $P(EW \mid CW)$ is estimated to characterize the noisy channel, known as the transliteration probability and $P(CW)$ is a language model to characterize the source language.

$$P(CW \mid EW) = P(EW \mid CW) P(CW) / P(EW). \quad (1)$$

Following the *translation-by-sound* principle, $P(EW \mid CW)$ can be approximated by the phonetic probability $P(ES \mid CS)$, which is given by Eq. (2).

$$P(ES \mid CS) = \max_{\Delta \in \Gamma} P(ES, \Delta \mid CS), \quad (2)$$

where Γ is the set of all possible alignment paths between *ES* and *CS*. To find the best alignment path Δ, one can resort to a dynamic warping algorithm (Myers and Rabiner, 1981). Assuming conditional independence of syllables in *ES* and *CS*, we have $P(ES \mid CS) = \prod_{k=1}^{K} P(e_{m_k} \mid s_{n_k})$ where *k* is the index of alignment. We rewrite Eq.(1) as,

$$P(CW \mid EW) \approx P(ES \mid CS) P(CW) / P(EW). \quad (3)$$

The language model $P(CW)$ in Eq.(3) can be represented by the *n*-gram statistics of the Chinese characters derived from a monolingual corpus. Using bigram to approximate the n-gram model, we have

$$P(CW) \approx P(w_1) \prod_{n=2}^{N} P(w_n \mid w_{n-1}). \quad (4)$$

Removing $P(EW)$ from Eq.(3) which is not a function of *CW*, a PSM Θ now consists of both $P(ES \mid CS)$ and $P(CW)$ parameters (Kuo *et al.*, 2007). We now look into the mathematic formulation for the learning of $P(ES \mid CS)$ parameters from a bilingual transliteration lexicon.

3.1 Batch Learning of PSM

A collection of manually selected or automatically extracted *E-C* pairs can form a transliteration lexicon. Given such a lexicon for training, the PSM parameters can be estimated in a batch mode. An initial PSM is bootstrapped using limited prior knowledge such as a small amount of transliterations, which may be obtained by exploiting co-occurrence information (Sproat *et al.*, 2006). Then we align the *E-C* pairs using the PSM Θ and derive syllable mapping statistics.

Suppose that we have the event counts $c_{i,j} = count(e_m = x_i, s_n = y_j)$, and $c_j = count(s_n = y_j)$ for a given transliteration lexicon D with alignments Λ. We would like to find the parameters $P_{i|j} = P(e_m = x_i \mid s_n = y_j)$, $< e_m, s_n > \in \Lambda$, that maximize the probability,

$$P(D,\Lambda \mid \Theta) = \prod_{\Lambda} P(e_m \mid s_n) = \prod_j \prod_i P_{i|j}^{c_{i,j}}, \qquad (5)$$

where $\Theta = \{P_{i|j}, i = 1,...,I, j = 1,...,J\}$, with maximum likelihood estimation (MLE) criteria, subject to the constraints of $\sum_i P_{i|j} = 1, \forall j$. Rewriting Eq.(5) in log-likelihood (LL)

$$LL(D,\Lambda \mid \Theta) = \sum_{\Lambda} \log P(e_m \mid s_n) = \sum_j \sum_i c_{i,j} \log P_{i|j} \qquad (6)$$

It is described as the *cross-entropy* of the true data distribution $c_{i,j}$ with regard to the PSM model. Given an alignment $\Delta \in \Lambda$, the MLE estimate of PSM is:

$$P_{i|j} = c_{i,j} / c_j. \qquad (7)$$

With a new PSM, one is able to arrive at a new alignment. This is formulated as an *expectation-maximization* (EM) process (Dempster, 1977), which assumes that there exists a mapping $D \to \Lambda$, where Λ is introduced as the latent information, also known as *missing* data in the EM literature. The EM algorithm maximizes the likelihood probability $P(D \mid \Theta)$ over Θ by exploiting $P(D \mid \Theta) = \sum_{\Lambda} P(D,\Lambda \mid \Theta)$.

The EM process guarantees non-decreasing likelihood probability $P(D \mid \Theta)$ through multiple EM steps until it converges. In the E-step, we derive the event counts $c_{i,j}$ and c_j by force-aligning all the *E-C* pairs in the training lexicon D using a PSM. In the M-step, we estimate the PSM parameters Θ by Eq.(7). The EM process also serves as a refining process to obtain the best alignment between the *E-C* syllables. In each EM cycle, the model is updated after observing the whole corpus D. An EM cycle is also called an iteration in batch learning. The batch learning process is described as follows and depicted in Figure 1.

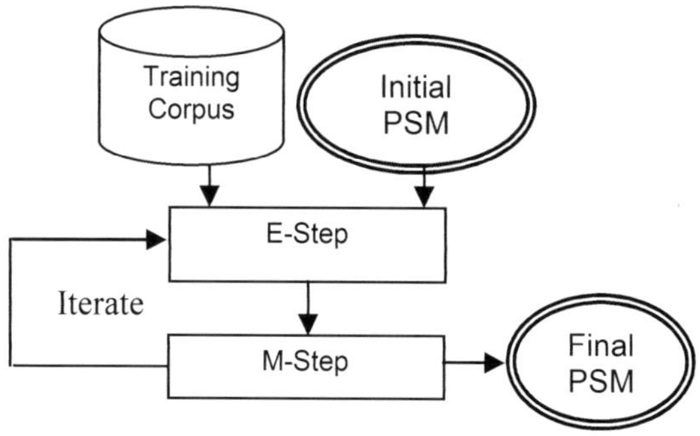

Figure 1. Batch learning of PSM

***Batch Learning Algorithm*:**

<u>Start:</u> Bootstrap PSM parameters $P_{i|j}$ using prior phonetic mapping knowledge;

<u>E-Step:</u> Force-align corpus D using $P_{i|j}$ to obtain Λ and hence the counts of $c_{i,j}$ and c_j;

<u>M-Step:</u> Re-estimate $P_{i|j} = c_{i,j} / c_j$ using the counts from E-Step;

<u>Iterate:</u> Repeat E-Step and M-Step until $P(D \mid \Theta)$ converges;

3.2 Incremental Learning of PSM

In batch learning all the training samples have to be collected in advance. In a dynamically changing environment, such as the Web, new samples always appear and it is impossible to collect all of them. Incremental learning (Zavaliagkos, 1995) is devised to achieve rapid adaptation towards the working environment by updating the model as learning samples arrive in sequence. It is believed that if the statistics for the E-step are incrementally collected and the parameters are frequently estimated, incremental learning converges quicker because the information from the new data contributes to the parameter estimation more effectively than the batch algorithm does (Gotoh *et al.*, 1998). In incremental learning, the model is typically updated progressively as the training samples become available and the number of incremental samples may vary from as few as one to as many as they are available. In the extreme case where all the learning samples are available and the updating is done after observing all of them, the incremental learning becomes batch learning. Therefore, the batch learning can be considered as a special case of the incremental learning.

The incremental learning can be formulated through maximum *a posteriori* (MAP) framework, also known as Bayesian learning, where we assume that the parameters Θ are random variables subject to a prior distribution. A possible candidate for the prior distribution of $P_{i|j}$ is the Dirichlet density over each of the parameters $P_{i|j}$ (Bacchiani *et al.*, 2006). Let $\Theta_j = \{P_{i|j}, i = 1,...,I\}$, we introduce,

$$P(\Theta_j) \propto \prod_i P_{i|j}^{\alpha h_{i|j} - 1}, \quad \forall j, \tag{8}$$

where $\sum_i h_{i|j} = 1$, and α, which can be empirically set, is a positive scalar. Assuming H is the set of hyperparameters, we have as many hyperparameters $h_{i|j} \in H$ as the parameters $P_{i|j}$. The probability of generating the aligned transliteration lexicon is obtained by integrating over the parameter space, $P(D) = \int P(D \mid \Theta) P(\Theta) d\Theta$.

This integration can be easily written down in a closed form due to the conjugacy between Dirichlet distribution $\prod_i P_{i|j}^{\alpha h_{i|j} - 1}$ and the multinomial distribution $\prod_i P_{i|j}^{c_{i,j}}$. Instead of finding Θ that maximizes $P(D \mid \Theta)$ with MLE, we maximize *a posteriori* (MAP) probability as follows:

$$\Theta_{MAP} = \arg\max_{\Theta} P(\Theta \mid D) = \arg\max_{\Theta} P(D \mid \Theta) P(\Theta) / P(D)$$
$$= \arg\max_{\Theta} P(D \mid \Theta) P(\Theta) \tag{9}$$

The MAP solution uses a distribution to model the uncertainty of the parameters Θ, while the MLE gives a point estimation (Jelinek, 1990; MacKay, 1994). We rewrite Eq.(9) as Eq.(10) using Eq.(5) and Eq.(8).

$$\Theta_j^{map} \approx \arg\max_{\Theta_j} \prod_i P_{i|j}^{c_{i,j} + \alpha h_{i|j} - 1} \tag{10}$$

Eq.(10) can be seen as a Dirichlet function of Θ given H, or a multinomial function of H given Θ. With given prior H, the MAP estimation is therefore similar to the MLE problem which is to find the mode of the kernel density in Eq.(10).

$$P_{i|j} = \lambda h_{i|j} + (1 - \lambda) f_{i|j}, \tag{11}$$

where $f_{i|j} = c_{i,j} / c_j$, $\lambda = \alpha / (\sum_i c_{i,j} + \alpha)$.

One can find that λ serves as a weighting factor between the prior and the current observations. The difference between MLE and MAP strategy lies in the fact that MAP introduces prior knowledge into the parameter updating formula. Eq.(11) assumes that the prior parameters H are known and static while the training samples are available all at once.

The idea of incremental learning is to benefit from the continuously developing history to update the static model towards the intended reality. As is often the case, the Web query results in an *on-line* application arrive in sequence. It is of practical use to devise such an incremental mechanism that adapts both parameters and the prior knowledge over time. The *quasi-Bayesian* (QB) learning method offers a solution to it (Bai and Li, 2006).

Let's break up a training corpus D into a sequence of sample subsets $D = \{D_1, D_2, ..., D_T\}$ and denote an accumulated sample subset $D^{(t)} = \{D_1, D_2, ..., D_t\}, 1 \le t \le T$ as an incremental corpus. Therefore, we have $D = D^{(T)}$. The QB method approximates the posterior probability $P(\Theta \mid D^{(t-1)})$ by the closest tractable prior density $P(\Theta \mid H^{(t-1)})$ with $H^{(t-1)}$ evolved from historical corpus $D^{(t-1)}$,

$$\Theta_{QB}^{(t)} = \arg\max_{\Theta} P(\Theta \mid D^{(t)})$$
$$\approx \arg\max_{\Theta} P(D_t \mid \Theta) P(\Theta \mid D^{(t-1)}) \tag{12}$$
$$= \arg\max_{\Theta} \prod_{i=1}^{I} P_{i|j}^{c_{i,j} + \alpha h_i^{(t-1)} - 1}, \quad \forall j.$$

QB estimation offers a recursive learning mechanism. Starting with a hyperparameter set $H^{(0)}$ and a corpus subset D_1, we estimate $H^{(1)}$ and $\Theta_{QB}^{(1)}$, then $H^{(2)}$ and $\Theta_{QB}^{(2)}$ and so on until $H^{(t)}$ and $\Theta_{QB}^{(t)}$ as observed samples arrive in sequence. The updating of parameters can be iterated between the reproducible prior and posterior estimates as in Eq. (13) and Eq. (14). Assuming $T \to \infty$, we have the following:

Incremental Learning Algorithm:

Start: Bootstrap $\Theta_{QB}^{(0)}$ and $H^{(0)}$ using prior phonetic mapping knowledge and set $t = 1$;

E-Step: Force-align corpus subset D_t using $\Theta_{QB}^{(t-1)}$, compute the event counts $c_{i,j}^{(t)}$ and reproduce prior parameters $H^{(t-1)} \to H^{(t)}$.

$$h_{i|j}^{(t)} = h_{i|j}^{(t-1)} + c_{i,j}^{(t)} / \alpha \tag{13}$$

M-Step: Re-estimate parameters $H^{(t)} \rightarrow \Theta_{QB}^{(t)}$ and $P_{i|j}$ using the counts from E-Step.

$$P_{i|j}^{(t)} = h_{i|j}^{(t)} / \sum_i h_{i|j}^{(t)} \quad (14)$$

EM cycle: Repeat E-Step and M-Step until $P(\Theta \mid D^{(t)})$ converges.

Iterate: Repeat T EM cycles covering the entire data set D in an iteration.

The algorithm updates the PSM as training samples become available. The scalar factor α can be seen as a forgetting factor. When α is big, the update of hyperparameters favors the prior. Otherwise, current observation is given more attention. As for the sample subset size $|D_t|$, if we set $|D_t| = 100$, each EM cycle updates Θ after observing every 100 samples. To be comparable with batch learning, we define an iteration here to be a sequence of EM cycles that covers the whole corpus D. If corpus D has a fixed size $|D^{(T)}|$, an iteration means T EM cycles in incremental learning.

4 Mining Transliterations from the Web

Since the Web is dynamically changing and new transliterations come out all the time, it is better to mine transliterations from the Web in an incremental way. Words transliterated by closely observing common guidelines are referred to as *regular* transliterations. However, in Web publishing, translators in different regions may not observe the same guidelines. Sometimes they skew the transliterations in different ways to introduce semantic implications, also known as wordplay, resulting in *casual* transliterations. *Casual* transliteration leads to multiple Chinese transliteration variants for the same English word. For example, "Disney" may be transliterated into "迪士尼/Di-Shi-Ni/[1]", "迪斯耐/Di-Si-Nai/" and "狄斯耐/Di-Si-Nai/".

Suppose that a sufficiently large, manually validated transliteration lexicon is available, a PSM can be built in a supervised manner. However, this method hinges on the availability of such a lexicon. Even if a lexicon is available, the derived model can only be as good as what the training lexicon offers. New transliterations, such as *casual* ones, may not be well handled. It is desirable to adapt the PSM as new transliterations become available, also referred to as the *learning-at-work* mechanism. Some solutions have been proposed recently along this direction (Kuo *et al.*, 2006). However, the effort was mainly devoted to mitigating the need of manual labeling. A dynamic *learning-at-work* mechanism for mining transliterations has not been well studied.

Here we are interested in an unsupervised learning process, in which we adapt the PSM as we extract transliterations. The *learning-at-work* framework is illustrated in Figure 2. As opposed to a manually labeled training corpus in Figure 1, we insert into the EM process an automatic transliteration extraction mechanism, *search and rank*, as shown in the left panel of Figure 2. The *search and rank* shortlists a set of transliterations from the Web query results or bilingual snippets.

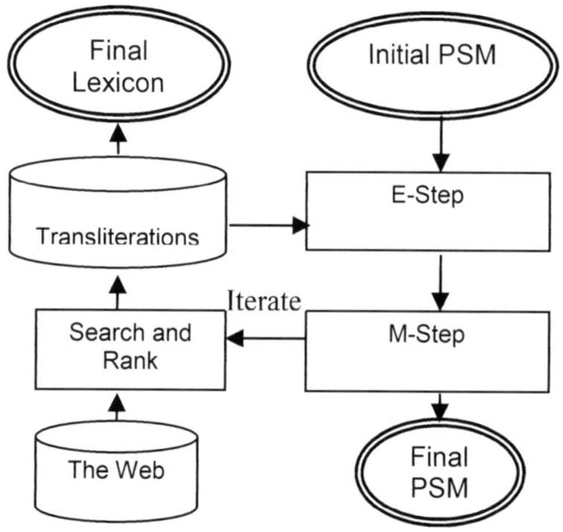

Figure 2. Diagram of unsupervised transliteration extraction – *learning-at-work*.

4.1 Search and Rank

We obtain bilingual snippets from the Web by iteratively submitting queries to the Web search engines (Brin and Page, 1998). Qualified sentences are extracted from the results of each query. Each qualified sentence has at least one English word.

Given a qualified sentence, first, the competing Chinese transliteration candidates are denoted as a set Ω, from which we would like to pick the most likely one. Second, we would like to know if there is indeed a Chinese transliteration CW in the close context of the English word EW.

We propose ranking the candidates using the PSM model to find the most likely CW for a given EW. The CW candidate that gives the highest posterior probability is considered the most probable

[1] The Chinese words are romanized in Hanyu Pinyin.

candidate CW'.

$$CW' = \arg\max_{CW \in \Omega} P(CW \mid EW) \approx \arg\max_{CW \in \Omega} P(ES \mid CS)P(CW) \quad (15)$$

The next step is to examine if CW' and EW indeed form a genuine *E-C* pair. We define the confidence of the *E-C* pair as the posterior odds similar to that in a hypothesis test under the Bayesian interpretation. We have H_0, which hypothesizes that CW' and EW form an *E-C* pair, and H_1, which hypothesizes otherwise, and use posterior odd σ (Kuo *et al.*, 2006) for hypothesis tests.

Our *search and rank* formulation can be seen as an extension to a prior work (Brill *et al.*, 2001). The posterior odd σ is used as the confidence score so that *E-C* pairs extracted from different contexts can be directly compared. In practice, we set a threshold for σ to decide on a cutoff point for *E-C* pairs short-listing. In this way, the *search and rank* is able to retrieve a collection of transliterations from the Web given a PSM.

4.2 Unsupervised Learning Strategy

Now we can carry out PSM learning as formulated in Section 3 using the transliterations as if they were manually validated. By unsupervised batch learning, we mean to re-estimate the PSM after *search and rank* over the whole database, i.e., in each iteration. Just as in supervised learning, one can expect the PSM performance to improve over multiple iterations. We report the *F*-measure at each iteration. The extracted transliterations also form a new training corpus in next iteration.

In contrast to the batch learning, incremental learning updates the PSM parameters as the training samples arrive in sequence. This is especially useful in Web mining. With the QB incremental optimization, one can think of an EM process that continuously re-estimates PSM parameters as the Web crawler discovers new "territories". In this way, the *search and rank* process gathers qualified training samples D_t after crawling a portion of the Web. Note that the incremental EM process updates parameters more often than batch learning does. To evaluate performance of both learning, we define an iteration to be T EM cycles in incremental learning on a training corpus $D = D^{(T)}$ as discussed in Section 3.2.

5 Experiments

To obtain the ground truth for performance evaluation, each possible transliteration pair is manually checked based on the following criteria: (i) only the phonetic transliteration is extracted to form a transliteration pair; (ii) multiple *E-C* pairs may appear in one sentence; (iii) an *EW* can have multiple valid Chinese transliterations and vice versa. The validation process results in a collection of qualified *E-C* pairs, also referred to as *distinct qualified transliteration pairs* (DQTPs), which form a transliteration lexicon.

To simulate the dynamic Web, we collected a Web corpus, which consists of about 500 MB of Web pages, referred to as SET1. From SET1, 80,094 qualified sentences were automatically extracted and 8,898 DQTPs were further selected with manual validation.

To establish a reference for performance benchmarking, we first initialize a PSM, referred to as *seed* PSM hereafter, using randomly selected 100 seed DQTPs. By exploiting the *seed* PSM on all 8,898 DQTPs, we train a PSM in a supervised batch mode and improve the PSM on SET1 after each iteration. The performance defined below in precision, recall and *F*-measure in the 6th iteration is reported in Table 1 and the *F*-measure is also shown in Figure 3.

$$precision = \#extracted\_DQTPs / \#extracted\_pairs,$$
$$recall = \#extracted\_DQTPs / \#total\_DQTPs,$$
$$F-measure = 2 \times recall \times precision / (recall + precision)$$

	Precision	Recall	F-measure
Closed-test	0.834	0.663	0.739

Table 1. The performance achieved by supervised batch learning on SET1.

We use this closed test (supervised batch learning) as the reference point for unsupervised experiments. Next we further implement two PSM learning strategies, namely unsupervised batch and unsupervised incremental learning.

5.1 Unsupervised Batch Learning

We begin with the same *seed* PSM. However, we use transliterations that are extracted automatically instead of manually validated DQTPs for training. Note that the transliterations are extracted and collected at the end of each iteration. It may differ from one iteration to another. After re-estimating the PSM in each iteration, we evaluate performance on SET1.

Comparing the two batch mode learning strategies in Figure 3, it is observed that learning substantially improves the *seed* PSM after the first iteration. Without surprise, the supervised learning consistently outperforms the unsupervised one, which reaches a plateau at 0.679 F-measure. This performance is considered as the baseline for comparison in this paper. The unsupervised batch learning presented here is similar to that in (Kuo *et al.*, 2006).

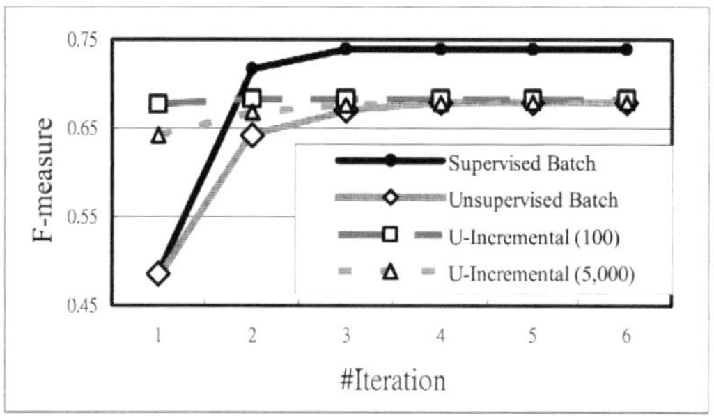

Figure 3. Comparison of F-measure over iterations (U-Incremental: Unsupervised Incremental).

5.2 Unsupervised Incremental Learning

We now formulate an *on-line*[2] unsupervised incremental learning algorithm:

(i) Start with the *seed* PSM, set $t=1$;
(ii) Extract $|D_t|$ quasi-transliterations pairs followed by E-Step in incremental learning algorithm;
(iii) Re-estimate PSM using $|D_t|$ (M-Step), $t=t+1$;
(iv) Repeat (ii) and (iii) to crawl over a corpus.

To simulate the *on-line* incremental learning just described, we train and test on SET1 because of the availability of gold standard and comparison with performance by batch mode. We empirically set $\alpha=0.5$ and study different $|D_t|$ settings. An iteration is defined as multiple cycles of steps (ii)-(iii) that screen through the whole SET1 once. We run multiple iterations.

The performance of incremental learning with $|D_t|=100$ and $|D_t|=5,000$ are reported in Figure 3. It is observed that incremental learning benefits from more frequent PSM updating. With $|D_t|=100$, it not only attains good *F*-measure in the first iteration, but also outperforms that of unsupervised batch learning along the EM process. The PSM updating becomes less frequent for larger $|D_t|$. When $|D_t|$ is set to be the whole corpus, then incremental learning becomes a batch mode learning, which is evidenced by $|D_t|=5,000$ and it performs close to the batch mode learning. The experiments in Figure 3 are considered closed tests. Next we move on to an actual *on-line* experiment.

5.3 Learning from the Live Web

In practice, it is possible to extract bilingual snippets of interest by repeatedly submitting queries to the Web. With the *learning-at-work* mechanism, we can mine the query results for up-to-date transliterations in an *on-line* environment. For example, by submitting "Amy" to search engines, we may get "Amy-愛咪/Ai-Mi/" and, as a by-product, "Jessica-潔西卡/Jie-Xi-Ka/" as well. In this way, new queries can be generated iteratively, thus new pairs are discovered.

Following the unsupervised incremental learning algorithm, we start the crawling with the same *seed* PSM as in Section 5.2. We adapt the PSM as every 100 quasi-transliterations are extracted, i.e. $|D_t|=100$. The crawling stops after accumulating 67,944 Web pages, where there are 100 snippets at most in a page, with 2,122,026 qualified sentences. We obtain 123,215 distinct *E-C* pairs when the crawling stops. For comparison, we also carry out unsupervised batch learning over the same 2,122,026 qualified sentences in a single iteration under such an *on-line* environment. As the gold standard for this live corpus is not available, we randomly select 500 quasi-transliteration pairs for manual checking of precision (see Table 2). It is found that incremental learning is more productive than batch learning in discovering transliteration pairs. This finding is consistent with the test results on SET1.

	Unsupervised Batch	Unsupervised Incremental
#distinct *E-C* pairs	67,708	123,215
Estimated Precision	0.758	0.768

Table 2. Comparison between the unsupervised batch and incremental learning from live Web.

The live Web corpus was used in transliteration extraction using active learning (Kuo *et al.*, 2006).

[2] In an actual *on-line* environment, we are not supposed to store documents, thus no iteration can take place.

Kuo *et al.* reported slightly better performance by annotating some samples manually and adapting the learning process in a batch manner. However, it is apparent that, in an *on-line* environment, the unsupervised learning is more suitable for discovering knowledge without resorting to human annotation; incremental learning is desirable as it does not require storing all documents in advance.

6 Conclusions

We have proposed a learning framework for mining *E-C* transliterations using bilingual snippets from a live Web corpus. In this *learning-at-work* framework, we formulate the PSM learning method and study strategies for PSM learning in both batch and incremental manners. The batch mode learning benefits from multiple iterations for improving performance, while the unsupervised incremental one, which does not require all the training data to be available in advance, adapts to the dynamically changing environment easily without compromising the performance. Unsupervised incremental learning provides a practical and effective solution to transliteration extraction from query results, which can be easily extended to other Web mining applications.

References

S. Bai and H. Li. 2006. Bayesian Learning of N-gram Statistical Language Modeling, In *Proc. of ICASSP*, pp. 1045-1048.

M. Bacchiani, B. Roark, M. Riley and R. Sproat. 2006. MAP Adaptation of Stochastic Grammars, Computer Speech and Language, 20(1), pp. 41-68.

E. Brill, G. Kacmarcik, C. Brockett. 2001. Automatically Harvesting Katakana-English Term Pairs from Search Engine Query Logs, In *Proc. of NLPPRS*, pp. 393-399.

S. Brin and L. Page. 1998. The Anatomy of a Large-scale Hypertextual Web Search Engine, In *Proc. of 7th WWW,* pp. 107-117.

A. P. Dempster, N. M. Laird and D. B. Rubin. 1977. Maximum Likelihood from Incomplete Data via the EM Algorithm, Journal of the Royal Statistical Society, Ser. B. Vol. 39, pp. 1-38.

P. Fung and L.-Y. Yee. 1998. An IR Approach for Translating New Words from Nonparallel, Comparable Texts, In *Proc. of 17th COLING and 36th ACL*, pp. 414-420.

Y. Gotoh, M. M. Hochberg and H. F. Silverman. 1998. Efficient Training Algorithms for HMM's Using Incremental Estimation, IEEE Trans. on Speech and Audio Processing, 6(6), pp. 539-547.

F. Jelinek. 1999. Self-organized Language Modeling for Speech Recognition, Readings in speech recognition, Morgan Kaufmann, pp. 450-506.

D. Jurafsky and J. H. Martin. 2000. Speech and Language Processing, pp. 102-120, Prentice-Hall, New Jersey.

K. Knight and J. Graehl. 1998. Machine Transliteration, Computational Linguistics, 24(4), pp. 599-612.

J.-S. Kuo, H. Li and Y.-K. Yang. 2006. Learning Transliteration Lexicons from the Web, In *Proc. of 44th ACL*, pp. 1129-1136.

J.-S. Kuo, H. Li and Y.-K. Yang. 2007. A Phonetic Similarity Model for Automatic Extraction of Transliteration Pairs, ACM TALIP, 6(2), pp. 1-24.

H. Li, M. Zhang and J. Su. 2004. A Joint Source Channel Model for Machine Transliteration, In *Proc. of 42nd ACL*, pp. 159-166.

W. Lam, R.-Z. Huang and P.-S. Cheung. 2004. Learning Phonetic Similarity for Matching Named Entity Translations and Mining New Translations, In *Proc. of 27th ACM SIGIR*, pp. 289-296.

D. MacKay and L. Peto. 1994. A Hierarchical Dirichlet Language Model, Natural Language Engineering, 1(3), pp.1-19.

C. S. Myers and L. R. Rabiner. 1981. A Comparative Study of Several Dynamic Time-warping Algorithms for Connected word Recognition, The Bell System Technical Journal, 60(7), pp. 1389-1409.

J.-Y. Nie, P. Isabelle, M. Simard and R. Durand. 1999. Cross-language Information Retrieval based on Parallel Texts and Automatic Mining of Parallel Text from the Web, In *Proc. of 22nd ACM SIGIR*, pp. 74-81.

R. Rapp. 1999. Automatic Identification of Word Translations from Unrelated English and German Corpora, In *Proc. of 37th ACL*, pp. 519-526.

R. Sproat, T. Tao and C. Zhai. 2006. Named Entity Transliteration with Comparable Corpora, In *Proc. of 44th ACL*, pp. 73-80.

G. Zavaliagkos, R. Schwartz, and J. Makhoul. 1995. Batch, Incremental and Instantaneous Adaptation Techniques for Speech Recognition, In *Proc. of ICASSP*, pp. 676-679.

An Effective Hybrid Machine Learning Approach for Coreference Resolution

Feiliang Ren
Natural Language Processing Lab
College of Information Science and Engineering
Northeastern University, P.R.China
renfeiliang@ise.neu.edu.cn

Jingbo Zhu
Natural Language Processing Lab
College of Information Science and Engineering
Northeastern University, P.R.China
zhujingbo@ise.neu.edu.cn

Abstract

We present a hybrid machine learning approach for coreference resolution. In our method, we use CRFs as basic training model, use active learning method to generate combined features so as to make existed features used more effectively; at last, we proposed a novel clustering algorithm which used both the linguistics knowledge and the statistical knowledge. We built a coreference resolution system based on the proposed method and evaluate its performance from three aspects: the contributions of active learning; the effects of different clustering algorithms; and the resolution performance of different kinds of NPs. Experimental results show that additional performance gain can be obtained by using active learning method; clustering algorithm has a great effect on coreference resolution's performance and our clustering algorithm is very effective; and the key of coreference resolution is to improve the performance of the normal noun's resolution, especially the pronoun's resolution.

1 Introduction

Coreference resolution is the process of determining whether two noun phrases (NPs) refer to the same entity in a document. It is an important task in natural language processing and can be classified into pronoun phrase (denoted as ***PRO***) resolution, normal noun phrase (denoted as ***NOM***) resolution, and named noun phrase (denoted as ***NAM***) resolution. Machine learning approaches recast this problem as a classification task based on constraints that are learned from an annotated corpus. Then a separate clustering mechanism is used to construct a partition on the set of NPs.

Previous machine learning approaches for coreference resolution (Soon et al, 2001; Ng et al, 2002; Florian et al, 2004, etc) usually selected a machine learning approach to train a classification model, used as many as possible features for the training of this classification model, and finally used a clustering algorithm to construct a partition on the set of NPs based on the statistical data obtained from trained classification model. Their experimental results showed that different kinds of features had different contributions for system's performance, and usually the more features used, the better performance obtained. But they rarely focused on how to make existed features used more effectively; besides, they proposed their own clustering algorithm respectively mainly used the statistical data obtained from trained classification model, they rarely used the linguistics knowledge when clustering different kinds of NPs. Also, there were fewer experiments conducted to find out the effect of a clustering algorithm on final system's performance.

In this paper, we propose a new hybrid machine learning method for coreference resolution. We use NP pairs to create training examples; use CRFs as a basic classification model, and use active learning method to generate some combined features so as to make existed features used more effectively; at last, cluster NPs into entities by a novel cascade clustering algorithm.

The rest of the paper is organized as follows. Section 2 presents our coreference resolution system in detail. Section 3 is our experiments and discussions. And at last, we conclude our work in section 4.

2 Coreference Resolution

There are three basic components for a coreference resolution system that uses machine learning approach: the training set creation, the feature selection, and the coreference clustering algorithm. We will introduce our methods for these components respectively as follows.

2.1 Training Set Creation

Previous researchers (Soon et al., 2001, Vincent Ng et al., 2002, etc) took different creation strategies for positive examples and negative examples. Because there were no experimental results showed that these kinds of example creation methods were helpful for system's performance, we create both positive examples and negative examples in a unified NP pair wise manner.

Given an input NP chain of an annotated document, select a NP in this NP chain from left to right one by one, and take every of its right side's NP, we generate a positive example if they refer to the same entity or a negative example if they don't refer to the same entity. For example, there is a NP chain n1-n2-n3-n4 found in document, we will generate following training examples: (n1-n2, ± 1), (n1-n3, ± 1), (n1-n4, ± 1), (n2-n3, ± 1), (n2-n4, ± 1), and (n3-n4, ± 1). Where $+1$ denotes that this is a positive example, and -1 denotes that this is a negative example.

2.2 Feature Sets

In our system, two kinds of features are used. One is atomic feature, the other is combined feature. We define the features that have only one generation condition as atomic features, and define the union of some atomic features as combined features.

2.2.1 Atomic Features

All of the atomic features used in our system are listed as follows.

String Match Feature (denoted as *Sm*): Its possible values are *exact, left, right, included*, *part*, *alias*, and *other*. If two NPs are exactly string matched, return *exact*; if one NP is the left substring of the other, return *left*; if one NP is the right substring of the other, return *right*; if all the characters in one NP are appeared in the other but not belong to set {*left, right*}, return *included*; if some (not all) characters in one NP are appeared in the other, return *part*; if one NP is the alias of the other, return *alias*; if two NPs don't have any common characters, return *other*.

Lexical Similarity Features (denoted as *Ls*): compute two NP's similarity and their head words' similarity using following formula 1.

$$Sim(n_1, n_2) = \frac{2 \times SameChar(n_1, n_2)}{Len(n_1) + Len(n_2)} \quad (1)$$

Here $SameChar(n_1, n_2)$ means the common characters' number in n_1 and n_2 ; $Len(n_i)$ is the total characters' number in n_i .

Edit Distance Features (denoted as *Ed*): compute two NP's edit distance and their head words' edit distance (Wagner and Fischer, 1974), and the possible values are *true* and *false*. If the edit distance of two NPs (or the head words of these two NPs) are less than or equal to 1, return *true*, else return *false*.

Distance Features (denoted as *Dis*): distance between two NPs in words, NPs, sentences, paragraphs, and characters.

Length Ratio Features (denoted as *Lr*): the length ratio of two NPs, and their head words. Their possible values belong to the range $(0,1]$.

NP's Semantic Features (denoted as *Sem*): the POSs of two NPs' head words; the types of the two NPs (***NAM***, ***NOM*** or ***PRO***); besides, if one of the NP is ***PRO***, the semantic features will also include this NP's gender information and plurality information.

Other Features (denoted as *Oth*): whether two NPs are completely made up of capital English characters; whether two NPs are completely made up of lowercase English characters; whether two NPs are completely made up of digits.

2.2.2 Combined Features Generated by Active Learning

During the process of model training for coreference resolution, we found that we had very fewer available resources compared with previous researchers. In their works, they usually had some extra knowledge-based features such as alias table, abbreviation table, *wordnet* and so on; or they had some extra in-house analysis tools such as proper name parser, chunk parser, rule-based shallow coreference resolution parser, and so on (Hal Daume III, etc, 2005; R.Florian, etc, 2004; Vincent Ng, etc, 2002; etc). Although we also collected some aliases and abbreviations, the amounts are very small compared with previous researchers'. We hope we can make up for this by making existed features used more effectively by active learning method.

Formally, active learning studies the closed-loop phenomenon of a learner selecting actions or making queries that influence what data are added to its training set. When actions or queries are selected properly, the data requirements for some problems decrease drastically (Angluin, 1988; Baum & Lang, 1991). In our system, we used a pool-based active learning framework that is similar as Manabu Sassano (2002) used, this is shown in figure 1.

1. Build an initial classifier
2. While teacher can ***correct examples based on feature combinations***
   a) Apply the current classifier to training examples
   b) Find ***m*** most ***informative*** training examples
   c) Have two teachers correct these examples based on feature combinations
   d) Add the feature combinations that are used by both of these two teachers to feature sets in CRFs and train a new classifier.

Figure 1: Our Active Learning Framework

In this active learning framework, an initial classifier is trained by CRFs [1] that uses only atomic features, and then two human teachers are asked to correct some selected wrong classified examples independently. During the process of correction, without any other available information, system only shows the examples that are made up of features to the human teachers; then these two human teachers have to use the information of some atomic features' combinations to decide whether two NPs refer to the same entity. We record all these atomic features' combinations that used by both of these human teachers, and take them as combined features.

For example, if both of these human teachers correct a wrong classified example based on the knowledge that "if two NPs are left substring matched, lexical similarity feature is greater than 0.5, I think they will refer to the same entity", the corresponding combined feature would be described as: "*Sm(NPs)-Ls(NPs)*", which denotes the human teachers made their decisions based on the combination information of "*String Match Features*" and "*Lexical Similarity Features*".

1. Select all the wrong classified examples whose CRFs' probability belongs to range [0.4, 0.6]
2. Sort these examples in decreasing order.
3. Select the top ***m*** examples

Figure 2: Selection Algorithm

In figure 1, "*information*" means the valuable data that can improve the system's performance after correcting their classification. The selection algorithm for "*informative*" is the most important component in an active learning framework. We designed it from the degree of correcting difficulty. We know 0.5 is a critical value for an example's classification. For a wrong classified example, the closer its probability value to 0.5, the easier for us to correct its classification. Following this, our selection algorithm for "informative" is designed as shown in figure 2.

When add new combined features won't lead to a performance improvement, we end active learning process. Totally we obtained 21 combined features from active learning. Some of them are listed in table 1.

Table 1: Some Combined Features

Sm(NPs)-Sm(HWs)-Ls(NPs)-Ls(HWs)
Sm(NPs)-Sm(HWs)-Ls(NPs)
Sm(NPs)-Sm(HWs)-Ls(HWs)
Sm(NPs)-Sm(HWs)-Lr(NPs)-Lr(HWs)
Sm(NPs)-Sm(HWs)-Lr(NPs)
Sm(NPs)-Sm(HWs)-Sem(HW1)-Sem(HW2)
Sm(NPs)-Sm(HWs)-Sem(NP1)-Sem(NP2)
Sm(NPs)-Sm(HWs)-Lr(HWs)
……

Here "*Sm(NPs)*" means the string match feature's value of two NPs, "*Sm(HWs)*" means the string match feature's value of two NPs' head words. "*HWs*" means the head words of two NPs. Combined feature "*Sm(NPs)-Sm(HWs)-Ls(NPs)*" means when correcting a wrong classified example, both these human teachers made their decisions based on the combination information of *Sm(NPs)*, *Sm(HWs)*, and *Ls(NPs)* . Other combined features have the similar explanation.

[1] http://www.chasen.org/~taku/software/CRF++/

And at last, we take all the atomic features and the combined features as final features to train the final CRFs classifier.

2.3 Clustering Algorithm

Formally, let $\{m_i : 1 \le i \le n\}$ be n NPs in a document. Let us define $S_a = \{N_{a1}, ..., N_{af}\}$ the set of NPs whose types are all ***NAM***s; define $S_o = \{N_{o1}, ..., N_{og}\}$ the set of NPs whose types are all ***NOM***s; define $S_p = \{N_{p1}, ..., N_{pk}\}$ the set of NPs whose types are all ***PRO***s. Let $g : i \mapsto j$ be the map from NP index i to entity index j. For a NP index $k (1 \le k \le n)$, let us define $J_k = \{g(1), ..., g(k-1)\}$ the set of indices of the partially-established entities before clustering m_k, and $E_k = \{e_t : t \in J_k\}$, the set of the partially-established entities. Let e_{ij} be the $j-th$ NP in $i-th$ entity. Let $prob(m_i, m_j)$ be the probability that m_i and m_j refer to the same entity, and $prob(m_i, m_j)$ can be trained from CRFs.

Given that E_k has been formed before clustering m_k, m_k can take two possible actions: if $g(k) \in J_k$, then the active NP m_k is said to *link* with the entity $e_{g(k)}$; otherwise it *starts* a new entity $e_{g(k)}$.

In this work, $P(L = 1 | E_k, m_k, A = t)$ is used to compute the link probability, where $t \in J_k$, L is 1 iff m_k links with e_t; the random variable A is the index of the partial entity to which m_k is linking.

Our clustering algorithm is shown in figure 3. The basic idea of our clustering algorithm is that ***NAM*s, *NOM***s and ***PRO***s have different abilities starting an entity. For ***NAM***s, they are inherent antecedents in entities, so we start entities based on them first.

For ***NOM***s, they have a higher ability of acting as antecedents in entities than ***PRO***s, but lower than ***NAM***s. We cluster them secondly, and add a ***NOM*** in an existed entity as long as their link probability is higher than a threshold. And during the process of the link probabilities computations, we select a NP in an existed entity carefully, and take these two NPs' link probability as the link probability between this ***NOM*** and current entity. The selection strategy is to try to make these link probabilities have the greatest distinction.

And for ***PROs***, they have the lowest ability of acting as antecedents in entities, most of the time, they won't be antecedents in entities; so we cluster them into an existed entity as long as there is a non-zero link probability.

3 Experiments and Discussions

Our experiments are conducted on Chinese EDR (Entity Detection and Recognize) &EMD (Entity Mention Detection) corpora from LDC. These corpora are the training data for ACE (Automatic Content Extraction) evaluation 2004 and ACE evaluation 2005. These corpora are annotated and can be used to train and test the coreference resolution task directly.

Input: $M = \{m_i : 1 \le i \le n\}$
Output: a partition E of the set M
Initialize: $H^0 \leftarrow \{e_i = \{\{m_i : m_i \in S_a\}\}\}$
if $\exists m_x \in e_c \cap m_y \in e_d$, $c \ne d$, and m_x is alias of m_y, then $H' \leftarrow H \setminus \{e_d\} \cup \{e_c \cup e_d\}$
foreach $m_k \in S_o$ that hasn't been clustered
  if e_{k0} is ***NAM*** and $\exists d$ makes $\sigma(e_{td}, NOM) \ne 0$
    $P = \arg\max_{e_t} \{prob(m_k, e_{td}) \times \sigma(e_{td}, NOM)\}_{|d-k|=\min}$
  esleif e_{k0} is ***NAM*** and $\forall d, \sigma(e_{td}, NOM) == 0$
    $P = \arg\max_{e_t} \{prob(m_k, e_{td}) \times \sigma(e_{td}, NAM)\}_{|d-k|=\min}$
  esleif e_{k0} is ***NOM***
    $P = \arg\max_{e_t} prob(m_k, e_{t0})$
  if $P \ge \theta$, $H' \leftarrow H \setminus \{e_t\} \cup \{e_t \cup \{m_k\}\}$
  else $H' \leftarrow H \cup \{m_k\}$
foreach $m_k \in S_p$ that hasn't been clustered
  $P = \arg\max_{m \in e_t} prob(m, m_k)$
  if $P > 0$, $H' \leftarrow H \setminus \{e_t\} \cup \{e_t \cup \{m_k\}\}$
  else $H' \leftarrow H \cup \{m_k\}$
return H

Figure 3: Our Clustering Algorithm

In ACE 2004 corpus, there are two types of documents: paper news (denoted as newswire) and broadcast news (denoted as broadca); for ACE 2005 corpus, a new type added: web log documents (denoted as weblogs). Totally there are 438 documents in ACE 2004 corpus and 636 documents in ACE 2005 corpus. We randomly divide these two corpora into two parts respectively, 75% of them for training CRFs model, and 25% of them for test. By this way, we get 354 documents for training and 84 documents for test in ACE 2004 corpus; and 513 documents for training and 123 documents for test in ACE 2005 corpus.

Some statistics of ACE2005 corpus and ACE2004 corpus are shown in table 2.

Our experiments were classified into three groups. Group 1 (denoted as ***ExperimentA***) is designed to evaluate the contributions of active learning for the system's performance. We developed two systems for ***ExperimentA***, one is a system that used only the atomic features for CRFs training and we took it as a baseline system, the other is a system that used both the atomic features and the combined features for CRFs training and we took it as our final system. The experimental results are shown in table 3 and table 4 for different corpus respectively. Bold font is the results of our final system, and normal font is the results of baseline system. Here we used the clustering algorithm as described in figure 3.

Group 2 (denoted as ***ExperimentB***) is designed to investigate the effects of different clustering algorithm for coreference resolution. We implemented another two clustering algorithms: *algorithm1* that is proposed by Ng et al. (2002) and *algorithm2* that is proposed by Florian et al. (2004). We compared the performance of them with our clustering algorithm and experimental results are shown in table 5.

Group 3 (denoted as ***ExperimentC***) is designed to evaluate the resolution performances of different kinds of NPs. We think this is very helpful for us to find out the difficulties and bottlenecks of coreference resolution; and also is helpful for our future work. Experimental results are shown in table 6.

In ***ExperimentB*** and ***ExperimentC***, we used both atomic features and combined features for CRFs classification model training. And in table5, table6 and table7, the data before "/" are experimental results for ACE2005 corpus and the data after "/" are experimental results for ACE2004 corpus.

In all of our experiments, we use recall, precision, and F-measure as evaluation metrics, and denoted as R, P, and F for short respectively.

Table 2: Statistics of ACE2005/2004 Corpora

	Training	Test
# of all documents	513/354	123/84
# of broadca	204/204	52/47
# of newswire	229/150	54/47
#of weblogs	80/0	17/0
# of characters	248972/164443	55263/35255
# of NPs	28173/18995	6257/3966
# of entities	12664/8723	2783/1828
# of ***neg*** examples	722919/488762	142949/89894
# of ***pos*** examples	72000/44682	15808/8935

Table3: ***ExperimentA*** for ACE2005 Corpora

	R	P	F
broadca	**79.0**/76.2	**75.4**/72.9	**77.2**/74.5
newswire	**73.2**/72.9	**68.7**/67.8	**70.9**/70.3
weblogs	**72.3**/68.5	**65.5**/63.3	**68.8**/65.8
total	**75.4**/73.7	**70.9**/69.3	**73.1**/71.4

Table4: ***ExperimentA*** for ACE2004 Corpora

	R	P	F
broadca	**74.7**/71.0	**72.4**/68.9	**73.5**/69.9
newswire	**77.7**/73.1	**73.0**/68.6	**75.2**/70.7
Total	**76.2**/72.0	**72.7**/68.7	**74.4**/70.4

Table5: ***ExperimentB*** for ACE2005/2004 Corpora

	R	P	F
algorithm1	61.0/63.5	59.5/62.8	60.2/63.2
algorithm2	61.0/62.4	60.7/62.8	60.9/62.6
Ours	**75.4/76.2**	**70.9/72.7**	**73.1/74.4**

Table6: ***ExperimentC*** for ACE2005/2004 Corpora

	R	P	F
NAM	80.5/81.4	77.9/79.2	79.2/80.1
NOM	62.6/62.5	54.4/56.8	58.2/59.5
PRO	28.4/29.8	22.7/24.0	25.2/26.6

From table 3 and table 4 we can see that the final system's performance made a notable improvement compared with the baseline system in both corpora. We know the only difference of these two systems is whether used active learning method. This indicates that by using active learning method, we make the existed features used more effectively and obtain additional performance gain accordingly. One may say that even without active learning method, he still can add some combined features during CRFs model training. But this can't guarantee it would make a performance improvement at anytime. Active learning method provides us a way that makes this combined features' selection process goes in a proper manner. Generally, a system can obtain an obvious performance improvement after several active learning iterations. We still noticed that the contributions of active learning for different kinds of documents are different. In ACE04 corpus, both kinds of documents' performance obtained almost equal improvements; in ACE05 corpus, there is almost no performance improvement for newswire documents, but broadcast documents' performance and web log documents' performance obtained greater improvements. We think this is because for different kinds of documents, they have different kinds of correcting rules (these rules refer to the combination methods of atomic features) for the wrong classified examples, some of these rules may be consistent, but some of them may be conflicting. Active learning mechanism will balance these conflicts and select a most appropriate global optimization for these rules. This can also explain why ACE04 corpus obtains more performance improvement than ACE05 corpus, because there are more kinds of documents in ACE05 corpus, and thus it is more likely to lead to rule conflicts during active learning process.

Experimental results in table 5 show that if other experimental conditions are the same, there are obvious differences among the performances with different clustering algorithms. This surprised us very much because both *algorithm1* and *algorithm2* worked very well in their own learning frameworks. We know R.Florian et al. (2004) first proposed *algorithm2* using maximum entropy model. Is this the reason for the poor performance of *algorithm2* and *algorithm1*? To make sure this, we conducted other experiments that changed the CRFs model to maximum entropy model [2] without changing any other conditions and the experimental results are shown in table 7.

The experimental results are the same: our clustering algorithm achieved better performance. We think this is mainly because the following reason, that in our clustering algorithm, we notice the fact that different kinds of NPs have different abilities of acting as antecedents in an entity, and take different clustering strategy for them respectively, this is obvious better than the methods that only use statistical data.

Table7: ***ExperimentB*** for ACE2005/2004 Corpora with ME Model

	R	P	F
algorithm1	48.9/48.3	44.2/50.3	46.4/49.3
algorithm2	57.4/59.5	52.3/61.4	54.7/60.4
Ours	**68.1/69.8**	**65.7/72.6**	**66.9/71.2**

We also noticed that the experimental results with maximum entropy model are poorer than with CRFs model. We think this maybe because that the combined features are obtained under CRFs model, thus they will be more suitable for CRFs model than for maximum entropy model, that is to say these obtained combined features don't play the same role in maximum entropy model as they do in CRFs model.

Experimental results in table 6 surprised us greatly. ***PRO*** resolution gets so poor a performance that it is only about 1/3 of the ***NAM*** resolution's performance. And ***NOM*** resolution's performance is also pessimistic, which reaches about 80% of the ***NAM*** resolution's performance. After analyses we found this is because there is too much confusing information for ***NOM***'s resolution and ***PRO***'s resolution and system can hardly distinguish them correctly with current features description for an example. For example, in a Chinese document, a ***NOM*** *"总统"* (means *president*) may refer to a person *A* at sometime, but refer to person *B* at another time, and there is no enough information for system to distinguish *A* and *B*. It is worse for ***PRO*** resolution because a ***PRO*** can refer to any ***NAM*** or ***NOM*** from a very long distance, there is little information for the system to distinguish which one it really refers to. For example, two ***PRO***s that both of whom are "*他*" (means *he*) , one refers to person *A*, the other refers to person *B*, even our human can hardly distinguish them, not to say the system.

Fortunately, generally there are more ***NAMs*** and ***NOMs*** in a document, but less ***PROs***. If they have similar amounts in a document, you can image how poor the performance of the coreference resolution system would be.

4 Conclusions

In this paper, we present a hybrid machine learning approach for coreference resolution task. It uses CRFs as a basic classification model and uses active learning method to generate some combined

[2] http://homepages.inf.ed.ac.uk/s0450736/maxent_toolkit.html

features to make existed features used more effectively; and we also proposed an effective clustering algorithm that used both the linguistics knowledge and the statistical knowledge. Experimental results show that additional performance gain can be obtained by using active learning method, clustering algorithm has a great effect on coreference resolution's performance and our clustering algorithm is very effective. Our experimental results also indicate the key of coreference resolution is to improve the performance of the ***NOM*** resolution, especially the ***PRO*** resolution; both of them remain challenges for a coreference resolution system.

Acknowledgments

We used the method proposed in this paper for Chinese EDR (Entity Detection and Recognition) task of ACE07 (Automatic Content Extraction 2007) and achieved very encouraging result.

And this work was supported in part by the National Natural Science Foundation of China under Grant No.60473140; the National 863 High-tech Project No.2006AA01Z154; the Program for New Century Excellent Talents in University No.NCET-05-0287; and the National 985 Project No.985-2-DB-C03.

Reference

Andrew Kachites McCallum and Kamal Nigam, 1998. Employing EM and pool-based active learning for text classification. In Proceedings of the Fifteenth International Conference on Machine Learning, pp 359-367

Cohn, D., Grahramani, Z., & Jordan, M.1996. Active learning with statistical models. Journal of Artificial Intelligence Research, 4. pp 129-145

Cynthia A.Thompson, Mary Leaine Califf, and Raymond J.Mooney. 1999. Active learning for natural language parsing and information extraction. In Proceedings of the Seventeenth International Conference on Machine Learning, pp 406-414

Hal Daume III and Daniel Marcu, 2005, A large-scale exploration of effective global features for a joint entity detection and tracking model. Proceedings of HLT/EMNLP, 2005

http://www.nist.gov/speech/tests/ace/ace07/doc, The ACE 2007 (ACE07) Evaluation Plan, Evaluation of the Detection and Recognition of ACE Entities, Values, Temporal Expressions, Relations and Events

John Lafferty, Andrew McCallum, and Fernando Pereira. 2001. Conditional random fields: Probabilistic models for segmenting and labeling sequence data. In International Conference on Machine Learingin(ICML01)

Lafferty, J., McCallum, A., & Pereira, F. 2001. Conditional random fields: Probabilistic models for segmenting and labeling sequence data. Proc. ICML

Manabu Sassano. 2002. An Empirical Study of Active Learning with Support Vector Machines for Japanese Word Segmentation. Proceeding of the 40th Annual Meeting of the Association for Computational Linguistics (ACL), 2002, pp 505-512

Min Tang, Xiaoqiang Luo, Salim Roukos.2002. Active Learning for Statistical Natural Language Parsing. Proceedings of the 40th Annual Meeting of the Association for Computational Linguistics (ACL), 2002, pp.120-127.

Pinto, D., McCallum, A., Lee, X., & Croft, W.B. 2003. combining classifiers in text categorization. SIGIR' 03: Proceedings of the Twenty-sixth Annual International ACM SIGIR Conference on Research and Development in Information Retrieval.

Radu Florian, Hongyan Jing, Nanda Kambhatla and Imed Zitouni, "Factoring Complex Models: A Case Study in Mention Detection", in Procedings of the 21st International Conference on Computational Linguistics and 44th Annual Meeting of the ACL, pages 473-480, Sydney, July 2006.

R Florian, H Hassan et al. 2004. A statistical model for multilingual entity detection and tracking. In Proc. Of HLT/NAACL-04, pp1-8

Sha, F., & Pereira, F. 2003. Shallow parsing with conditional random fields. Proceedings of Human Language Technology, NAACL.

Simon Tong, Daphne Koller. 2001. Support Vector Machine Active Learning with Applications to Text Classification. Journal of Machine Learning Research,(2001) pp45-66.

V.Ng and C.Cardie. 2002. Improving machine learning approaches to coreference resolution. In Proceedings of the ACL'02, pp.104-111.

W.M.Soon, H.T.Ng, et al.2001. A Machine Learning Approach to Coreference Resolution of Noun Phrases. Computational Linguistics, 27(4):521-544

Use of Event Types for Temporal Relation Identification in Chinese Text

Yuchang Cheng, Masayuki Asahara and Yuji Matsumoto
Graduate School of Information Science
Nara Institute of Science and Technology
8916-5 Takayama, Ikoma, Nara 630-0192, Japan
{yuchan-c,masayu-a,matsu}@is.naist.jp

Abstract

This paper investigates a machine learning approach for identification of temporal relation between events in Chinese text. We proposed a temporal relation annotation guideline (Cheng, 2007) and constructed temporal information annotated corpora. However, our previous criteria did not deal with various uses of Chinese verbs. For supplementing the previous version of our criteria, we introduce attributes of verbs that describe event types. We illustrate the attributes by the different examples of verb usages. We perform an experiment to evaluate the effect of our event type attributes in the temporal relation identification. As far as we know, this is the first work of temporal relation identification between verbs in Chinese texts. The result shows that the use of the attributes of verbs can improve the annotation accuracy.

1 Introduction

Extracting temporal information in documents is a useful technique for many NLP applications such as question answering, text summarization, machine translation, and so on. The temporal information is coded in three types of expressions: 1. temporal expressions, which describe time or period in the actual or hypothetical world; 2. event or situation expressions that occur at a time point or that last for a period of time; 3. temporal relations, which describe the ordering relation between an event expression and a temporal expression, or between two event expressions.

There are many researches dealing with the temporal expressions and event expressions. Extracting temporal expressions is a subtask of Named Entity Recognition (IREX committee, 1999) and is widely studied in many languages. Normalizing temporal expressions is investigated in evaluation workshops (Chinchor, 1997). Event semantics is investigated in linguistics and AI fields (Bach, 1986). However, researches at temporal relation extraction are still limited. Temporal relation extraction includes the following issues: identifying events, anchoring events on the timeline, ordering events, and reasoning with contextually underspecified temporal expressions. To extract temporal relations, several knowledge resources are necessary, such as tense and aspect of verbs, temporal adverbs, and world knowledge (Mani, et al., 2006).

In English, TimeBank (Pustejovsky, et al., 2006), a temporal information annotated corpus, is available to machine learning approaches for automatically extracting temporal relation. In Chinese, Li (2004) proposed a machine learning based method for temporal relation identification, but they considered the relation between adjacent verbs in a small scale corpus. There is no publicly available Chinese resource for temporal information processing. We proposed (Cheng, 2007) a dependency structure based method to annotate temporal relations manually on a limited set of event pairs and extend the relations using inference rules. In our previous research, the dependency structure helps to detect subordinate and coordinate structures in sentences. Our proposed criteria can reduce the manual effort for annotating the temporal relation tagged corpus.

Our research focuses on the relations between events where they are assumed to be described by verbs. Verbs in an article can represent events in actual world (which describe actual situations or actions) and events in hypothetical world (which describe possible situations, imagination or background knowledge). However, our previous research does not define the class of event types. Our

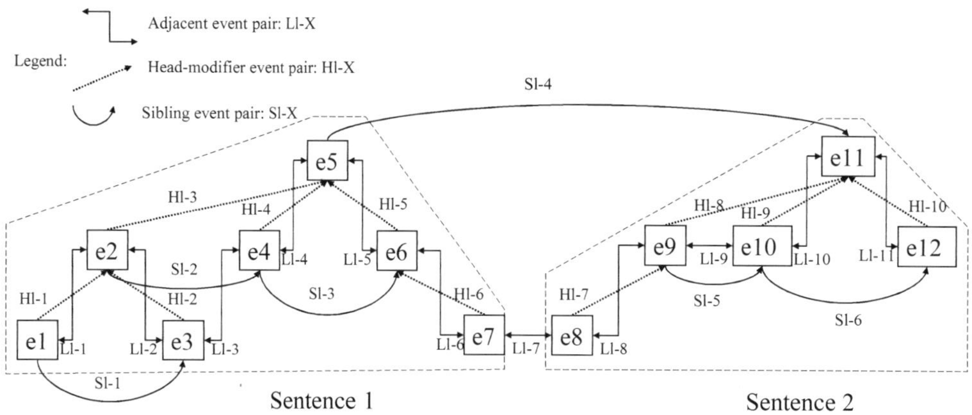

Figure 1: The example of annotating the temporal relations between events.

previous annotation guideline requires annotators to decide the attributes of temporal relations of a verb by annotators' own judgment but does not describe the difference between events (verbs) in actual and hypothetical world.

In this paper, we attempt to give the definition of actual / hypothetical world events (verbs). We collect usages of verbs in Penn Chinese treebank and classify them to actual / hypothetical worlds. We add another attribute to our previous criteria. Then we train the temporal relation annotated corpus to investigate the effect of using the event types for automatic annotation.

In the next section, we describe the criteria of temporal relations between events that are proposed in our previous research (Cheng, 2007). In section 3, we discuss the event types of verbs and define the actual / hypothetical world events. In section 4, we perform an experiment of a machine learning based temporal relation identifier with and without the event type information. Finally, we discuss the results of experiments and our future direction.

2 Temporal relations between events

We propose an annotation guideline for developing a Chinese temporal relation annotated corpus. The guideline is based on TimeML (Saurí, 2005) and focuses on the temporal relations between events. To reduce manual effort, we introduce several constraints on the original TimeML. First, we restrict the definition of events to verbs. Second, we focus on three types of event pairs according to syntactic dependency structure.

2.1 The definition of the events

According to the TimeML guideline for English, verbs, nominalized verbs, adjectives, predicative and prepositional phrases can represent events. However, to recognize an instance of nominalized verb represents whether an event or not is difficult in Chinese articles. Chunking phrases and clauses is another difficult process in Chinese. To simplify the process of recognizing events, the criteria only regard verbs as events.

2.2 Three types of event pairs

The criteria of temporal relation between events include three types of event pairs in the complete graph as follows:

- RLP (Relation to Linear Preceding event): Relation between the focus event and the adjacent event at the immediately proceeding position. (Relation of adjacent event pair).
- RTA (Relation to Tree Ancestor event): Relation between the focus event and the ancestor event in a dependency structure (Relation of Head-modifier event pair).
- RTP (Relation to Tree Preceding event): Relation between the focus event and its sibling event in a dependency structure (Relation of Sibling event pair).

The first type stands for the adjacent event pairs. The second and third types are the head-modifier event pairs and the sibling event pairs in dependency tree representation of a sentence. Figure 1 describes the relation of three types of event pairs in an article. There are two sentences with twelve events (from e1 to e12) in the figure and the polygons with dashed-lines show the boundary of sentences. The angle-line links show adjacent event pairs (from Ll-1 to Ll-11). The dotted-line links show head-modifier event pairs (from Hl-1 to Hl-10) and the curve links show sibling event pairs (from Sl-1 to Sl-6). The first type (adjacent event pairs) and the other two types (head-modifier or sibling event pairs) are not exclusive. An event pair can be a head-modifier event pairs and can be a head-modifier event at the same time.

The adjacent event pair links and the sibling event pair links can be used to connect the temporal relations between sentences. The links Sl-4 and Ll-7 span two sentences in the example.

Subordinate event pairs are head-modifier relations and coordinate event pairs are sibling relations. Using dependency structure can help to extract subordinate relations and coordinate relations in a sentence.

2.3 Deficiency of our previous criteria

Our criteria can reduce manual effort of temporal relation annotation. However, our previous guideline does not distinguish actual world and hypothetical world events. Because all verbs in the previous guideline are regarded as events, verbs of hypothetical world events are also included in the events. For example: (the italicized words in our examples indicate verbs)

- (a) 工業區/*成立*/後/大量/*吸引*/外資 (after the industrial estate ***was established***, it ***attracted*** a great deal of foreign capital)
- (b) 工業區/*成立*/後/可能/大量/*吸引*/外資 (after the industrial estate ***is established***, it can ***attract*** a great deal of foreign capital)

The difference between examples (a) and (b) is only with or without the word "可能 (can)", which governs a verb phrase and explains a possible situation. It should be noted that verbs in Chinese do not have morphological change. The complete meaning of verbs in the examples should consider the global context in the article. The example (a) explains an actual world event that the industrial estate attracted a great deal of foreign capital. However, in example (b), the word "可能 (can)" changes the phrase "大量/吸引/外資 (to attract a great deal of foreign capital)" into a hypothetical world event. This clause presents a possibility and does not indicate an event in the actual world.

Considering the temporal relation between the verbs "成立(establish)" and "吸引(attract)", the temporal relation in the example (a) means that the event 成立(establish) occurs before the event 吸引(attract). On the other hand, in the example (b), the verb "吸引(attract)" indicates a possibility. We cannot make sure if it could really happen. We regard that the temporal relation in the example (b) is unidentifiable. In the previous guideline, we request annotators to decide the temporal relation between them. However we do not classify the difference between actual and hypothetical worlds. The annotators annotate even some incomprehensible temporal relations (such as the relation in example (b)) with the tag "unknown". We clarify the issue by introducing event types to verbs.

Aside form the problem of actual and hypothetical world events, verbs in our temporal relation annotated corpus still include some incomprehensible events (We consider these in the next section). For solving these problems, we investigated different types of events (verbs) in the Penn Chinese Treebank (Palmer, 2005) then give a clear classification of event types. We use this classification of events to annotate events in the temporal relation tagged corpus.

3 Event types of verbs

Our criteria restrict events to verbs according to the POS-tag of Penn Chinese Treebank. Therefore, all the words tagged with the POS-tags (Xia, 2000), "VA", "VE", "VC", and "VV" are the "event candidates". However, these POS-tags include not only actual world events but also hypothetical world events, modifiers of nouns, and subsegments of named entities. We will exemplify these situations in this section.

3.1 Verbs of actual world events

The "event" that we want to annotate is an action or situation that has happened or will definitely happen in the actual world. We define these events as actual world events. For example:

- (c) 市場/*發生*/火災 (A fire ***occurred*** in the market.)
- (d) 市政府/大樓/將於/年底/*完工* (The construction work of the city hall will ***finish*** at the end of the year.)
- (e) 金融/市場/運行/*平穩* (The function of financial market is ***smooth.***)

The verbs in these examples represent actual world events. We want to distinguish between these events and hypothetical world events.

The example (c) is a general instance of an actual world event. The verb "發生 (happen)" in the sentence indicates an occurrence of an event. The verb "完工 (finish)" in example (d) is a confirmative result that definitely happens. The word "將於 (will)" indicates that the sentence describes a future statement. If there is no other statement that describes an accident event in the context, we can trust the event in the example (d) is an actual world event.

In Chinese, an adjective can be a predicate without a copula (corresponding to the verb "be"). The example (e) contains no copula. Still, the adjective "平穩 (smooth)" is a predicate and represents an actual world situation. This kind of adjective is the POS-tag "VA" in Penn Chinese Treebank and also can represent an actual world event.

3.2 Verbs of hypothetical world events

Sometime verbs indicate hypothetical world events. In such situations, verbs describe a possibility, a statement of ability, anticipation, a request or an inconclusive future. For example:

- (b) 工業區/*成立*/後/可能/大量/*吸引*/外資 (after the industrial estate ***is established***, it can ***attract*** a great deal of foreign capital)
- (g) 新港口/能/*停靠*/大型油輪 (A big oil tanker can ***berth*** at the new port)
- (h) 他們/*希望*/政府/*訂立*/相關/法案 (They ***wish*** the government to ***legislate*** against affiliated bill)
- (i) 政府/*要求*/工廠/*改進*/設施 (The government ***requires*** the factory to ***amend*** their equipments)
- (j) 此/技術/*有助於*/未來/*開發*/新藥 (this technology can ***help*** to ***develop*** a new kind of medicine)

The verb "吸引 (attract)" in example (b) explains a possibility that "may" occur after a confirmative result "成立 (establish)" in future. We cannot decide the temporal relation between the actual world event "成立 (establish)" and the possible event "吸引 (attract)" in the example (b), because we do not know if the event "吸引 (attract)" will realize.

The verb "停靠 (berth)" in example (g) explains the capacity of the new port. The verb "停靠 (berth)" does not indicate truth or a confirmative result. We cannot confirm when an oil tanker will berth at the new port. This verb represents a hypothetical world event. The verb "訂立 (legislate)" in the example (h) and the verb "改進(amend)" in the example (i) explain a wish and a request. Even the sentences describe that the government (in the example (h)) or the factory (in the example (i)) was required to do something; the descriptions do not show any evidence that the request will be executed. Although the wish and request will be realized in future, we cannot identify the time point of the realization of these events. Therefore we should consider that these verbs represent hypothetical world events.

The verb "開發 (develop)" in the example (j) explains an inconclusive plan in future. The developed technology can be used for a new development plan. However, we also cannot make sure if the development plan will be realized or not. We cannot identify the verb "開發 (develop)" on a timeline. Since the verb represents a hypothetical world event.

These examples (from the examples (b), (g) to (j)) indicate hypothetical world events. However, as we introduced in section 2.3 (the examples (a) and (b)), the instances with different types of events have the same context in local structure (the phrase "大量/吸引/外資 (to attract a great deal of foreign capital)"). The difference between the example (a) and the example (b) is that the word "*可能 (can)*" exists or not. To distinguish an actual world event and a hypothetical world event with similar local context, the dependency structure analysis is quite helpful.

3.3 Copula verbs

There are two special POS-tags of verbs in Penn Chinese Treebank, VC and VE. These verbs are copulas in Chinese. The copula verb (such as the verb "是 (be)") indicates existence and corresponds to "be" in English. In TimeML, these copulas are not considered as an independent verb. It is included in another verb phrase or in a nominal phrase that represents an event. However, the copula verb "是 (be)" is an independent verb in Penn Chinese Treebank. We should investigate how to deal with this copula verb. For example:

- (k) 舊/法律/*是*/三年前/*修訂*/的 (The older version of bill ***was legislated*** at three years ago.)

- (l) 該/公司/***是***/世界上/最大/的/電力公司 (The company ***is*** the largest electric power company in the world.)

Considering the use of copula in Penn Chinese Treebank, sentences that include copula verbs can be distinguished to two types. The copula verbs describe existence. The existence could be a verb phrase (the example (k)) or a nominal phrase (the example (l)). In the example (k), the verb phrase "三年前/修訂 (was legislated at three years ago)" represents an event that the copula verb accentuates the existence of the verb phrase. Although there are two verbs in the example (k), the sentence only includes an event which is the verb phrase "三年前/修訂 (was legislated at three years ago)".

According to the dependency structure of sentence, copula verbs represent the root of the dependency structure and the head of a verb phrase that modifies a copula verb. We define a pair of a copula and a verb that modifies the copula as a "copula phrase". Therefore we regard the copula verb in the example (k) as the main verb of the verb phrase "修訂 (legislate)" and it represents an actual world event[1].

The copula verb "是 (be)" in the example (l) accentuates the truth of the nominal phrase "世界上/最大/的/電力公司 (the largest electric power company in the world)". According to the discussion in the previous paragraph, the meaning of this copula comes from the nominal phrase. We can recognize the nominal phrase as a truth at the time point "NOW" (the company is largest in the world now). However, this phrase does not indicate any specific period of time that the fact holds. We can regard it as the background knowledge and it does not include an event. To identify the temporal relation between this noun phrase and other actual world event is impossible[2]. We also regard this copula verb as a hypothetical world event.

3.4 Non-event verbs

There are several types of words that have a verbal POS-tag but do not represent events. These words include non-event predicative adjectives and named entities.

In Chinese, adjectives can be predicates of a sentence without verbs. This kind of adjectives are predicative adjective and have a POS-tag "VA" in Penn Chinese Treebank. These predicative adjectives indicate situations. However, some instances in the Treebank are close to normal adjectives. We should distinguish the difference between the predicative adjectives that describe situations and predicative adjectives that are normal adjectives. For example:

- (e) 金融/市場/運行/*平穩* (The function of financial market is ***smooth.***)
- (n)*提供*/*新*/的/動力 (***To provide*** a ***new*** kind of power)

The adjective "平穩 (smooth)" in the example (e) indicates a situation. We regard this adjective as an actual world event. However, the adjective "新 (new)" in the example (n) is a modifier of the noun "動力 (power)". This adjective do not indicate a situation, therefore it dose not represent an event.

Another situation of non-event verbs is a verb in a named entity. Because of the strategy of the POS-tagging of Penn Chinese Treebank, a named entity is separated to several words and these words are tagged independently. For example:

- (o) "*解放*/剛果/民主/同盟 (Alliance of Democratic Forces for ***Liberating*** Congo-Zaire)"

The example (o) shows a named entity that includes a word "解放 (liberate)" has the POS-tag "VV". However, this verb does not represent an actual event or a hypothetical event. It is a substring of the named entity. We define this kind of verbs as non-event verbs.

3.5 Attribute of event types

Figure 2 summarizes the event types of verbs in section 3.1-3.4. We divide the verbs roughly into two types "actual world" and "hypothetical world". Each type includes several sub-types. We annotate these two event types of verbs to our previous temporal relation annotated corpus. The definition of these event types in previous sections is a guideline for our annotators. This new attribute has two

[1] Whether the copula verbs are actual world events or hypothetical world events depend on the modifier verb phrases.

[2] We cannot know when the company became the largest one on the world. And other events in the context distribute in a shorter period on a timeline. Therefore to compare the existence period of the truth and other events is impossible. However, if a temporal expression with a passed time period in the context, the truth could have a boundary of occurrence time. Then the copula can be recognized as an actual world event.

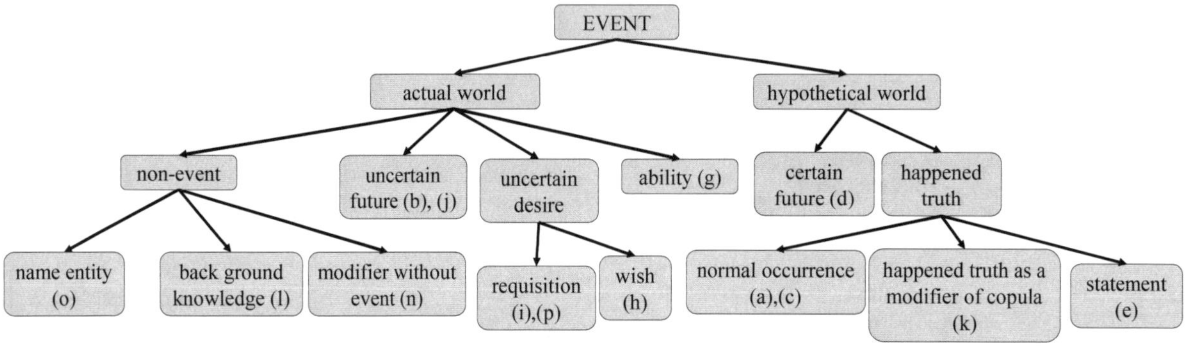

Note: the characters in the brackets refer to the examples of each event type

Figure 2: The classifications of event types

values "actual world" and "hypothetical world". Although the types of values are coarse-grained, this attribute can describe whether a verb can be recognized as an event with understandable temporal relation on the timeline or not.

However, the value "hypothetical world" of the event types means not only that the verbs with this value are temporal relation un-recognizable events, but also that the verbs with this value are "locally recognizable" events. For example:

- (p) 他們/***希望***/政府/***增加***/預算/來/***修補***/堤防 (They ***wish*** the government to ***increase*** budget to ***repair*** the bank)

The verb "希望 (wish)" governs the verb phrase "政府/增加/預算/來/修補/堤防 (the government increases budget to repair the bank)". Therefore the verb phrase represents a hypothetical world event (because we do not know if the government will do it or not). However, considering the local context of the verb phrase, it includes two verbs that have a causal relation between them. The event "增加 (increase)" should occur before the event "修補 (repair)"[3]. The temporal relation between the two verbs exists in the local context. We do not ignore this kind of temporal relations and annotate them. The temporal relation between the verb "增加 (increase)" and the verb "修補 (repair)" is not unknown but the temporal relation between the verbs "增加 (increase)" and the verb "希望 (wish)" is unknown.

Therefore, we regard the attribute of event type as a "bridge" between an actual world and a hypothetical world. The event in the actual world means that we can identify the temporal relation between an event and the other occurred events in an actual world. The temporal relations between a hypothetical world event and an actual world event can only be identified in a hypothetical world. Figure 3 describes this concept. The index on each event indicates the linear ordering of the event mention in the article. The two events with rectangles represent the actual world and the four events with diamond shapes represent the hypothetical world. There is no understandable temporal relation between actual and hypothetical worlds (for example the relation between the event 1 and event 2). The events in hypothetical world have their temporal relation with other events in the same hypothetical world. However, a hypothetical world is independent to other hypothetical worlds. Therefore, the temporal relation between event 2 and event 3 understandable but the relation between event 3 and event 4 are unknown. We ask our annotators to annotate the understandable temporal relations in each hypothetical world because the instances of the local context are useful in analyzing the temporal relation between events in actual world by machine learning.

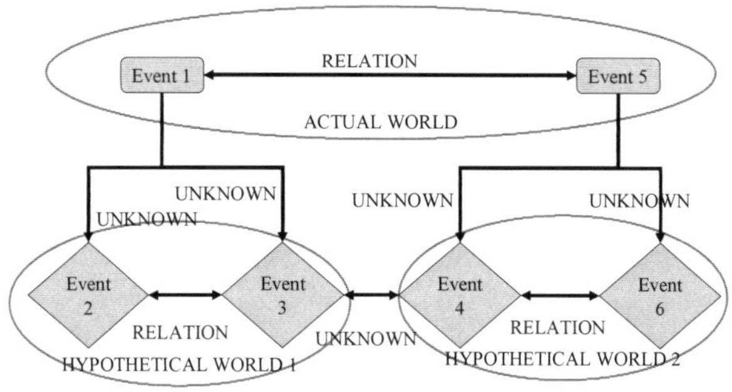

Figure 3: The actual world and hypothetical worlds

4 Evaluation Experiments

[3] The government must increase the budget and pass the deliberation in the congress, and then the budget can be used to repair the bank.

	RLP		RTA		RTP	
	Train	Test	Train	Test	Train	Test
after	2487	278	580	81	925	101
before	1273	139	1864	191	372	36
simultaneous	1391	75	1011	63	525	20
overlap	212	24	96	15	85	2
hypothetical			1587	163		
copula-existence			417	39		
Unknown	2157	216			704	75
Total	7520	732	5553	552	2611	234
Event Types	Train (7520 verbs)			Test (732 verbs)		
	actual world: 4584			actual world: 453		
	hypothetical world: 2936			hypothetical world: 279		

Table 1: The distribution of our data set

After we manually annotate the event type of verbs on our temporal relation tagged corpus, we use support vector machines as machine learner to compose a temporal relation identifier. We perform an experiment to investigate the effect of the event type information.

4.1 The data set

We annotated a part of Penn Chinese Treebank with our previous criteria. The temporal relation tagged corpus includes 7520 verbs. Each verb has three types of temporal relation that we introduce in section 2.3. We annotate the event type information manually and refine some ambiguous instances. For efficiency, we introduce grouping on the temporal relation classes. Our criteria defined ten classes of temporal relation values. We compose three types of temporal relation identifiers (RLP, RTA and RTP) and an event type classifier.

To discriminate the event types of verbs, we add two possible values of temporal relations, the value "hypothetical" and "copula-existence". The value "hypothetical" is introduced in the temporal relation type "RTA". If the verb represents a hypothetical world event or non-event, the verb is enclosed into the hypothetical world. The verb in hypothetical world cannot have a RLP relation (Relation of adjacent event pair) between hypothetical and actual worlds. However, for recognizing the verb that is the root event of the hypothetical world, we annotate the RTA relation (Relation of adjacent event pair) of the root event in hypothetical world as the value "hypothetical". The value "copula-existence" is introduced to annotate the event emphasized by the copula verb. If the copula verb governs a verb phrase with several verbs, the root event of the verb phrase has the value "copula-existence".

The possible values of three types of temporal relations and event types in our experiment are summarized as follows:

- Event types: actual world and hypothetical world
- RLP: after (includes the values "after" and "begun-by" in our criteria), before (includes the values "before" and "end-by" in our criteria), simultaneous, overlap (includes the values "overlap", "overlapped-by", "include", "during" our criteria)
- RTA: after, before, simultaneous, overlap, unknown, copula-existence, hypothetical
- RTP: after, before, simultaneous, overlap

The training data for SVMs includes 151 articles with 49620 words and 7520 verbs and the testing data is collected from articles in Penn Chinese Treebank other than training data (testing data includes 50 short articles with 5010 words and 732 verbs). The basic information of our corpus and the distribution of the value of attributes in our training and testing data are shown in Table 1. It should be noted that the number of the attributes of the data ignore some negligible instances. Such as, if a verb does not have sibling verbs in the dependency structure, to consider the attribute "RTP (Relation between focus event and its sibling event)" is unnecessary. Therefore the total numbers of the attribute "RTA" and the attribute "RTP" are less than the number of all verbs.

4.2 Experiment

We train each classifier (event types, RLP, RTA and RTP) by an independent model. The features for machine learning are also tuned independently. We evaluate the accuracy of automatic annotation of event types and temporal relations with and without our event types. We use our event type tag as a feature of the three temporal relations. Other features for SVM analyzer to annotate the three types of temporal relations include the morphological information of the focus event pair and the dependency structure of the sentence. These features can be extracted from the dependency structures automatically.

The results are shown in Table 2. The abbreviations "R", "P" and "F" mean "Recall", "Precision" and "F-measure". The row "Accuracy w/o event type" means the results of the temporal relations annotating without using the event type as a feature. Other rows use the event type which is annotated

	RLP			RTA			RTP		
	R	P	F	R	P	F	R	P	F
after	0.70	0.62	0.65	0.45	0.64	0.52	0.71	0.63	0.67
before	0.45	0.51	0.50	0.81	0.68	0.73	0.42	0.52	0.46
simultaneous	0.32	0.35	0.33	0.31	0.32	0.32	0.32	0.35	0.33
overlap	0.45	1	0.51	0.6	0.81	0.69	0.29	1	0.45
hypothetical				0.57	0.68	0.62			
copula-existence				0.80	0.67	0.72			
unknown	0.73	0.69	0.71				0.74	0.68	0.70
Accuracy	0.62			0.63			0.61		
Accuracy w/o Event type	0.61			0.60			0.61		

Event Types	actual world			hypothetical world		
R /P /F	0.93	0.91	0.92	0.78	0.76	0.77
Accuracy	0.83					

Table 2: The results of our experiment

by a machine learning-based analyzer as a feature. Because there is no similar related research that analyzes temporal relation between Chinese verbs based on machine learning, we cannot make any comparison. We discuss the accuracy of temporal relation annotating with and without using our event type according to the result of our experiment.

4.2 Discussions

Table 2 shows that the model with the result of the event type classifier is better than that without using the result of the event type classifier. However, the improvement of using event types is limited. The reason might be the accuracy of event type is as low as 83%. To improve the performance of event type annotation helps to improve the relation annotation.

There is no research based on the same data set and corpus guideline, therefore we can not compare the result to other research. However, in the shared task: "TempEval[4] Temporal Relation Identification" (Verhagen, 2007), the task "temporal relations between matrix verbs" resembles the goal of our corpus. The F-measure in TempEval shared task distribute between 40%~50%. The result of the shared task also shows the difficulty of automatic temporal relation analysis.

5 Conclusions and future directions

We propose a machine learning-based temporal relation identification method. This is the first work of the temporal relation identification between verbs in Chinese texts. To deal with the deficiency in our previous temporal relation annotating criteria, we newly introduce the event types of Chinese verb. The result of evaluation experiments shows that the event type information helps to improve the accuracy of the identifier.

A deficient of our experiment is that we do not use semantic information as features for machine learner. Semantic information of temporal and event expressions is important for recognizing temporal relations between events. As a future research, we would like to introduce causal relation knowledge of verbs (this is similar to VerbOcean (Chklovski, 2004)). We are collecting this kind of verb pairs and expect that this causal relation helps to improve the performance of automatic annotation.

References

Emmon Bach. 1986. *the algebra of events*. Linguistics and Philosophy 9.

Yuchang Cheng, et al. 2007. *Constructing a Temporal Relation Tagged Corpus of Chinese based on Dependency Structure Analysis*. TIME 2007.

Timothy Chklovski and Patrick Pantel. 2004. *VerbOcean: Mining the Web for Fine-Grained Semantic Verb Relations*. EMNLP 2004.

Nancy Chinchor. 1997. *MUC-7 named entity task definition*. http://www.itl.nist.gov/iaui/894.02/related_projects/muc/proceedings/muc_7_proceedings/overview.html.

Wenjie Li, et al. 2004. *Applying Machine Learning to Chinese Temporal Relation Resolution*. ACL 2004.

Inderjeet Mani, et al. 2006. *Machine Learning of Temporal Relations*. COLING/ACL 2006.

IREX Committee. 1999. *Named entity extraction task definition*. http://nlp.cs.nyu.edu/irex/NE/df990214.txt, 1999.

Martha Palmer, et al. 2005. *Chinese Treebank 5.1*. http://www.ldc.upenn.edu/. LDC.

James Pustejovsky, et al. 2006. *TimeBank 1.2*. http://www.ldc.upenn.edu/. LDC.

Roser Saurí, et al. 2005. *TimeML Annotation Guidelines*. http://www.timeml.org/.

Marc Verhagen, et al. 2007. *SemEval-2007 Task 15: TempEval Temporal Relation Identification*. ACL 2007 Workshop: SemEval-2007.

Fei Xia. 2000. *The Part-Of-Speech Tagging Guidelines for the Penn Chinese Treebank*. http://www.cis.upenn.edu/~chinese/ctb.html.

[4] This shared task deals with English news articles.(TimeBank 1.2)

Chinese Word Sense Disambiguation with PageRank and HowNet

Jinghua Wang
Beijing University of Posts and Telecommunications
Beijing, China
wjh_smile@163.com

Jianyi Liu
Beijing University of Posts and Telecommunications
Beijing, China
jianyilui@sohu.com

Ping Zhang
Shenyang Normal University
Shenyang, China
pinney58@163.com

Abstract

Word sense disambiguation is a basic problem in natural language processing. This paper proposed an unsupervised word sense disambiguation method based PageRank and HowNet. In the method, a free text is firstly represented as a sememe graph with sememes as vertices and relatedness of sememes as weighted edges based on HowNet. Then UW-PageRank is applied on the sememe graph to score the importance of sememes. Score of each definition of one word can be computed from the score of sememes it contains. Finally, the highest scored definition is assigned to the word. This approach is tested on SENSEVAL-3 and the experimental results prove practical and effective.

1 Introduction

Word sense disambiguation, whose purpose is to identify the correct sense of a word in context, is one of the most important problems in natural language processing. There are two different approaches: knowledge-based and corpus-based (Montoyo, 2005). Knowledge-based method disambiguates words by matching context with information from a prescribed knowledge source, such as WordNet and HowNet. Corpus-based methods are also divided into two kinds: unsupervised and supervised (Lu Z, 2007). Unsupervised methods cluster words into some sets which indicate the same meaning, but they can not give an exact explanation. Supervised machine-learning method learns from annotated sense examples. Though corpus-based approach usually has better performance, the mount of words it can disambiguate essentially relies on the size of training corpus, while knowledge-based approach has the advantage of providing larger coverage. Knowledge-based methods for word sense disambiguation are usually applicable to all words in the text, while corpus-based techniques usually target only few selected word for which large corpora are made available (Mihalcea, 2004).

This paper presents an unsupervised word sense disambiguation algorithm based on HowNet. Words' definition in HowNet is composed of some sememes which are the smallest, unambiguous sense unit. First, a free text is represented as a sememe graph, in which sememes are defined as vertices and relatedness of sememes are defined as weighted edges. Then UW-PageRank is applied on this graph to score the importance of sememes. Score of each definition of one word can be deduced from the score of sememes it contains. Finally, the highest scored definition is assigned to the word. This algorithm needs no corpus, and is able to disambiguate all the words in the text at one time. The experiment result shows that our algorithm is effective and practical.

2 HowNet

HowNet (Dong, Z. D, 2000) is not only a machine readable dictionary, but also a knowledge base which organizes words or concepts as they represent in the object world. It has been widely used in word sense disambiguation and pruning, text categorization, text clustering, text retrieval, machine translation, etc (Dong, Z. D, 2007).

2.1 The content and structure of HowNet

HowNet is an online common-sense knowledge based unveiling inter-conceptual relations and inter-attribute relations of concepts as connoting in lexicons of the Chinese and English equivalents. There are over 16000 word records in the dictionary. This is an example

No.=017625	No.=017630
W_C=打	W_C=打
G_C=V	G_C=V
E_C=打鼓	E_C=打酱油
W_E=hit	W_E=buy
G_E=V	G_E=V
DEF=beat|打	DEF=buy|买，commercial|商

This is two of the concepts of word "打": "No." is the entry number of the concept in the dictionary; "G_C" is the part of speech of this concept in Chinese, and "G_E" is that in English; "E_C" is the example of the concept; "W_E" is the concept in English; "DEF" is the definition.

Definitions of words are composed of a series of sememes (usually more than one，like DEF No.017630 contains "buy|买" and "commercial|商")，like "beat|打" which is the smallest unambiguous unit of concept. First sememe of the definition like "buy|买" of DEF No.017630 is the main attribution of the definition. Sememes have been classified into 8 categories, such as attribute, entity, event role and feature, event, quantity value, quantity, secondary feature and syntax. Sememes in one category form a tree structure with hypernymy / hyponymy relation. Sememes construct concepts, e.g. definition, so the word sense disambiguation task of assigning definition to word can be done through the computation of sememes.

2.2 The similarity of sememes

The tree structure of sememes makes it possible to judge the relatedness of them with a precision mathematical method. Rada (Rada, R, 1989) defined the conceptual distance between any two concepts as the shortest path through a semantic network. The shortest path is the one which includes the fewest number of intermediate concepts. With Rada's algorithm, the more similar two concepts are, the smaller their shortest path is, and so we use the reciprocal of the length of shortest path as the similarity. Leacock and Chodorow (Leacock, C, 1998) define it as follows:

$$sim_{lch}(c_1, c_2) = \max[-\log(length(c_1, c_2)/(2D))$$

where *length(c1, c2)* is the shortest path length between the two concepts and D is the maximum depth of the taxonomy.

Wu and Palmer (Wu, Z., 1994) define another formula to measure the similarity

$$sim_{wup}(c_1, c_2) = \frac{2 \cdot depth(lcs(c_1, c_2))}{depth(c_1) + depth(c_2)}$$

depth is the distance from the concept node to the root of the hierarchy. *lcs(c1,c2)* is the most specific concept that two concepts have in common, that is the lowest common subsumer.

3 PageRank on Sememe Graph

PageRank is an algorithm of deciding the importance of vertices in a graph. Sememes from HowNet can be viewed as an undirected weighted graph, which defines sememes as vertices, relations of sememes as edges and the relatedness of connected sememes as the weights of edges. Because PageRank formula is defined for directed graph, a modified PageRank formula is applied to use on the undirected weighted graph from HowNet.

3.1 PageRank

PageRank (Page, L., 1998) which is widely used by search engines for ranking web pages based on the importance of the pages on the web is an algorithm essentially for deciding the importance of vertices within a graph. The main idea is that: in a directed graph, when one vertex links to another one, it is casting a vote for that other vertex. The more votes one vertex gets, the more important this vertex is. PageRank also takes account the voter: the more important the voter is, the more important the vote itself is. In one word, the score associated with a vertex is determined based on the votes that are cast for it, and the score of the vertex casting these votes. So this is the definition:

Let G=(V,E) be a directed graph with the set of vertices V and set of edges E, when E is a subset of V×V. For a given vertex V_i, let $In(V_i)$ be the set of vertices that point to it, and let $Out(V_i)$ be the set of edges going out of vertex V_i. The PageRank score of vertex V_i is

$$S(V_i) = (1-d) + d * \sum_{j \in In(V_i)} \frac{S(V_j)}{|Out(V_j)|}$$

d is a damping factor that can be set between 0 and 1,and usually set at 0.85 which is the value we use in this paper (Mihalcea, R., 2004).

PageRank starts from arbitrary values assigned to each vertex in the graph, and ends when the convergence below a given threshold is achieved. Experiments proved that it usually stops computing within 30 iterations (Mihalcea, R., 2004).

PageRank can be also applied on undirected graph, in which case the out-degree of a vertex is equal to the in-degree of the vertex.

3.2 PageRank on sememe graph

Sememes from HowNet can be organized in a graph, in which sememes are defined as vertices, and similarity of connected sememes are defined as weight of edges. The graph can be constructed as an undirected weighted graph.

We applied PageRank on the graph with a modified formula

$$S(V_i) = (1-d) + d * \sum_{j \in C(V_i)} \frac{weight(E_{ij}) \cdot S(V_j)}{|D(V_j)|}$$

C(Vi)is the set of edges connecting with V_j, weight(E_{ij})is the weight of edge E_{ij} connecting vertex V_i and V_j, and D(V_j) is the degree of V_j. This formula is named UW-PageRank. In sememe graph, we define sememes as vertices, relations of sememes as edges and the relatedness of connected sememes as the weights of edges. UW-PageRank is applied on this graph to measure the importance of the sememes. The higher score one sememe gets, the more important it is.

4 Word sense disambiguation based on PageRank

To disambiguate words in the text, firstly the text is converted to an undirected weighted sememe graph based on HowNet. The sememes which are from all the definitions for all the words in the text form the vertices of the graph and they are connected by edges whose weight is the similarity of the two sememes. Then, we use UW-PageRank to measure the importance of the vertex in the graph, so all the sememes are scored. So each definition of one word can be scored based on the score of the sememes it contains. Finally, the highest scored definition is assigned to the word as its meaning.

4.1 Text representation as a graph

To use PageRank algorithm to do disambiguation, a graph which represents the text and interconnects the words with meaningful relations should be built first. All the words in the text should be POS tagged first, and then find all the definitions pertaining to the word in HowNet with its POS. Different sememes from these definitions form the vertices of the graph. Edges are added between the vertices whose weights are the similarity of the sememes. The similarity can be measured by the algorithm in Section 2.2. As mentioned in Section 2.1, all the sememes in HowNet are divided into eight categories, and in each category, sememes are connected in a tree structure. So based on the algorithms in Section 2.2, each two sememes in one category, i.e. in one tree, have a similarity more than 0, but if they are in different category, they will have a similarity equal to 0. As a result, a text will be represented in a sememe graph that is composed of several small separate fully connected graphs.

Assumed that a text containing "word1 word2 word3" is to be represented in a graph. The definition (DEF) and sememes for each word are listed in Table 1.

Table 1. " *Word1 Word2Word3*"

Word	Definition	Sememes
Word1	DEF11	S1,S5
	DEF12	S2
	DEF13	S8
Word2	DEF21	S6
	DEF22	S7,S9
Word3	DEF31	S3
	DEF32	S4

Sememes are linked together with the weight of relatedness. For example, S1 and S2 are connected with an edge weighted 0.3.The relation of word, DEF and sememes is represented in Figure1, and sememe graph is in Figure 2.

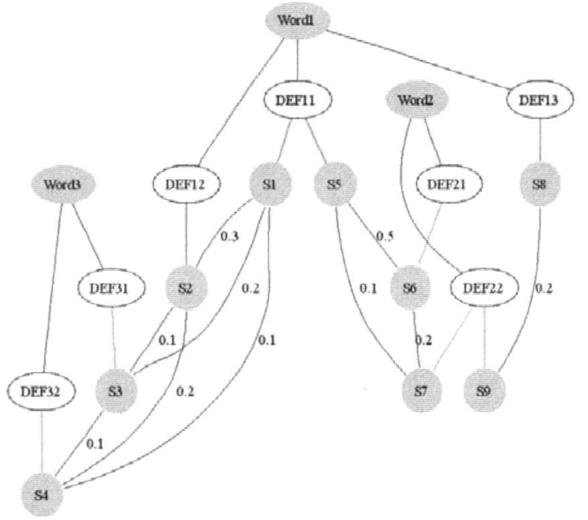

Figure 1. Word-DEF-Sememe Relation

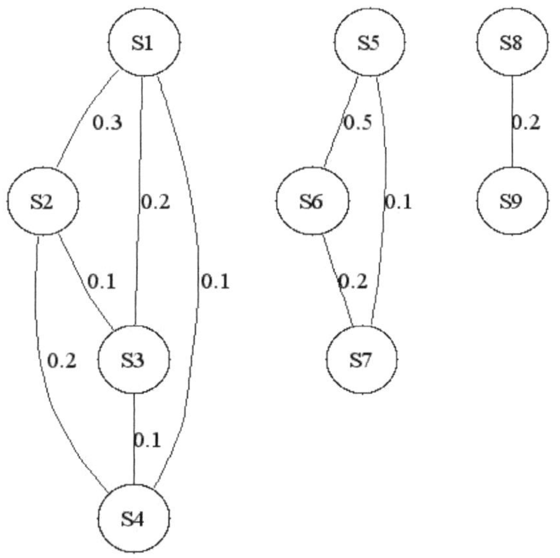

Figure 2. Sememe Graph

4.2 Word sense disambiguation based on PageRank

Text has been represented in a sememe graph with sememes as vertices and similarity of sememes as the weight of the edges. Then, UW-PageRank is used to measure the importance of the vertex, i.e. sememes in the graph. The score of all the vertices in Figure 1 is in Table 2.

Table 2. Score of Sememes

Vertex	S1	S2	S3	S4	S5
UW-PageRank Score	0.179	0.175	0.170	0.165	0.202
Vertex	S6	S7	S8	S9	
UW-PageRank Score	0.208	0.176	0.181	0.181	

Each definition of the words is scored based on the score of the sememes it contains.

$$Sense(Word) = \arg\max_{1 \le i \le m}(Score(DEF_i))$$

$DEF_i \in Word$, DEF_i is the i sense of the word.

We use two methods to score the definition:

Mean method

HowNet uses sememes to construct definitions, so the score of the definition can be measured through an average score of all the sememes it contains. And we chose the definition of the highest score as the result.

$$Score(DEF) = \frac{1}{n}\sum_{1 \le i \le n} Score(S_i)$$

$S_i \in DEF$, S_i is the i sememe of DEF.

First Sememe method

First sememe of one DEF is defined as the most important meaning of the DEF. So we use another method to assign one DEF to one word taking first sememe into consideration. For all the DEF of one word, if one first sememe of one DEF gets the highest score, the DEF is assigned to the word.

$$Score(DEF) = Score(FirstSememe)$$

If several DEFs have the same first sememe or have the same score, we sort all the other sememes are from high score to low score, then comparison is made among this sememes from the beginning to the end until one of the sememes has the highest score among them, and finally the DEF containing this sememe is assigned to the word.

The performance of the two methods will be tested and compared in Section5.

With the "Means" (M) and "First Sememe" (FS) methods, text in Section 4.1 gets the result in Table 3.

Table3. Result of "*Word1 Word2 Word3*"

Word	Definition	Score (M)	Result(M)	Result(FS)
Word1	DEF11	0.191	DEF11	DEF13
	DEF12	0.175		
	DEF13	0.181		
Word2	DEF21	0.208	DEF21	DEF21
	DEF22	0.179		
Word3	DEF31	0.170	DEF31	DEF31
	DEF32	0.165		

Table 4. Experimental Result

Word	Baseline	R+M	L +M	W+M	R+FS	L +FS	W+FS	Li
把握	0.25	**0.53**	**0.53**	**0.53**	**0.53**	**0.53**	**0.53**	0.32
材料	0.33	**0.6**	0.5	**0.6**	0.4	0.4	0.3	0.74
老	0.1	**0.42**	**0.42**	0.46	0.35	0.35	0.38	0.26
没有	0.25	0.73	**0.75**	0.56	0.67	**0.75**	0.56	0.39
突出	0.17	0.5	0.57	0.64	0.43	0.5	0.64	**0.67**
研究	0.33	**0.47**	0.27	0.13	**0.47**	0.27	0.13	0.27
Average Precision	0.24	**0.54**	0.51	0.49	0.48	0.47	0.42	0.44

5 Experiment and evaluation

We chose 96 instances of six words from SENSEVAl-3 Chinese corpus as the test corpus. Words are POS tagged. We use precision as the measure of performance and random tagging as the baseline. We crossly use Rada's (R), Leacock & Chodorowp's (L), and Wu and Palmer's (W) methods to measure the similarity of sememes with mean method (M) and first sememe (FS) scoring the DEF. The precision of the combination algorithm is listed in Table 4.

Li (Li W., 2005) used naive bayes classifier with features extracted from People's Daily News to do word sense disambiguation on SENSEVAL-3. The precision is listed in line "Li" of table as a comparison.

The average precision of our algorithm is around two times higher than the baseline, and 5 of the 6 combination algorithm gets better performance than Li. And for 5/6 word case, our algorithm gets the best performance. Among the three methods of measure the similarity of sememes, Rada's method gets the best performance. And between the two methods of scoring definition, "Mean method" works better, which indicates that although the first sememe is the most important meaning of one definition, the other sememes are also very important, and the importance of other sememes also should be taken into consideration while scoring the definition. Of all the combination of algorithms, "Rada + Mean" gets the best performance, which takes a reasonable way to measure the similarity of two sememes and comprehensively scores the definition based on the importance of its sememes in the sememe graph from the whole text.

6 Related works

Many works in Chinese word sense disambiguation with HowNet. Chen Hao (Chen Hao, 2005) brought up a k-means cluster method base on HowNet, which firstly convert contexts that include ambiguous words into context vectors; then, the definitions of ambiguous words in Hownet can be determined by calculating the similarity between these context vectors. To do disambiguation, Yan Rong (Yan Rong, 2006) first extracted some most relative words from the text based on the co-occurrence, then calculate the similarity between each definition of ambiguous word and its relative words, and finally find the most similar definition as its meaning. The similarity of definitions is measured by the weighted mean of the similarity of sememes, and the similarity of sememes is measured by a modified Rada's formula. Gong YongEn (Gong YongEn, 2006) used a similar method with Yan, and more over, he took recurrence of sememes into consideration. Compare with those methods, our method has a more precious sememes' similarity measure method, and make full use of the structure of its tree structure by representing text in graph and use UW-PageRank to judge sememes' importance in the whole text, that is the most obvious difference from them. Mihalceal (Mihalceal, 2004) first provide the semantic graph method to do word sense disambiguation, but her work is totally on English with WordNet, which is definitely different in meaning representation from HowNet. WordNet uses synsets to group similar concepts together and differentiate them, while HowNet use a close set of sememes to construct concept definitions. In Mihalceal's method, the vertexes of graph are synsets, and in ours are sememes. And after measure the importance of sememes, an additional strategy is used to judge the score of definition based on the sememes.

7 Conclusion

An unsupervised method is applied to word sense disambiguation based on HowNet. First, a free text is represented as a sememe graph with sememes as vertices and relatedness of sememes as weighted edges. Then UW-PageRank is applied on this graph to score the importance of sememes. Score of each definition of one word can be deduced from the score of sememes it contains. Finally, the highest scored definition is assigned to the word. Our algorithm is tested on SENSEVAL-3 and the experimental results prove our algorithm to be practical and effective.

Acknowledgment

This study is supported by Beijing Natural Science Foundation of (4073037) and Ministry of Education Doctor Foundation (20060013007).

References

Chen hao, He Tingting, Ji Donghong, Quan Changqing, 2005. *An Unsupervised Approach to Chinese Word Sense Disambiguation Based on Hownet*, Computational Linguistics and Chinese Language Processing, Vol. 10, No. 4, pp. 473-482

Dong, Z.D., Dong, Q.2000. "Hownet," http://keenage.com.

Dong Zhendong, Dong Qiang, Hao Changling, 2007. *Theoretical Findings of HowNet*, Journal of Chinese Information Processing, Vol. 21, No. 4, P3-9

Gong Y., Yuan C., Wu G., 2006. *Word Sense Disambiguation Algorithm Based on Semantic Information*, Application Research of Computers, 41-43.

Leacock, C., Chodorow, M., 1998.*Combing local context and WordNet Similarity for word sense identification*, in: C.Fellbaum (Ed.), WordNet: An electronic lexical database, MIT Press, 305-332

Li W., Lu Q., Li W., 2005. *Integrating Collocation Features in Chinese Word Sense Disambiguation*, Integrating Collocation Features in Chinese Word Sense Disambiguation. In Proceedings of the Fourth Sighan Workshop on Chinese Language Processing, 87-94.

Lu Z., Liu T., Li, S., 2007. *Chinese word sense disambiguation based on extension theory*, Journal of Harbin Institute of Technology, Vol.38 No.12, 2026-2035

Mihalcea, R., Tarau, P., Figa, E., 2004. *PageRank on Semantic Networks, with application to Word Sense Disambiguation*, in Proceedings of The 20st International Conference on Computational Linguistics

Montoyo, A., Suarez, A., Rigau, G. and Palomar, M. 2005. Combining Knowledge- and Corpus-based Word-Sense-Disambiguation Methods, Volume 23, Journal of Machine learning research , 299-330.

Page, L., Brin, S., Motwani, R., and wingorad, T., 1998. *The pagerank citation ranking: Bringing order to the web Technical report,* Stanford Digital Library Technologies Project.

Rada, R., Mili,E,.Bicknell, Blettner, M., 1989. *Development and application of a metric on semantic nets*, IEEE Transactions on Systems, Man and Cybernetics 19(1) 17-30

Wu, Z., Plamer, M., 1994. *Verb semantics and lexical selection*, in 32nd Annual Meeting of the Association for Computational Linguistics, Las Cruces, New Mexico, 133-138

Yan R., Zhang L., 2006. *New Chinese Word Sense Disambiguation Method*, Computer Technology and Development, Vol. 16 No.3, 22-25

Stochastic Dependency Parsing Based on A* Admissible Search

Bor-shen Lin

National Taiwan University of Science and Technology / No. 43, Keelung Road, Section 4, Taipei, Taiwan

bslin@cs.ntust.edu.tw

Abstract

Dependency parsing has gained attention in natural language understanding because the representation of dependency tree is simple, compact and direct such that robust partial understanding and task portability can be achieved more easily. However, many dependency parsers make hard decisions with local information while selecting among the next parse states. As a consequence, though the obtained dependency trees are good in some sense, the N-best output is not guaranteed to be globally optimal in general.

In this paper, a stochastic dependency parsing scheme based on A* admissible search is formally presented. By well representing the parse state and appropriately designing the cost and heuristic functions, dependency parsing can be modeled as an A* search problem, and solved with a generic algorithm of state space search. When evaluated on the Chinese Tree Bank, this parser can obtain 85.99% dependency accuracy at 68.39% sentence accuracy, and 14.62% node ratio for dynamic heuristic. This parser can output N-best dependency trees, and integrate the semantic processing into the search process easily.

1 Introduction

Constituency grammar has long been the main way for describing the sentence structure of natural language for decades. The phrase structure of sentences can be analyzed by such parsing algorithms as Earley or CYK algorithms (Allen, 1995; Jurafsky and Martin 2001). To parse sentences with constituency grammar, a set of grammar rules written in linguistics is indispensable, while a corpus of tree bank annotated manually is also necessary if stochastic parsing scheme is adopted. In addition, the many non-terminal or phrasal nodes make it sophisticated to further interpret or disambiguate the parse trees since deep linguistic knowledge is often required. All these factors make language understanding very difficult, labor-intensive and not easy to be ported to various tasks.

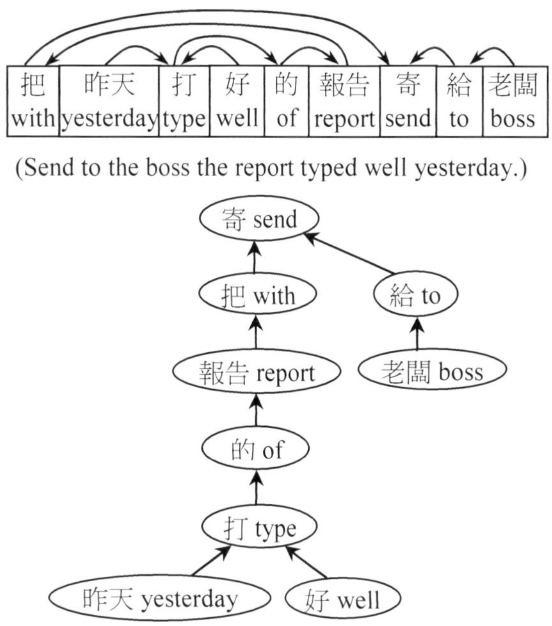

Figure 1. An example of dependency parsing with unlabeled dependency tree.

Dependency grammar, on the other hand, describes the syntactic and semantic relationships among lexical terms directly with binary head-modifier links. Such representation is very simple, compact, direct, and therefore helpful for simplifying the process of language understanding and increasing task portability. Figure 1 shows an example of dependency parsing for the Chinese sentence "把昨天打好的報告寄給老闆" (meaning "send to the boss the report typed well yesterday"). According to the binary head-modifier links, it is pretty easy to transform the dependency tree into the predicate "send(to:boss,object:report(typed(yesterday,well))) " for further interpretation or interaction, since the semantic gap between them is slight and the mappings are thus quite direct. Furthermore, robust partial understanding can be achieved easily when full parse is not obtainable, and measured precisely by simply counting the correct attachments on the dependency tree (Ohno et al., 2004). All these will not be so simple provided that conventional constituency grammar is used.

In the dependency parsing paradigm, several deterministic, stochastic or machine-learning-based parsing algorithms have been proposed (Eisner, 1996; Covington 2001; Kudo and Matsumoto, 2002; Yamada and Matsumoto, 2003; Nivre 2003; Nivre and Scholz, 2004; Chen et al., 2005). Many of them make hard decisions with local information while selecting among next parse states. As a consequence, though the obtained dependency trees are good in some sense, the N-best output is not guaranteed to be globally optimal in general (Klein and Manning, 2003).

On the other hand, A* search that guarantees optimality has been applied to many areas including AI. Klein and Manning (2003) proposed to use A* search in PCFG parsing. Dienes et al. depicted primarily the idea of applying A* search to dependency parsing, but there is not yet formal evaluation results and discussions based on the literatures we have (Dienes et al., 2003).

In this paper, a stochastic dependency parsing scheme based on A* admissible search is formally presented. By well representing the parse state and appropriately designing the cost and heuristic functions, dependency parsing can be modeled as an A* search problem, and solved with a generic algorithm of state space search. This parser has been tested on the Chinese Tree Bank (Chen et al., 1999), and 85.99% dependency accuracy at 68.39% sentence accuracy can be obtained. Among three types of proposed admissible heuristics, dynamic heuristic can achieve the highest efficiency with node ratio 14.62%. This parser can output N-best dependency trees, and integrate the semantic processing into the search process easily.

2 Fundamentals of A* Search

Search is an important issue in AI area, since the solutions of many problems could be automated if they could be modeled as search problems on state space (Russell and Norvig, 2003). A well known example is the traveling salesperson problem, as shown in the example of Figure 2. In this section basic constituents of A* search will be depicted.

2.1 State Representation

State representation is the first step for modeling the problem domain. It involves not only designing the data structure of search state but indicating the way a state can be uniquely identified. This is definitely not a trivial issue, and depends on the how the problem is defined. In Figure 2, for example, search state cannot be represented simply with the current city, because traveling salesperson problem requires every city has to be visited exactly once. The two nodes of city E on level 2 in Figure 2, with paths A-B-E and A-C-E respectively, are therefore regarded as different search states, and generate their successor states individually. The node E with the path A-C-E, for example, can generate successor B, but the one with the path A-B-E cannot due to reentry of city B. In other words, the search state here is the path, including all cities visited so far, instead of the current city. However, if the problem is changed as finding the shortest path from city A to city F, the two paths A-B-E and A-C-E can then be merged into a single node of city E with shorter path tracked. In such case, the search state will then be the current city instead of the path.

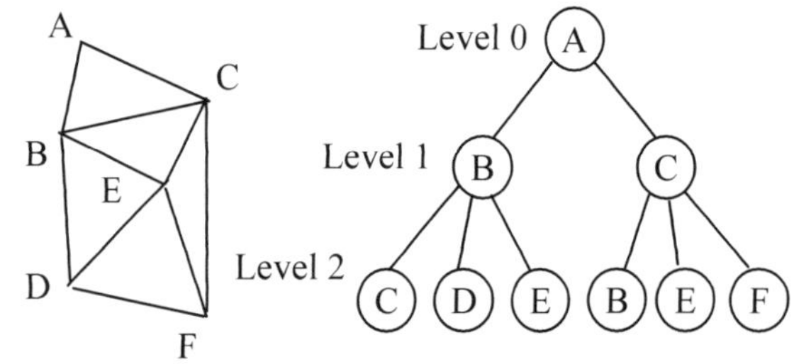

Figure 2. An example of state space search for traveling salesperson problem from initial city A.

In addition, for state representation three issues need to be further addressed.

- Initial state: what the initial state is.
- State transition: how successor states are generated from the current state.
- Goal state: to judge whether the goal state is achieved or not.

In the above example in Figure 2, the initial state is the path containing city A only. The state transition is to visit next cities from the current city under the constraint of no reentry. The goal states are any paths that depart from city A and pass every city exactly once.

2.2 State Space Search

With the state well represented, two data structures are utilized to guide the search.

- An open list (a priority queue, denoted as *open* in Figure 3) used for tracking those states not yet spanned.
- A closed list (denoted as *closed* in Figure 3) used for tracking those states visited so far to avoid the reentry of the same states.

Then, a generic algorithm for state space search, with pseudo codes in object-oriented style shown in Figure 3, is performed to find the goal states. The initial state is first inserted into the queue, and an iterative search procedure (denoted as *search()* in Figure 3) is then called. For each iteration in the search procedure, the search state is popped from the queue and inspected one by one. If it is the goal state, the procedure terminates and returns the goal state. Otherwise the successors of the current state are generated, and inserted into the queue individually according to the priority provided not yet visited. The search procedure could be called multiple times if more than one goal states are desired.

Note that the algorithm in Figure 3 is generic enough to be adapted for various search strategies, including depth first search, breadth first search, best first search, algorithm A, algorithm A* and so on, by simply providing different evaluation function *f(n)* of search state *n* for prioritizing the queue. For depth first search, for example, those states with the highest depth will have higher priority and be inserted at the front of the queue, while for breadth first search at the back.

```
open.add(initial);
goal = search();
search() {
    while(true) {
        state = open.pop();
        if(state.isGoal()) return state;
        successors = state.getSuccessors();
        for(successor in successors) {
            if(!closed.contains(successor)) {
                closed.add(successor);
                open.add(successor);
            }
        }
    }
}
```

Figure 3. Generic algorithm for state space search.

2.3 Optimality and Efficiency

If the evaluation function $f(n)$ satisfies

$$f(n) = g(n) + h(n),$$

where $g(n)$ is the real cost from the initial state to the current state n and $h(n)$ is the heuristic estimate of the cost from the current state n to the goal state, such type of algorithm is called algorithm A. If further, the constraint of admissibility for $h(n)$ holds, i.e.,

$$h(n) \leqq h^*(n),$$

where $h^*(n)$ is the true minimum cost from current state n to the goal state, then optimality can be guaranteed, or equivalently, the goal state obtained first will give minimum cost. Such type of algorithm is called algorithm A*. It can be proved that for algorithm A*, the closer the heuristic $h(n)$ is to the true minimum cost, $h^*(n)$, the higher the search efficiency is.

3 A*-based Dependency Parser

In this section, how dependency parsing is modeled as an A* search problem will be depicted in detail.

3.1 Formulation

First, let $\boldsymbol{W} = \{W_1, W_2, ..., W_n\}$ denote the word list (sentence) to be parsed, where W_i denotes the i-th word in the list. And, each word W_i is expressed in the form,

$W = (w, t)$ (1)

where w is the lexical term and t is the part-of-speech tag. A dependency database can first be built by extracting the dependency links among words from a corpus of tree bank. Given the dependency database, a directed dependency graph ***G*** indicating valid links for the word list ***W*** can be constructed, as shown in the example of Figure 4. The direction of the link here indicates the direction of modification. Link $W_3 \rightarrow W_2$ in Figure 4, for example, means W_3 can modify (or be attached to) W_2. The dependency graph ***G*** will be used for directing the state transition during search.

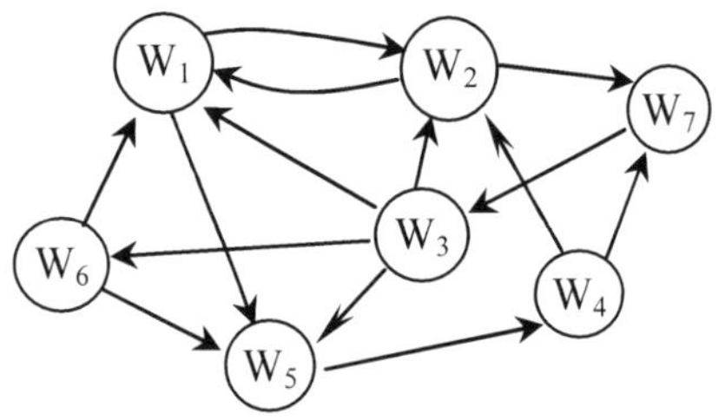

Figure 4. Example dependency graph.

3.2 Representation of Parse State

Since the goal of dependency parsing is to find the dependency tree, the search state can therefore be represented as the dependency tree constructed so far (denoted as ***T***). Besides, a set containing those words not yet attached to the dependency tree (denoted as ***C***, meaning "to be consumed") can be generated dynamically by excluding those words on the dependency tree ***T*** from word list ***W***. The three issues depicted in Section 2.1 are then addressed as follows.

- Initial state: the dependency tree ***T*** is empty and the set ***C*** contains all words in list ***W***.
- State transition: a word is extracted from ***C*** and attached onto some node on the dependency tree ***T***, and a successor state ***T'*** and ***C'*** is then generated. Whether an attachment is valid or not is determined according to the dependency graph ***G***, under the constraints of uniqueness (any word has at most one head) and projectivity[1] (Covington 2001, Nivre 2003).
- Goal state: the set ***C*** is empty while all words in ***W*** are attached onto the dependency tree ***T***.

With the parse state represented well, the generic algorithm for state space search depicted in Section 2.2 can then be performed to find the N-best dependency trees. A partial search space based on the dependency graph ***G*** in Figure 4 is displayed in Figure 5, in which R denotes the root node of dependency tree. As shown in Figure 5, for each search state (denoted by the ovals enclosed with double-lines), only a link in form of $W_j \rightarrow R$ or $W_j \rightarrow W_i$ is actually tracked Through tracing the search tree back from the current state, all links can be obtained, and the overall dependency tree ***T*** can be constructed accordingly. For the search state $W_3 \rightarrow W_2$ in Figure 5, for example, the links $W_1 \rightarrow R$, $W_2 \rightarrow W_1$ and $W_3 \rightarrow W_2$ are obtained through back tracing, which can then construct the dependency tree, $W_3 \rightarrow W_2 \rightarrow W_1 \rightarrow R$, as can be seen on the left-hand side of Figure 5. This is similar to the case of traveling salesperson problem in Figure 2, in which only the current city is tracked for each state, but the path that identifies the search state uniquely can be obtained by back tracing.

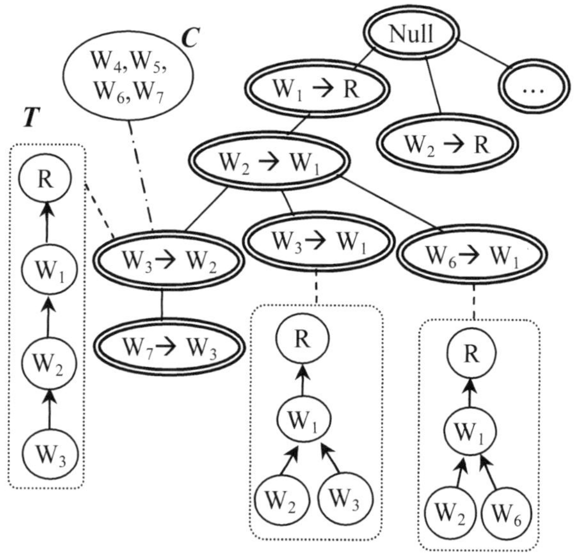

Figure 5. A partial search space where some search states are associated with their dependency trees with dashed lines.

[1] The projective constraint for new attachment is imposed by those attachments already on the dependency tree. Each attachment already on the tree forms a non-crossing region between its head and modifier to constrain new attachments for those words located within that region.

3.3 Cost Function

For given word list $\boldsymbol{W}$, the dependency tree $\boldsymbol{T}$ with the highest probability $P(\boldsymbol{T})$ is desired, where

$$P(\boldsymbol{T}) = \{\Pi\, P(W_l \rightarrow R)\} \cdot \{\Pi\, P(W_j \rightarrow W_i)\} \qquad (2)$$

The first term corresponds to those attachments on the root node of dependency tree (i.e. headless words), while the second term corresponds to the other attachments. In A* search, the optimal goal state obtained is guaranteed to give the minimal cost. So, if the cost function, $g(n)$, is defined as the minus logarithm of $P(\boldsymbol{T})$,

$$\begin{aligned} g(n) &\equiv -log\,(P(\boldsymbol{T})) \\ &= \Sigma\,(-log(P(W_l \rightarrow R))) + \Sigma\,(-log(P(W_j \rightarrow W_i))) \\ &\equiv \Sigma\, step\text{-}cost \qquad (3) \end{aligned}$$

then the A* search algorithm that minimizes the cost $g(n)$ will eventually maximizes the probability of the dependency tree, $P(\boldsymbol{T})$. Here the minus logarithms of the probabilities in Equation (3), $-log(P(W_l \rightarrow R))$ and $-log(P(W_j \rightarrow W_i))$, can be regarded as the step cost for each attachment (or link) accumulated during search. Furthermore, since each word is expressed with a lexical term and a part-of-speech tag as shown in Equation (1), the probability for each link can be depicted as,

$$P(W_l \rightarrow R) = P(W_l \mid R) = P(t_l|R) \cdot P(w_l|t_l) \qquad (4)$$

$$P(W_j \rightarrow W_i) = P(W_j \mid W_i) = P(t_j|t_i) \cdot P(w_j|t_j) \qquad (5)$$

assuming the word list $\boldsymbol{W}$ is generated by the Baysian networks in Figure 6(a) and 6(b) respectively. Note that here the probability for a link $P(W_j \rightarrow W_i)$ involves not only the lexical terms w_j and w_i but also the part-of-speech tags t_j and t_i, and is denoted as link bigram. Such formulation can be generalized to high order link n-grams. Figure 6(c), for example, displays the Baysian network for the link $W_k \rightarrow W_j$ conditioned on $W_j \rightarrow W_i$, based on which the link trigram is defined as

$$\begin{aligned} &P(W_k \rightarrow W_j \mid W_j \rightarrow W_i) = P(W_k \mid W_i, W_j) \\ &= P(t_k \mid t_i, t_j) \cdot P(w_k \mid t_k). \qquad (6) \end{aligned}$$

When comparing Figure 6(c) with Figure 6(d), the Baysian networks for link trigram $P(W_k \mid W_i, W_j)$ and conventional linear trigram $P(W_{i+2} \mid W_i, W_{i+1})$ respectively, it could be found that link n-gram is flexible for long-distance stochastic dependencies, though the two topologies look similar. Undoubtedly, the Baysian networks in Figure 6 appear too simple to model the real statistics precisely. In the link $W_j \rightarrow W_i$, for example, W_j might depend on not only its parent W_i but the children of W_i (Eisner, 1996). Also, the direction ($sgn(i\text{-}j)$) and the distance ($|i\text{-}j|$) of modification between W_i and W_j might be important (Ohno et al., 2004). All these factors could be taken into account by simply including the minus logarithms of the corresponding probabilities into the step cost.

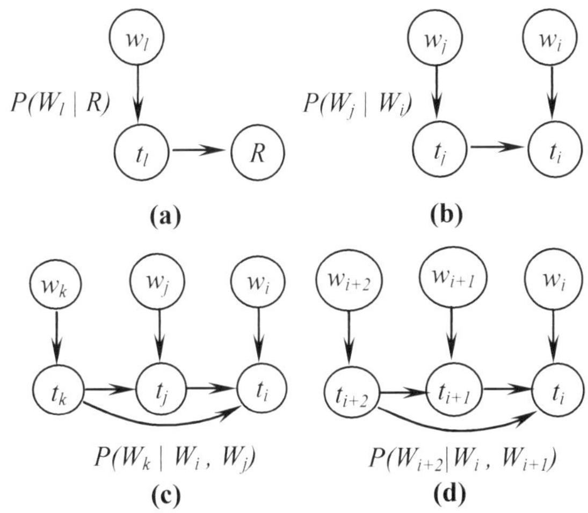

Figure 6. Baysian networks of (a) link unigram (b) link bigram (c) link trigram (d) linear trigram.

3.4 Heuristic Function

In A* search, the evaluation function $f(n)$ consists of $g(n)$, the real cost from the initial state to the current state n, and $h(n)$, the cost estimated heuristically from the current state n to the goal state. Now for dependency parsing, $g(n)$ defined in Equation (3) is the accumulated cost for those attachments on current dependency tree $\boldsymbol{T}$, while $h(n)$ is the predicted cost of the attachments for the words in $\boldsymbol{C}$ which have not yet been attached. Since $h(n) \leqq h^*(n)$ has to hold for admissibility, it is necessary to estimate $h(n)$ conservatively enough so as not to exceed the true minimum cost $h^*(n)$. To achieve higher search efficiency, however, it is preferred to estimate $h(n)$ more aggressively such that $h(n)$ can be as close to $h^*(n)$ as possible. Therefore, in this paper, $h(n)$ is estimated with *the minimum of minus logarithms of link n-grams* for each word in $\boldsymbol{C}$, with different levels of constraints described below.

- Global heuristic: the minimum is static, and can be calculated in advance before parsing any sentence by considering all link n-grams for each word.
- Local heuristic: the minimum is calculated according to the dependency graph ***G*** of current parsing sentence by considering all possible link n-grams with respect to ***G***.
- Dynamic heuristic: the minimum is calculated dynamically according to current dependency tree ***T*** during parsing by considering only projective link n-grams with respect to ***G*** for current dependency tree ***T***.

By virtue of taking the minimum of minus logarithms of link n-grams, admissibility can be guaranteed for these heuristics. The latter with stricter constraints on finding the minimum can give more precise estimate of cost (with higher $h(n)$) than the former, and is thus expected to be more efficient, as will be discussed in the next section.

4 Experiments

The stochastic dependency parsing scheme proposed in this paper has been first tested on the Chinese Tree Bank 3.0 licensed by Academia Sinica, Taiwan, with six sets of data collected from different sources (Chen et al., 1999). Head-modifier links (with lexical term and part-of-speech tag) can be extracted from the tree bank since it is produced by a head-driven parser (Chen, 1996). In our experiments, One set, named as *oral.check*, containing 4156 sentences manually transcribed from dialogue database is used to train the dependency database, link statistics including conditional probabilities, link unigrams and bigrams as shown in Equation (4) and (5), and so on. Another set, named as *ev.check*, containing 1797 sentences in text books of elementary school is used to test the A*-based dependency parser. Note here the training corpus and testing corpus are of different domains, and each word in test sentences is transcribed into (w, t) format with lexical term w and associated part-of-speech tag t.

4.1 Coverage Rate

The number of occurrences and the coverage rate for the conditional probability $P(w_j|t_j)$, link unigram $P(t_j)$ and link bigram $P(t_j|t_i)$ respectively are shown in Table 1. As can be seen in this table, the coverage rate for $P(w_j|t_j)$ is as low as 50.8%, since the training and testing domains are quite different. The coverage rates for link unigram and bigram, however, can be up to 94.06% and 84.88% respectively. This implies that, the link probabilities can be estimated more appropriately and contribute more in finding the dependency trees. To handle the issue of data sparseness, in the following experiments a simple n-gram backoff mechanism is utilized for smoothing.

No. of occurrences	$P(w_j\|t_j)$	$P(t_j)$	$P(t_j\|t_i)$
Training corpus	8137	120	3383
Testing corpus	2791	101	1468
Overlaps	1418	95	1246
Coverage rate	50.80%	94.06%	84.88%

Table 1. Coverage rates for link statistics.

4.2 Parsing Accuracy

The experiment settings for dependency parsing are depicted as below. The first, denoted as BASE, is the baseline setting, while the others describe the search conditions applied to the baseline incrementally. The heuristic $h(n)$ used here is the dynamic heuristic.

- BASE: baseline with the cost defined in Equation (3), (4) and (5).
- RP: root penalty for every root attachment $W_l \rightarrow R$ is included into the step cost.
- DIR: the statistics for the direction of modification, $P(D|W_j \rightarrow W_i)=P(D|t_i, t_j)$, is included into the step cost where $D \equiv sgn(j-i)$.
- NA: the statistics for the number of attachments (or valence), $P(N_i|W_i)=P(N_i|t_i)$, is included into the step cost and updated incrementally for every new attachment onto W_i. N_i is the current number of words attached to W_i.
- REJ: the obtained dependency trees are inspected one by one, and rejected if any of the conditions occurs: (a) the modifiers for conjunction word (e.g. "和", meaning "and") belong to different part-of-speech categories (incorrect meaning) (b) illegal use of "的" (meaning "of") as leaf node (incomplete meaning).

The baseline setting with Equation (3), (4) and (5) is based on the Baysian networks depicted in Figure 6(a) and 6(b). Finer statistics could be applied in the settings RP, DIR and NA. The setting RP, for example, can restrain the number of headless words. The setting DIR can take into account the cost due to the direction of modification, since it in fact matters[2], but the link probability $P(W_j \rightarrow W_i)$ in Equation (5) cannot differentiate between the two directions. The distance of modification, |j-i|, might matter too, but is not considered here due to quite limited amount of training data. The setting NA can include the cost due to the number of attachments. Verbs, for example, often require more attachments, and may produce lower cost for higher number of attachments. Here for simplification, the statistics of $P(N_i|t_i)$ are gathered only for N_i = 0,1,2, and >=3, respectively. In addition to using finer statistics, it is also feasible to use semantic or lexical rules to reject the dependency trees with incorrect or incomplete meanings. In the setting REJ, two rules are utilized. One is, the conjunction word should have modifiers in the same part-of-speech category, while the other is, the word "的" must have at least one modifier.

		No. of Accurate Sentences	SA	DA
Cross Domain	BASE	867	48.25%	77.42%
	+ RP	1039	57.82%	80.74%
	+ DIR	1102	61.32%	82.72%
	+ NA	1211	67.39%	85.21%
	+ REJ	1229	68.39%	85.99%
Within Domain	BASE	1109	61.71%	85.93%
	+ RP	1314	73.12%	89.91%
	+ DIR	1340	74.57%	90.66%
	+ NA	1476	82.16%	92.81%
	+ REJ	1484	82.58%	93.20%

Table 2. Parsing accuracy for various settings.

The parsing performance can be measured with sentence accuracy (SA) and dependency accuracy (DA). Table 2 shows the experimental results for the above settings. The results for within-domain test by using the set *ev.check* for both training and testing are also listed here for comparison. It can be found in this table that, the performance of cross-domain test is not so good for the baseline setting, but can be persistently improved when finer statistics are applied. Rejection of incorrect or incomplete dependency trees is also helpful (REJ), though very few semantic or lexical constraints are utilized here. When the constraints of all settings are applied, 85.99% dependency accuracy can be obtained at 68.39% sentence accuracy.

4.3 N-best Output

Note that due to data sparseness and the limitation of simplified Baysian networks, some parsing errors are intrinsic and difficult to avoid. Figure 7 shows the parsing result for a clause "吃晚飯的時候" (meaning "at the time for eating dinner"). The incorrect parsing result on the right-hand side (meaning "to eat the time of dinner") is syntactically correct and inevitable in fact, since the link probabilities ($P(t_j)$ or $P(t_j|t_i)$) dominate over the conditional probabilities ($P(w_j|t_j)$), as illustrated in Section 4.1. Such problem could possibly be alleviated to some extent if deep semantic constraints (e.g. a transitive verb may require a subject and an object) or lexical constraints (e.g. some adjectives may modify only specific nouns) could be utilized for rejection while reprocessing the N-best output.

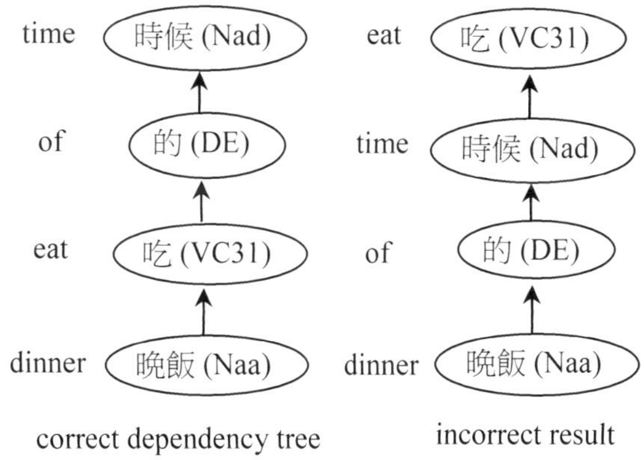

Figure 7. The parsing result for the clause "吃晚飯的時候" (time for eating dinner).

Table 3 shows the experimental results of N-best output for the setting REJ. In Table 3 it can be seen that higher sentence accuracy, 80.08%, for top-5 output can be achieved, which implies large space for improvement in N-best processing.

	Top 1	Top 2	Top 3	Top 4	Top 5
SA	68.39%	75.24%	78.02%	79.41%	80.08%

Table 3. Sentence accuracy for N-best output.

[2] In the Chinese phrase "在(in)…前面(front)", for example, "在" is the head while "前面" is the modifier, and "前面" always modifies "在" backwards.

4.4 Search Efficiency

The search efficiency for each test sentence can be measured heuristically by the order of complexity, defined as

$$C = log_n N \qquad (7)$$

where n is number of words in the test sentence and N is the total number of the search nodes for that sentence. C_{ave} is then used to denote the average complexity over all test sentences. In addition, N_{all} is the total number of search nodes for all test sentences, and can produce the node ratio R_N when normalized. The experimental results for different heuristics depicted in Section 3.4 are shown in Table 4. As can be observed in this table, much higher search efficiency can be obtained for more precise heuristic estimate, but with compatible top 1 sentence accuracy. For dynamic heuristic with real-time estimate of the cost according to the current dependency tree, the highest efficiency can be obtained at 2.38 average complexity and 14.62% node ratio, respectively.

Heuristic	SA	C_{ave}	N_{all}	R_N
None	68.84%	2.91	4748268	100%
Global	68.34%	2.82	3417766	66.29%
Local	68.50%	2.39	841716	17.73%
Dynamic	68.39%	2.38	694193	14.62%

Table 4. Search efficiency for different heuristics.

5 Conclusions

We have presented a stochastic dependency parsing scheme based on A* admissible search, and verified its parsing accuracy and search efficiency on the Chinese Tree Bank 3.0. 85.99% dependency accuracy at 68.39% sentence accuracy can be obtained under cross-domain test. Among three types of admissible heuristics proposed, dynamic heuristic can achieve the highest efficiency with node ratio 14.62%. This parser can output N-best dependency trees, and reprocess them flexibly with more semantic constraints so as to achieve higher parsing accuracy. This parsing scheme is the basis for natural language understanding in our research project on dialogue systems for mission delegation tasks. We plan to perform comparative studies with other non-stochastic approaches, and evaluate our approach on the shared task of dependency parsing.

References

Allen James, 1995. *Natural Language Understanding*, The Benjamin/Cummings Publishing Company.

Chen K. J. 1996. *A Model for Robust Chinese Parser*, Computational Linguistics and Chinese Language Processing, Vol. 1, no. 1, pp. 183-205.

Chen K. J., et al. 1999. *The CKIP Chinese Treebank: Guidelines for Annotation*, ATALA Workshop – Treebanks, Paris, pp. 85-96.

Chen Yuchang, Asahara Masayuki and Matsumoto Yuji. 2005. Machine Learning-based Dependency Analyzer for Chinese, ICCC-2005.

Covington Michael A. 2001. *A Fundamental Algorithm for Dependency Parsing*, Proc. of the 39th Annual ACM Southeast Conference, pp. 95-102.

Dienes Peter, Koller Alexander and Kuhlmann Macro. 2003. *Statistical A* Dependency Parsing*, Proc. Workshop on Prospects and Advances in the Syntax/Semantics Interface.

Eisner Jason M. 1996. *Three Probabilistic Models for Dependency Parsing: An Exploration*, Proc. COLING, pp. 340-345.

Jurafsky Daniel and Martin James H. 2001. *Speech and Language Processing*, Prentice Hall, NJ.

Klein Dan and Manning Christopher D. 2003. *A* Parsing: Fast Exact Viterbi Parse Selection*, Proc. NAACL/HLT.

Klein Dan and Manning Christopher D. 2003. *Fast Exact Inference with a Factored Model for Natural Language Parsing*, Proc. Advances in Neural Information Processing Systems.

Kudo Taku and Matsumoto Yuji. 2002. *Japanese Dependency Analysis using Cascaded Chunking*, Proc. CONLL.

Nivre Joakim, 2003, *An Efficient Algorithm for Projective Dependency Parsing*, Proc. International Workshop on Parsing Technologies (IWPT).

Nivre Joakim and Scholz Mario. 2004. *Deterministic Dependency Parsing of English Text*, Proc. COLING.

Ohno Tomohiro, et al, 2004. *Robust Dependency Parsing of Spontaneous Japanese Speech and Its Evaluation*, Proc. ICSLP.

Russell S. and Norvig P. 2003. *Artificial Intelligence: A Modern Approach*, Prentice Hall.

Yamada Hiroyasu and Matsumoto Yuji. 2003. *Statistical Dependency Analysis with Support Vector Machines*, Proc. IWPT

Analyzing Chinese Synthetic Words with Tree-based Information and a Survey on Chinese Morphologically Derived Words

Jia Lu
Nara Institute of Science and Technology
jia-l@is.naist.jp

Masayuki Asahara
Nara Institute of Science and Technology
masayu-a@is.naist.jp

Yuji Matsumoto
Nara Institute of Science and Technology
matsu@is.naist.jp

Abstract

The lack of internal information of Chinese synthetic words has become a crucial problem for Chinese morphological analysis systems which will face various needs of segmentation standards for upper NLP applications in the future. In this paper, we first categorize Chinese synthetic words into several types according to their inside semantic and syntactic structure, and then propose a method to represent these inside information of word by applying a tree-based structure. Then we try to automatically identify the inner morphological structure of 3-character synthetic words by using a large corpus and try to add syntactic tags to their internal structure. We believe that this tree-based word internal information could be useful in specifying a Chinese synthetic word segmentation standard.

1 Introduction

Chinese word segmentation has always been a difficult and challenging task in Chinese language processing. Several Chinese morphological analysis systems have been developed by different research groups and they all have quite good performance when doing segmentation of written Chinese. But there still remain some problems. The biggest one is that each research group has its own segmentation standard for their system, which means that there is no single segmentation standard for all tagged corpora which can be agreeable across different research groups. And we believe that this situation slows down the progress of Chinese NLP research.

Among all the differences of segmentation standards, the segmentation method for Chinese synthetic words is the most controversial part because Chinese synthetic words have a quite complex structure and should be represented by several segmention levels according to the needs of upper applications such as MT, IR and IME.

For instance, a long(upper level) segmentation unit may simplify syntactic analysis and IME application but a small(lower level) segmentation unit might be better for information retrieval or word-based statistical summarization. But for now, no Chinese morphological analysis system can do all kinds of these work with only one segmentation standard.

Furthermore, although every segmentation system has good performance, in the analysis of real world text, there are still many out-of-vocabulary words which could not be easily recognized because of the flexibility of Chinese synthetic word construction, especially proper names that could always appear as synthetic words.

In order to make our Chinese morphological analysis system to recognize more out-of-vocabulary words and to fit different kinds of NLP applications, we try to analyze the structure of the internal information of Chinese synthetic words, categorize them into semantic and syntactic types and store these information into a synthetic word dictionary by representing them with a kind of tree structure built on our system dictionary.

In this paper, we first make the definition of Chinese synthetic words and classify them into several categories in Section 2. In Section 3, two previous researches on Chinese synthetic words will be introduced. Then we propose a tree-based method for analyzing Chinese synthetic words and make a survey focused on 3-character morphological derived words to get the features for future machine learning process. In Section 4, we do an experiment by using SVM classifier to annotate 3-character morphologically derived words. Finally, Section 5 shows how this method could benefit Chinese morphological analysis and our future work.

2 Detailed study of Chinese synthetic words

2.1 Definition of Chinese words

There has always been a common belief that Chinese 'doesn't have words', but instead has 'characters', or that Chinese 'has no morphology' and so is 'morphologically impoverished', because in Chinese a 'word' is by no means a clear and intuitive notion. But actually for native Chinese speakers, they know that words are those lexical entries which represent a complete concept and occur innately in the form of specific language rules based on the speaker's mental lexicon.

Though there are a lot of ways to classify Chinese words, we believe that Chinese words should be first divided into single-morpheme words and synthetic words according to the way of construction of their internal parts.

Single-morpheme words are those that could not be divided into smaller parts when representing as the whole concept. In other words, if we divide single morpheme words into characters or parts, the meaning of individual parts become independent and does not indicate any connection with the meaning of the original word. Following are the three different types of single-morpheme words:

①one-character words:
人[human], 马[horse], 车[vehicle]

②one-morpheme words:
鹌鹑[quail], 翡翠[jadeite]
鸳鸯[mandarin duck]

③transliteration words:
比萨[pizza], 肯德基[Kentucky]
阿司匹林[aspirin]

The first kind is obvious single words in that an ordinary character in Chinese stands for an independent morpheme with one or several senses. The second kind shows those words which are composed of several characters and always used as a whole. For the last kind, as can be seen from the above examples, if we divide 肯德基[Kentucky] into '肯[can]', '德[moral]' and '基[base]', it definitely can not indicate the meaning of the well-known fried chicken restaurant chain from those three characters. So these three kinds of single-morpheme words should be segmented as one word in any morphological analysis systems.

However, it becomes much more complicated when dealing with synthetic words. Generally, synthetic words are the type of words which are composed of single-morpheme words and represent a new entity or meaning which can be indicated from the internal constituents. According to this definition, if we divide synthetic words into smaller parts, we could still somehow guess the original meaning from the meaning of internal parts despite the fact that it may not be a very precise one. For example the word 司机[driver]. If we don't know the meaning of '司机', but we do know the meaning of '司' is 'control' and the meaning of '机' is 'machine'. Then we can guess the meaning of '司机' may be connected with 'control' and 'machine', and actually the real meaning is the person who drives(controls) a car(machine).

In Chinese language, according to the encoding standard of GB2312, there are about 6,763 commonly used characters. And in our own system dictionary which has about 129,440 word entries, the number of one-character words is only 6,188 (about 4.78%). From these figures, we know that most Chinese words belong to synthetic words and a deep analysis for synthetic words is necessary for Chinese language processing.

2.2 Classification of Chinese synthetic words

The Synthetic words may be understood as the result or 'output' of a word-formation rule in Chinese language. Classification of these Chinese synthetic words is a difficult task because the 'formation rule' is not so obvious and sometimes even a native speaker can not determine which category a word

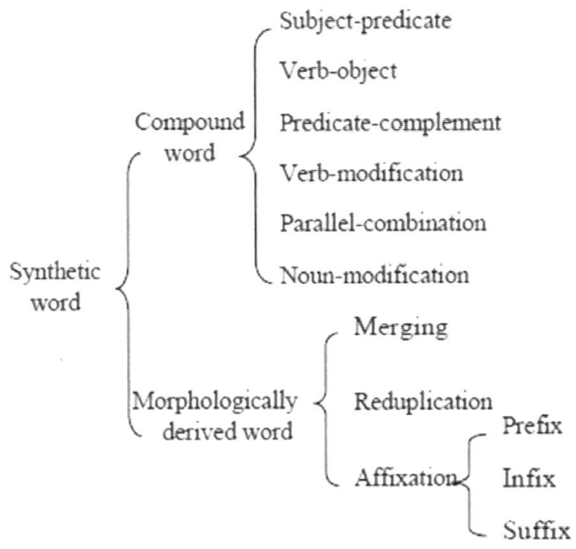

Figure 1: Types of Chinese synthetic words

should belong to. However, since it is quite important to understand the structure of Chinese words, there have been a lot of research on classification of Chinese synthetic words from both linguistic and computational points of view until now. Each of them has divided synthetic words into different categories according to their own criteria. In our research, based on our experience on Chinese morphological analysis and unknown word detection, we divide Chinese synthetic words into the categories as shown in Figure 1 to help us understand the inner constituents of them.

2.3 Compound words

Compound words, whose internal constituents have some syntactic relations with each other, can be divided into the following six kinds according to (Yuanjian He, 2004).

- Subject-predicate[主谓式]

  words that only have subject and predicate parts. This type is subdivided into two types: SV and VS.

  VS: 搬运/工[porter], 裁判/员[referee]

  SV: 胃/下垂[gastroptosia], 地/震[earthquake]

- Verb-object[动宾式]

  words that have verb and object parts, which contains two types: VO and OV.

  OV: 党/代表[representative of party]

  VO: 理/发[haircut], 反/政府[anti-government]

- Verb-modification[动词偏正式]

  words that have a verb part and an adjunct part which are neither subject nor object of the verb. The adjunct part always shows the property of the verb part or be the media of the verb's action.This type contains VX and XV.

  VX: 放大/器[amplifier], 冲印/店[print shop]

  XV: 自动/控制[automatic control]

  批/发[wholesale]

- Predicate-complement[述补式]

  words that have a verb part and a complement part, which shows the result, direction or aspect of the action. This type also have two kinds: VV and VA.

  VV: 跑/出来[running out of]

  打发/掉[get rid of]

  VA: 染/红[dyeing red]

- Parallel-combination[联合式]

  words that have a coordinate structure where the meanings of constituents are same, similar, related or opposite.

  Example: 开/关[switch], 学/习[learning]

  国/家[nation], 兄/弟[brother]

  中/日/韩[China, Japan and Korea]

- Noun-modification[名词偏正式]

  words that have a noun part which is the root of the word, and a modification part which shows the property of the noun part.

  Example: 电/脑[computer], 书/架[book shelf]

  汽车/站[bus stop]

Here we have made some compromises with these categories mentioned above based on the simplicity of machine learning process and our experience on tagging compund words. For example, we only define SV and VS as the subject-predicate type because it will make machine learning process much easier when it comes to those words with a structure like SVO or SVX. Futhermore, in the case that a word with an internal constituent which has both NN and VV parts of speech, even human annotators can not easily tell which type this word should be categarized into between noun-modification and verb-modification. So we tagged all these words to verb-modification when they have an internal part with both NN and VV parts of speech.

2.4 Morphologically derived words

Morphologically derived words are those which have specific word formation. It can be categoried into the following types:

- Merging

  words that are composed of two adjacent and semantically related words, which have some characters in common. It could be seen as a kind of abbreviation.

  Example: 中学+小学➔中小学 [middle and preliminary school]

  上文+下文➔上下文[context]

  北京市+市长➔北京市长 [mayer of Beijing city]

- Reduplication

  words that contain some reduplicated characters. There are eight main patterns of reduplication: AA, ABAB, AABB, AXA, AXAY, XAYA, AAB and ABB.

  Example: 听/听[listen], 雄/赳赳[valiantly]

  研究/研究[research]

- Affixation

  words that are composed of a word and an affix(either a prefix, a suffix or an infix).

  Example: 副主席[vice president]
  总工程师[Executive Engineer]

  看不到[can't see]
  听得见[can hear]

  调查局[bureau of investigation]
  安全厅[security agency]

2.5 Exceptions

Apart from compound words and morphologically derived words, there still exist some types of words which need discussion about whether they belong to synthetic words or not. However, we can use some other methods like time expression extraction or named entity recognition to deal with these kinds of words.

- Abbreviations

  expressions that have a short appearance, but stand for a long term.

  Example: 中共➔中国共产党 [Communist Party of China]

- Factoids

  expressions that indicate date, time, number, money, score or range. This kind of expressions have a large variation in their appearance.

  Example: 2007.1.30

  五点半[five thirty]

  三块五毛六[3.56 yuan]

- Idioms, proverbs, sayings and poems

  expressions that usually consist of more than three characters and always have a special meaning.

  Example: 门可罗雀[sparsely visited]

  先天下之忧而忧 [be the First to bear hardships]

3 Previous research and tree-based method

3.1 Previous research

Until now, there is little specific research on Chinese synthetic words. However, every institution has its own way of dealing with synthetic words in their segmentation standard when doing Chinese morphological analysis. There are two main previous researches on the analysis of Chinese synthetic words.

The first one is done by Microsoft (Andi Wu, 2003) by creating a customizable segmentation system of Chinese morphologically derived words. This system uses a parameter driven method which can divide synthetic words into different levels of word components based on some pre-defined rules, according to the needs of different NLP application. For instance, in machine translation, we will translate '烤面包器' into 'toaster' if our system dictionary has this kind of information. But if we do not have this entry in our dictionary, we have to split '烤面包器[toaster]' into lower level such as '烤[bake] / 面包[bread] / 器[machine]', the translation of which will probably give us some information about the original meaning of the whole word. Although this system achieves higher score than other systems that do not have synthetic analysis, it only takes morphologically derived words into account, which means it does not contain information about internal syntactic relations.

The second one (C. Huang, 1997) is actually a proposal of segmentation standard rather than a detailed synthetic word analysis research. It is first used by Sinica when doing the tagging task of Chinese word segmentation. If the tagging object is a synthetic word, one tag among w0, w1 and w2, which stand for 'faithful', 'truthful' and 'graceful', will be selected for it. For example, if we have a synthetic word '北京市安全厅[security agency of Beijing city]', this tagging method will divide the word as follows:

<w2>
<w1><w0>北京</w0><w0>市</w0></w1>
<w1><w0>安全</w0><w0>厅</w0></w1>
</w2>

Again, this kind of method does not take word internal syntactic relations into account either. Furthermore, it even does not have the POS information of different levels of word, thus can not be used to construct a customizable system.

3.2 Synthetic word analysis with tree-based structure information

For specifying consistent Chinese segmentation standard for our morphological analysis system and fertilizing the information of our dictionary, we propose a synthetic word analysis method with tree-based structure information.

We assume that words which are already in our current system dictionary could be word components of other out-of-vocabulary synthetic words. So the first thing to do is to classify all synthetic words in our current dictionary into the categories defined in section 2.2. Because intuitively most 2-character words, though they could have internal syntactic relations, are often used as single words by native speakers and have already been registered as lexical entries in our Chinese dictionary, we can first classify all 3-character words into those categories and link their internal components to 1-character words and 2-character words which are already in our dictionary.

After finishing the internal structure annotation for 3-character words, we can easily construct 4-character or 5-character words' structure by using 3-character and 2-character words' information and store these structure information into synthetic word dictionary.

Finally, when we get a long synthetic word, we can build a tree structure recursively like in Figure 2 by using the constituent words' internal structures, which have already been stored in our synthetic word dictionary.

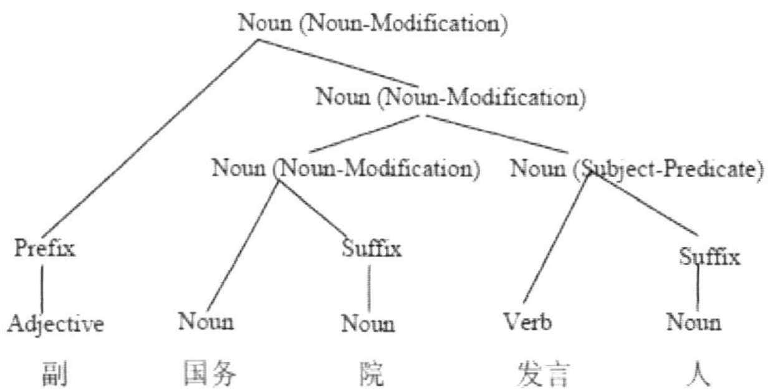

Figure 2: Synthetic word tree of '副国务院发言人 [vice spokesman of State Department]'

When constructing this kind of tree, we can use some rules which have the following form:

A + B➔ Category
or A + B + C➔ Category

where A, B and C are parts of speech, affixation or other properties of word components.

3.3 Annotation of morphologically derived words in system dictionary

Usually, in Chinese, 2-character words are thought and used as single words by native speakers. And words which have more than two characters are often synthetic words which can be categorized into compound words or morphologically derived words. So during our work of analyzing Chinese synthetic words, we first choose 3-character words as our main target in that starting from 3-character words will give us a good chain effect when analyzing words which have more than three characters.

At first, there is no other resource at hand except for the morphological analysis system dictionary with 129440 entries. Because a standard set with all category information of Chinese synthetic words is needed in further research, we first extracted 1000 3-character words from our dictionary and annotated them by hand according to the categories introduced in section 2. As the result of human annotation, Table 1 and 2 show the distribution of compound words and morphologically derived words. In Table 1, although about 6% of the 1000 words are single-morpheme words, we still can see that noun-modification words occupy the largest part (62.9%) in synthetic words from a syntactic point of view. Table 2 gives us the information that most synthetic words (83%) have an internal structure with a suffix.

subject-predicate	4.8%
verb-object	2.0%
verb-modification	21.3%
predicate-complement	3.2%
parallel-combination	0.2%
noun-modification	62.9%
single-morpheme word	5.4%

Table 1: Compound words in 1000 words

prefix	infix	suffix	merging	reduplication
9.0%	0.5%	83.0%	1.5%	0.2%

Table 2: Morphologically derived words in 1000 words

Since most 3-character Chinese words have the structure such as 'two+one' or 'one+two' character formation, it is obvious that we should first look at noun-modification words with frequently used suffixes as the beginning of our analysis. We could get a list of characters of possible affixation from this process too. Furthermore, we also find that parallel-combination words and reduplication words tend to have some fixed structures which makes them easy to recognize.

4 Experiment on Morphologically derived words

In order to apply our proposed tree-based analysis method, we first have to annotate all 3-character words in our dictionary with their internal parts linked to 2-character and 1-character words. Because most Chinese 3-character words have prefix or suffix structure, we assume that it will be much efficient for us to annotate 3-character words if we can classify them from the aspect of morphologically derived words.

Because we don't have any other useful resources except Chinese Gigaword(CGW), We first computed mutual information for all 3-character words in two ways by referencing the CGW. For example, if we have a word ABC and we assume that A, C, AB and BC are all independent entries in our dictionary, we compute the mutual information Mi-pre for A and BC, and the mutual information Mi-suf for AB and C.

Since A, C, AB and BC are all independent words, if the result shows Mi-pre<Mi-suf, we could say that the relation between A and BC is more independent than the relation between AB and C, which means it is more possible that A and some other 2-character word XY cound form the word AXY. So the possibility of A being a prefix is greater than the possibility of C being a suffix. Then we could conclude that the word ABC has a prefix internal structure. Otherwise, we could say it has suffix internal structure.

After this process, we got a Mi(Mi-pre or Mi-suf) and a possible internal structure(prefix or suffix) for every 3-character word in system dictionary. By comparing these results to the 1000 extracted words whose internal structure has been already known, we can easily get the correct ones whose possible internal structure is the same as the ones annotated by hand.

Except for the ones which have infix, merging or redplication structure, there are 920 words in the 1000 extracted words which are tagged as prefix or suffix structure by hand. After comparing, we got

676 out of 920 words(73.48%), which was divided correctly by only looking at the internal mutual information in a large corpus(Chinese Gigaword).

The above result shows that overall accuracy is quite low by only taking account the internal mutual information when classifying prefix and suffix structure. Some examples of wrongly classified words are shown in Table 3.

words	Mi-pre	Mi-suf	result
个体户	7.024e-07	9.981e-07	个 / 体户
水彩画	1.084e-06	1.171e-05	水 / 彩画
宝莲灯	1.384e-05	1.978e-05	宝 / 莲灯
交响曲	1.993e-06	2.440e-06	交 / 响曲
大批量	8.971e-08	6.762e-08	大批 / 量

Table 3: Examples of wrongly divided words by only using mutual information

As shown in Table 3, most uncorrect ones are words having suffix internal structure but wrongly classified to have prefix internal structure. This is because we only counted the frequencies of internal parts of words without considerring their properties such as parts of speech and the frequencies that the internal parts show out at a particular position, etc.

In order to improve the whole accuracy when recognizing prefix or suffix internal structure automatically, we used an SVM classifier with the following features(in the case of 3-character string ABC):

1.internal part: A, C, BC, AB, ABC

2.pos of each internal part:
pos(A), pos(C), pos(BC), pos(AB), pos(ABC)

3.frequency of each part in Chinese Gigaword:
fre(A), fre(C), fre(BC), fre(AB), fre(ABC)

4.mutual information of internal part:
Mi-pre(A-BC), Mi-suf(AB-C)

(In the actual classification process, we set the frequency range by 2000 and the mutual information range by $\log_{10}$)

After dividing 80% of 920 words into traning set and 20% into testing set, the accuracy of SVM classifier is 94.02%. The precision and recall are shown in the first row of Table 4. Because the above experiment(A) did not take the existence of 2-character words in system dictionary into account, we then add these features and run the SVM classifier again. Finally we get the result of experiment(B) shown in the second row of Table 4.

Exp	Acc. (%)	F	Prefix(%)		Suffix(%)	
			Rec.	Pre.	Rec.	Pre.
A	94.02	0.56	38.89	100.0	100.0	93.79
B	94.57	0.67	55.56	83.33	98.80	95.35

Table 4: Results of Recall and Precision for words which have prefix or suffix structure

This result is quite unbalanced because there are only a few intances of prefixes both in training(72/736=9.78%) and testing(18/184=9.78%) sets. This is the reason of low recall in classifying instances of prefixes. The following words are the ones which were wrongly classified.

主色调，土坷垃，大批量，小卖部，山大王
市中心，菲军方，零备件，学联会，罗影剧

It turns out that these words contains mainly two types: the first type contains word like '大批量', a prefix structure word whose last character has a quite high probability to be a suffix. This makes it difficult for SVM to determine to which class the whole word should be classified; an example of the second type is suffix structure word like '罗影剧', whose front part '罗影' does not appear in the Chinese Gigaword independently, which in the end make it unsure for SVM to classify it into suffix structure word.

Though there are some words that were wrongly categorized, we still got a overall accuracy of 94.57% which would be much higher if we recursively use SVMs for classification. We believe that this method could classify morphologically derived words quite efficiently if we add some more rules for recognizing merging and reduplication words. And by applying the tree-based method, we could use this method on words with more than 3 characters in future.

5 Conclusion and future work

This paper proposed a tree-based method for analyzing Chinese synthetic words by constructing a Chinese synthetic word dictionary. This method is based on the classification of Chinese synthetic words both from syntactic and morphological ways. After annotating and investigating the distribution of one thousand 3-character words, we used frequencies and mutual information as features from Chinese Gigaword for machine learning. With these features, we tried to classify morphologically derived words into prefix or suffix internal structure by using SVM classifier.

For future work, we have to take other morphological internal structures into account and try to classify all synthetic words into morphologically derived word categories. Then, we should also find some thesaurus that contain syntactic information of words or characters to help us analyze the compound words' internal structure. Finally, after gathering the information of Chinese synthetic words from both syntactic and morphological aspect, we will build a Chinese synthetic word dictionary and try to use it to improve the performance of our morphological analysis system and unknown word extraction.

References

[Andi Wu2003] Andi Wu. 2003. *Customizable Segmentation of Morphologically Derived Words in Chinese.* Vol.8, No.1, February 2003, pp. 1-28 Computational Linguistics and Chinese Language Processing

[C. Huang1997] C. Huang, K. Chen and L. Chang 1997. *Segmentation standard for Chinese natural language processing.* International Journal of Computational Linguistics and Chinese Language Processing

[Chooi-Ling Goh2006] Chooi-Ling Goh, Jia Lu, Yuchang Cheng, Masayuki Asahara and Yuji Matsumoto 2006. *The Construction of a Dictionary for a Two-layer Chinese Morphological Analyzer.* PACLIC 2006

[Hiroshi Nakagawa, Hiroyuki Kojima, Akira Maeda2004] Hiroshi Nakagawa, Hiroyuki Kojima, Akira Maeda 2004. *Chinese Term Extraction from Web Pages Based on Compound word Productivity.* Third SIGHAN Workshop on Chinese Language Processing, ACL 2004

[Huihsin Tseng and Keh-Jiann Chen2002] Huihsin Tseng and Keh-Jiann Chen 2002. *Design of Chinese Morphological Analyzer.* First SIGHAN Workshop 2002

[Jerome L. Packard2000] Jerome L. Packard 2000. *The Morphology of Chinese-A Linguistic and Cognitive Approach.*

[Keh-Jiann Chen, Chao-jan Chen2000] Keh-Jiann Chen, Chao-jan Chen 2000. *Automatic Semantic Classification for Chinese Unknown Compound Nouns.* ACL 2000

[Shengfen Luo and Maosong Sun2003] Shengfen Luo and Maosong Sun 2003. *Two-character Chinese Word Extraction Based on Hybrid of Internal and Contextual Measures.* ACL 2003

[Yuanjian He2004] Yuanjian He 2004. 汉语真假复合词-从普遍语法原则看汉语复合词的语序、类型及结构. The Chinese University of Hong Kong

Which Performs Better on In-Vocabulary Word Segmentation: Based on Word or Character?

Zhenxing Wang[1,2], Changning Huang[2] and Jingbo Zhu[1]
1 Institute of Computer Software and Theory, Northeastern University, Shenyang, China, 110004
2 Microsoft Research Asia, 49, Zhichun Road, Haidian District, Beijing, China, 100080
zxwang@ics.neu.edu.cn
v-cnh@microsoft.com
zhujingbo@mail.neu.edu.cn

Abstract*

Since the first Chinese Word Segmentation (CWS) Bakeoff on 2003, CWS has experienced a prominent flourish because Bakeoff provides a platform for the participants, which helps them recognize the merits and drawbacks of their segmenters. However, the evaluation metric of bakeoff is not sufficient enough to measure the performance thoroughly, sometimes even misleading. One typical example caused by this insufficiency is that there is a popular belief existing in the research field that segmentation based on word can yield a better result than character-based tagging (CT) on in-vocabulary (IV) word segmentation even within closed tests of Bakeoff. Many efforts were paid to balance the performance on IV and out-of-vocabulary (OOV) words by combining these two methods according to this belief. In this paper, we provide a more detailed evaluation metric of IV and OOV words than Bakeoff to analyze CT method and combination method, which is a typical way to seek such balance. Our evaluation metric shows that CT outperforms dictionary-based (or so called word-based in general) segmentation on both IV and OOV words within Bakeoff closed tests. Furthermore, our analysis shows that using confidence measure to combine the two segmentation results should be under certain limitation.

1 Introduction

Chinese Word Segmentation (CWS) has been witnessed a prominent progress in the last three Bakeoffs (Sproat and Emerson, 2003), (Emerson, 2005), (Levow, 2006). One of the reasons for this progress is that Bakeoff provides standard corpora and objective metric, which makes the result of each system comparable. Through those evaluations researchers can recognize the advantage and disadvantage of their methods and improve their systems accordingly. However, in the evaluation metric of Bakeoff, only the overall F measure, precision, recall, IV (in-vocabulary) recall and OOV (out-of-vocabulary) recall are included and such a metric is not sufficient to give a completely measure on the performance, especially when the performance on IV and OOV word segmentation need to be evaluated. An important issue is that segmentation based on which, word or character, can yield the better performance on IV words. We give a detailed explanation about this issue as following.

Since CWS was firstly treated as a character-based tagging task (we call it "CT" for short hereafter) in (Xue and Converse, 2002), this method has been widely accepted and further developed by researchers (Peng et al., 2004), (Tseng et al., 2005), (Low et al., 2005), (Zhao et al., 2006). Relatively to dictionary-based

* The work is done when the first author is working in MSRA as an intern.

segmentation (we call it "DS" for short hereafter), CT method can achieve a higher accuracy on OOV word recognition and a better performance of segmentation in whole. Thus, CT has drawn more and more attention and became the dominant method in the Bakeoff 2005 and 2006.

Although CT has shown its merits in word segmentation task, some researchers still hold the belief that on IV words DS can perform better than CT even in the restriction of Bakeoff closed test. Consequently, many strategies are proposed to balance the IV and OOV performance (Goh et al., 2005), (Zhang et al., 2006a). Among these strategies, the confidence measure used to combine the results of CT and DS is a straight-forward one, which is introduced in (Zhang et al., 2006a). The basic assumption of such combination is that DS method performs better on IV words and Zhang derives this belief from the fact that DS achieves higher IV recall rate as Table 1 shows. In which AS, CityU, MSRA and PKU are four corpora used in Bakeoff 2005 (also see Table 2 for detail). We provide a more detailed evaluation metric to analyze these two methods, including precision and F measure of IV and OOV respectively and our experiments show that CT outperforms DS on both IV and OOV words within Bakeoff closed test. The precision and F measure are existing metrics and the definitions of them are clear. Here we just employ them to evaluate segmentation results. Furthermore, our error analysis on the results of combination reveals that confidence measure in (Zhang et al., 2006a) has a representation flaw and we propose an EIV tag method to revise it. Finally, we give an empirical comparison between existing pure CT method and combination, which shows that pure CT method can produce state-of-the-art results on both IV word and overall segmentation.

Corpus	R_{IV}		R_{OOV}	
	DS	CT	DS	CT
AS	0.982	0.967	0.038	0.647
CityU	0.989	0.967	0.164	0.736
MSRA	0.993	0.972	0.048	0.716
PKU	0.981	0.955	0.408	0.754

Table 1 IV and OOV recall in (Zhang et al., 2006a)

The rest of this paper is organized as follows. In Section 2, we give a brief introduction to Zhang's DS method and subword-based tagging, which is a special CT method. And by comparing the results of this special CT method and DS according our detailed metric, we show that CT performs better on both IV and OOV. We review in Section 3 how confidence measure works and indicate its representation flaw. Furthermore, an "EIV" tag method is proposed to revise the confidence measure. In Section 4, the experimental results of existing pure CT method are demonstrated to compare with combination result, based on which we discuss the related work. In Section 5, we conclude the contributions of this paper and discuss the future work.

2 Comparison between DS and CT Based on Detailed Metric

We proposed a detailed evaluation metric for IV and OOV word identification in this section and experiments based on the new metric show that CT outperforms DS not only on OOV words but also on IV words with F-measure of IV. All the experiments in this paper conform to the constraints of closed test in Bakeoff 2005 (Emerson, 2005). It means that any resource beyond the training corpus is excluded. We first review how DS and CT work and then present our evaluation metric and experiment results. There is one thing should be emphasized, by comparing DS and CT result we just want to verify that our new metric can show the performance on IV words more objectively. Since either DS or CT implementation has specific setting here we should not extend the comparison result to a general sense between those generative models and discriminative models.

2.1 Dictionary-based segmentation

For the dictionary-based word segmentation, we collect a dictionary from training corpus first. Instead of Maximum Match, trigram language model[2] trained on training corpus is employed for disambiguation. During the disambiguation procedure, a beam search decoder is used to seek the most possible segmentation. Since the setting in our paper is consistent with the closed test of

[2] Language model used in this paper is SLRIM from http://www.speech.sri.com/projects/srilm/

Bakeoff, we can only use the information we learn from training corpus though other open resources may be helpful to improve the performance further. For detail, the decoder reads characters from the input sentence one at a time, and generates candidate segmentations incrementally. At each stage, the next incoming character is combined with an existing candidate in two different ways to generate new candidates: it is either appended to the last word in the candidate, or taken as the start of a new word. This method guarantees exhaustive generation of possible segmentations for any input sentence. However, the exponential time and space of the length of the input sentence are needed for such a search and it is always intractable in practice. Thus, we use the trigram language model to select top B (B is a constant predefined before search and in our experiment 3 is used) best candidates with highest probability at each stage so that the search algorithm can work in practice. Finally, when the whole sentence has been read, the best candidate with the highest probability will be selected as the segmentation result. Here, the term "dictionary-based" is exactly the method implemented in (Zhang et al., 2006a), it does not mean the generative language model in general.

2.2 Character-based tagging

Under CT scheme, each character in one sentence is labeled as 'B' if it is the beginning of a word, 'O' tag means the current character is a single-character word, other character is labeled as 'I'. For example, "全中国 (whole China)" is labeled as "全 (whole)/O 中 (central)/B 国 (country)/I".

In (Zhang et al., 2006a), the above CT method is developed as subword-based tagging. First, the most frequent multi-character words and all single characters in training corpus are collected as subwords. During the subword-based tagging, a subword is viewed as an unit instead of several separate characters and given only one tag. For example, in subword-based tagging, "全中国 (whole China)" is labeled as "全 (whole)/O 中国 (China)/O", if the word "中国 (China)" is collected as a subword. As the preprocessing, both training and test corpora are segmented by maximum match with subword set as dictionary. After this preprocessing, every sentence in both training and test corpora becomes subword sequence. Finally, the tagger is trained by CRFs approach[3] on the training data. Although word information is integrated into this method, it still works in the scheme of "IOB" tagging. Thus, we still call subword-based tagging as a special CT method and in the reminder of this paper "CT" means subword-based tagging in Zhang's paper and "Pure CT" means CT without subword.

2.3 A detailed evaluation metric

In this paper, data provided by Bakeoff 2005 is used in our experiments in order to compare with the published results in (Zhang et al., 2006a). The statistics of the corpora for Bakeoff 2005 are listed in Table 2 (Emerson, 2005).

Corpus	Encoding	#Training words	#Test words	OOV rate
AS	Big5	5.45M	122K	0.043
CityU	Big5	1.46M	41K	0.074
MSRA	GB	2.37M	107K	0.026
PKU	GB	1.1M	104K	0.058

Table 2 Corpora statistics of Bakeoff 2005

Evaluation standard is also provided by Bakeoff, including overall precision, recall, F measure, IV recall and OOV recall (Sproat and Emerson, 2003), (Emerson, 2005). However, some important metrics, such as F measure and precision of both IV and OOV words are omitted, which are necessary when the performance of IV or OOV word identification need to be judged. Thus, in order to judge the results of each experiment, a more detailed evaluation with precision and F measure of both IV and OOV words included is used. To calculate the IV and OOV precision and recall, we firstly divide words of the segmenter's output and gold data into IV word and OOV word sets respectively with the dictionary collected from the training corpus. Then, for IV and OOV word sets respectively, the IV (or OOV) recall is the proportion of the correctly segmented IV (or OOV) word tokens to all IV (or OOV) word tokens in the gold data, and IV (or OOV) precision is the proportion of the correctly segmented IV

[3] CRF tagger in this paper is implemented by CRF++ downloaded from http://crfpp.sourceforge.net/

(or OOV) word tokens to all IV (or OOV) word tokens in the segmenter's output. One thing have to be emphasized is that the single character in test corpus will be defined as OOV if it does not appear in training corpus. We will see later in this section, by this evaluation, some facts covered by the bakeoff evaluation can be illustrated by our new evaluation metric.

Here, we repeat two experiments described in (Zhang et al., 2006a), namely dictionary-based approach and subword-based tagging. For CT method, top 2000 most frequent multi-character words and all single characters in training corpus are selected as subwords and the feature templates used for CRF model is listed in Table 3. We present all the segmentation results in Table 6 to see the strength and weakness of each method conveniently.

Based on IV and OOV recall as we show in Table 1, Zhang argues that the DS performs better on IV word identification while CT performs better on OOV words. But we can see from the results in Table 6 (the lines about DS and CT), the IV precision of DS approach is much lower than that of CT on all the four corpora, which also causes a lower F measure of IV. The reason for low IV precision of DS is that many OOV words are segmented into two IV words by DS. For example, OOV word "歌唱班(choral)" is segmented into"歌唱(sing) 班(class)" by DS. These wrongly identified IV words increase the number of all IV words in the segmenter's output and cause the low IV precision of the DS result. Since the F measure of IV is a more reasonable metric of performance of IV than IV recall only, Table 6 shows that CT method outperforms the DS on IV word segmentation over all four corpora. The comparison also shows that CT outperforms the DS on OOV and overall segmentation as well.

Type	Feature	Function
Unigram	C_{-2}, C_{-1}, C_0, C_1, C_2	Previous two, current and next two subword
Bigram	$C_{-2}\,C_{-1}$, $C_{-1}\,C_0$, $C_0\,C_1$, $C_1\,C_2$	Two adjacent subwords
Jump	$C_{-1}\,C_1$	Previous character and next subwords

Table 3 Feature templates used for CRF in our experiments

3 Balance between IV and OOV Performance

There are other strategies such as (Goh et al., 2005) trying to seek balance between IV and OOV performance. In (Goh et al, 2005), information in a dictionary is used in a statistical model. In this way, the dictionary-based approach and the statistical model are combined. We choose the confidence measure to study because it is straight-forward. We show in this section that there is a representation flaw in the formula of confidence measure in (Zhang et al., 2006a). And we propose an "EIV" tag method to solve this problem. Our experiments show that confidence measure with EIV tag outperforms CT and DS alone.

3.1 Confidence measure

Confidence Measure (CM) means to seek an optimal tradeoff between performance on IV and OOV words. The basic idea of CM comes from the belief that CT performs better on OOV words while DS performs better on IV words. When both results of CT and DS are available, the CM can be calculated according to the following formula in (Zhang et al., 2006a):

$$\mathrm{CM}(t_{iob} \mid w) = \alpha CM_{iob}(t_{iob} \mid w) + (1-\alpha)\delta(t_w, t_{iob})_{ng}$$

Here, w is a subword, t_{iob} is "IOB" tag given by CT and t_w is "IOB" tag generated by DS. In the first term of the right hand side of the formula, $CM_{iob}(t_{iob} \mid w)$ is the marginal probability of t_{iob} (we call this marginal probability "MP" for short). And in the second term, $\delta(t_w, t_{iob})_{ng}$ is a Kronecker delta function, returning 1 if and only if t_w and t_{iob} are identical, else returning 0. But if $\delta(t_w, t_{iob})_{ng} = 1$, there is no requirement of replacement at all. While if $\delta(t_w, t_{iob})_{ng} = 0$, when $t_w \neq t_{iob}$, CM depends on the first term of its right hand side only and α is unnecessary to be set as a weight. Finally, α in the formula is a weight to seek balance between CT tag and DS tag. Another parameter here is a threshold t for the CM. If CM is less than t, t_w replaces t_{iob} as the final tag, otherwise t_{iob} will be remained as the final tag. However, two parameters in the CM, namely α and t, are unnecessary, because when MP is greater than or equal to t/α, t_{iob} will be kept, otherwise it will be replaced with t_w. Thus, the CM ultimately is the marginal probability of the "IOB" tag (MP). In the experiment of this paper, MP is used as CM because it is equivalent to Zhang's CM but more convenient to express.

3.2 Experiments and error analysis about combination

We repeat the experiments about CM in Zhang's paper (Zhang et al., 2006a) and show that there is a representation flaw in the CM formula. Furthermore, we propose an EIV tag method to make CM yield a better result.

In this paper, α = 0.8 and t = 0.7 (Parameters in two papers, Zhang et al. 2006a and Zhang et al. 2006b, are different. And our parameters are consistent with Zhang et al. 2006b which is confirmed by Dr Zhang through email) are used in CM, namely MP= 0.875 is the threshold. Here, in Table 4, we provide some statistics on the results of CT when MP is less than 0.875. From Table 4 we can see that even with MP less than 0.875, most of the subwords are still tagged correctly by CT and should not be revised by DS result. Besides, lots of the subwords with low MP contained by OOV words in test data, especially for the corpus whose OOV rate is high (i.e. on CityU corpus more than one third subwords with low MP belong to OOV word) and performance on OOV recognition is the advantage of CT rather than that of DS approach. Thus when combining the results of the two methods, it is the t_{iob} should be maintained if the subword is contained by an OOV word. Therefore, the CM formula seems somewhat unreasonable.

The error analysis about how many original errors are eliminated and how many new errors are introduced by CM is provided in Table 5 (the columns about CM). Table 5 illustrates that, after combining the two results, most original errors on IV words are corrected because DS can achieve higher IV recall as described in Zhang's paper. But on OOV part, more new errors are introduced by CM and these new errors decrease the precision of the IV words. For example, the OOV words "警卫队员 (guard member)" and "设计费 (design fee)" is recognized correctly by CT but with low CM. In the combining procedure, these words are wrongly split as IV errors: "警卫 (guard) 队员 (member)" and "设计 (design) 费 (fee)". Thus, for two corpora (i.e. CityU and AS), F measure of IV and overall F measure decreases since there are more new errors introduced than original ones eliminated and only on the other two corpora (MSRA and PKU), overall F measure of combination method is higher than CT alone, which is shown in Table 6 by the lines about combination.

3.3 EIV tag method

Since combining the two results by CM may produce an even worse performance in some case, it is worthy to study how to use this CM to get an enhanced result. Intuitively, if we can change only the CT tags of the subwords which contained in IV word while keep the CT tags of those contained in OOV words unchanged, we will improve the final result according to our error analysis in Table 5. Unfortunately, only from the test data, we can get the information whether a subword contained in an IV word, just as what we do to get Table 4. However, we can get an approximate estimation from DS result. When using subwords to re-segment DS result[4], all the fractions re-segmented out of multiple-character words, including both multiple-character words and single characters, will be given an "EIV" tag, which means that the current multiple-character word or single character is contained in an IV word with high probability. For example, "人力资源 (human resource)" in DS result is a whole word. However, only "资源 (resource)" belongs to the subword set, so during the re-segmentation "人力资源 (human resource)" will be re-segmented as "人 (people) 力 (force) 资源 (resource)". All these three fractions will be labeled with an "EIV" tag respectively. It is reasonable because all the multiple-character words in the DS result can match an IV word. After this procedure, when combining

[4] For the detail, please refer to (Zhang et al., 2006a).

Corpus	AS	CityU	MSRA	PKU
# subword tokens belong to IV	10010	4404	9552	9619
# subword tokens belong to IV and tagged correctly by CT	7452	3434	7452	7213
# subword tokens belong to IV and tagged wrongly by CT	2558	970	2100	2406
# subword tokens belong to OOV	5924	2524	2685	3580
# subword tokens belong to OOV and tagged correctly by CT	3177	1656	1725	2208
# subword tokens belong to OOV and tagged wrongly by CT	2747	868	960	1372

Table 4 Results of CT when MP is less than 0.875

Corpus	AS		CityU		MSRA		PKU	
Method	CM	EIV	CM	EIV	CM	EIV	CM	EIV
#original errors eliminated on IV	1905	1003	904	469	1959	1077	1923	1187
#original errors eliminated on OOV	755	75	155	80	104	30	230	76
#original errors eliminated totally	2660	1078	1059	549	2063	1107	2153	1263
#new errors introduced on IV	441	185	80	50	148	68	211	118
#new errors introduced on OOV	2487	77	1320	103	1517	57	1681	58
# new errors introduced totally	2928	262	1400	153	1665	125	1892	176

Table 5 Error analysis of confidence measure with and without EIV tag

the two results, only the CT tag with EIV tags and low MP will be replaced by DS tag, otherwise the original CT tag will be maintained. Under this condition the errors introduced by OOV will not happen and enhanced results are listed in Table 6 lines about EIV. We can see that on all four corpora the overall F measure of EIV result is higher than that of CT alone, which show that our EIV method works well. Now, let's check what changes happened in the number of error tags after EIV condition added into the CM. We can see from the Table 5 columns about EIV, there are more errors eliminated than the new errors introduced after EIV condition added into CM and most CT tags of subwords contained in OOV words maintained unchanged as we supposed. And then, our results (in Table 6 lines about EIV) are comparable with that in Zhang's paper. Thus, there may be some similar strategies in Zhang's CM too but not presented in Zhang's paper.

4 Discussion and Related Works

Although the method such as confidence measure can be helpful at some circumstance, our experiment shows that pure character-based tagging (pure CT) can work well with reasonable features and tag set. In (Zhao et al., 2006), an enhanced CRF tag set is proposed to distinguish different positions in the multi-character words when the word length is less than 6. In this method, feature templates are almost the same as shown in Table 3 with a 3-character window and a 6-tag set {B, B2, B3, M, E, O} is used. Here, tag B and E stand for the first and the last position in a multi-character word, respectively. S stands up a single-character word. B2 and B3 stand for the second and the third position in a multi-character word, whose length is larger than two-character or three-character. M stands for the fourth or more rear position in a multi-character word, whose length is larger than four-character.

In Table 6, the lines about "pure CT" provide the results generated by pure CT with 6-tag set. We can see from the Table 6 this pure CT approach achieves the state-of-the-art results on all the corpora. On three of the four corpora (AS, MSRA and PKU) this pure CT method gets the best result. Even on IV word, this pure CT approach outperforms Zhang's CT method and produces comparable results with combination with EIV tags, which shows that pure CT method can perform well on IV words too. Moreover, this character-based tagging approach is more clear and simple than the confidence measure method.

Although character-based tagging became mainstream approach in the last two Bakeoffs, it does not mean that word information is valueless in Chinese word segmentation. A word-based perceptron algorithm is proposed recently (Zhang and Clark, 2007), which views Chinese word segmentation task from a new angle instead of character-based tagging and gets comparable results with the best results of Bakeoff.

Corpus	Method	R	P	F	R_{IV}	P_{IV}	F_{IV}	R_{OOV}	P_{OOV}	F_{OOV}
AS	DS	0.943	0.881	0.911	0.984	0.892	0.935	0.044	0.217	0.076
	CT	0.954	0.938	0.946	0.967	0.960	0.964	0.666	0.606	0.635
	Combination	0.958	0.929	0.943	0.980	0.945	0.962	0.487	0.593	0.535
	EIV tag	0.960	0.942	0.951	0.973	0.962	0.968	0.667	0.624	0.645
	Pure CT	0.958	0.947	0.953	0.971	0.963	0.967	0.682	0.618	0.648
CityU	DS	0.928	0.848	0.886	0.989	0.865	0.923	0.162	0.353	0.223
	CT	0.947	0.940	0.944	0.963	0.964	0.964	0.739	0.717	0.728
	Combination	0.954	0.922	0.938	0.984	0.938	0.961	0.581	0.693	0.632
	EIV tag	0.953	0.949	0.951	0.970	0.968	0.969	0.744	0.750	0.747
	Pure CT	0.947	0.948	0.948	0.967	0.973	0.970	0.692	0.660	0.676
MSRA	DS	0.969	0.927	0.947	0.994	0.930	0.961	0.036	0.358	0.066
	CT	0.963	0.964	0.963	0.970	0.979	0.975	0.698	0.662	0.680
	Combination	0.977	0.961	0.969	0.990	0.970	0.980	0.511	0.653	0.574
	EIV tag	0.972	0.970	0.971	0.980	0.982	0.981	0.696	0.679	0.688
	Pure CT	0.972	0.975	0.973	0.978	0.986	0.982	0.750	0.632	0.686
PKU	DS	0.948	0.911	0.929	0.981	0.920	0.950	0.403	0.711	0.515
	CT	0.944	0.945	0.945	0.955	0.966	0.961	0.763	0.727	0.745
	Combination	0.955	0.942	0.949	0.973	0.953	0.963	0.664	0.782	0.718
	EIV tag	0.950	0.952	0.951	0.961	0.970	0.966	0.768	0.753	0.760
	Pure CT	0.946	0.957	0.951	0.956	0.973	0.964	0.672	0.580	0.623

Table 6 Results of different approach used in our experiments (White background lines are the results we repeat Zhang's methods and they have some trivial difference with Table 1.)

Therefore, the most important thing worth to pay attention in future study is how to integrate linguistic information into the statistical model effectively, no matter character or word information.

5 Conclusions and Future Work

In this paper, we first provided a detailed evaluation metric, which provides the necessary information to judge the performance of each method on IV and OOV word identification. Second, by this evaluation metric, we show that character-based tagging outperforms dictionary-based segmentation not only on OOV words but also on IV words within Bakeoff closed tests. Furthermore, our experiments show that confidence measure in Zhang's paper has a representation flaw and we propose an EIV tag method to revise the combination. Finally, our experiments show that pure character-based approach also can achieve good IV word and overall performance. Perhaps, there are two reasons that existing combination results don't outperform the pure CT. One is that most information contained in statistic language model is already captured by the CT feature templates in CRF framework. The other is that confidence measure may not be the effective way to combine the DS and CT results.

In the future work, our research will focus on how to integrate word information into CRF features rather than using it to modify the results of CRF tagging. In this way, we can capture the word information meanwhile avoid destroying the optimal output of CRF tagging.

Acknowledgement

The authors appreciate Dr. Hai Zhao in City University of Hong Kong and Dr. Ruiqiang Zhang in Spoken Language Communications Lab, ATR, Japan providing a lot of help for this paper. Thank those reviewers who gave the valuable comment to improve this paper.

References

Thomas Emerson. 2005. The Second International Chinese Word Segmentation Bakeoff. In *Proceedings of the Fourth SIGHAN Workshop on Chinese Language Processing*, pages 123-133, Jeju Island, Korea:

Chooi-Ling Goh, Masayuku Asahara and Yuji Matsumoto. 2005. Chinese Word Segmentatin by Classification of Characters. *Computational Linguistics and*

Chinese Language Processing, Vol. 10(3): pages 381-396.

Gina-Anne Levow. 2006. The Third International Chinese Language Processing Bakeoff: Word Segmentation and Named Entity Recognition. In *Proceedings of the Fifth SIGHAN Workshop on Chinese Language Processing* , pages 108-117, Sydney: July.

Jin Kiat Low, Hwee Tou Ng, and Wenyuan Guo. 2005. A Maximum Entropy Approach to Chinese Word Segmentation. In *Proceedings of the Fourth SIGHAN Workshop on Chinese Language Processing*, pages 161-164, Jeju Island, Korea.

Fuchun Peng, Fangfang Feng, and Andrew McCallum. 2004. Chinese segmentation and new word detection using conditional random fields. In COLING 2004, pages 562–568. Geneva, Switzerland.

Richard Sproat and Thomas Emerson. 2003. The First International Chinese Word Segmentation Bakeoff. In *Proceedings of the Second SIGHAN Workshop on Chinese Language Processing*, pages 133-143, Sapporo, Japan: July 11-12,

Huihsin Tseng, Pichuan Chang et al. 2005. A Conditional Random Field Word Segmenter for SIGHAN Bakeoff 2005. In *Proceedings of the Fourth SIGHAN Workshop on Chinese Language Processing*, pages 168-171, Jeju Island, Korea.

Neinwen Xue and Susan P. Converse. 2002. Combining Classifiers for Chinese Word Segmentation. In *Proceedings of the First SIGHAN Workshop on Chinese Language Processing*, pages 63-70, Taipei, Taiwan.

Ruiqiang Zhang, Genichiro Kikui and Eiichiro Sumita. 2006a. Subword-based Tagging by Conditional Random Fields for Chinese Word Segmentation. In *Proceedings of the Human Language Technology Conference of the NAACL, Companion volume*, pages 193-196. New York, USA.

Ruiqiang Zhang, Genichiro Kikui and Eiichiro Sumita. 2006b. Subword-based Tagging for Confidence-dependent Chinese Word Segmentaion. In *Proceedings of the COLING/ACL, Main Conference Poster Sessions*, pages 961-968. Sydney, Australia.

Yue Zhang and Stephen Clark. 2007. Chinese Segmentation with a Word-Based Perceptron Algorithm. In *Proceedings of the 45th Annual Meeting of the Association for Computational Linguistics,* pages 840-847. Prague, Czech Republic.

Hai Zhao, Changning Huang et al. 2006. Effective Tag Set Selection in Chinese Word Segmentation via Conditional Random Field Modeling. In *Proceedings of PACLIC-20.* pages 87-94. Wuhan, China, Novemeber.

The Fourth International Chinese Language Processing Bakeoff: Chinese Word Segmentation, Named Entity Recognition and Chinese POS Tagging

Guangjin Jin
Institute of Applied linguistics
M.O.E., P.R.C.
No.51, Chaonei Nanxiaojie
Dong Cheng District, Beijing, China
guangjin2000@163.com

Xiao Chen
Dept of Chinese, Translation & Linguistics
City University of Hong Kong
83 Tat Chee Avenue
Kowloon, Hong Kong, China
cxiao2@student.cityu.edu.hk

Abstract

The Fourth International Chinese Language Processing Bakeoff was held in 2007 to assess the state of the art in three important tasks: Chinese word segmentation, named entity recognition and Chinese POS tagging. Twenty-eight groups submitted result sets in the three tasks across two tracks and a total of seven corpora. Strong results have been found in all the tasks as well as continuing challenges.

1 Introduction

Chinese is a kind of language which does not use word delimiters in its writing system. Now a days, under the background of information explosion, many application oriented natural language processing task become more and more important, such as parsing and machine translation. Chinese tokenization, as the foundation of many downstream processing tasks, has attracted lots of research interest. However, it is still a significant challenge for all the researchers.

SIGHAN, the Special Interest Group for Chinese Language Processing of the Association for Computational Linguistics, conducted three prior word segmentation bakeoffs, in 2003, 2005 and 2006(Sproat and Emerson, 2003; Emerson, 2005; Levow, 2006), which established benchmarks for word segmentation and named entity recognition. The bakeoff presentations at SIGHAN workshops highlighted new approaches in this field.

The fourth bakeoff was jointly held with the First CIPS Chinese Language Processing Evaluation in the summer of 2007, and co-organized by SIGHAN, Chinese LDC, and the Verifying Center of Chinese Language and Character Standards of the State Language Commission of P.R.C. In this bakeoff, we continue the Chinese word segmentation and named entity recognition tasks. Furthermore, a new evaluation task has been augmented, the task for Chinese POS tagging. In this evaluation task, a participating system will take a given segmented corpus as the input, and only the POS tagging performance will be evaluated. Both closed and open track are available for this task.

2 Details of the Evaluation

2.1 Corpora

Seven corpora were provided for the evaluation: five in Simplified characters and two in traditional characters. The Simplified character corpora were provided by Microsoft Research Asia (MSRA) for NER, by University of Pennsylvania/University of Colorado (CTB) for WS and POS tagging, by Peking University for NER and POS tagging, by Shanxi University for WS. The Traditional character corpora were provided by City University of Hong Kong (CITYU) for WS, NER and POS tagging, by the Chinese Knowledge Information Processing Laboratory (CKIP) of the Academia Sinica, Taiwan for WS and POS tagging. Each data provider offered separate training and test corpora. Statistical information for each corpus appears in Table1. All data providers were requested to supply the training and test corpora in both the standard local encoding and in Unicode (UTF-16). For all providers, missing encodings were transcoded by the organizers using the appropriate software. Primary training and truth data for word segmentation were generated by the organizers via a C++ program by uniforming sentence end tags and delimiters. For test data, all tags removed except sentence end tags.

Comparable XML format data was also provided for all corpora and all tasks. Except as noted above, no additional changes were made to the data furnished by the providers.

Table 1: Corpora for Bakeoff-4

Source	Encoding	CWS	NER	TAG[a]
CITYU	BIG5HKSCS/UTF-16	√	√	√
CKIP	BIG5/UTF-16	√		√
CTB	GB/UTF-16	√		√
MSRA	GB/UTF-16		√	
NCC	GB/UTF-16	√		√
PKU	GB/UTF-16			√
SXU	GB/UTF-16	√		

[a]TAG:Chinese POS tagging

2.2 Rules and Procedures

The fourth Bakeoff followed the structure of the former three word segmentation bakeoffs. The only difference is that participating groups ("sites") registered online and for those who could not access our web site, email registration is acceptable; On registration, all the groups are asked to identify the corpora and tasks of interest. Training data was released for download from the online registration system on August 25, 2007. Test data was released on September 25, 2007 and results were due 12:00 Beijing Time on September 28, 2007. Scores for all submitted runs were emailed to the individual groups on October 15, and were made available to all groups on a web page a few days later.

Groups could participate in either or both of two tracks for each task and corpus:

In the open track, participants could use any external data they chose in addition to the provided training data. Groups were required to specify this information in their system descriptions.

In the closed track, participants could only use information found in the provided training data. Groups were required to submit fully automatic runs and were prohibited from testing on corpora which they had previously used.

Scoring was performed automatically using a C++ program. In cases where naming errors or minor divergences from required file formats arose, a mix of manual intervention and automatic conversion was employed to enable scoring. The primary scoring program was made available to participants for follow up experiments.

3 Participating sites

A total of 42 sites registered, and 28 submitted results for scoring. A summary of participating groups with task and track information appears in Table 2. A total of 263 official runs were scored: 166 for word segmentation, 33 for named entity recognition and 64 for POS tagging.

4 Results and Discussion

4.1 Word Segmentation Results & Discussion

There are five corpus provided in the CWS track. The statistics for these corpora are in Table 3. We introduce a type-token ration(TTR) to indicate the vocabulary diversity in each corpus.

To provide a basis for comparison, we computed baseline and possible topline scores for each of the corpora. The baseline was constructed by left-to-right maximal match algorithm, using the training corpus vocabulary. The topline employed the same procedure, but instead used the test vocabulary. These results are shown in Tables 5 and 6. For the CWS task, we computed the following measures: recall (R), precision (P), equally weighted F-measure ($F = 2PR/(P + R)$), the recall, precision and F-measure on OOV (R_{OOV}, P_{OOV}, F_{OOV}), and recall, precision and F-measure on in vocabulary words (R_{IV}, P_{IV}, F_{IV}). In and out of vocabulary status are defined relative to the training corpus. Following previous bakeoffs, we employ the Central Limit Theorem for Bernoulli trials (Grinstead and

Site ID	Site Name	CITYU CWS	CKIP CWS	CTB CWS	NCC CWS	SXU CWS	CITYU NER	MSRA NER	CITYU TAG	CKIP TAG	CTB TAG	NCC TAG	PKU TAG
1	Institute of Automation, Chinese Academy of Sciences							O					
2	City University of Hong Kong	C	C	C	C	C	C(a-b) O	C O					
3	Computing Laboratory, University of Oxford	O	O	O	O	O							
5	Dept. of Decision Sciences, The Chinese University of Hong Kong	C	C O	C	C O(a-b)	C							
7	Nara Institute of Science and Technology, JAPAN	C(a-d)	C(a-d)	C(a-d)	C(a-d)	C(a-d)							
8	Nanjing Normal University	C	C(a-b)	C(a-b) O(a-c)		C(a-d) O(a-c)							
9	National Central University			C	C	C			C	C	C	C	C
11	Institute of software, Chinese Academy of Sciences							O					
14	School of Computer and Information Technology, Shanxi University				O								
15	Tungnan University	C	C										
16	Department of Chinese, Translation and Linguistics, City University of Hong Kong									C	C	C	C
18	Institute of Computational Linguistics, EECS,Peking University	C(a-b)	C	C	C(a-c)	C(a-c)	C(a-c)	C(a-b) O(a-b)					
19	NiCT/ATR	C	C	C	C	C			C	C	C	C	C
21	Faculty of Science and Technology of University of Macau, INESC Macau	C(a-d)	C(a-b)	C(a-d)	C(a-b)	C(a-b)	C(a-b)		C(a-b)				
22	Center of Intelligence Science and Technology Research of Beijing University of Posts and Telecommunications			O	O	O		O(a-b)			O	O	O
23	The Chinese University of Hong Kong						O	O					
24	France Telecom R&D Beijing Co. Ltd	C(a-b) O(a-b)	C(a-b) O(a-b)	C(a-b) O(a-b)	C(a-b)	C(a-b)	C O	C O	C	C	C	C	
26	Microsoft Research Asia and Northeastern University of China	C	C	C	C	C							
27	Simon Fraser University	C	C	C	C	C							
28	State Key Laboratory of Machine Perception, Center for Information Science, School of Electronics Engineering & Computer Science, Peking University	C O	C O	C O(a-b)	C O	C O	C O	C	C O	C O	C O	C O	C O
29	ITNLP Lab, Computer Science of Technology, Harbin Institute of Technology				C O			O				C	C O
30	Yahoo! Inc								C(a-b)	C(a-b)		C(a-b)	C(a-b)
31	Dalian University of Technology	O	O	C(a-d) O(a-b)	C(a-d) O(a-b)	C(a-d) O(a-b)		CO			C(a-b) O(a-b)	C(a-b) O(a-b)	C(a-c) O(a-b)
33	Pohang University of Science and Technology	C	C	C	C	C							
34	NOKIA(CHINA) INVESTMENT CO.,LTD. Nokia research center, Beijing				C O	C							
37	Fudan university			C	C	C		C					C
39	Language Computer Corporation	O	O	O	O	O	O	O	O	O	O	O	O

Table 2: Participating Sites by Corpus, Task, and Track

Snell, 1997) to compute 95% confidence interval as $\pm 2\sqrt{\frac{p(1-p)}{n}}$.

Chinese Word Segmentation results for all runs grouped by corpus and track appear in Tables 6-15; all tables are sorted by F-score.

Across all corpora, the best closed track F-score was achieved in the SXU corpus at 0.9623.In the open track, two systems that has exceeded the topline in the CTB corpus, and there are also three runs approaching the topline. This might because of the overlapping of testing data in this bakeoff and the training data in the last bakeoff.

According to the statistics on all the corpus for this bakeoff, there is no clear negative linear correlation between the OOV rate of a corpus and the highest score achieved on it, since the OOV words are not the only obstacle for segmentation systems to overcome.

There are some difference in the segmentation scoring system between this bakeoff and the former ones. The precision and F-measure for both IV and OOV are appended. It could be observed that, from the result tables in every corpus, the highest total F-measure is always coming up with the highest OOV and IV F-measure rather than the recall of them. So, we consider the F-measure of both IV and OOV words a more powerful indicator for the performance of the segmentation systems in some sense.

4.2 Named Entity Recognition Results & Discussion

There are only two corpus CITYU and MSRA for named entity recognition task in this bakeoff. For statistics, we compute the OOV rate of named entities for each corpus, which denotes the proportion of named entities in testing data that are not seen in training corpus.

For each submission for named entity recognition, like the former bakeoff, we compute overall phrase precision (P), recall(R), and F-measure (F), as well as the F-measure for each entity type (PER,ORG,LOC). The only difference is the recall and precision for each entity type is appended.

We compute a baseline for each corpus as in the bakeoff-3. A left-to-right maximum match algorithm was applied on the testing data with a named entity list generated from the training data. This algorithm only detects those named entities with one unique tag in training data, others are considered as incorrectly tagged. These scores for all NER corpora are found in Table 18.

Named entity recognition results for all runs grouped by corpus and track appear in Tables 19-22; all tables are sorted by F-score.

It is shown in the result table that the baseline and the system performance for MSRA corpus are better than those for CITYU corpus. However,the statistics is showing that the number of named entities in CITYU training corpus is twice as large as the number in MSRA corpus. The system performance for these two corpus are consist with the OOV rate for these two corpora. Therefore,it seems that OOV named entities is a principal challenge for named entity recognition systems. Furthermore, the F-measure of organization name recognition is the lowest one in every participant's result on every corpus. This phenomenon is potentially implying that the organization name is the most difficult one among the three categories of named entities.

There are several systems participating both the closed and open track on the same corpus. All of them perform better in the open track. This phenomenon is implying that proper external information can strongly affect the performance of named entity recognition system.

since the testing data MSRA is a subset of the training data for last bakeoff, two sites have achieved novelly high scores in the open track.

4.3 POS Tagging Result & Discussion

There are five corpora in the Chinese POS tagging task, each of them is built on different tag set and tagging standard. For statistics and evaluation, we define several terms for this task:

- Multi-tag words: the words that been assigned more than one POS-tag in either the training corpus or testing corpus. For instance, if an IV

Table 3: Chinese Word Segmentation Training and Truth data statistics

	Training			Truth				
Source	Token	WT[a]	TTR[b]	Token	WT	TTR	OOV[c]	$\mathcal{R}_{OOV}$[d]
CITYU	1092687	43639	0.0399	235631	23303	0.0989	19382	0.0823
CKIP	721549	48114	0.0667	90678	14662	0.1617	6718	0.0741
CTB	642246	42159	0.0656	80700	12188	0.1510	4480	0.0555
NCC	913466	58592	0.0641	152354	21352	0.1401	7218	0.0474
SXU	528238	32484	0.0614	113527	12428	0.1095	5815	0.0512

Table 4: Chinese Word Segmentation Baseline

Source	R	P	F	R_{OOV}	P_{OOV}	F_{OOV}	R_{IV}	P_{IV}	F_{IV}
CITYU	.9006	.8225	.8598	.0970	.2262	.1358	.9727	.8424	.9029
CKIP	.8978	.8232	.8589	.0208	.0678	.0319	.9680	.8393	.8990
CTB	.8864	.8427	.8640	.0283	.0769	.0414	.9369	.8579	.8956
NCC	.9200	.8716	.8951	.0273	.1858	.0476	.9644	.8761	.9181
SXU	.9238	.8679	.8949	.0251	.0867	.0389	.9723	.8789	.9232

Table 5: Chinese Word Segmentation Topline

Source	R	P	F	R_{OOV}	P_{OOV}	F_{OOV}	R_{IV}	P_{IV}	F_{IV}
CITYU	.9787	.9840	.9813	.9917	.9678	.9796	.9775	.9855	.9815
CKIP	.9823	.9880	.9852	.9932	.9642	.9784	.9815	.9900	.9857
CTB	.9710	.9825	.9767	.9920	.9707	.9812	.9698	.9832	.9764
NCC	.9735	.9817	.9776	.9933	.9203	.9554	.9725	.9850	.9787
SXU	.9820	.9867	.9844	.9942	.9480	.9705	.9813	.9890	.9851

Table 6: CITYU: Word Segmentation: Closed Track

ID	RunID	R	Cr	P	Cp	F	R_{OOV}	P_{OOV}	F_{OOV}	R_{IV}	P_{IV}	F_{IV}
2		.9526	.000875	.9493	.000903	.9510	.7495	.7912	.7698	.9708	.9626	.9667
5		.9513	.000887	.9430	.000955	.9471	.7339	.7752	.7540	.9707	.9570	.9638
8		.9465	.000927	.9443	.000945	.9454	.7721	.7244	.7475	.9621	.9653	.9637
24	a	.9450	.000939	.9437	.000949	.9443	.7716	.7099	.7395	.9605	.9666	.9636
26		.9490	.000906	.9372	.000999	.9430	.6780	.7591	.7163	.9733	.9511	.9621
18	b	.9421	.000962	.9339	.001023	.9380	.7074	.7050	.7062	.9631	.9543	.9587
28		.9367	.001003	.9377	.000996	.9372	.6295	.7394	.6800	.9642	.9526	.9584
27		.9386	.000988	.9325	.001033	.9355	.6708	.6840	.6773	.9626	.9541	.9584
18	a	.9296	.001054	.9290	.001058	.9293	.6862	.6541	.6698	.9514	.9549	.9532
33		.9285	.001061	.9261	.001077	.9273	.6866	.6326	.6585	.9502	.9548	.9525
7	c	.9237	.001093	.9234	.001095	.9236	.6830	.5934	.6350	.9453	.9579	.9516
7	b	.9237	.001093	.9234	.001095	.9236	.6830	.5934	.6350	.9453	.9579	.9516
7	a	.9238	.001093	.9234	.001095	.9236	.6830	.5934	.6351	.9453	.9579	.9516
7	d	.9197	.001119	.9169	.001137	.9183	.6558	.5690	.6093	.9434	.9532	.9483
15		.9191	.001123	.9014	.001228	.9102	.5466	.5588	.5527	.9525	.9308	.9415
21	b	.9219	.001105	.8951	.001262	.9083	.4703	.5899	.5234	.9624	.9159	.9386
21	a	.9221	.001104	.8947	.001264	.9082	.4697	.5891	.5227	.9627	.9155	.9385
21	d	.9120	.001167	.8974	.001250	.9047	.5263	.5333	.5297	.9466	.9290	.9377
19		.8884	.001296	.8817	.001330	.8850	.6114	.6030	.6072	.9133	.9069	.9101
21	c	.0155	.000509	.0155	.000508	.0155	.0047	.0049	.0048	.0165	.0164	.0165

Table 7: CITYU: Word Segmentation: Open Track

ID	RunID	R	Cr	P	Cp	F	R_{OOV}	P_{OOV}	F_{OOV}	R_{IV}	P_{IV}	F_{IV}
24	a	.9670	.000736	.9725	.000674	.9697	.8988	.8525	.8750	.9731	.9839	.9785
24	b	.9657	.000750	.9715	.000685	.9686	.8963	.8411	.8678	.9719	.9841	.9780
39		.9181	.001129	.9024	.001222	.9102	.6656	.5843	.6223	.9407	.9346	.9377
28		.8860	.001309	.9349	.001016	.9098	.6595	.5657	.6090	.9063	.9764	.9401
3		.0445	.000862	.0446	.000863	.0446	.0226	.0229	.0227	.0465	.0466	.0465

[a]WT: word type.

[b]TTR: type-token ratio = type count / token count.

[c]OOV: number of OOV.

[d]$\mathcal{R}_{OOV}$: OOV Rate

Table 8: CKIP: Word Segmentation: Closed Track

ID	RunID	R	Cr	P	Cp	F	R_{OOV}	P_{OOV}	F_{OOV}	R_{IV}	P_{IV}	F_{IV}
2		.9501	.001445	.9440	.001527	.9470	.7404	.7649	.7524	.9669	.9577	.9623
26		.9497	.001451	.9361	.001624	.9429	.6556	.7481	.6988	.9732	.9490	.9610
5		.9455	.001507	.9371	.001612	.9413	.7004	.7373	.7184	.9651	.9521	.9586
28		.9383	.001597	.9396	.001582	.9390	.6962	.6780	.6870	.9577	.9612	.9594
19		.9432	.001536	.9333	.001657	.9383	.6882	.6885	.6883	.9637	.9527	.9581
8	a	.9412	.001562	.9345	.001643	.9378	.7228	.6688	.6948	.9586	.9575	.9580
18		.9369	.001615	.9270	.001727	.9319	.6636	.6624	.6630	.9587	.9480	.9533
24	a	.9345	.001643	.9289	.001707	.9317	.7124	.6602	.6853	.9522	.9521	.9522
24	b	.9336	.001653	.9277	.001720	.9306	.7091	.6589	.6831	.9515	.9508	.9512
27		.9354	.001632	.9173	.001828	.9263	.5521	.6877	.6125	.9661	.9316	.9485
8	b	.9247	.001753	.9162	.001840	.9204	.6859	.5896	.6341	.9438	.9467	.9452
33		.9241	.001758	.9165	.001836	.9203	.6746	.6195	.6459	.9441	.9424	.9432
7	c	.9233	.001767	.9161	.001841	.9197	.6801	.5846	.6287	.9428	.9471	.9449
7	a	.9233	.001767	.9162	.001840	.9197	.6801	.5849	.6289	.9428	.9471	.9450
7	d	.9224	.001777	.9153	.001849	.9188	.6672	.5732	.6166	.9428	.9473	.9450
15		.9150	.001852	.9001	.001991	.9075	.4751	.5689	.5178	.9502	.9216	.9356
21	b	.9074	.001925	.8897	.002080	.8985	.4405	.5020	.4692	.9447	.9161	.9302
21	a	.9076	.001923	.8896	.002081	.8985	.4406	.5028	.4697	.9449	.9159	.9302
7	b	.8588	.002312	.8850	.002118	.8717	.6204	.4183	.4997	.8779	.9447	.9101

Table 9: CKIP: Word Segmentation: Open Track

ID	RunID	R	Cr	P	Cp	F	R_{OOV}	P_{OOV}	F_{OOV}	R_{IV}	P_{IV}	F_{IV}
5		.9586	.001323	.9541	.001389	.9563	.7804	.8050	.7925	.9728	.9656	.9692
28		.9507	.001438	.9503	.001443	.9505	.7391	.7704	.7544	.9676	.964	.9658
24	b	.9367	.001616	.9360	.001625	.9364	.7527	.6911	.7206	.9515	.9575	.9545
24	a	.9324	.001667	.9326	.001665	.9325	.7459	.6631	.7021	.9473	.9571	.9522
39		.9218	.001782	.8960	.002027	.9087	.6454	.5901	.6165	.944	.9221	.9329
3		.3977	.003245	.3944	.003240	.3961	.3405	.3359	.3382	.4025	.3994	.4009

Table 10: CTB: Word Segmentation: Closed Track

ID	RunID	R	Cr	P	Cp	F	R_{OOV}	P_{OOV}	F_{OOV}	R_{IV}	P_{IV}	F_{IV}
2		.9583	.001408	.9596	.001386	.9589	.7730	.7761	.7745	.9691	.9704	.9697
26		.9538	.001477	.9527	.001493	.9533	.7031	.7491	.7254	.9685	.9639	.9662
31	b	.9505	.001527	.9528	.001492	.9517	.7580	.6886	.7216	.9618	.9701	.9659
31	a	.9503	.001529	.9520	.001505	.9512	.7540	.6845	.7176	.9619	.9694	.9656
27		.9494	.001543	.9508	.001522	.9501	.7208	.7012	.7108	.9628	.9659	.9644
18		.9487	.001553	.9514	.001513	.9500	.7507	.6753	.7110	.9603	.9696	.9650
8	b	.9482	.001560	.9516	.001511	.9499	.7596	.6740	.7142	.9592	.9702	.9647
8	a	.9481	.001561	.9514	.001513	.9498	.7614	.6742	.7152	.9591	.9700	.9645
31	d	.9487	.001552	.9509	.001520	.9498	.7583	.6812	.7177	.9599	.9687	.9643
9		.9471	.001575	.9500	.001533	.9486	.7670	.6736	.7173	.9577	.9688	.9632
24	a	.9451	.001603	.9521	.001503	.9486	.7694	.6714	.7171	.9555	.9713	.9633
31	c	.9495	.001542	.9474	.001571	.9485	.6638	.7456	.7023	.9663	.9579	.9621
28		.9429	.001633	.9535	.001481	.9482	.7536	.6661	.7072	.954	.9730	.9634
24	b	.9456	.001596	.9492	.001545	.9474	.7565	.6613	.7057	.9567	.9688	.9627
5		.9434	.001626	.9459	.001592	.9447	.6911	.6883	.6897	.9582	.9612	.9597
37		.9459	.001592	.9418	.001648	.9439	.6589	.6698	.6643	.9628	.9574	.9601
33		.9402	.001669	.9433	.001628	.9417	.7317	.6517	.6894	.9524	.9628	.9576
7	c	.9350	.001736	.9378	.001700	.9364	.7132	.5796	.6395	.9480	.9641	.9560
7	a	.9350	.001735	.9379	.001699	.9364	.7132	.5800	.6397	.9480	.9642	.9560
7	d	.9342	.001745	.9366	.001715	.9354	.6998	.5706	.6286	.9480	.9634	.9556
7	b	.9099	.002015	.9250	.001854	.9174	.6911	.4834	.5689	.9227	.9638	.9428
21	b	.9077	.002037	.9078	.002037	.9077	.4728	.5603	.5128	.9333	.9248	.9290
21	a	.9078	.002037	.9073	.002041	.9075	.4703	.5583	.5105	.9335	.9244	.9289
21	d	.8992	.002119	.9063	.002051	.9027	.5301	.5029	.5161	.9209	.9316	.9262
21	c	.8992	.002119	.9062	.002052	.9027	.5299	.5029	.5160	.9210	.9315	.9262
19		.8773	.002310	.8788	.002297	.8780	.6714	.5886	.6273	.8894	.8985	.8939

Table 11: CTB: Word Segmentation: Open Track

ID	RunID	R	Cr	P	Cp	F	R_{OOV}	P_{OOV}	F_{OOV}	R_{IV}	P_{IV}	F_{IV}
28	a	.9914	.000648	.9926	.000602	.9920	.9685	.9623	.9654	.9928	.9944	.9936
24	a	.9760	.001077	.9826	.000920	.9793	.9420	.8655	.9021	.9780	.9902	.9840
31	a	.9766	.001065	.9721	.001158	.9743	.9089	.8553	.8813	.9805	.9794	.9800
24	b	.9702	.001196	.9753	.001092	.9728	.9145	.8361	.8736	.9735	.9844	.9789
28	b	.9665	.001266	.9738	.001123	.9702	.8821	.8857	.8839	.9715	.9790	.9753
31	b	.9589	.001397	.9612	.001359	.9601	.7922	.7902	.7912	.9687	.9713	.9700
3		.9485	.001556	.9498	.001536	.9491	.7261	.6769	.7006	.9615	.9672	.9643
39		.9461	.001590	.9372	.001707	.9416	.7223	.6764	.6986	.9592	.9535	.9563
8	a	.9370	.001710	.9321	.001770	.9346	.6556	.6139	.6341	.9535	.9521	.9528
8	b	.9270	.001831	.9319	.001773	.9294	.6576	.6099	.6329	.9428	.9525	.9476
22		.9251	.001853	.9261	.001841	.9256	.5967	.7337	.6581	.9444	.9352	.9398
8	c	.9089	.002025	.8346	.002615	.8702	.2011	.3336	.2509	.9505	.8505	.8977

Table 12: NCC: Word Segmentation: Closed Track

ID	RunID	R	Cr	P	Cp	F	R_{OOV}	P_{OOV}	F_{OOV}	R_{IV}	P_{IV}	F_{IV}
2		.9402	.001214	.9407	.001210	.9405	.6179	.5984	.6080	.9562	.9583	.9573
26		.9452	.001166	.9320	.001289	.9386	.4502	.6196	.5215	.9698	.9430	.9562
5		.9365	.001249	.9365	.001249	.9365	.6158	.5542	.5834	.9524	.9577	.9551
34		.9417	.001200	.9272	.001331	.9344	.4001	.6454	.4940	.9687	.9356	.9518
31	b	.9387	.001229	.9301	.001306	.9344	.5561	.5728	.5643	.9577	.9472	.9524
31	a	.9389	.001226	.9298	.001309	.9343	.5556	.5743	.5648	.9580	.9467	.9523
37		.9396	.001220	.9286	.001319	.9341	.5007	.5411	.5201	.9614	.9462	.9537
19		.9328	.001282	.9353	.001260	.9340	.5907	.5218	.5542	.9498	.9588	.9543
31	d	.9307	.001301	.9318	.001292	.9312	.6309	.5222	.5715	.9456	.9566	.9511
31	c	.9380	.001235	.9223	.001371	.9301	.4709	.6247	.5370	.9613	.9331	.947
24	a	.9251	.001348	.9347	.001266	.9299	.6577	.4968	.5660	.9384	.9643	.9512
27		.9300	.001307	.9291	.001314	.9296	.5459	.5138	.5294	.9491	.9511	.9501
24	b	.9246	.001352	.9332	.001279	.9289	.6524	.4932	.5617	.9381	.9629	.9503
28		.9193	.001395	.9378	.001237	.9285	.6516	.4833	.5549	.9326	.9695	.9507
18	b	.9278	.001326	.9250	.001349	.9264	.5529	.4966	.5232	.9464	.9488	.9476
29		.9268	.001334	.9260	.001341	.9264	.6094	.4948	.5462	.9426	.9527	.9476
18	a	.9278	.001326	.9249	.001350	.9263	.5486	.4940	.5199	.9466	.9488	.9477
18	c	.9264	.001338	.9241	.001356	.9253	.5707	.4977	.5317	.9441	.9486	.9463
9		.9236	.001361	.9269	.001333	.9252	.6474	.4941	.5604	.9373	.9556	.9464
7	c	.9086	.001476	.9110	.001459	.9098	.5957	.4080	.4843	.9241	.9485	.9361
7	d	.9071	.001487	.9106	.001461	.9088	.5907	.3987	.4761	.9228	.9494	.9359
21	a	.8997	.001539	.8992	.001542	.8995	.4232	.3710	.3954	.9234	.9294	.9264
21	b	.8995	.001540	.8992	.001542	.8994	.4224	.3702	.3946	.9233	.9295	.9264
7	a	.7804	.002121	.8581	.001788	.8174	.5409	.2134	.3060	.7924	.9561	.8666
7	b	.7747	.002140	.8513	.001823	.8112	.5405	.2014	.2935	.7864	.9568	.8633
33		.3082	.002367	.3073	.002365	.3078	.2217	.1678	.1910	.3125	.3166	.3145

Table 13: NCC: Word Segmentation: Open Track

ID	RunID	R	Cr	P	Cp	F	R_{OOV}	P_{OOV}	F_{OOV}	R_{IV}	P_{IV}	F_{IV}
34		.9735	.000823	.9779	.000753	.9757	.8893	.8867	.8880	.9777	.9824	.9800
22		.9568	.001041	.9616	.000984	.9592	.8264	.8144	.8204	.9633	.9691	.9662
31	b	.9620	.000980	.9496	.001120	.9557	.6337	.7673	.6941	.9783	.9569	.9675
31	a	.9528	.001086	.9478	.001139	.9503	.7109	.7619	.7355	.9648	.9563	.9606
5	a	.9440	.001177	.9517	.001098	.9478	.7305	.6381	.6812	.9547	.9698	.9622
5	b	.9376	.001239	.9521	.001093	.9448	.7826	.6110	.6862	.9453	.9745	.9597
14		.9446	.001171	.9263	.001339	.9354	.4643	.7160	.5633	.9685	.9328	.9503
3		.9324	.001286	.9349	.001263	.9337	.6070	.5296	.5657	.9486	.9583	.9534
28		.9191	.001396	.9380	.001235	.9285	.6543	.4840	.5564	.9323	.9697	.9506
29		.9268	.001334	.9279	.001325	.9273	.6265	.5032	.5581	.9417	.9546	.9481
39		.9323	.001287	.9134	.001440	.9228	.6075	.5820	.5945	.9485	.9303	.9393

Table 14: SXU: Word Segmentation: Closed Track

ID	RunID	R	Cr	P	Cp	F	R_{OOV}	P_{OOV}	F_{OOV}	R_{IV}	P_{IV}	F_{IV}
2		.9622	.001132	.9625	.001127	.9623	.7429	.7159	.7292	.974	.9764	.9752
26		.9623	.001131	.9554	.001225	.9588	.6454	.7022	.6726	.9794	.9678	.9736
28		.9549	.001231	.9611	.001148	.9580	.6626	.6639	.6632	.9707	.9772	.9739
18	b	.9543	.001239	.9568	.001206	.9556	.7273	.6232	.6712	.9666	.9781	.9723
5		.9558	.001219	.9552	.001228	.9555	.6922	.6638	.6777	.9701	.9716	.9708
24	a	.9523	.001264	.9569	.001205	.9546	.7506	.6129	.6748	.9632	.9801	.9716
18	c	.9528	.001258	.9560	.001217	.9544	.7369	.6164	.6713	.9645	.9782	.9713
31	a	.9594	.001171	.9493	.001302	.9543	.6653	.6694	.6674	.9753	.9642	.9697
8	a	.9534	.001250	.9544	.001238	.9539	.7395	.6275	.6789	.9650	.9754	.9702
8	b	.9536	.001248	.9541	.001242	.9538	.7352	.6287	.6778	.9654	.9748	.9701
31	d	.9535	.001249	.9532	.001253	.9533	.7305	.6257	.6741	.9656	.9740	.9698
31	b	.9593	.001173	.9474	.001324	.9533	.6463	.6749	.6603	.9762	.9613	.9687
18	a	.9518	.001270	.9547	.001234	.9533	.7020	.6020	.6481	.9653	.9772	.9712
8	d	.9512	.001278	.9553	.001226	.9532	.7462	.6275	.6817	.9623	.9767	.9694
8	c	.9509	.001282	.9544	.001238	.9526	.7396	.6281	.6793	.9623	.9754	.9688
24	b	.9499	.001295	.9536	.001249	.9517	.7271	.5966	.6554	.9619	.9774	.9696
27		.9514	.001276	.9511	.001279	.9512	.6834	.6202	.6502	.9658	.9709	.9684
9		.9505	.001287	.9515	.001275	.9510	.7326	.6106	.6660	.9623	.9738	.9680
37		.9554	.001224	.9459	.001342	.9507	.6206	.6113	.6159	.9735	.9641	.9688
34		.9558	.001220	.9442	.001362	.9500	.5176	.6966	.5939	.9794	.9539	.9665
31	c	.9558	.001219	.9441	.001363	.9499	.5788	.7154	.6399	.9762	.9539	.9649
33		.9387	.001423	.9392	.001418	.9390	.6741	.5627	.6134	.9530	.9638	.9584
7	a	.9378	.001434	.9390	.001420	.9384	.6731	.5110	.5810	.9520	.9701	.9610
7	b	.9376	.001435	.9391	.001419	.9383	.6729	.5107	.5807	.9519	.9701	.9609
7	c	.9377	.001434	.9389	.001421	.9383	.6731	.5110	.5810	.9520	.9699	.9609
7	d	.9360	.001452	.9369	.001443	.9365	.6550	.4949	.5638	.9512	.9691	.9600
21	b	.9185	.001624	.9107	.001692	.9146	.4898	.4423	.4648	.9416	.9386	.9401
21	a	.9185	.001624	.9106	.001693	.9145	.4886	.4414	.4638	.9417	.9386	.9401
19		.7820	.002450	.7793	.002460	.7807	.4969	.3538	.4133	.7976	.8125	.8050

Table 15: SXU: Word Segmentation: Open Track

ID	RunID	R	Cr	P	Cp	F	R_{OOV}	P_{OOV}	F_{OOV}	R_{IV}	P_{IV}	F_{IV}
31	a	.9768	.000894	.9703	.001007	.9735	.7825	.8415	.8109	.9872	.9767	.9820
31	b	.9738	.000948	.9620	.001134	.9679	.7089	.8040	.7534	.9881	.9694	.9786
28		.9547	.001233	.9622	.001132	.9584	.6705	.6628	.6666	.9701	.9787	.9744
8	a	.9545	.001236	.9572	.001201	.9559	.7543	.6400	.6925	.9654	.9776	.9714
8	b	.9639	.001108	.9479	.001319	.9558	.6103	.7089	.6559	.9829	.9587	.9707
8	c	.9586	.001182	.9467	.001333	.9526	.6126	.6967	.6519	.9773	.9583	.9677
39		.9575	.001197	.9461	.001339	.9518	.7274	.6920	.7093	.9699	.9604	.9652
3		.9516	.001273	.9515	.001275	.9516	.6843	.6174	.6491	.9661	.9716	.9688
22		.8777	.001945	.8705	.001993	.8741	.5621	.6371	.5972	.8947	.8815	.8880

word has only one POS-tag in the training corpus, but has other POS-tags in the testing corpus, it is a multi-tag word.

- OOV tag: If a tag of a word is found in the test corpus, but not in the training corpus, or the word itself is an OOV word, the corresponding word-tag pair is called OOV tag.
- IV tag: if the pair of word and tag does occur in the training corpus, the pair is called IV tag.
- IV multi-tag words: the multi-tag words that occurred in training data.

For each submission, we compute total accuracy (A_{Total}),IV recall (R_{IV}), OOV recall (R_{OOV}), and IV Multi-tag word recall ($R_{MT_{IV}}$) for evaluation. The formula for total accuracy is: $A_{Total} = \frac{N_{correct}}{N_{truth}}$, where $N_{correct}$ denotes the number of words that are correctly tagged, and N_{truth} denotes the number of words in the truth corpus.

The recall for IV, OOV and IV Multi-tag words are supposed to indicate participating system's performance on these three categories.

As Chinese word segmentation task, a baseline and a topline for each corpus are computed to reflect

Table 16: Named Entity Recognition Training and Truth data statistics

	Training				Truth			
Source	NE[a]	PER[b]	LOC[c]	ORG[d]	NE	PER	LOC	ORG
CITYU	66255	16552	36213	13490	13014	4940	4847	3227
MSRA	37811	9028	18522	10261	7707	1864	3658	2185

Table 17: Named Entity Recognition Truth data OOV statistics

	NE		PER		LOC		ORG	
Source	OOV	$\mathcal{R}_{OOV}$[e]	OOV	$\mathcal{R}_{OOV}$	OOV	$\mathcal{R}_{OOV}$	OOV	$\mathcal{R}_{OOV}$
CITYU	6354	0.4882	3878	0.7850	900	0.1857	1576	0.4884
MSRA	1651	0.2142	564	0.3026	315	0.0861	772	0.3533

Table 18: Named Entity Recognition Baseline

Source	R	P	F	R_{PER}	P_{PER}	F_{PER}	R_{LOC}	P_{LOC}	F_{LOC}	R_{ORG}	P_{ORG}	F_{ORG}
CITYU	.4912	.7562	.5955	.2130	.7056	.3272	.7681	.8438	.8042	.5011	.6341	.5598
MSRA	.5451	.6937	.6105	.6459	.9205	.7591	.4513	.7847	.5731	.6160	.5091	.5575

Table 19: CITYU: Named Entity Recognition: Closed Track

ID	RunID	R	P	F	R_{PER}	P_{PER}	F_{PER}	R_{LOC}	P_{LOC}	F_{LOC}	R_{ORG}	P_{ORG}	F_{ORG}
24		.8247	.8768	.8499	.8615	.9240	.8917	.9098	.8612	.8848	.6402	.8221	.7199
2	a	.7556	.8850	.8152	.7688	.9165	.8362	.8659	.8695	.8677	.5699	.8589	.6852
2	b	.7541	.8846	.8142	.7638	.9167	.8333	.8675	.8684	.8680	.5689	.8596	.6847
18	c	.7608	.8751	.8140	.7771	.9143	.8401	.8692	.8551	.8621	.5730	.8451	.6829
28		.7570	.8585	.8046	.7682	.8976	.8279	.8750	.8314	.8526	.5624	.8462	.6757
18	b	.7286	.8933	.8026	.7306	.9254	.8165	.8535	.8789	.8660	.5380	.8650	.6634
18	a	.7277	.8926	.8017	.7287	.9252	.8153	.8529	.8781	.8653	.5380	.8633	.6628
21	a	.0874	.1058	.0957	.0656	.0962	.0780	.1388	.1200	.1288	.0437	.0789	.0562
21	b	.0211	.0326	.0256	.0128	.0218	.0161	.0390	.0433	.0410	.0068	.0192	.0101

Table 20: CITYU: Named Entity Recognition: Open Track

ID	RunID	R	P	F	R_{PER}	P_{PER}	F_{PER}	R_{LOC}	P_{LOC}	F_{LOC}	R_{ORG}	P_{ORG}	F_{ORG}
23		.8743	.9342	.9033	.9526	.9721	.9623	.9342	.9235	.9288	.6644	.8805	.7573
2		.8579	.9179	.8869	.8822	.9449	.9125	.9336	.9099	.9216	.7072	.8852	.7862
28		.8826	.8826	.8826	.9168	.8947	.9056	.9329	.8942	.9132	.7546	.8411	.7955
24		.8975	.8616	.8792	.9474	.9153	.9311	.9389	.8966	.9173	.7589	.7274	.7428
39		.7163	.8000	.7559	.7180	.8194	.7653	.8389	.7845	.8108	.5296	.7986	.6369

Table 21: MSRA: Named Entity Recognition: Closed Track

ID	RunID	R	P	F	R_{PER}	P_{PER}	F_{PER}	R_{LOC}	P_{LOC}	F_{LOC}	R_{ORG}	P_{ORG}	F_{ORG}
24		.9186	.9377	.9281	.9437	.9665	.9549	.9423	.9428	.9426	.8577	.9036	.8800
18	b	.8862	.9304	.9078	.9195	.9651	.9418	.9043	.9379	.9208	.8275	.8871	.8563
2		.8779	.9274	.9020	.9029	.9628	.9319	.9101	.9341	.9219	.8027	.8841	.8414
18	a	.8752	.9255	.8996	.9040	.9618	.9320	.8991	.9346	.9165	.8105	.8780	.8429
28		.8822	.9156	.8986	.9126	.9461	.9290	.9079	.9248	.9163	.8133	.8724	.8418
31		.8058	.9107	.8550	.9029	.9519	.9268	.8185	.9278	.8697	.7016	.8405	.7648
37		.8331	.8730	.8526	.8557	.8084	.8314	.8576	.9138	.8848	.7730	.8666	.8171

[a] NE: Number of Named Entities.
[b] PER: Number of Person names.
[c] LOC: Number of Location names.
[d] ORG: Number of Organization names
[e] $\mathcal{R}_{OOV}$:OOV rate

Table 22: MSRA: Named Entity Recognition: Open Track

ID	RunID	R	P	F	R_{PER}	P_{PER}	F_{PER}	R_{LOC}	P_{LOC}	F_{LOC}	R_{ORG}	P_{ORG}	F_{ORG}
24		.9995	.9982	.9988	1	.9989	.9995	.9997	.9975	.9986	.9986	.9986	.9986
2		.9961	.9956	.9958	1	1	1	.9992	.9929	.9960	.9876	.9963	.9920
1		.9377	.9603	.9489	.9657	.9574	.9615	.9593	.9769	.9680	.8778	.9338	.9049
23		.9111	.9471	.9288	.9458	.9833	.9642	.9336	.9397	.9366	.8439	.9280	.8840
18	a	.9135	.9321	.9227	.9560	.9601	.9581	.9221	.9388	.9304	.8627	.8959	.8790
18	b	.9084	.9278	.9180	.9544	.9575	.9559	.9169	.9322	.9245	.8549	.8938	.8739
22	b	.8675	.9163	.8912	.9217	.9630	.9419	.8445	.9352	.8875	.8600	.8502	.8551
29		.8791	.9035	.8911	.9549	.9498	.9524	.9194	.9129	.9161	.7469	.8408	.7911
11		.8674	.9003	.8836	.9083	.9216	.9149	.8989	.9166	.9077	.7799	.8516	.8141
31		.8238	.9038	.8619	.9206	.9517	.9359	.8362	.9424	.8862	.7204	.7966	.7565
22	a	.8452	.8720	.8584	.8734	.9498	.9100	.8710	.8909	.8808	.7780	.7798	.7789
39		.7890	.8347	.8112	.8771	.9196	.8979	.8365	.8331	.8348	.6343	.7557	.6897

the different degree of difficulty of tagging individual corpora. The algorithm of baseline and topline is briefly described as follows: Baseline indicates the different degree of difficulty of tagging individual corpus.

The baseline of each corpus is calculated by generating a list of words and POS tags from the training corpus, then: 1. tagging those IV words in the testing corpus which have only one POS tag in the list. 2. for those IV words that have not only one tag in training corpus, the unique most frequent tag in training corpus will be assigned to them. 3. for each IV word that does not have a unique most frequent tag in training corpus, one of its tag which is most frequent in the overall phase is assigned to it; 4. for those words that do not fall into any of the former three categories are assigned with a overall most frequent tag.

The topline algorithm is similar to baseline, instead the list of words and POS tags is generated from testing corpus.

Chinese POS tagging results for all runs grouped by corpus and track appear in Tables 27-36; all tables are sorted by A_{Total}.

The baseline and topline has shown that, with preliminary knowledge and mechanical algorithm, it is easy to achieve an accuracy over approximately 0.85. When excluding the effect caused by OOV tags, the accuracy can even be over 0.93.

There are two kind of problem in POS tagging task we should cope with: multi tag disambiguation and unknown words guessing. We could consider that the value of (topline - baseline) is the accuracy drop caused by unknown words guessing, and the value of (1 - topline) is the accuracy drop caused by multi tag disambiguation. The average of these two value is 0.0628 and 0.0600, therefore these two kind of problem can equally affect the performance of POS tagging system.

For this reason, unlike the topline of Chinese word segmentation, the topline of Chinese POS tagging could be easily exceeded by tagging systems, because the algorithm of this topline just excludes the effect of OOV tags, which is not a dominant determinant in this task.

In closed track, the highest total accuracy is achieved in the NCC corpus which has the lowest OOV tag rate, and the lowest total accuracy is achieved in the CITYU corpus which has the highest OOV tag rate.

Most of the participants outperformed baseline, some have exceeded topline. When comparing the OOV recall and IV multi tag word recall with topline, participant's system can easily approaching or surpass the IV multi tag word recall, but none system could successfully approach the OOV recall. This might because participant's systems do better in solving the multi tag disambiguation problem than in coping with the unknown words guessing problem.

5 Conclusions & Future Directions

The Fourth SIGHAN Chinese Language Processing Bakeoff successfully brought together a collection of 28 strong research groups to assess the progress of research in three important tasks, Chinese word segmentation, named entity recognition and Chinese POS tagging, that in turn enable other important language processing technologies. The individual group presentations at the SIGHAN workshop will detail the approaches that yielded strong performance for both tasks. Issues of out-of-vocabulary word handling, annotation consistency and unknown guessing all continue to challenge system designers and bakeoff organizers alike.

In future analysis, we hope to develop additional analysis tools to better assess progress in these fundamental tasks, in a more corpus independent fashion. Such developments will guide the planning of future evaluations.

Finally, while Chinese word segmentation, named entity recognition and Chinese POS tagging are important in themselves, these three enabling technologies are also the foundation of those upper level applications such as parsing, reference resolution or machine translation. To evaluate the impact of improvement in these three technologies on the subsequent applications is still the future work for this evaluation.

6 Acknowledgements

We gratefully acknowledge the generous assistance of the organizations listed below who provided the data for this bakeoff; without their support, it could not have taken place:

- City University of Hong Kong, Hong Kong;
- Chinese Knowledge Information Processing Group, Academia Sinica, Taiwan;
- Institute of Applied linguistics, M.O.E., China;
- Microsoft Research Asia, China;
- Peking University, China;
- Shanxi University, China;
- University of Colorado, USA;

We also thank Olivia Oi Yee Kwong, the co-organizers of the sixth SIGHAN workshop, in conjunction with which this bakeoff takes place, and Yongsheng Guo from Institute of Applied Linguistics, M.O.E., P.R.C. who has made great effort for this bakeoff.

Professor Changning Huang merits special thanks for his help in this bakeoff. Finally, we thank all the participating sites who enabled the success of this bakeoff.

Table 25: Chinese POS tagging Baseline

Source	A_{Total}[a]	R_{IV}[b]	R_{OOV}[c]	$R_{MT_{IV}}$[d]
CITYU	.8425	.9021	.2543	.8083
CKIP	.8861	.9451	.2814	.8740
CTB	.8609	.8967	.3313	.8057
NCC	.9159	.9543	.2242	.8636
PKU	.8809	.9237	.2038	.8296

Table 26: Chinese POS tagging Topline

Source	A_{Total}	R_{IV}	R_{OOV}	$R_{MT_{IV}}$
CITYU	.9310	.9330	.9107	.8727
CKIP	.9606	.9597	.9699	.9103
CTB	.9147	.9120	.9555	.8369
NCC	.9588	.9593	.9507	.8822
PKU	.9351	.9354	.9305	.8600

Table 27: CITYU:POS tagging Closed Track

ID	RunID	A_{Total}	R_{IV}	R_{OOV}	$R_{MT_{IV}}$
30	b	.8951	.9389	.4637	.8745
30	a	.8929	.9367	.4608	.8705
28		.8905	.9328	.4733	.8687
9		.8865	.9326	.4322	.8707
19		.8693	.9284	.2868	.8585
24		.8564	.9149	.2805	.8506
21	b	.2793	.2969	.1051	.2538
21	a	.1890	.2031	.0550	.1704

Table 28: CITYU:POS tagging Open Track

ID	RunID	A_{Total}	R_{IV}	R_{OOV}	$R_{MT_{IV}}$
28		.8900	.9329	.4670	.8695
39		.8669	.9089	.4537	.8495

Table 29: CKIP:POS tagging Closed Track

ID	RunID	A_{Total}	R_{IV}	R_{OOV}	$R_{MT_{IV}}$
30	b	.9295	.9629	.5869	.9123
30	a	.9286	.9618	.5875	.9099
28		.9220	.9556	.5772	.9088
9		.9160	.9504	.5631	.9065
16		.9124	.9549	.4756	.8953
19		.8994	.9561	.3169	.9001
24		.8793	.9334	.3247	.8943

[a] A_{Total}: total accuracy
[b] R_{IV}: IV recall
[c] R_{OOV}: OOV recall
[d] $R_{MT_{IV}}$: MT_{IV} recall

Table 23: Chinese POS tagging Training data statistics

Source	Token	WT	TT[a]	ATN[b]	MT_{IV}[c]	$\mathcal{R}_{MT_{IV}}$[d]
CITYU	1092687	43639	44	1.2588	585056	0.5354
CKIP	721551	48045	60	1.0851	335017	0.4643
CTB	642246	42133	37	1.1690	334317	0.5205
NCC	535023	45108	60	1.0673	178078	0.3328
PKU	1116754	55178	103	1.1194	490243	0.4390

Table 24: Chinese POS tagging Truth data statistics

Source	Token	WT	TT	ATN	OOV	$\mathcal{R}_{OOV}$[e]	MT_{IV}	$\mathcal{R}_{MT_{IV}}$
CITYU	184314	17827	43	1.1446	16977	0.0921	92934	0.5042
CKIP	91071	15331	63	1.0530	8085	0.0888	38640	0.4243
CTB	59955	9797	35	1.1227	3794	0.0633	30513	0.5089
NCC	102344	17493	55	1.0675	5392	0.0527	33853	0.3308
PKU	156407	17643	103	1.1270	9295	0.0594	68065	0.4352

[a] TT: number of tag type.

[b] ATN: Average Tag Number per word.

[c] MT_{IV}: number of IV Multi-Tag word

[d] $\mathcal{R}_{MT_{IV}}$: coverage rate of IV Multi-Tag words

[e] $\mathcal{R}_{OOV}$: OOV tag rate

Table 30: CKIP:POS tagging Open Track

ID	RunID	A_{Total}	R_{IV}	R_{OOV}	$R_{MT_{IV}}$
28		.9211	.9542	.5813	.9082
39		.9004	.9327	.5686	.8936

Table 31: CTB:POS tagging Closed Track

ID	RunID	A_{Total}	R_{IV}	R_{OOV}	$R_{MT_{IV}}$
28		.9428	.9557	.7522	.9197
9		.9401	.9554	.7135	.9183
16		.9234	.9507	.5200	.9051
24		.9203	.9460	.5390	.9055
19		.9133	.9438	.4620	.8983
31	a	.9088	.9374	.4866	.8805
31	b	.8065	.8608	.0040	.7395

Table 32: CTB:POS tagging Open Track

ID	RunID	A_{Total}	R_{IV}	R_{OOV}	$R_{MT_{IV}}$
22		.9689	.9767	.8537	.9554
28		.9646	.9714	.8648	.9495
39		.9271	.9400	.7354	.9016
31	a	.9120	.9374	.5361	.8805
31	b	.8076	.8608	.0206	.7396

Table 33: NCC:POS tagging Closed Track

ID	RunID	A_{Total}	R_{IV}	R_{OOV}	$R_{MT_{IV}}$
30	b	.9541	.9738	.5998	.9195
30	a	.9525	.9717	.6059	.9135
28		.9494	.9690	.5959	.9129
9		.9456	.9658	.5822	.9116
16		.9395	.9690	.4086	.9059
19		.9336	.9687	.3017	.9050
31	a	.9313	.9604	.4080	.8809
29		.9277	.9664	.2329	.9000
24		.9172	.9498	.3312	.8963
31	b	.8940	.9303	.2411	.7948

Table 34: NCC:POS tagging Open Track

ID	RunID	A_{Total}	R_{IV}	R_{OOV}	$R_{MT_{IV}}$
28		.9496	.9694	.5938	.9141
31	a	.9326	.9604	.4336	.8809
39		.9280	.9477	.5749	.8954
22		.9096	.9377	.4045	.8935
31	b	.8940	.9303	.2411	.7948
25		.0836	.0855	.0488	.0645

Table 35: PKU:POS tagging Closed Track

ID	RunID	A_{Total}	R_{IV}	R_{OOV}	$R_{MT_{IV}}$
30	b	.9450	.9679	.5818	.9252
30	a	.9420	.9648	.5813	.9184
28		.9396	.9608	.6036	.9173
9		.9368	.9591	.5832	.9173
16		.9266	.9574	.4386	.9079
29		.9113	.9518	.2708	.8958
37		.9065	.9269	.5836	.8903
31	a	.9053	.9451	.2751	.8758
19		.8815	.9158	.3386	.8897
31	b	.8527	.8936	.2043	.7646
31	c	.8450	.8855	.2039	.7471

Table 36: PKU:POS tagging Open Track

ID	RunID	A_{Total}	R_{IV}	R_{OOV}	$R_{MT_{IV}}$
28		.9411	.9622	.6057	.9200
31	a	.9329	.9518	.6332	.8972
29		.9197	.9512	.4222	.8990
39		.9134	.9341	.5862	.8894
31	b	.8427	.8935	.0398	.7643
22		.6649	.6796	.4308	.6495

References

Thomas Emerson. 2005. The second international Chinese word segmentation bakeoff. In *Proceedings of the Fourth SIGHAN Workshop on Chinese Language Processing*, pages 123–133, Jeju Island, Korea.

Charles Grinstead and J. Laurie Snell. 1997. *Introduction to Probability*. American Mathematical Society, Providence, RI.

Gina-Anne Levow. 2006. The third international chinese language processing bakeoff: Word segmentation and named entity recognition. In *Proceedings of the Fifth SIGHAN Workshop on Chinese Language Processing*, pages 108–117, Sydney, Australia, July. Association for Computational Linguistics.

Richard Sproat and Thomas Emerson. 2003. The first international Chinese word segmentation bakeoff. In *The Second SIGHAN Workshop on Chinese Language Processing*, pages 133–143, Sapporo, Japan.

A Two-Stage Approach to Chinese Part-of-Speech Tagging

Aitao Chen
Yahoo! Inc.
701 First Avenue
Sunnyvale, CA 94089
aitao@yahoo-inc.com

Ya Zhang
Yahoo! Inc.
701 First Avenue
Sunnyvale, CA 94089
yazhang@yahoo-inc.com

Gordon Sun
Yahoo! Inc.
701 First Avenue
Sunnyvale, CA 94089
gzsun@yahoo-inc.com

Abstract

This paper describes a Chinese part-of-speech tagging system based on the maximum entropy model. It presents a novel two-stage approach to using the part-of-speech tags of the words on both sides of the current word in Chinese part-of-speech tagging. The system is evaluated on four corpora at the Fourth SIGHAN Bakeoff in the close track of the Chinese part-of-speech tagging task.

1 Introduction

A part-of-speech tagger typically assigns a tag to each word in a sentence sequentially from left to right or in reverse order. When the words are tagged from left to right, the part-of-speech tags assigned to the previous words are available to the tagging of the current word, but not the tags of the following words. And when words are tagged from right to left, only the tags of the words on the right side are available to the tagging of the current word. We expect the use of the tags of the words on both sides of the current word should improve the tagging of the current word. In this paper, we present a novel two-stage approach to using the tags of the words on both sides of the current word in tagging the current word. We train two maximum entropy part-of-speech taggers on the same training data. The difference between the two taggers is that the second tagger uses features involving the tags of the words on both sides of the current word, while the first tagger uses the tags of only the previous words. Both taggers assign tags to words from left to right. In tagging a new sentence, the first tagger is applied to the testing data, and then the second tagger is applied to the output of the first tagger to produce the final results.

We participated in the Chinese part-of-speech tagging task at the Fourth International Chinese Language Processing Bakeoff. Our Chinese part-of-speech taggers were trained only on the training data provided to the participants, and evaluated on four corpora in the close track of the part-of-speech tagging task. The words in both the training and testing data sets are already segmented into words.

2 Maximum Entropy POS Tagger

Maximum entropy model is a machine learning algorithm that has been applied to a range of natural language processing tasks, including part-of-speech tagging (Ratnaparkhi, 1996). Our Chinese part-of-speech taggers are based on the maximum entropy model.

2.1 Maximum Entropy Model

The conditional maximum entropy model (Berger, et. al., 1996) has the form

$$p(y \mid x) = \frac{1}{Z(x)} \exp(\sum_k \lambda_k f_k(x, y))$$

where $Z(x) = \sum_y p(y \mid x)$ is a normalization factor, and λ_k is a weight parameter associated with feature $f_k(x, y)$. In the context of part-of-speech tagging, y is the POS tag assigned to a word, and x represents the contextual information regarding the word in consideration, such as the surrounding words. A feature is a real-valued, typically binary, function. For example, we may define a binary feature which takes the value 1 if the current word of X is 'story' and its POS tag is 'NNS'; and 0 otherwise. Given a set of training examples, the log likelihood of the model with Gaussian prior (Chen and Rosenfeld, 1999) has the form

$$L(\lambda) = \sum_i \log p(y^{(i)} \mid x^{(i)}) - \sum_k \frac{\lambda_k^2}{2\sigma^2} + const$$

Malouf (2002) compared iterative procedures such as *Generalized Iterative Scaling (GIS)* and *Improved Iterative Scaling (IIS)* with numerical optimization techniques like limited-memory BFGS (L-BFGS) for estimating the maximum entropy model parameters and found that L-BFGS outperforms the other methods. The use of L-BFGS requires the computation of the gradient of the log likelihood function. The first derivative with respect to parameter λ_k is given by

$$\frac{\partial L(\lambda)}{\partial \lambda_k} = E_{\tilde{p}} f_k(x, y) - E_p f_k(x, y) - \frac{\lambda_k}{\sigma^2}$$

where the first term $E_{\tilde{p}} f_k$ is the feature expectation with the empirical model, and the second term $E_p f_k$ is the feature expectation with respect to the model. In our model training, we used L-BFGS to estimate the model parameters by maximizing $L(\lambda)$ on the training data.

2.2 Features

The feature templates used in our part-of-speech taggers are presented in Table 1 and Table 2.

Word	$w_{i-2}, w_{i-1}, w_i, w_{i+1}, w_{i+2}$ $w_{i-2}w_{i-1}, w_{i-1}w_i, w_iw_{i+1}, w_{i+1}w_{i+2},$ $w_{i-1}w_{i+1}, w_{i-1}w_iw_{i+1}$
Tag	$t_{i-1}, t_{i-2}t_{i-1}$
Word/Tag	$t_{i-1}w_i, t_{i-2}w_i$
Special	*FirstChar*, *LastChar*, *Length*, *ForeighWord*

Table 1: Feature templates used in the first stage POS tagger.

Tag	$t_{i+1}, t_{i+1}t_{i+2}, t_{i-1}t_{i+1}$
Word/Tag	w_it_{i+1}, w_it_{i+2}

Table 2: Additional feature templates used in the second stage POS tagger.

The features are grouped into four categories. The first category contains features involving word tokens only; the second category consists of features involving tags only; the third category has features involving both word tokens and tags. And the last category has four special features. In the feature templates, w_i denotes the current word, w_{i-2} the second word to the left, w_{i-1} the previous word, w_{i+1} the next word, w_{i+2} the second word to the right of the current word, and t_i denotes the part-of-speech tag assigned to the word w_i. The *FirstChar* refers to the initial character of a word, and the *LastChar* the final character of a word. The *Length* denotes the length of a word in terms of byte. And the feature *ForeignWord* indicates whether or not a word is a foreign word. Table 2 shows additional feature templates involving the part-of-speech tags of the following one or two words. The features involving the tags of the words in the right contexts are used only in the second maximum entropy POS tagger. Features are generated from the training data according to the feature templates presented in Table 1 and Table 2.

2.3 Training Models

The four training corpora we received for the Chinese part-of-speech tagging task include the Academia Sinica corpus (**CKIP**), the City University of Hong Kong corpus (**CityU**), the National Chinese Corpus (**NCC**), and the Peking University corpus (**PKU**). The CKIP corpus and the CityU corpus contain texts in traditional Chinese, while the NCC corpus and the PKU corpus contain texts in simplified Chinese. The texts in all four training corpora are segmented into words according to different word segmentation guidelines. And the words in all training corpora are labeled with part-of-speech tags using different tag sets.

Two maximum entropy POS taggers were trained on each of the four corpora using our own implementation of the maximum entropy model. The first-stage POS tagger was trained with only the feature templates presented in Table 1, while the second-stage POS tagger with the feature templates presented in both Table 1 and Table 2.

All the first-stage POS taggers, one for each corpus, were trained with the same feature templates shown in Table 1, and all the second-stage POS taggers were trained with the same feature templates shown in Table 1 and Table 2. The feature templates are not necessarily optimal for each individual corpus. For simplicity, we chose to apply the same feature templates to all four corpora.

The same parameter settings were applied in the training of all eight POS taggers. More specifically, no feature selection was performed. All features, including features occurring just once in the training data, were retained. The sigma square σ^2 was set to 5.0. And the training process was terminated when the ratio of the likelihood difference between the current iteration and the previous iteration over the likelihood of the current iteration is below the pre-defined threshold or the maximum number of iterations, which was set to 400, is reached. Both the first-stage POS tagger and the second-stage POS tagger were trained on the same corpus.

2.4 Testing the Models

The POS tagger assigns a part-of-speech tag to each word in a new sentence such that the tag sequence maximizes the probability $p(Y|X)$, where X is the input sentence, and Y the POS tags assigned to X. The decoder implements the beam search procedure described in (Ratnaparkhi, 1996). At each word position, the decoder keeps the top n best tag sequences up to that position. The decoder also uses a word/tag dictionary, consisting of the words in the training data and the tags assigned to each word in the training data. During the decoding phase, if a word in the new sentence is found in the training data, only the tags that are assigned to that word in the training corpus are considered. Otherwise, all the tags in the tag set are considered for a new word. So the tagger will not assign to a word, found in the training data, a tag that is never assigned to that word in the training data, even if that word should be assigned a new tag that was never assigned to the word in the training data. A word/tag dictionary is automatically built by collecting all the words in the training corpus and the tags assigned to every word in the training corpus.

The final output is produced in two steps. The first-stage POS tagger is applied on the testing data, and then the second-stage POS tagger is applied on the output of the first POS tagger. The second-stage tagger uses features involving POS tags of the following one or two words. The features involving the tags of following one or two words may be erroneous, since the tags assigned to the following one or two words by the first-stage tagger may be incorrect.

3 Evaluation Results

Five corpora are provided for the Chinese part-of-speech tagging task at the forth SIGHAN bakeoff. We selected four corpora, two in simplified Chinese and two in traditional Chinese.

Corpus	Training size (tokens)	Tagset size	No. of tags per token type
CityU	1,092,687	44	1.2587
CKIP	721,551	60	1.1086
NCC	535,023	60	1.0658
PKU	1,116,754	103	1.1194

Table 3: Training corpus size.

Table 3 shows the training corpus size, the tagset size, and the average number of tags per token type. The NCC tagset has 60 tags, but nine of the tags occurred only once in the training corpus. In all four corpora, most of the unique tokens have only a single tag. The percentage of token types having single tag is 83.29% in CityU corpus; 91.09 in CKIP corpus; 94.67 in NCC corpus; and 90.27% in PKU corpus. The proportion of token types having single tag in CityU corpus is much lower than in NCC corpus. In the NCC corpus, the organization names, location names, and a sequence of English words are all treated as single token, and these long single tokens are not ambiguous and are assigned to a single part-of-speech tag in the corpus.

corpus	Baseline	Testing size	Token/tag OOV-R
CityU	0.8433	184,314	0.0921
CKIP	0.8865	91,071	0.0897
NCC	0.9159	102,344	0.0527
PKU	0.8805	156,407	0.0594

Table 4: The testing data size and the baseline performance.

The baseline performance is computed by assigning the most likely tag to each word in the testing data. When a word in the testing data is found in the training corpus, it is assigned the tag that is most frequently assigned to that word in the training corpus. A new word in the testing data is assigned the most frequent tag found in the training corpus, which is the common noun in all four corpora. The baseline performances of the four testing data sets are presented in Table 4, which also shows the percentage of new token/tag in the testing data sets.

Our POS taggers are evaluated on four testing data sets, one corresponding to each training corpus. We trained eight POS taggers, two on each training corpus, and submitted eight runs in total on the Chinese part-of-speech tagging task, two runs on each testing data set. The first run, labeled 'a' in Table 5, is produced using the first-stage tagger, and the second run, labeled 'b' in Table 5, is the output of the second-stage tagger, which is applied to the output of the first tagger. For all of our runs, only the provided training data are used. Table 5 shows the official evaluation results of the eight runs we submitted in the close track. The third column, labeled 'Total-A', shows the accuracy of the eight runs. The accuracy is the proportion of correctly tagged words in a testing data set. Only one tag is assigned to every word in the testing data set. The remaining three labels, 'IV-R', 'OOV-R', and 'MT-R', may be defined in The Fourth SIGHAN Bakeoff overview paper.

Corpus	Run ID	Total-A	IV-R	OOV-R	MT-R
CityU	a	0.8929	0.9367	0.4608	0.8705
CityU	b	0.8951	0.9389	0.4637	0.8745
CKIP	a	0.9286	0.9618	0.5875	0.9099
CKIP	b	0.9295	0.9629	0.5869	0.9123
NCC	a	0.9525	0.9717	0.6059	0.9135
NCC	b	0.9541	0.9738	0.5998	0.9195
PKU	a	0.9420	0.9648	0.5813	0.9148
PKU	b	0.9450	0.9679	0.5818	0.9252

Table 5: Official evaluation results of eight runs in the close track of the Chinese part-of-speech tagging task.

4 Discussions

A Chinese verb can function as a noun, and vice versa, without suffix change. In PKU corpus, a verb is labeled with the tag 'v', and a verb that functions as a noun is labeled with the tag 'vn'. In the PKU-b run, almost half of the incorrectly tagged verbs (v) were tagged as verbal noun (vn), and slightly more than half of the incorrectly tagged verbal nouns (vn) were tagged as verb (v).

The accuracy of our best runs on all four corpora is much higher than the baseline performance. On the PKU corpus, the accuracy is increased from the baseline performance of 0.8805 to 0.9450, an improvement of 7.33% over the baseline. The second-stage tagging increased the accuracy on all four corpora. On the PKU corpus, the accuracy is increased by about 0.32% over the first-stage tagging. The improvement may not seem to be large; however, it corresponds to an error reduction by 5.4%.

That the accuracy on the CityU corpus is the lowest among all four corpora is not surprising, given that the CityU testing data set has the highest out-of-vocabulary rate, and the CityU training corpus has the highest average number of tags assigned to each token type. Furthermore, the CityU training corpus has the lowest percentage of tokens with only one tag. The POS tagging task on CityU corpus seems to be most challenging among the four corpora.

5 Conclusions

We have described a Chinese part-of-speech tagger with maximum entropy modeling. The tagger with rich lexical and morphological features significantly outperforms the baseline system which assigns to a word the most likely tag assigned to that word in the training corpus. The use of features involving the part-of-speech tags of the following words further improves the performance of the tagger.

References

Adam L. Berger, Stephen A. Della Pietra, and Vincent J. Della Pietra. 1996. A Maximum Entropy Approach to Natural Language Processing. *Computational Linguistics,* 22(1):39-71.

Stanley F. Chen, and Ronald Rosenfeld. 1999. *A Gaussion Prior for Smoothing Maximum Entropy Models*, Technical Report CMU-CS-99-108, Carnegie Mellon University.

Rober Malouf. 2002. *A Comparison of Algorithms for Maximum Entropy Parameter Estimation*, Proceedings of CoNLL-2002.

Adwait Ratnaparkhi. 1996. *A Maximum Entropy Model for Part-of-Speech Tagging*, Proceedings of the Conference on Empirical Methods in Natural Language Processing, pp 133-142.

NOKIA Research Center Beijing Chinese Word Segmentation System for the SIGHAN Bakeoff 2007

Jiang LI[1, 2], Rile HU[1], Guohua ZHANG[1], Yuezhong TANG[1], Zhanjiang SONG[1] and Xia WANG[1]
NOKIA Research Center, Beijing[1]
Beijing University of Posts and Telecommunications[2]
{ext-jiang.1.li, ext-rile.hu,ext-guohua.zhang,yuezhong.tang, zhanjiang.song,xia.s.wang}@nokia.com

Abstract

This paper presents the Chinese word segmentation system developed by NOKIA Research Center (NRC), which was evaluated in the Fourth International Chinese Language Processing Bakeoff and the First CIPS Chinese Language Processing Evaluation organized by SIGHAN. In our system, a preprocessing module was used to discover the out-of-vocabulary words which occur repeatedly in the text, then an improved n-gram model was used for segmentation and some post processing strategies are adopted in system to recognize the organization names and new words. We took part in three tracks, which are called the open and closed track on corpora State Language Commission of P.R.C. (NCC), and closed track on corpora Shanxi University (SXU). Our system achieved good performance, especially in the open track on NCC, our system ranks 1st among 11 systems.

1 Introduction

Chinese word segmentation is an essential and core technology in Chinese language processing, and generally it is the first stage for later processing, such as machine translation, text summarization, information retrieval and etc. The topic of Chinese word segmentation has been researched for many years. Many approaches have been developed to solve the problems under this topic. Among these approaches, statistical approaches are most widely used.

Our system based on a pragmatic approach, integrating a lot of features and information, the framework is similar to (Jianfeng Gao, 2005). In our system, the model is simplified to n-gram architecture. First, all the possible paths of segmentation will be considered and each of the candidate word will be categorized into a certain type. Second, each word will be given a value; each type has different computational strategy and is processed in different ways. At last, all the possible paths of segmentation are calculated and the best path is selected as the final result.

N-gram language model is a generative model, and it could express the correlation of the context word very well. But it is powerless to detect the out-of-vocabulary word (OOV). In the post-processing module, we detect the OOV through some Chinese character information instead of the word information. In addition, to deal with the long organization names in NCC corpus, a module for combining organization name is adopted.

The remainder of this paper is organized as follow: section 2 describes our system in detail; section 3 presents the experiment results and analysis; in last section we give our conclusions and future research directions.

2 System Description

The basic architecture of our system is shown in figure 1, and the detailed description of each module is provided in the following subsections.

2.1 Framework

The input of the system is text to be segmented. First, the system scans the text and finds out the character strings appear many times but not lexicon words. These strings are called recurring-OOV. Second, all the candidate words are categorized into different types and the optimal path is calculated by Viterbi algorithm. Finally, some post-processing strategies are used to modify the results: NW detection is used to merge two single characters as a new word, and organization combination is provided to combine some words as an organization name.

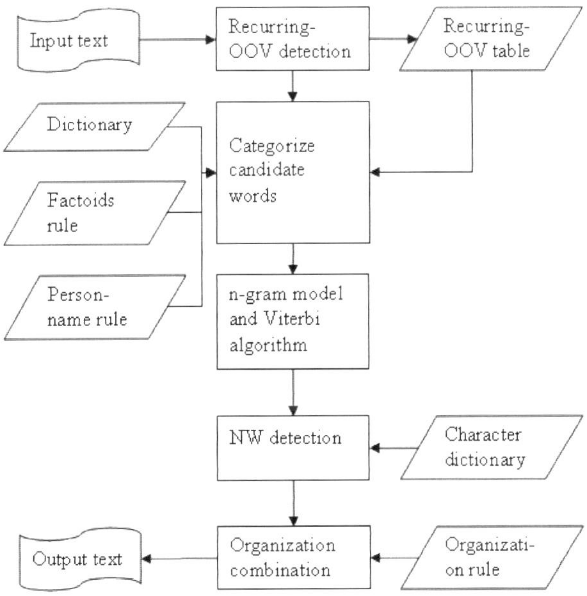

Figure 1: Framework of system

2.2 Recurring-OOV Detection

We found that there are some words which appear many times in different position of the context. For example, a verb "说给" appears 2 times in a sentence, "这是… 说给大臣、太监听的，说给普天下劳苦大众的部分…", and a person name "杨宇霆" appears in different sentences, "杨宇霆感到身边四术士神机妙算…" "…杨宇霆向常荫槐使了个眼色…". These words are defined as Recurring-OOV.

Therefore, without any prior knowledge, the Chinese text is scanned; the sentence of the text is compared with itself and compared with others which were close to it for finding out the repeated strings. All these repeated character strings were saved in list. Not all of them are considered as the candidates of OOV word. Only 2-character or 3-character repeated strings are considered as the candidates of OOV words. And some simple rules are used to avoid some wrong classification. For example, if there is a repeated string contains character "的", which is a high frequent one-character word, this repeated string is not considered as a recurring OOV.

A value (probability) will be given to each Recurring-OOV. Two factors will be considered in the value evaluation：

1. The repeating times of the Recurring-OOV in the testing corpus. The more it repeats, the bigger the value will be.
2. Character-based statistical information and some other information are also considered to calculate the probability of this string to be a word. The computing method is described in Section 2.5, NW Detection.

2.3 Word Categorization

In our system, Chinese words are categorized into a set of types as follows:

1. Lexicon Words (LW). The words in this type can be found in the library we get from the training corpus.
2. Factoids (FT). This type includes the English letter, Arabic numerals and etc.
3. Named Entity (NE). This type includes person name and location name. Being different from the Gao's system, the organization detection is a post processing in our system.
4. Recurring-OOV. This type is described in the section 2.2.
5. Others.

2.4 N-gram Model

Each candidate word W_i is relegated to a type T_j and assigned a value $P(W_i|T_j)$. The transfer probability between word-types is also assigned a value $P(T_{j-1}|T_j)$. We assume that $W = W_1W_2 \ldots W_n$ is a word sequence, the segmentation module's task is to find out the most likely word sequence among all possible paths:

$$W^* = \arg\max \prod P(W_i|T_j)P(T_{j-1}|T_j) \qquad (1)$$

Viterbi algorithm is used to search the optimized path described in Equation (1).

2.5 NW Detection

This module is used to detect the New Words, which "refer to OOV words that are neither recognized as named entities or factoids" (Jianfeng Gao, 2005). And in particular, we only consider the 2-character words for the reason that 2-character words are the most common in Chinese language.

We identify the new words through some features of Chinese character information:

1. The probability of a character occurring in the left/right position.

In fact, most Chinese characters have their favorite position. For example, "这" almost occurs in the left, "径" almost occurs in the right and "的" always compose a single word by itself. So the string "这x" is much more possible to be a new word than "x这", and string "的x" is not likely to be a word.

2. The similarity of different characters.

If two characters often occur in the same position with the same character to form a word, it is considered that the two characters are similar, or there is a short distance between them. For example, the character "这" is very similar to "那" in respect that they are almost in the left position with some same characters, such as "里", "么", to construct the word "这里","那里","这么","那么". So if we know the "这边" is a word, we can speculate the string "那边" is also a word.

The strict mathematical formula which used to describe the similarity of characters is reported in (Rile Hu, 2006).

2.6 Organization combination

The organization name is recognized as a long word in the NCC corpus, but during the n-gram processing, these long words will be segmented into several shorter words. In our system, the organization names are combined in this module. First, a list of suffix-words of organization name, such as "公司" "集团", is selected from the training set. Second, the string that has been segmented in previous module is searched to find out the suffix-word, which is considered as a candidate of organization name. At last, we estimate the possibility of the candidate string and judge it is an organization name or not.

3 Evaluation Results

3.1 Results

We took part in three segmentation tasks in Bakeoff-2007, which are named as the open and closed track on corpora State Language Commission of P.R.C. (NCC), and closed track on corpora Shanxi University (SXU).

Precision (P), Recall (R) and F-measure (F) are adopted to measure the performance of word segmentation system. In addition, OOV Recall (R_{OOV}), OOV Precision (P_{OOV}) and OOV F-measure (F_{OOV}) are very important indicators which reflect the system's ability to deal with the OOV words.

The results of our system in three tasks are shown in Table 1.

Table 1: Test set results on NCC, SXU

Corpus	NCC-O	NCC-C	SXU-C
R	0.9735	0.9417	0.9558
P	0.9779	0.9272	0.9442
F	0.9757	0.9344	0.95
R_{OOV}	0.8893	0.4001	0.5176
P_{OOV}	0.8867	0.6454	0.6966
F_{OOV}	0.888	0.494	0.5939
R_{IV}	0.9777	0.9687	0.9794
P_{IV}	0.9824	0.9356	0.9539
F_{IV}	0.98	0.9518	0.9665

3.2 NCC Open Track

For the open track of NCC, an external corpus is used for training and the size of training set is about 54M. In addition, there are some special dictionary were added to identify some special words. For example, an idiom dictionary is used to find the idioms and a personal-name dictionary is used to identify the common Chinese names.

3.3 Error Analysis

Apart from ranking 1st in NCC open test, our system got not so good results in NCC close test and SXU close test.

The comparison between our system results and best results in bakeoff-2007 are shown in table 2.

Table 2: The comparison between our system results and best results

Type	F-Measures	
	Bakeoff-2007	Our system
NCC-O	0.9757	0.9757
NCC-C	0.9405	0.9344
SXU-C	0.9623	0.95

Table 3: The comparison between our system results and best Top 3 results in OOV identification

		R_{OOV}	P_{OOV}	F_{OOV}
NCC-C	Our	0.4001	0.6454	0.494
	1st	0.6179	0.5984	0.608
	2nd	0.4502	0.6196	0.5215
	3rd	0.6158	0.5542	0.5834
SXU-C	Our	0.5176	0.6966	0.5939
	1st	0.7429	0.7159	0.7292
	2nd	0.6454	0.7022	0.6726
	3rd	0.6626	0.6639	0.6632

In table 3, 1st, 2nd and 3rd are the best Top 3 systems in the test. It shows that in the close track in NCC, the OOV Precision of our system is the best, but the OOV Recall is the worst in all the four system. Similarly, in the close track in SXU, the OOV Precision is very close to the best one, and the OOV Recall is the worst. It means that our system is too cautious in identifying the OOV words.

Our system was carefully tuned on NCC training set. The NCC training set contains articles from many domains; the OOV words can not be easily detected. Therefore, in parameter tuning, we raise the threshold of OOV. This strategy increases the precision of the OOV detection, but decreases the recall of this. And we also use some simple rules to filter the OOV candidates. These rules can easily pick out the wrongly detected OOVs, but at the same time, they remove some correct candidates by mistake.

The performance of our system is good in NCC close test but not so good in SXU close test. This means that our strategies for OOV detection is too cautious for SXU close test.

4 Conclusion and Future Work

In this paper, a detailed description on a Chinese word segmentation system is presented. N-gram model is adopted as the language model, and some preprocessing and post processing methods are integrated as a unified framework. The evaluation results show the efficiency of our approaches.

In future research, we will continue to enhance our system with other new techniques, especially we will focus on improving the recall of OOV words.

References

Jianfeng Gao, Mu Li, Andi Wu and Chang-Ning Huang. 2005. Chinese Word Segmentation and Named Entity Recognition: A Pragmatic Approach. Computational Linguistics, Vol.31(4): 531-574.

Hai Zhao, Chang-Ning Huang and Mu Li. 2006. An Improved Chinese Word Segmentation System with Conditional Random Field. Proceedings of the fifth SIGHAN Workshop on Chinese Language Processing, 162-165. Sydney, Australia.

Adwait Ratnaparkni. 1996. A Maximum Entropy Part-of-speech Tagger. In Proceedings of the Empirical Method in Natural Language Processing Conference, 133-142. University of Pennsylvania.

JK Low, HT Ng, W Guo. 2005. A Maximum Entropy Approach to Chinese Word Segmentation. Proceedings of the fourth SIGHAN Workshop on Chinese Language Processing. Jeju Island, Korea.

Manning, Christopher D. and Hinrich Schutze. 1999. Foundations of Statistical Natural Language Processing. The MIT Press, Cambridge, Massachusetts, London, England.

Nianwen Xue. 2003. Chinese word segmentation as character tagging. International Journal of Computational Linguistics and Chinese Language Processing, 8(1).

Rile Hu, Chengqing Zong, and Bo Xu. An Approach to Automatic Acquisition of Translation Templates Based on Phrase Structure Extraction and Alignment. *IEEE Transaction on Speech and Audio Processing*. Vol. 14, No.5, September 2006.

Chinese Word Segmentation and Named Entity Recognition Based on Conditional Random Fields

Xinnian Mao
France Telecom R&D Center (Beijing), Beijing, 100080, P.R.China
xinnian.mao@orange-ftgroup.com

Saike He
University of Posts and Telecommunications, Beijing, 100876, P.R.China

Sencheng Bao
University of Posts and Telecommunications, Beijing, 100876, P.R.China

Yuan Dong[1,2]
[1]France Telecom R&D Center (Beijing), Beijing, 100080, P.R.China
[2]University of Posts and Telecommunications, Beijing, 100876, P.R.China
yuan.dong@orange-ftgroup.com

Haila Wang
France Telecom R&D Center (Beijing), Beijing, 100080, P.R.China
haila.wang@orange-ftgroup.com

Abstract

Chinese word segmentation (CWS), named entity recognition (NER) and part-of-speech tagging is the lexical processing in Chinese language. This paper describes the work on these tasks done by France Telecom Team (Beijing) at the fourth International Chinese Language Processing Bakeoff. In particular, we employ Conditional Random Fields with different features for these tasks. In order to improve NER relatively low recall; we exploit non-local features and alleviate class imbalanced distribution on NER dataset to enhance the recall and keep its relatively high precision. Some other post-processing measures such as consistency checking and transformation-based error-driven learning are used to improve word segmentation performance. Our systems participated in most CWS and POS tagging evaluations and all the NER tracks. As a result, our NER system achieves the first ranks on MSRA open track and MSRA/CityU closed track. Our CWS system achieves the first rank on CityU open track, which means that our systems achieve state-of-the-art performance on Chinese lexical processing.

1 Introduction

Different from most European languages, there is no space to mark word boundary between Chinese characters, so Chinese word segmentation (CWS) is the first step for Chinese language processing. From another point that there is no capitalization information to indicate entity boundary, which makes Chinese named entity recognition (NER) more difficult than European languages. And part-of-speech tagging (POS tagging) provides valuable information for deep language processing such as parsing, semantic role labeling and etc. This paper presents recent research progress on CWS, NER and POS tagging done by France Telecom Team (Beijing). Recently, Conditional Random Fields[1] (CRFs) (Lafferty et al., 2001) have been successfully employed in various natural language processing tasks and achieve the state-of-the-art performance, in our system, we use it as the basic framework and incorporate some other post-processing measures for CWS, NER and POS tagging tasks.

2 Chinese Named Entity Recognition

NER is always limited by its lower recall due to the imbalanced distribution where the NONE class dominates the entity classes. Classifiers built on such dataset typically have a higher precision and a lower recall and tend to overproduce the NONE

[1] We use the CRF++ V4.5 software from http://chasen.org/~taku/software/CRF++/

class (Kambhatla, 2006). Taking SIGHAN Bakeoff 2006 (Levow, 2006) as an example, the recall is lower about 5% than the precision for each submitted system on MSRA and CityU closed track. If we could improve NER recall but keep its relatively high precision, the overall F-measure will be improved as a result. We design two kinds of effective features: 0/1 features and non-local features to achieve this objective. Our final systems utilize these features together with the local features to perform NER task.

2.1 Local Features

The local features are character-based and are instantiated from the following temples:

Unigram: C_n (n=-2,-1, 0, 1, 2).

Bigram: C_nC_{n+1} (n=-2,-1, 0, 1) and $C_{-1}C_1$.

Where C_0 is the current character, C_1 the next character, C_2 the second character after C_0, C_{-1} the character preceding C_0, and C_{-2} the second character before C_0.

2.2 0/1 Features

In order to alleviate the imbalanced class distribution, we assign 1 to all the characters which are labeled as entity and 0 to all the characters which are labeled as *NONE* in training data. In such way, the class distribution can be alleviated greatly, taking Bakeoff 2006 MSRA NER training data for example, if we label the corpus with 10 classes, the class distribution is 0.81(B-PER):1.70(B-LOC):0.95(B-ORG):0.81(I-PER):0.88(I-LOC):2.87(I-ORG):0.76(E-PER):1.42(E-LOC):0.94(E-ORG):88.86(NONE), if we change the label scheme to 2 labels (0/1), the class distribution is 11.14 (entity):88.86(*NONE*). We train the 0/1 CRFs tagger using the local features alone. For the 0/1 features, during the training stage, they are assigned with 2-fold cross validation, and during the testing stage, they are assigned with the 0/1 tagger.

2.3 Non-local Features

Most empirical approaches including CRFs currently employed in NER task make decision only on local context for extract inference, which is based on the data independent assumption. But often this assumption does not hold because non-local dependencies are prevalent in natural language (including the NER task). How to utilize the non-local dependencies is a key issue in NER task. Up to now, few researches have been devoted to this issue; existing works mainly focus on using the non-local information for improving NER label consistency (Krishnan and Manning, 2006). There are two methods to use non-local information. One is to add additional edges to graphical model structure to represent the distant dependencies and the other is to encode the non-locality with non-local features. In the first approach, heuristic rules are used to find the dependencies (Bunescu and Mooney, 2004) or penalties for label inconsistency are required to handset ad-hoc (Finkel et al., 2005). Furthermore, high computational cost is spent for approximate inference. In order to establish the long dependencies easily and overcome the disadvantage of the approximate inference, Krishnan and Manning (2006) propose a two-stage approach using CRFs framework with extract inference. They represent the non-locality with non-local features, and extract them from the output of the first stage CRF with local context alone; then they incorporate the non-local features into the second CRF. But the features in this approach are only used to improve label consistency in European languages. Similar with their work encoding the non-local information with non-local feature, and we also exploit the non-local features under two-stage architecture. Different from their features are activated on the recognized entities coming from the first CRF, the non-local features we design are used to recall more missed entities which are seen in the training data or unseen entities but some of their occurrences being recognized correctly in the first stage, so our non-local features are activated on the raw character sequence.

Different NER in European languages, where entity semantic classification is more difficult compared with boundary detection, in Chinese, the situation is opposite. So we encode different useful information for Chinese NER two subtasks: entity boundary detection and entity semantic classification. Three kinds of non-local features are designed; they are fired on the token sequences if they are matched with certain entity in the entity list in forward maximum matching (FMM) way.

Token-position features (NF1): These refer to the position information (start, middle and last) assigned to the token sequence which is matched with the entity list exactly. These features enable us to capture the dependencies between the identical candidate entities and their boundaries.

Entity-majority features (NF2): These refer to the majority label assigned to the token sequence which is matched with the entity list exactly. These features enable us to capture the dependencies between the identical entities and their classes, so that the same candidate entities of different occurrences can be recalled favorably, and their label consistencies can be considered too.

Token-position & entity-majority features (NF3): These features capture non-local information from NF1 and NF2 simultaneously. They take into account the entity boundary and semantic class information at the same time.

Figure 1 shows the flow of using non-local features under CRFs framework in two-stage architecture. The first CRF is trained with local features alone, and then we test the testing data with the first CRF and get the entities plus their type from the output. The second CRF utilizes the 0/1 features and the non-local features derived from the entity list which is merged by the output of the first CRF from the testing data and the entities extracted directly from the training data. We compare the three kinds of non-local features on MSRA and CityU closed track in SIGHAN 2006 and we find that the NF3 is the best (Mao etc, 2007). So we only incorporate the NF3 into our final NER system.

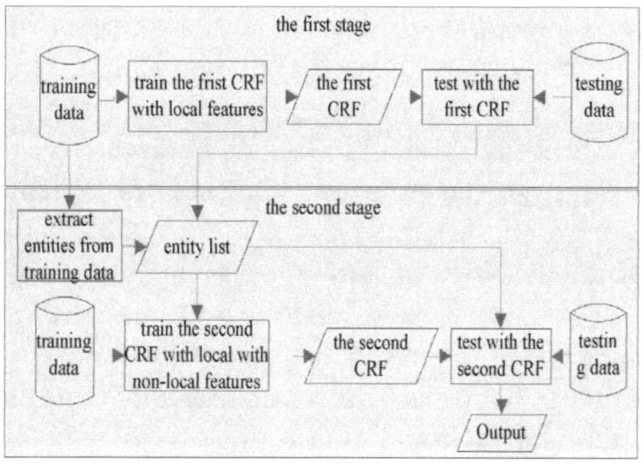

Figure 1. The flow using non-local features in two-stage architecture

2.4 Results

We employ BIOE1 label scheme for the NER task because we found it performs better than IOB2 on Bakeoff 2006 (Levow, 2006) NER MSRA and CityU corpora. Table 1 presents the official results on the MSRA and CityU corpus. The F-measure on MSRA open track is so high just because the testing data in Bakeoff 2007 is part of its Bakeoff 2006 training dataset and we utilize this corpus for training the final CRFs classifier. The F-measure on CityU open track is not much superior to its closed track because we only use its Bakeoff 2006 corpus to train the 0/1 CRFs, but not use the Bakeoff 2006 corpus to train final classifier.

Run ID	F-Score	Run ID	F-Score
cityu_c	84.99	cityu_o	87.92
msra_c	92.81	msra_o	99.88

Table 1: The official results on NER closed(c) tracks and open(o) tracks

3 Chinese Word Segmentation

Type	Feature
Unigram	C_n (n=-2,-1, 0, 1, 2).
Bigram	C_nC_{n+1} (n=-2,-1,0, 1)
Jump	$C_{-1}C_1$
Punc	Pu (C_0)
Date, Digit, Letter	$T_{-1}T_0T_1$

Table 2: The features used in our CWS systems

Table 2 lists the features we used in our CWS systems. After the raw corpus is processed by CRFs, two other post-processing measures are performed. We utilize transformation-based error-driven learning (TBL)[2] to further improve CWS and perform consistency checking among different occurrences of a particular character sequence. For TBL, we use the template defined in (He et al.). Our CWS system participate almost all the tracks and table 3 lists the official results.

Run ID	F-Score	Run ID	F-Score
cityu_c_a	94.43	cityu_o_a	96.97
cityu_c_b	error (94.31)	cityu_o_b	96.86
ckip_c_a	93.17	ckip_o_a	93.25
ckip_c_b	93.06	ckip_o_b	93.64
ctb_c_a	94.86	ctb_o_a	97.93
ctb_c_b	94.74	ctb_o_b	97.28
ncc_c_a	92.99	sxu_c_a	95.46
ncc_c_b	92.89	sxu_c_b	95.17

Table 3: The official results on CWS closed(c) tracks and open(o) tracks

In the table 3, run (a) means that we only perform consistency checking; run (b) means that

[2] We use the TBL software from http://nlp.cs.jhu.edu/~rflorian/fntbl/index.html

TBL is performed after consistency checking is done. We make a mistake on cityu_c_b because we rename cityu_c_a as cityu_c_b, so the two results are the same, after we correct the mistake and score again; we achieve an F-measure of 94.31%.

In the closed tracks, we first train initial CRFs with 3-fold cross-validation; then we test the training data (three parts) with the three trained CRFs, we train the TBL learner on the training data compared it with the testing result from the initial CRFs. The consistency checking is inspired by (Ng and Low, 2004). Table 4 lists the corpus used to train the CRFs and TBL learner in the open tracks.

	CRFs	TBL
CityU	2005,2006,2007	2003
CKIP	2007	2006
CTB	2006,2007	2007

Table 4. Corpora used to train the CRFs classifier and the TBL learner

In the open track, we collect the consistency list from all its correspondent Bakeoff corpora, the gazetteer extract from People Daily 2000 and idioms, slang from GKB. From the table 3 in the closed test, we can confirm that TBL may not improve CWS performance, while in most cases, performance will surely draw back. The reason lies in the fact that the learning capability of CRFs is superior to that of TBL, if they are trained with the same corpus, TBL may modify some correctly tags by CRFs. This can be seen from Table 3 that results without TBL (in run (a)) are almost superior to that with TBL (in run (b)).

4 Part-of-speech Tagging

For POS tagging task, apart from the local features same as used in NER, two other features are designed to improve the performance.

- Ambiguous part-of-speech: this feature is true when the word has more than 2 kinds of part-of-speech.
- Major part-of-speech: The feature is assigned as the major part-of-speech for any word. We do not assign the value to the new words.

Table 5 shows the performance in the closed tracks. Because we only used the simple features and do not process the unknown word specially, our performance is not satisfactory.

Run ID	F-Score	Run ID	F-Score
cityu_c	87.93	ctb_c	92.03
ckip_c	87.93	ncc_c	91.72
ctb_c	92.03		

Table 5: The official results on POS tagging in closed tracks

References

R. Bunescu and R. J. Mooney. 2004. Collective Information Extraction with Relational Markov Networks. In *Proceedings of the 42nd ACL*, 439–446.

J. Finkel, T. Grenager, and C. D. Manning. 2005. Incorporating Non-local Information into Information Extraction Systems by Gibbs Sampling. In *Proceedings of the 42nd ACL*, 363–370.

Nan He, Xinnian Mao, Yuan Dong, Haila Wang, 2007. Transformation-based Error-driven Learning as Post-processing for Chinese Word Segmentation, In *Proceedings of the 7th International Conference on Chinese Computing*, 46-51, Wuhan, China.

N. Kambhatla. 2006. Minority Vote: At-Least-N Voting Improves Recall for Extracting Relations. In *Proceeding of the 44th ACL*, 460–466.

V. Krishnan and C. D Manning. 2006. An Effective Two-Stage Model for Exploiting Non-Local Dependencies in Named Entity Recognition. In *Proceedings of the 44th ACL*, 1121–1128.

J. Lafferty, A. McCallum, and F. Pereira. 2001. Conditional Random Fields: Probabilistic Models for Segmenting and Labeling Sequence Data. In *Proceedings of the 18th ICML*, 282–289, San Francisco, CA.

G. Levow. 2006. The Third International Chinese Language Processing Bakeoff: Word Segmentation and Named Entity Recognition. In *Proceedings of SIGHAN-2006*, 108-117. Sydney, Australia.

Xinnian Mao, Xu Wei, Yuan Dong, Saike He and Haila Wang, 2007. Using Non-local Features to Improve Named Entity Recognition Recall, In *Proceedings of the 21th Pacific Asia Conference on Language, Information and Computation*, 303-310, Seoul, Korea.

Hwee Tou Ng, Jin Kiat Low, 2004. Chinese Part-of-Speech Tagging: One-at-a-Time or All at Once? Word-based or Character based? In *Proceedings of the Conference on Empirical Methods in Natural Language Processing*, Spain.

BUPT Systems in the SIGHAN Bakeoff 2007

Ying Qin Caixia Yuan Jiashen Sun Xiaojie Wang
Center of Intelligent Science and Technology Research
Beijing University of Posts and Telecommunications
Beijing, 100876, China
qinyingmail@163.com, yuancx@gmail.com,
b.bigart911@gmail.com, xjwang@bupt.edu.cn

Abstract

Chinese Word Segmentation(WS), Name Entity Recognition(NER) and Part-Of-Speech(POS) are three important Chinese Corpus annotation tasks. With the great improvement in these annotations on some corpus, now, the robustness, a capability of keeping good performances for a system by automatically fitting the different corpus and standards, become a focal problem. This paper introduces the work on robustness of WS and POS annotation systems from Beijing University of Posts and Telecommunications(BUPT), and two NER systems. The WS system combines a basic WS tagger with an adaptor used to fit a specific standard given. POS taggers are built for different standards under a two step frame, both steps use ME but with incremental features. A multiple knowledge source system and a less knowledge Conditional Random Field (CRF) based systems are used for NER. Experiments show that our WS and POS systems are robust.

1 Introduction

In the last SIGHAN bakeoff, there is no single system consistently outperforms the others on different test standards of Chinese WS and NER standards(Sproat and Emerson, 2003). Performances of some systems varied significantly on different corpus and different standards, this kind of systems can not satisfy demands in practical applications. The robustness, a capability of keeping good performances for a system by automatically fitting the different corpus and standard, thus become a focal problem in WS and NER, it is the same for Chinese Part-of-Speech(POS) task which is new in the SIGHAN bakeoff 2007.

It is worthy to distinguish two kinds of different robustness, one is for different corpus (from different sources or different domain and so on) under a same standard, we call it corpus robustness, and another is for different standards (for different application goals or demands and so on) for a same corpus. We call it standard robustness. The SIGHAN bakeoff series seems to focus more on later. We think corpus robustness should be received more attentions in the near future.

We participant all simplified Chinese track on WS, NER and POS task in the SIGHAN bakeoff 2007. There are more than two tracks for WS and POS. This gives us a chance to test the robustness of our systems. This paper reports our WS, NER and POS systems in the SIGHAN Bakeoff 2007, especially on the work of achieving robustness of WS and POS systems.

This paper is arranged as follows, we introduce our WS, NER and POS system separately in section 2, section 3 and section 4, experiments and results are listed in section 5, finally we draw some conclusions.

2 Word Segmentation

WS system includes three sequent steps, which are basic segmentation, disambiguation and out-of vocabulary (OOV) recognition. In each step, we construct a basic work unit first, and then have an adaptor to tune the basic unit to fit different standards.

2.1 Basic Segmentation

For constructing a basic work unit for WS, a common wordlist containing words ratified by four different segmentation standards (from SXU, NCC, PKU and CTB separately) are built. We finally get 64,000 words including about 1500 known entity words as the common wordlist. A forward-backward maximum matching algorithm with the common wordlist is employed as the common unit of our basic segmentor.

To cater for different characteristics in different segmentation standards, we construct another wordlist containing words for each specification. A wordlist based adaptor is built to implement the tuning task after basic segmentation.

2.2 Disambiguation

Disambiguation of overlapping Ambiguity (OA) is a major task in this step.

Strings with OA are also detected during basic forward-backward maximum matching in basic WS step. These strings are common OA strings for different standards. Class-based bigram model is applied to resolve the ambiguities. In class-based bigram, all named entities, all punctuation and factoids is one class respectively and each word is one class. We train the bigram transition probability based on the corpus of Chinese People's Daily 2000 newswire.

For corpus from different standards, overlapping ambiguity strings with less than 3 overlapping chain are extracted from each train corpus. We do not work on all of them but on some strings with a frequency that is bigger than a given value. A disambiguation adaptor using the highest probability segmentations is built for OA strings from each different standard.

2.3 OOV Recognition

In OOV recognition, we have a similar model which consists of a common part based on common characteristics and an individual part automatically constructed for each standard.

We divide OOV into factoid which contains non-Chinese characters like date, time, ordinal number, cardinal number, phone number, email address and non-factoid.

Factoid is recognized by an automaton. To compatible to different standards, we also built core automata and several adaptors.

Non-factoid is tackled by a unified character-based segmentation model based on CRF. We first transform the WS training dataset into character-based two columns format as the training dataset in NER task. The right column is a boundary tag of each character. The boundary tags are B I and S, which B is the tag of the first character of a word which contains more than two characters, I is the other non-initial characters in a word, S is for the single character word. Then the transformed training data is used to train the CRF model. Features in the model are current character and other three characters within the context and bigrams.

The trigger of non-factoid recognition is continual single character string excluding all the punctuations in a line after basic word matching, disambiguation and factoid incorporation. The model will tell whether these consecutive characters can form multi-character words in a given context.

At last, several rules are used to recognize some proper names separated by coordinate characters like "、", "和", "与" and symbol " • " in foreign person names.

3 Named Entity Recognition

We built two NER systems separately. One is a unified named entity model based on CRF. It used only a little knowledge include a small scale of entity dictionary, a few linguistic rules to process some special cases such as coordinate relation in corpus and some special symbols like dot among a transliteration foreign person name.

Another one is an individual model for each kind of entity based on Maximum Entropy where more rules found from corpus are used on entity boundary detection. Some details on this model can be found in Suxiang Zhang et al 2006.

4 POS Tagging

In POS, we construct POS taggers for different standards under a two steps frame, both steps use ME but with incremental features. First, we use normal features based Maximum Entropy (ME) to train a basic model, and then join some probabilistic features acquired from error analysis to training a finer model.

4.1 Normal Features for ME

In the first step of feature selection for ME tagger, we select contextual syntactic features for all words basing on a series of incremental experiments.

For shrinking the search space, the model only assigns each word a label occurred in the training data. That is, the model builds a subset of all POS tags for each token and restricts all possible labels of a word within a small candidate set, which greatly saves computing cost.

We enlarged PKU training corpus by using one month of Peking University's China Daily corpus (June in 2003) and CTB training corpus by using CTB 2.0 data which includes 325 passages.

To adapt with the given training corpus, the samples whose labels are not included in the standard training data were omitted firstly. After preprocessing, we get two sets of training samples for PKU and CTB with 1178 thousands tokens and 206 thousands tokens respectively. But the NCC test remains its original data due to we have no corpus with this standard.

4.2 Probabilistic feature for ME

By detecting the label errors when training and testing using syntactic features such as words around the current tokens and tags of previous tokens, words with multiple possible tags are obviously error-prone. We thus define some probabilistic features especially for multi-tag words.

We find labels of these tokens are most closely related to POS tag of word immediately previous to them. For instance, in corpus of Peking University, word "Report" has three different tags of "n(noun), v(verb), vn(noun verb)". But when we taken into account its immediately previous words, we can find that when previous word's label is "q(quantifier)", "Report" is labeled as "n" with a frequency of 91.67%, "v" with a frequency of 8.33% and "vn" with a frequency of 0.0%. We can assume that "Report" is labeled as "n" with the 91.67% probability when previous word's label is "q", and so on.

Such probability is calculated from the whole training data and is viewed as discriminating probabilistic feature when choosing among the multiple tags for each word. But for words with only one possible tag, no matter what the label of previous word is, the label for them is always the tag occurred in the training data.

5 Experiments

We participant all simplified Chinese tracks on WS, NER and POS task in the SIGHAN bakeoff 2007. Our systems only deal with Chinese in GBK code. There are some mistakes in some results submitted to bakeoff organizer due to coding transform from GBK to UTF-16. We then use WS evaluation program in the SIGHAN bakeoff 2006 to re-evaluate WS system using same corpus, as for POS, since there is no POS evaluation in the SIGHAN bakeoff 2006, we implement a evaluation using ourselves' program using same corpus.

Table 1 shows evaluation results of WS using evaluation programs from both the SIGHAN bakeoff 2007 and the SIGHAN bakeoff 2006. Table 2 lists evaluation results of NER using evaluation program from the SIGHAN bakeoff 2007. Table 3 gives evaluation results of POS using evaluation programs from both the SIGHAN bakeoff 2007 and ourselves(BUPT).

Track	UTF-16 (SIGHAN4)	GBK (SIGHAN 3)
CTB	0.9256	0.950
SXU	0.8741	0.969
NCC	0.9592	0.972

Table 1. WS results (F-measure)

SIGHAN 4	R	P	F
System-1	0.8452	0.872	0.8584
System-2	0.8675	0.9163	0.8912

Table 2. NER results (F-measure)

Track	UTF-16 (SIGHAN 4)	GBK (BUPT)
CTB	0.9689	0.9689
NCC	0.9096	0.9096
PKU	0.6649	0.9462

Table 3. POS Results (F-measure)

From the table 1 and Table 3, we can find our system is robust enough. WS system keeps at a relatively steady performance. Difference in POS between NCC and other two tracks is mainly due to the difference of the training corpus.

6 Conclusion

Recently, the robustness, a capability of keeping good performances for a system by automatically fitting the different corpus and standards, become a focal problem. This paper introduces our WS, NER and POS systems, especially on how they can get a robust performance.

The SIGHAN bakeoff series seems to focus more on standard robustness. We think corpus robustness should be received more attentions in the near future.

Acknowledgement

Thanks to Zhang Yan, Zhang Bichuan, Zhang Taozheng, Liu Haipeng and Jiang Huixing for all the work they done to make the WS, NER and POS systems go on wheels in a very short time.

References

Berger, A., Della Pietra, S. and Della Pietra, V.: A Maximum Entropy Approach to Natural Language Processing. *Computational Linguistics*. 22(1): pp 39-71, 1996.

Thomas Emerson. 2005. The Second International Chinese Word Segmentation Bakeoff. In *Proceedings of the Fourth SIGHAN Workshop on Chinese Language Processing*, Jeju Island, Republic of Korea.

NanYuan Liang. 1987 A Written Chinese Segmentation system– CDWS. *Journal of Chinese Information Processing*, Vol.2: 44-52

YaJuan Lv, Tie-jun Zhao, et al. 2001. Leveled unknown Chinese Words resolution by dynamic programming. *Journal Information Processing*, 15(1): 28-33.

Yintang Yan, XiaoQiang Zhou. 2000. Study of Segmentation Strategy on Ambiguous Phrases of Overlapping Type *Journal of The China Society For Scientific and Technical Information* Vol. 19 , №6

Richard Sproat and Thomas Emerson. 2003. The First International Chinese Word Segmentation Bakeoff. In *Proceedings of the Second SIGHAN Workshop on Chinese Language Processing*, Sapporo, Japan.

Caixia Yuan, Xiaojie Wang, Yixin Zhong. Some Improvements on Maximum Entropy Based Chinese POS Tagging. *The Journal of China Universities of Posts and Telecommunications*, Vol. 13, pp 99-103, 2006.

Suxiang Zhang, Xiaojie Wang, Juan Wen, Ying Qin, Yixin Zhong. A Probabilistic Feature Based Maximum Entropy Model for Chinese Named Entity Recognition, in *proceedings of 21st International Conference on the Computer Processing of Oriental Languages*,December 17-19, 2006, Singapore.

The Character-based CRF Segmenter of MSRA&NEU for the 4th Bakeoff

Zhenxing Wang[1,2], Changning Huang[2] and Jingbo Zhu[1]
1 Institute of Computer Software and Theory, Northeastern University, Shenyang, China, 110004
2 Microsoft Research Asia, 49, Zhichun Road, Haidian District, Beijing, China, 100080
zxwang@ics.neu.edu.cn
v-cnh@microsoft.com
zhujingbo@mail.neu.edu.cn

Abstract

This paper describes the Chinese Word Segmenter for the fourth International Chinese Language Processing Bakeoff. Base on Conditional Random Field (CRF) model, a basic segmenter is designed as a problem of character-based tagging. To further improve the performance of our segmenter, we employ a word-based approach to increase the in-vocabulary (IV) word recall and a post-processing to increase the out-of-vocabulary (OOV) word recall. We participate in the word segmentation closed test on all five corpora and our system achieved four second best and one the fifth in all the five corpora.

1 Introduction

Since Chinese Word Segmentation was firstly treated as a character-based tagging task in (Xue and Converse, 2002), this method has been widely accepted and further developed by researchers (Peng et al., 2004), (Tseng et al., 2005), (Low et al., 2005), (Zhao et al., 2006). Thus, as a powerful sequence tagging model, CRF became the dominant method in the Bakeoff 2006 (Levow, 2006).

In this paper, we improve basic segmenter under the CRF work frame in two aspects, namely IV and OOV identification respectively. We use the result from word-based segmentation to revise the CRF output so that we gain a higher IV word recall. For the OOV part a post-processing rule is proposed to find those OOV words which are wrongly segmented into several fractions. Our system performs well in the Fourth Bakeoff, achieving four second best and on the fifth in all the five corpora. In the following of this paper, we describe our method in more detail.

The rest of this paper is organized as follows. In Section 2, we first give a brief review to the basic CRF tagging approach and then we propose our methods to improve IV and OOV performance respectively. In Section 3 we give the experiment results on the fourth Bakeoff corpora to show that our method is effective to improve the performance of the segmenter. In Section 4, we conclude our work.

2 Our Word Segmentation System

In this section, we describe our system in more detail. Our system includes three modules: a basic CRF tagger, a word-base segmenter to improve the IV recall and a post-processing rule to improve the OOV recall. In the following of this section, we introduce these three modules respectively.

2.1 Basic CRF tagger

Sequence tagging approach treat Word Segmentation task as a labeling problem. Every character in input sentences will be given a label which indicates whether this character is a word boundary. Our basic CRF[1] tagger is almost the same as the system described in (Zhao et al., 2006) except we add a feature to incorporate word information, which is learned from training corpus.

[1] CRF tagger in this paper is implemented by CRF++ which is downloaded from http://crfpp.sourceforge.net/

Type	Feature	Function
Unigram	C_{-1}, C_0, C_1	Previous, current and next character
Bigram	$C_{-1}\,C_0$, $C_0\,C_1$	Two adjacent character
Jump	$C_{-1}\,C_1$	Previous character and next character
Word Flag	$F_0\,F_1$	Whether adjacent characters form an IV word

Table 1 Feature templates used for CRF in our system

Under the CRF tagging scheme, each character in one sentence will be given a label by CRF model to indicate which position this character occupies in a word. In our system, CRF tag set is proposed to distinguish different positions in the multi-character words when the word length is less than 6, namely 6-tag set {B, B2, B3, M, E, O}. Here, Tag B and E stand for the first and the last position in a multi-character word, respectively. S stands up a single-character word. B2 and B3 stand for the second and the third position in a multi-character word, whose length is larger than two-character or three-character. M stands for the fourth or more rear position in a multi-character word, whose length is larger than four-character.

We add a new feature, which also used in maximum entropy model for word segmentation task by (Low et al., 2005), to the feature templates for CRF model while keep the other features same as (Zhao et al., 2006). The feature templates are defined in table 1. In the feature template, only the Word Flag feature needs an explanation. The binary function $F_0 = 1$ if and only if $C_{-1}\,C_0$ form a IV word, else $F_0 = 0$ and $F_1 = 1$ if and only if $C_0\,C_1$ form a IV word, else $F_1 = 0$.

2.2 Word based segmenter and revise rules

For the word-based word segmentation, we collect dictionary from training corpus first. Instead of Maximum Match, trigram language model [2] trained on training corpus is employed for disambiguation. During the disambiguation procedure, a beam search decoder is used to seek the most possible segmentation. For detail, the decoder reads characters from the input sentence one at a time, and generates candidate segmentations incrementally. At each stage, the next incoming character is combined with an existing candidate in two different ways to generate new candidates: it is either appended to the last word in the candidate, or taken as the start of a new word. This method guarantees exhaustive generation of possible segmentations for any input sentence. However, the exponential time and space of the length of the input sentence are needed for such a search and it is always intractable in practice. Thus, we use the trigram language model to select top B (B is a constant predefined before search and in our experiment 3 is used) best candidates with highest probability at each stage so that the search algorithm can work in practice. Finally, when the whole sentence has been read, the best candidate with the highest probability will be selected as the segmentation result.

After we get word-based segmentation result, we use it to revise the CRF tagging result similar to (Zhang et al., 2006). Since word-based segmentation result also corresponds to a tag sequence according to the 6-tag set, we now have two tags for each character, word-based tag (WT) and CRF tag (CT). Which tag will be kept as the final result depends on Marginal Probability (MP) of the CT.

Here, we give a short explanation about what is the MP of the CT. Suppose there is a sentence $C = c_0 c_1 ... c_M$, where c_i is the character this sentence containing. CRF model gives this sentence a optimal tag sequence $T = t_0 t_1 ... t_M$, where t_i is the tag for c_i. If $t_i = t$ and $t \in \{B, B_2, B_3, M, E, S\}$, the MP of t_i is defined as:

$$\mathrm{MP}(t_i = t) = \frac{\sum_{T, t_i = t} P(T \mid C)}{\sum_T P(T \mid C)}$$

Here, $P(T \mid C)$ is the conditional probability given by CRF model. For more detail about how to calculate this conditional probability, please refer to (Lafferty et al., 2001).

Assume that the tag assigned to the current character is CT by CRF and WT by word-based segmenter respectively. The rules under which we revise CRF result with word-based result is that if MP(CT) of a character is less than a predefined threshold and WT is not "S", the WT of this character will be kept as the final result, else the CT of the character will be kept as the final result.

[2] Language model used in this paper is SLRIM downloaded from http://www.speech.sri.com/projects/srilm/

The restriction that WT should not be "S" is reasonable because word-based segmentation is incapable to recognize the OOV word and always segments OOV word into single characters. Besides CRF model is better at dealing with OOV word than our word-based segmentation. When WT is "S" it is possible that current word is an OOV word and segmented into single character wrongly by the word-based segmenter, so the CT of the character should be kept under such situation. For more detail about this analysis please refer to (Wang et al., 2008).

2.3 Post-processing rule

The rules we described in last subsection is helpful to improve the IV word recall and now we introduce our post-processing rule to improve the OOV recall.

Our post-processing rule is designed to deal with one typical type of OOV errors, namely an OOV word wrongly segmented into several parts. In practice many OOV errors belong to such type.

The rule is quite simple. When we read a sentence from the result we get by the last step, we also kept the last N sentences in memory, in our system we set N equals to 20. We do this because adjacent sentences are always relevant and some named entity likely occurs repeatedly in these sentences. Then, we scan these sentences to find all n-grams (n from 2 to 7) and count their occurrence. If certain n-gram appears more than a threshold and this n-gram never appears in training corpus, the n-gram will be selected as a word candidate. Then, we filter these word candidates according to the context entropy (Luo and Song, 2004). Assume w is a word candidate appears n times in the current sentence and last N sentences and $\alpha = \{a_0, a_1, ..., a_l\}$ is the set of left side characters of w. Left Context Entropy (LCE) can be defined as:

$$LCE(w) = \frac{1}{n} \sum_{a_i \in \alpha} C(a_i, w) \log \frac{n}{C(a_i, w)}$$

Here, $C(a_i, w)$ is the count of concurrence of a_i and w. For the Right Context Entropy, the definition is the same except change left into right. Now, we define Context Entropy (CE) of a word candidate w as $\min(LCE(w), RCE(w))$. The word candidates with CE larger than a predefined threshold will be bind as a whole word in test corpus no matter what tag sequence the segmenter giving it. If a shorter n-gram is contained in a longer n-gram and both of them satisfy the above condition, the shorter n-gram will be overlooked and the longer n-gram is bind as a whole word.

3 Evaluation of Our System

On the corpora of the Fourth Bakeoff, we evaluate our system. We carry out our evaluation on the closed tracks. It means that we do not use any additional knowledge beyond the training corpus. The thresholds set for MP and CE on each corpus are tuned on left-out data of training corpus by cross validation. To analyze our methods on IV and OOV words, we use a detailed evaluation metric than Bakeoff 2006 (Levow, 2006) which includes Foov and Fiv. Our results are shown in Table 2. In Table 2, the row "Basic Model" means the results produced by our basic CRF tagger, the row "+IV" means the results produced by the combination of CRF tagger and word-based segmenter and the row "+IV+OOV" means the result we get by executing post-processing rule on the combination results. The F measure of the basic CRF tagger alone in the Table 2 is within the top three in the closed tests except Cityu. Performance on Cityu corpus is not so good because the inconsistencies existing in Cityu training and test corpora. In the training corpus the quotation marks are 「」 while in test corpus quotation marks are " " , which never apper in the training corpus. As a reult, a lot of errors were caused by quotation marks. For example, the following four character "事業" were combined as a one word in our result and fragment "越位" was tagged as two words "越 and 位" . Because CRF tagger never met " and " in training corpus so the tagger gave the most common tags, namely B and E to the quotation marks, which cause segmentation errors not only on quotation marks themselves but also on the characters adjacent to them. We remove these inconsistencies munually and got the F measure 0.5 percentage higer than the rusult in table 2. This result is within the top three in the closed tests. On all the five corpora, our "+IV" module can increase the Fiv and our "+OOV" module can increase Foov respectively. However, these improvements are not significant.

Corpus	Method	R	P	F	R_{OOV}	P_{OOV}	F_{OOV}	R_{IV}	P_{IV}	F_{IV}
CKIP	Basic Model	0.946	0.923	0.940	0.651	0.719	0.683	0.969	0.948	0.958
	+ IV	0.949	0.935	0.942	0.647	0.741	0.691	0.973	0.948	0.960
	+ IV + OOV	0.950	0.936	0.943	0.656	0.748	0.699	0.973	0.949	0.961
CityU	Basic Model	0.944	0.934	0.939	0.654	0.721	0.686	0.970	0.951	0.960
	+ IV	0.946	0.936	0.941	0.655	0.738	0.694	0.972	0.951	0.962
	+ IV + OOV	0.949	0.937	0.943	0.678	0.759	0.716	0.973	0.951	0.962
CTB	Basic Model	0.953	0.951	0.952	0.703	0.727	0.715	0.967	0.964	0.965
	+ IV	0.954	0.952	0.953	0.697	0.747	0.721	0.969	0.963	0.966
	+ IV + OOV	0.954	0.953	0.953	0.703	0.749	0.725	0.969	0.964	0.966
NCC	Basic Model	0.940	0.928	0.934	0.438	0.580	0.499	0.965	0.940	0.952
	+ IV	0.944	0.930	0.936	0.434	0.603	0.504	0.969	0.941	0.955
	+ IV + OOV	0.945	0.932	0.939	0.450	0.620	0.522	0.970	0.943	0.956
SXU	Basic Model	0.960	0.953	0.956	0.636	0.674	0.654	0.977	0.967	0.972
	+ IV	0.962	0.955	0.958	0.637	0.696	0.665	0.980	0.967	0.973
	+ IV + OOV	0.962	0.955	0.959	0.645	0.702	0.673	0.979	0.968	0.974

Table 2 performance each step of our system achieves

4 Conclusions and Future Work

In this paper, we propose a three-stage strategy in Chinese Word Segmentation. Based on the results produced by basic CRF, our word-based segmentation module and post-processing module are designed to improve IV and OOV performance respectively. The results above show that our system achieves the state-of-the-art performance. Since only the CRF tagger is good enough as we shown in our experiment, in the future work we will pay effort on the semi-supervised learning for CRF model in order to mining more useful information from training and test corpus for CRF tagger.

References

John Lafferty, Andrew McCallum, and Fernando Pereira. 2001. Conditional random fields: probabilistic models for segmenting and labeling sequence data. *In Proceedings of ICML-2001*, pages 591–598.

Gina-Anne Levow. 2006. The Third International Chinese Language Processing Bakeoff: Word Segmentation and Named Entity Recognition. In *Proceedings of the Fifth SIGHAN Workshop on Chinese Language Processing* , pages 108-117, Sydney: July.

Jin Kiat Low, Hwee Tou Ng, and Wenyuan Guo. 2005. A Maximum Entropy Approach to Chinese Word Segmentation. In *Proceedings of the Fourth SIGHAN Workshop on Chinese Language Processing*, pages 161-164, Jeju Island, Korea.

Zhiyong Luo, Rou Song, 2004. "An integrated method for Chinese unknown word extraction", In *Proceedings of Third SIGHAN Workshop on Chinese Language Processing*, pages 148-154. Barcelona, Spain.

Fuchun Peng, Fangfang Feng, and Andrew McCallum. 2004. Chinese segmentation and new word detection using conditional random fields. In COLING 2004, pages 562–568. Geneva, Switzerland.

Huihsin Tseng, Pichuan Chang et al. 2005. A Conditional Random Field Word Segmenter for SIGHAN Bakeoff 2005. In *Proceedings of the Fourth SIGHAN Workshop on Chinese Language Processing*, pages 168-171, Jeju Island, Korea.

Zhenxing Wang, Changning Huang and Jingbo Zhu. 2008. Which Performs Better on In-Vocabulary Word Segmentation: Based on Word or Character? In *Proceeding of the Sixth Sighan Workshop on Chinese Language Processing*. To be published.

Neinwen Xue and Susan P. Converse. 2002. Combining Classifiers for Chinese Word Segmentation. In *Proceedings of the First SIGHAN Workshop on Chinese Language Processing*, pages 63-70, Taipei, Taiwan.

Ruiqiang Zhang, Genichiro Kikui and Eiichiro Sumita. 2006. Subword-based Tagging by Conditional Random Fields for Chinese Word Segmentation. In *Proceedings of the Human Language Technology Conference of the NAACL, Companion volume*, pages 193-196. New York, USA.

Hai Zhao, Changning Huang et al. 2006. Effective Tag Set Selection in Chinese Word Segmentation via Conditional Random Field Modeling. In *Proceedings of PACLIC-20.* pages 87-94. Wuhan, China, Novemeber.

Chinese NER Using CRFs and Logic for the Fourth SIGHAN Bakeoff *

Xiaofeng Yu **Wai Lam** **Shing-Kit Chan** **Yiu Kei Wu** **Bo Chen**

Information Systems Laboratory
Department of Systems Engineering & Engineering Management
The Chinese University of Hong Kong
Shatin, N.T., Hong Kong
{xfyu,wlam,skchan,ykwu,bchen}@se.cuhk.edu.hk

Abstract

We report a high-performance Chinese NER system that incorporates Conditional Random Fields (CRFs) and first-order logic for the fourth SIGHAN Chinese language processing bakeoff (SIGHAN-6). Using current state-of-the-art CRFs along with a set of well-engineered features for Chinese NER as the base model, we consider distinct linguistic characteristics in Chinese named entities by introducing various types of domain knowledge into Markov Logic Networks (MLNs), an effective combination of first-order logic and probabilistic graphical models for validation and error correction of entities. Our submitted results achieved consistently high performance, including the first place on the CityU open track and fourth place on the MSRA open track respectively, which show both the attractiveness and effectiveness of our proposed model.

1 Introduction

We participated in the Chinese named entity recognition (NER) task for the fourth SIGHAN Chinese language processing bakeoff (SIGHAN-6). We submitted results for the open track of the NER task. Our official results achieved consistently high performance, including the first place on the CityU open track and fourth place on the MSRA open track. This paper presents an overview of our system due to space limit. A more detailed description of our model is presented in (Yu *et al.*, 2008).

Our Chinese NER system combines the strength of two graphical discriminative models, Conditional Random Fields (CRFs) and Markov Logic Networks (MLNs). First, we employ CRFs, a discriminatively trained undirected graphical model which has been shown to be an effective approach to segmenting and labeling sequence data, as our base system. Second, we model the linguistic and structural information in Chinese named entity composition. We exploit a variety of domain knowledge which can capture essential characteristics of Chinese named entities into Markov Logic Networks (MLNs), a powerful combination of first-order logic and probability, to (1) validate and correct errors made in the base system and (2) find and extract new entity candidates. These domain knowledge is easy to obtain and can be well and concisely formulated in first-order logic and incorporated into MLNs.

* The work described in this paper is substantially supported by grants from the Research Grant Council of the Hong Kong Special Administrative Region, China (Project Nos: CUHK 4179/03E, CUHK4193/04E, and CUHK4128/07) and the Direct Grant of the Faculty of Engineering, CUHK (Project Codes: 2050363 and 2050391). This work is also affiliated with the Microsoft-CUHK Joint Laboratory for Human-centric Computing and Interface Technologies.

2 Conditional Random Fields as Base Model

Conditional Random Fields (CRFs) (Lafferty *et al.*, 2001) are undirected graphical models trained to maximize the conditional probability of the desired outputs given the corresponding inputs. CRFs have been shown to perform well on Chinese NER shared task on SIGHAN-4 (Zhou *et al.* (2006), Chen *et al.* (2006a), Chen *et al.* (2006b)). We employ CRFs as the base model in our framework. In this base model, we design features similar to the state-of-the-art CRF models for Chinese NER. We use character features, word segmentation features, part-of-speech (POS) features, and dictionary features, as described below.

Character features: These features are the current character, 2 characters preceding the current character and 2 following the current character. We extend the window size to 7 but find that it slightly hurts. The reason is that CRFs can deal with non-independent features. A larger window size may introduce noisy and irrelevant features.

Word segmentation and POS features: We train our own model for conducting Chinese word segmentation and POS tagging. We employ a unified framework to integrate cascaded Chinese word segmentation and POS tagging tasks by joint decoding that guards against violations of those hard-constraints imposed by segmentation task based on dual-layer CRFs introduced by Shi and Wang (2007).

We separately train the Chinese word segmentation and POS tagging CRF models using 8-month and 2-month PKU 2000 corpus, respectively. The original PKU 2000 corpus contains more than 100 different POS tags. To reduce the training time for POS tagging experiment, we merge some similar tags and obtain only 42 tags finally. For example, {ia, ib, id, in, iv}→i. We use the same features as described in (Shi and Wang, 2007), except that we do not use the HowNet features for word segmentation. Instead, we use max-matching segmentation features based on a word dictionary. This dictionary contains 445456 words which are extracted from People's Daily corpus (January-June, 1998), CityU, MSRA, and PKU word segmentation training corpora in SIGHAN-6. For decoding, we first perform individual decoding for each task. We then set 10-best segmentation and POS tagging results for reranking and joint decoding in order to find the most probable joint decodings for both tasks.

Dictionary features: We obtain a named entity dictionary extracted from People's Daily 1998 corpus and PKU 2000 corpus, which contains 68305 PERs, 28408 LOCs and 55596 ORGs. We use the max-matching algorithm to search whether a string exists in this dictionary.

In summary, we list the features used for our CRF base model in Table 1. Besides the unigram feature template, CRFs also allow bigram feature template. With this template, a combination of the current output token and previous output token (bigram) is automatically generated.

We use CRF++ toolkit (version 0.48) (Kudo, 2005) in our experiments. We find that setting the cut-off threshold f for the features not only decreases the training time, but improves the NER performance. CRFs can use the features that occurs no less than f times in the given training data. We set $f = 5$ in our system.

We extend the **BIO** representation for the chunk tag which was employed in the CoNLL-2002 and CoNLL-2003 evaluations. We use the **BIOES** representation in which each character is tagged as either the beginning of a named entity (**B** tag), a character inside a named entity (**I** tag), the last character in an entity (**E** tag), single-character entities (**S** tag), or a character outside a named entity (**O** tag). We find that **BIOES** representation is more informative and yields better results than **BIO** representation.

3 Markov Logic Networks as Error Correction Model

Even though the CRF model is able to accommodate a large number of well-engineered features which can be easily obtained across languages, some NEs, especially LOCs and ORGs are difficult to identify due to the lack of linguistic or structural characteristics.

Table 1: Feature template for CRF model.

Character features	(1.1) $C_n, n \in [-2, 2]$
	(1.2) $C_nC_{n+1}, n \in [-2, 1]$
Word features	(1.3) $W_n, n \in [-3, 3]$
	(1.4) $W_nW_{n+1}, n \in [-3, 2]$
POS features	(1.5) $P_n, n \in [-3, 3]$
	(1.6) $P_nP_{n+1}, n \in [-3, 2]$
Dictionary features	(1.7) $D_n, n \in [-2, 2]$
	(1.8) $D_nD_{n+1}, n \in [-2, 1]$
	(1.9) $D_{-1}D_{+1}$

We incorporate domain knowledge that can be well formulated into first-order logic to extract entity candidates from CRF results. Then, the Markov Logic Networks (MLNs), an undirected graphical model for *statistical relational learning*, is used to validate and correct the errors made in the base model.

MLNs conduct *relational learning* by incorporating first-order logic into probabilistic graphical models under a single coherent framework (Richardson and Domingos, 2006). Traditional first-order logic is a set of hard constraints in which a world violates even one formula has zero probability. The advantage of MLNs is to soften these constraints so that when the fewer formulae a world violates, the more probable it is. MLNs have been applied to tackle the problems of gene interaction discovery from biomedical texts and citation entity resolution from citation texts with state-of-the-art performance (Riedel and Klein (2005), Singla and Domingos (2006)).

We use the Alchemy system (Beta version) (Kok *et al.*, 2005) in our experiment, which is a software package providing a series of algorithms for statistical relational learning and probabilistic logic inference, based on the Markov logic representation.

3.1 Domain Knowledge

We extract 165 location salient words and 843 organization salient words from Wikipedia and the LDC Chinese-English bi-directional NE lists compiled from Xinhua News database. We also make a punctuation list which contains 18 items and some stopwords which Chinese NEs cannot contain. We extract new NE candidates from the CRF results according to the following consideration:

- If a chunk (a series of continuous characters) occurs in the training data as a PER or a LOC or an ORG, then this chunk should be a PER or a LOC or an ORG in the testing data. In general, a unique string is defined as a PER, it cannot be a LOC somewhere else.

- If a tagged entity ends with a location salient word, it is a LOC. If a tagged entity ends with an organization salient word, it is an ORG.

Table 2: Statistics of NER training and testing corpora.

Corpus	Training NEs	PERs/LOCs/ORGs	Testing NEs	PERs/LOCs/ORGs
CityU	66255	16552/36213/13490	13014	4940/4847/3227
MSRA	37811	9028/18522/10261	7707	1864/3658/2185

NEs: Number of named entities; PERs: Number of person names;
LOCs: Number of location names; ORGs: Number of organization names.

Table 3: OOV Rate of NER testing corpora.

Corpus	Overall (IVs/OOVs/OOV-Rate)	PER (IVs/OOVs/OOV-Rate)	LOC (IVs/OOVs/OOV-Rate)	ORG (IVs/OOVs/OOV-Rate)
CityU	6660/6354/0.4882	1062/3878/0.7850	3947/900/0.1857	1651/1576/0.4884
MSRA	6056/1651/0.2142	1300/564/0.3026	3343/315/0.0861	1413/772/0.3533

IVs: number of IV (named entities in vocabulary); OOVs: number of OOV
(named entities out of vocabulary); OOV-Rate: ratio of named entities out of vocabulary.

- If a tagged entity is close to a subsequent location salient word, probably they should be combined together as a LOC. The closer they are, the more likely that they should be combined.
- If a series of consecutive tagged entities are close to a subsequent organization salient word, they should probably be combined together as an ORG because an ORG may contain multiple PERs, LOCs and ORGs.
- Similarly, if there exists a series of consecutive tagged entities and the last one is tagged as an ORG, it is likely that all of them should be combined as an ORG.
- Entity length restriction: all kinds of tagged entities cannot exceed 25 Chinese characters.
- Stopword restriction: intuitively, all tagged entities cannot comprise any stopword.
- Punctuation restriction: in general, all tagged entities cannot span any punctuation.
- Since all NEs are proper nouns, the tagged entities should end with noun words.
- For a chunk with low conditional probabilities, all the above assumptions are adopted.

3.2 First-Order Logic Construction

All the above domain knowledge can also be formulated as first-order logic to construct the structure of MLNs. First-order formulae are recursively constructed from atomic formulae using logical connectives and quantifiers. Atomic formulae are constructed using *constants*, *variables*, *functions*, and *predicates*.

For example, we use the predicate `organization(candidate)` to specify whether a candidate is an ORG. If "中国政府/China Government" is mis-tagged as a LOC by the CRF model, but it contains the organization salient word "政府/Government". The corresponding formula `endwith(r, p)`∧`orgsalientword(p)` ⇒`organization(r)` means if a tagged entity `r` ends with an organization salient word `p`, then it is extracted as a new ORG entity. Typically only a small number (e.g., 10-20) of formulae are needed. We declare 14 *predicates* and 15 first-order formulae according to the domain knowledge mentioned in Section 3.1.

3.3 Training and Inference for Named Entity Correction

Each extracted new NE candidate is represented by one or more strings appearing as arguments of ground atoms in the database. The goal of NE prediction is to determine whether the candidates are entities and the types of entities (query predicates), given the evidence predicates and other relations that can be deterministically derived from the database.

We extract all the NEs from the official training corpora, and then convert them to the first-order logic representation according to the domain knowledge. The MLN training database that consists of predicates, constants, and ground atoms was built automatically. We also extract new entity candidates from CRF results and construct MLN testing database in the same way.

During MLN learning, each formula is converted to Conjunctive Normal Form (CNF), and a weight is learned for each of its clauses. These weights reflect how often the clauses are actually observed in the training data. Inference is performed by grounding the minimal subset of the network required for answering the query predicates. Conducting maximum a posteriori (MAP) inference which finds the most likely values of a set of variables given the values of observed variables can be performed via approximate solution using Markov chain Monte Carlo (MCMC) algorithms. Gibbs sampling can be adopted by sampling each non-evidence variable in turn given its Markov blanket, and counting the fraction of samples that each variable is in each state.

4 Experiment Details

4.1 Data and Preprocessing

The training corpora provided by the SIGHAN bakeoff organizers were in the CoNLL two column format, with one Chinese character per line and hand-annotated named entity chunks in the second column. The CityU corpus was traditional Chinese. We converted this corpus to simplified Chinese and we used UTF-8 encoding in all the experiments so that all the resources (e.g., word dictionary and named entity dictionary) are compatible in our

Table 4: Official results on CityU and MSRA open tracks.

	Precision	*Recall*	$F_{\beta=1}$
CityU			
PER	97.21%	95.26%	96.23
LOC	92.35%	93.42%	92.88
ORG	88.05%	66.44%	75.73
Overall	93.42%	87.43%	90.33
MSRA			
PER	98.33%	94.58%	96.42
LOC	93.97%	93.36%	93.66
ORG	92.80%	84.39%	88.40
Overall	94.71%	91.11%	92.88

system.

Table 2 shows the statistics of NER training and testing corpora and Table 3 shows the OOV (Out of Vocabulary) rate of NER testing corpora [1]. The number of NEs in CityU corpus is almost twice as many as that in MSRA corpus. The OOV rate in CityU corpus is much higher than in MSRA corpus for PERs, LOCs and ORGs. These numbers indicate that NER on CityU corpus is much more difficult to handle.

4.2 Model Development

We performed holdout methodology to develop our model. We randomly selected 5000 sentences from CityU training corpus for development testing and the rest for training. We did the same thing for MSRA training corpus.

To avoid overfitting for CRF model, we penalized the log-likelihood by the commonly used zero-mean Gaussian prior over the parameters. Also, the MLNs were trained using a Gaussian prior with zero mean and unit variance on each weight to penalize the pseudo-likelihood, and with the weights initialized at the mode of the prior (zero).

We found an optimal value for the parameter c [2] for CRFs. Using held-out data, we tested all c values, $c \in [0.2, 2.2]$, with an incremental step of 0.4. Finally, we set $c = 1.8$ for CityU corpus and $c = 1.0$ for MSRA corpus.

5 Official Results

Table 4 presents the results obtained on the official CityU and MSRA test sets. Our results are consistently good: we obtained the first place on the CityU open track (90.33 overall F-measure) and fourth place on the MSRA open track (92.88 overall F-measure) respectively. The lower F-measure obtained on CityU corpus can be attributed to the higher OOV rate of this corpus.

6 Conclusion

We have described a Chinese NER system incorporating probabilistic graphical models and first-order logic which achieves state-of-the-art performance on the open track of SIGHAN-6. We exploited domain knowledge which can capture the essential features of Chinese NER and can be concisely formulated in MLNs, allowing the training and inference algorithms to be directly applied to them. Our proposed framework can also be extendable to NER for other languages, due to the simplicity of the domain knowledge we could access.

[1]The NER on the PKU corpus was cancelled by the organizer due to the tagging inconsistency of this corpus.

[2]This parameter trades the balance between overfitting and underfitting. With larger c value, CRF tends to overfit to the give training corpus. The results will significantly be influenced by this parameter

References

Aitao Chen, Fuchun Peng, Roy Shan, and Gordon Sun. Chinese named entity recognition with conditional probabilistic models. In *5th SIGHAN Workshop on Chinese Language Processing*, Australia, July 2006.

Wenliang Chen, Yujie Zhang, and Hitoshi Isahara. Chinese named entity recognition with conditional random fields. In *5th SIGHAN Workshop on Chinese Language Processing*, Australia, July 2006.

Stanley Kok, Parag Singla, Matthew Richardson, and Pedro Domingos. The Alchemy system for statistical relational AI. Technical report, Department of Computer Science and Engineering, University of Washington, Seattle, WA, 2005. http://www.cs.washington.edu/ai/alchemy.

Taku Kudo. CRF++: Yet another CRF tool kit. http://crfpp.sourceforge.net/, 2005.

John Lafferty, Andrew McCallum, and Fernando Pereira. Conditional random fields: Probabilistic models for segmenting and labeling sequence data. In *Proceedings of ICML-01*, pages 282–289. Morgan Kaufmann, San Francisco, CA, 2001.

Matthew Richardson and Pedro Domingos. Markov logic networks. *Machine Learning*, 62(1-2):107–136, 2006.

Sebastian Riedel and Ewan Klein. Genic interaction extraction with semantic and syntactic chains. In *Proceedings of the Learning Language in Logic Workshop (LLL-05)*, pages 69–74, 2005.

Yanxin Shi and Mengqiu Wang. A dual-layer CRFs based joint decoding method for cascaded segmentation and labeling tasks. In *Proceedings of IJCAI-07*, pages 1707–1712, Hyderabad, India, 2007.

Parag Singla and Pedro Domingos. Entity resolution with Markov logic. In *Proceedings of ICDM-06*, pages 572–582, Hong Kong, 2006.

Xiaofeng Yu, Wai Lam, and Shing-Kit Chan. A framework based on graphical models with logic for Chinese named entity recognition. In *Proceedings of IJCNLP-08*, Hyderabad, India, 2008. To appear.

Junsheng Zhou, Liang He, Xinyu Dai, and Jiajun Chen. Chinese named entity recognition with a multi-phase model. In *5th SIGHAN Workshop on Chinese Language Processing*, Australia, July 2006.

Unsupervised Segmentation Helps Supervised Learning of Character Tagging for Word Segmentation and Named Entity Recognition

Hai Zhao and Chunyu Kit
Department of Chinese, Translation and Linguistics
City University of Hong Kong
Tat Chee Ave., Kowloon, Hong Kong
Email: {haizhao, ctckit}@cityu.edu.hk

Abstract

This paper describes a novel character tagging approach to Chinese word segmentation and named entity recognition (NER) for our participation in Bakeoff-4.[1] It integrates unsupervised segmentation and conditional random fields (CRFs) learning successfully, using similar character tags and feature templates for both word segmentation and NER. It ranks at the top in all closed tests of word segmentation and gives promising results for all closed and open NER tasks in the Bakeoff. Tag set selection and unsupervised segmentation play a critical role in this success.

1 Introduction

A number of recent studies show that character sequence labeling is a simple but effective formulation of Chinese word segmentation and name entity recognition for machine learning (Xue, 2003; Low et al., 2005; Zhao et al., 2006a; Chen et al., 2006). Character tagging becomes a prevailing technique for this kind of labeling task for Chinese language processing, following the current trend of applying machine learning as a core technology in the field of natural language processing. In particular, when a full-fledged general-purpose sequence learning model such as CRFs is involved, the only work to do for a given application is to identify an ideal set of features and hyperparameters for the purpose of achieving the best learning model that we can with available training data. Our work in this aspect provides a solid foundation for applying an unsupervised segmentation criterion to enrich the supervised CRFs learning for further performance enhancement on both word segmentation and NER.

This paper is intended to present the research for our participation in Bakeoff-4, with a highlight on our strategy to select character tags and feature templates for CRFs learning. Particularly worth mentioning is the simplicity of our system in contrast to its success. The rest of the paper is organized as follows. The next section presents the technical details of the system and Section 3 its evaluation results. Section 4 looks into a few issues concerning character tag set, unsupervised segmentation, and available name entities (NEs) as features for open NER test. Section 5 concludes the paper.

2 System Description

Following our previous work (Zhao et al., 2006a; Zhao et al., 2006b; Zhao and Kit, 2007), we continue to apply the order-1 linear chain CRFs (Lafferty et al., 2001) as our learning model for Bakeoff-4. Specifically, we use its implementation CRF++ by Taku Kudo[2] freely available for research purpose. We opt for a similar set of character tags and feature templates for both word segmentation and NER.

In addition, two key techniques that we have explored in our previous work are applied. One is to introduce more tags in the hope of utilizing more precise contextual information to achieve more pre-

[1]The Fourth International Chinese Language Processing Bakeoff & the First CIPS Chinese Language Processing Evaluation, at http://www.china-language.gov.cn/bakeoff08/bakeoff-08_basic.html.

[2]http://crfpp.sourceforge.net/

Table 1: An exmaple of NE tagging for a character sequence

Characters	爱	乐	乐	团	到	沪	访	问	演	出
Tags	B-ORG	B_2-ORG	B_3-ORG	E-ORG	O	S-LOC	O	O	O	O

Table 2: Illustration of character tagging

Word length	Tag sequence for a word
1	S
2	B E
3	B B_2 E
4	B B_2 B_3 E
5	B B_2 B_3 M E
$\geqslant 6$	B B_2 B_3 M $\cdots$ M E

cise labeling results. This also optimizes the active features for the CRFs training. The other is to integrate the unsupervised segmentation outputs into CRFs as features. It assumes no word boundary information in the training and test corpora for NER.

2.1 Tag Set

Our previous work shows that a 6-tag set enables the CRFs learning of character tagging to achieve a better segmentation performance than others (Zhao et al., 2006a; Zhao et al., 2006b). So we keep using this tag set for Bakeoff-4. Its six tags are B, B_2, B_3, M, E and S. Table 2 illustrates how characters in words of various lengths are tagged with this tag set.

For NER, we need to tell apart three types of NEs, namely, *person*, *location* and *organization* names. Correspondingly, the six tags are also adapted for characters in these NEs but distinguished by the suffixes -PER, -LOC and -ORG. For example, a character in a person name may be tagged with either B-PER, B_2-PER, B_3-PER, M-PER, E-PER, or S-PER. Plus an additional tag "O" for none NE characters, altogether we have 19 tags for NER. An example of NE tagging is illustrated in Table 1.

2.2 Feature Templates

We use not only a similar tag set but also the same set of feature templates for both the word segmentation and NER closed tests in Bakeoff-4. Six n-gram templates, namely, C_{-1}, C_0, C_1, $C_{-1}C_0$, C_0C_1, $C_{-1}C_1$, are selected as features, where C stands for a character and the subscripts -1, 0 and 1 for the previous, current and next character, respectively.

In addition to these n-gram features, unsupervised segmentation outputs are also used as features, for the purpose of providing more word boundary information via global statistics derived from all unlabeled texts of the training and test corpora. The basic idea is to inform a supervised leaner of which substrings are recognized as word candidates by a given unsupervised segmentation criterion and how likely they are to be true words in terms of that criterion (Zhao and Kit, 2007; Kit and Zhao, 2007).

We adopt the *accessor variety* (AV) (Feng et al., 2004a; Feng et al., 2004b) as our unsupervised segmentation criterion. It formulates an idea similar to linguist Harris' (1955; 1970) for segmenting utterances of an unfamiliar language into morphemes to facilitate word extraction from Chinese raw texts. It is found more effective than other criteria in supporting CRFs learning of character tagging for word segmentation (Zhao and Kit, 2007). The AV value of a substring s is defined as

$$AV(s) = \min\{L_{av}(s), R_{av}(s)\},$$

where the left and right AV values $L_{av}(s)$ and $R_{av}(s)$ are defined, respectively, as the numbers of its distinct predecessor and successor characters.

In our work, AV values for word candidates are derived from an unlabeled corpus by substring counting, which can be efficiently carried out with the aid of the *suffix array* representation (Manber and Myers, 1993; Kit and Wilks, 1998). Heuristic rules are applied in Feng et al.'s work to remove insignificant substrings. We do not use any such rule.

Multiple feature templates are used to represent word candidates of various lengths identified by the AV criterion. For the sake of efficiency, all candidates longer than five characters are given up. To accommodate the word likelihood information, we need to extend the feature representation in (Zhao and Kit, 2007), where only the candidate substrings are used as features for word segmentation. Formally put, our new feature function for a word can-

Table 3: Training corpora for assistant learners

Track	CityU NER	MSRA NER
Ass. Seg.	CityU (Bakeoff-1 to 4)	MSRA (Bakeoff-2)
ANER-1	CityU(Bakeoff-3)	CityU(Bakeoff-3)
ANER-2	MSRA(Bakeoff-3)	CityU(Bakeoff-4)

Table 4: NE lists from Chinese Wikipedia

Category	Number
Place name suffix	85
Chinese place name	6,367
Foreign place name	1,626
Chinese family name	573
Most common Chinese family name	109
Foreign name	2,591
Chinese university	515

Table 5: Segmentation results for previous Bakeoffs

Bakeoff-1		AS	CityU	CTB	PKU
−AV	F	.9727	.9473	.8720	.9558
	R_{OOV}[a]	.7907	.7576	.7022	.7078
+AV	F	.9725	.9554	.9023	.9612
	R_{OOV}	.7597	.7616	.7502	.7208
Bakeoff-2		AS	CityU	MSRA	PKU
−AV	F	.9534	.9476	.9735	.9515
	R_{OOV}	.6812	.6920	.7496	.6720
+AV	F	.9570	.9610	.9758	.9540
	R_{OOV}	.6993	.7540	.7446	.6765
Bakeoff-3		AS	CityU	CTB	MSRA
−AV	F	.9538	.9691	.9322	.9608
	R_{OOV}	.6699	.7815	.7095	.6658
+AV	F	.9586	.9747	.9431	.9660
	R_{OOV}	.6935	.8005	.7608	.6620

[a]Recall of out-of-vocabulary (OOV) words.

didate s with a score $AV(s)$ is defined as

$$f_n(s) = t, \text{ if } 2^t \leq AV(s) < 2^{t+1},$$

where t is an integer to logarithmize the score. This is to alleviate the sparse data problem by narrowing down the feature representation involved. Note that t is used as a feature value rather than a parameter for the CRFs training in our system. For an overlap character of several word candidates, we only choose the one with the greatest AV score to activate the above feature function for that character. It is in this way that the unsupervised segmentation outcomes are fit into the CRFs learning.

2.3 Features for Open NER

Three extra groups of feature template are used for the open NER beyond those for the closed.

The first group includes three segmentation feature templates. One is character type feature template $T(C_{-1})T(C_0)T(C_1)$, where $T(C)$ is the type of character C. For this, five character types are defined, namdely, number, foreign letter, punctuation, date and time, and others. The other two are generated respectively by two assistant segmenters (Zhao et al., 2006a), a maximal matching segmenter based on a dictionary from Peking University[3] and a CRFs segmenter using the 6-tag set and the six n-gram feature templates for training.

The second group comes from the outputs of two assistant NE recognizers (ANERs), both trained with a corresponding 6-tag set and the same six n-gram feature templates. They share a similar feature representation as the assistant segmenter. Table 3 lists the training corpora for the assistant CRFs segmenter and the ANERs for various open NER tests.

The third group consists of feature templates generated from seven NE lists acquired from Chinese Wikipedia.[4] The categories and numbers of these NE items are summarized in Table 4.

3 Evaluation Results

The performance of both word segmentation and NER is measured in terms of the F-measure $F = 2RP/(R + P)$, where R and P are the recall and precision of segmentation or NER.

We tested the techniques described above with the previous Bakeoffs' data[5] (Sproat and Emerson, 2003; Emerson, 2005; Levow, 2006). The evaluation results for the closed tests of word segmentation are reported in Table 5 and those for the NER on two corpora of Bakeoff-3 are in the upper part of Table 7. '+/–AV' indicates whether AV features are applied.

For Bakeoff-4, we participated in all five closed tracks of word segmentation, namely, CityU, CKIP, CTB, NCC, and SXU, and in all closed and open NER tracks of CityU and MSRA.[6] The evaluation

[3]It consists of about 108K words of one to four charactersslong, available at http://ccl.pku.edu.cn/doubtfire/Course/Chinese%20Information%20Processing/Source_Code/Chapter_8/Lexicon_full.zip.

[4]http://zh.wikipedia.org/wiki/首页

[5]http://www.sighan.org

[6]We declare that our team has never been exposed to the

Table 6: Evaluation results of word segmentation on Bakeoff-4 data sets

Feature	Data	F	P	R	F_{IV}[a]	P_{IV}	R_{IV}	F_{OOV}	P_{OOV}	R_{OOV}
–AV (n-gram)	CityU	.9426	.9410	.9441	.9640	.9636	.9645	.7063	.6960	.7168
	CKIP	.9421	.9387	.9454	.9607	.9581	.9633	.7113	.7013	.7216
	CTB	**.9634**	.9641	.9627	.9738	.9761	.9715	.7924	.7719	.8141
	NCC	.9333	.9356	.9311	.9536	.9612	.9461	.5678	.5182	.6280
	SXU	.9552	.9559	.9544	.9721	.9767	.9675	.6640	.6223	.7116
+AV*[b]	CityU	.9510	.9493	.9526	.9667	.9626	.9708	.7698	.7912	.7495
	CKIP	.9470	.9440	.9501	.9623	.9577	.9669	.7524	.7649	.7404
	CTB	**.9589**	.9596	.9583	.9697	.9704	.9691	.7745	.7761	.7730
	NCC	.9405	.9407	.9402	.9573	.9583	.9562	.6080	.5984	.6179
	SXU	.9623	.9625	.9622	.9752	.9764	.9740	.7292	.7159	.7429

[a]F-score for in-vocabulary (IV) words.

[b]Henceforth the official evaluation results in Bakeoff-4 are marked with "*".

Table 7: NER evaluation results

Track	Setting	F_{PER}	F_{LOC}	F_{ORG}	F_{NE}
		Bakeoff-3			
CityU	–AV	.8849	.9219	.7905	.8807
	+AV	.9063	.9281	.7981	.8918
MSRA	–AV	.7851	.9072	.8242	.8525
	+AV	.8171	.9139	.8164	.8630
		Bakeoff-4			
CityU	–AV	.8222	.8682	.6801	.8092
	+AV*	.8362	.8677	.6852	.8152
	$Open_1$*	.9125	.9216	.7862	.8869
	$Open_2$	.9137	.9214	.7853	.8870
MSRA	–AV	.9221	.9193	.8367	.8968
	+AV*	.9319	.9219	.8414	.9020
	Open*	1.000	.9960	.9920	.9958
	$Open_1$[a]	.9710	.9601	.9352	.9558
	$Open_2$[b]	.9699	.9581	.9359	.9548

[a]For our official submission to Bakeoff-4, we also used an ANER trained on the MSRA NER training corpus of Bakeoff-3. This makes our official evaluation results extremely high but trivial, for a part of this corpus is used as the MSRA NER test corpus for Bakeoff-4. Presented here are the results without using this ANER.

[b]$Open_2$ is the result of $Open_1$ using no NE list feature.

results of word segmentation and NER for our system are presented in Tables 6 and 7, respectively.

For the purpose of comparison, the word segmentation performance of our system on Bakeoff-4 data using the 2- and 4-tag sets and the best corresponding n-gram feature templates as in (Tsai et al., 2006; Low et al., 2005) are presented in Table 8.[7] This comparison reconfirms the conclusion in (Zhao et al., 2006b) about tag set selection for character tagging for word segmentation that the 6-tag set is more effective than others, each with its own best corresponding feature template set.

Table 8: Segmentation F-scores by different tag sets

AV	Tags	CityU	CKIP	CTB	NCC	SXU
–	2	.9303	.9277	.9434	.9198	.9454
	4	.9370	.9348	.9481	.9280	.9512
	6	.9426	.9421	.9634	.9333	.9552
+	2	.9382	.9319	.9451	.9239	.9485
	4	.9482	.9423	.9527	.9356	.9593
	6	.9510	.9470	.9589	.9405	.9623

4 Discussion

4.1 Tag Set and Computational Cost

Using more labels in CRFs learning is expected to bring in performance enhancement. Inevitably, however, it also leads to a huge rise of computational cost for model training. We conducted a series of experiments to study the computational cost of CRFs training with different tag sets using Bakeoff-3 data. The experimental results are given in Table 9, showing that the 6-tag set costs nearly twice as much time as the 4-tag set and about three times as the 2-tag set. Fortunately, its memory cost with the six n-gram feature templates remains very close to that of the 2- and 4-tag sets with the n-gram feature template sets from (Tsai et al., 2006; Xue, 2003).

However, a 2-tag set is popular in use for word segmentation and NER for the reason that CRFs training is very computationally expensive and a large tag set would make the situation worse. Cer-

CityU data sets in any other situation than the Bakeoff.

[7]The templates for the 2-tag set, adopted from (Tsai et al., 2006), include C_{-2}, C_{-1}, C_0, C_1, $C_{-3}C_{-1}$, $C_{-2}C_0$, $C_{-2}C_{-1}$, $C_{-1}C_0$, $C_{-1}C_1$ and C_0C_1. Those for the 4-tag set, adopted from (Xue, 2003) and (Low et al., 2005), include C_{-2}, C_{-1}, C_0, C_1, C_2, $C_{-2}C_{-1}$, $C_{-1}C_0$, $C_{-1}C_1$, $C_0C_1$and C_1C_2.

Table 9: Comparison of computational cost

Tags	Templates	AS	CityU	CTB	MSRA
Training time (Minutes)					
2	Tsai	112	52	16	35
4	Xue	206	79	28	73
6	Zhao	402	146	47	117
Feature numbers ($\times 10^6$)					
2	Tsai	13.2	7.3	3.1	5.5
4	Xue	16.1	9.0	3.9	6.8
6	Zhao	15.6	8.8	3.8	6.6
Memory cost (Giga bytes)					
2	Tsai	5.4	2.4	0.9	1.8
4	Xue	6.6	2.8	1.1	2.2
6	Zhao	6.4	2.7	1.0	2.1

tainly, a possible way out of this problem is the computer hardware advancement, which is predicted by Moore's Law (Moore, 1965) to be improving at an exponential rate in general, including processing speed and memory capacity. Specifically, CPU can be made twice faster every other year or even 18 months. It is predictable that computational cost will not be a problem for CRFs training soon, and the advantages of using a larger tag set as in our approach will be shared by more others.

4.2 Unsupervised Segmentation Features

Our evaluation results show that the unsupervised segmentation features bring in performance improvement on both word segmentation and NER for all tracks except CTB segmentation, as highlighted in Table 6. We are unable explain this yet, and can only attribute it to some unique text characteristics of the CTB segmented corpus. An unsupervised segmentation criterion provides a kind of global information over the whole text of a corpus (Zhao and Kit, 2007). Its effectiveness is certainly sensitive to text characteristics.

Quite a number of other unsupervised segmentation criteria are available for word discovery in unlabeled texts, e.g., boundary entropy (Tung and Lee, 1994; Chang and Su, 1997; Huang and Powers, 2003; Jin and Tanaka-Ishii, 2006) and description-length-gain (DLG) (Kit and Wilks, 1999). We found that among them AV could help the CRFs model to achieve a better performance than others, although the overall unsupervised segmentation by DLG was slightly better than that by AV. Combining any two of these criteria did not give any further performance improvement. This is why we have opted for AV for Bakeoff-4.

4.3 NE List Features for Open NER

We realize that the NE lists available to us are far from sufficient for coping with all NEs in Bakeoff-4. It is reasonable that using richer external NE lists gives a better NER performance in many cases (Zhang et al., 2006). Surprisingly, however, the NE list features used in our NER do not lead to any significant performance improvement, according to the evaluation results in Table 7. This is certainly another issue for our further inspection.

5 Conclusion

Without doubt our achievements in Bakeoff-4 owes not only to the careful selection of character tag set and feature templates for exerting the strength of CRFs learning but also to the effectiveness of our unsupervised segmentation approach. It is for the sake of simplicity that similar sets of character tags and feature templates are applied to two distinctive labeling tasks, word segmentation and NER. Relying on little preprocessing and postprocessing, our system simply follows the plain training and test routines of machine learning practice with the CRFs model and achieves the best or nearly the best results for all tracks of Bakeoff-4 in which we participated. Simple is beautiful, as Albert Einstein said, "Everything should be made as simple as possible, but not one bit simpler." Our evaluation results also provide evidence that simple can be powerful too.

Acknowledgements

The research described in this paper was supported by the Research Grants Council of Hong Kong S.A.R., China, through the CERG grant 9040861 (CityU 1318/03H) and by City University of Hong Kong through the Strategic Research Grant 7002037. Dr. Hai Zhao was supported by a Postdoctoral Research Fellowship in the Department of Chinese, Translation and Linguistics, City University of Hong Kong.

References

Jing-Shin Chang and Keh-Yih Su. 1997. An unsupervised iterative method for Chinese new lexicon extraction. *Computational Linguistics and Chinese Language Processing*, 2(2):97–148.

Wenliang Chen, Yujie Zhang, and Hitoshi Isahara. 2006. Chinese named entity recognition with conditional random fields. In *SIGHAN-5*, pages 118–121, Sydney, Australia, July 22-23.

Thomas Emerson. 2005. The second international Chinese word segmentation bakeoff. In *SIGHAN-4*, pages 123–133, Jeju Island, Korea, October 14-15.

Haodi Feng, Kang Chen, Xiaotie Deng, and Weimin Zheng. 2004a. Accessor variety criteria for Chinese word extraction. *Computational Linguistics*, 30(1):75–93.

Haodi Feng, Kang Chen, Chunyu Kit, and Xiaotie Deng. 2004b. Unsupervised segmentation of Chinese corpus using accessor variety. In *First International Joint Conference on Natural Language Processing* (IJCNLP-04), pages 255–261, Sanya, Hainan Island, China, March 22-24. Also in K. Y. Su, J. Tsujii, J. H. Lee & O. Y. Kwong (eds.), *Natural Language Processing - IJCNLP 2004*, LNAI 3248, pages 694-703. Springer.

Zellig Sabbetai Harris. 1955. From phoneme to morpheme. *Language*, 31(2):190–222.

Zellig Sabbetai Harris. 1970. Morpheme boundaries within words. In *Papers in Structural and Transformational Linguistics*, page 68 - 77.

Jin Hu Huang and David Powers. 2003. Chinese word segmentation based on contextual entropy. In Dong Hong Ji and Kim-Ten Lua, editors, *PACLIC - 17*, pages 152–158, Sentosa, Singapore, October, 1-3. COLIPS Publication.

Zhihui Jin and Kumiko Tanaka-Ishii. 2006. Unsupervised segmentation of Chinese text by use of branching entropy. In *COLING/ACL–2006*, pages 428–435, Sidney, Australia, July 17-21.

Chunyu Kit and Yorick Wilks. 1998. The virtual corpus approach to deriving n-gram statistics from large scale corpora. In Changning Huang, editor, *Proceedings of 1998 International Conference on Chinese Information Processing Conference*, pages 223–229, Beijing, Nov. 18-20.

Chunyu Kit and Yorick Wilks. 1999. Unsupervised learning of word boundary with description length gain. In M. Osborne and E. T. K. Sang, editors, *CoNLL-99*, pages 1–6, Bergen, Norway.

Chunyu Kit and Hai Zhao. 2007. Improving Chinese word segmentation with description length gain. In *2007 International Conference on Artificial Intelligence* (ICAI'07), Las Vegas, June 25-28.

John D. Lafferty, Andrew McCallum, and Fernando C. N. Pereira. 2001. Conditional random fields: Probabilistic models for segmenting and labeling sequence data. In *ICML'2001*, pages 282–289, San Francisco, CA.

Gina-Anne Levow. 2006. The third international Chinese language processing bakeoff: Word segmentation and named entity recognition. In *SIGHAN-5*, pages 108–117, Sydney, Australia, July 22-23.

Jin Kiat Low, Hwee Tou Ng, and Wenyuan Guo. 2005. A maximum entropy approach to Chinese word segmentation. In *SIGHAN-4*, pages 161–164, Jeju Island, Korea, October 14-15.

Udi Manber and Gene Myers. 1993. Suffix arrays: A new method for on-line string searches. *SIAM Journal on Computing*, 22(5):935–948.

Gordon E. Moore. 1965. Cramming more components onto integrated circuits. *Electronics*, 3(8), April 19.

Richard Sproat and Thomas Emerson. 2003. The first international Chinese word segmentation bakeoff. In *SIGHAN-2*, pages 133–143, Sapporo, Japan.

Richard Tzong-Han Tsai, Hsieh-Chuan Hung, Cheng-Lung Sung, Hong-Jie Dai, and Wen-Lian Hsu. 2006. On closed task of Chinese word segmentation: An improved CRF model coupled with character clustering and automatically generated template matching. In *SIGHAN-5*, pages 108–117, Sydney, Australia, July 22-23.

Cheng-Huang Tung and His-Jian Lee. 1994. Identification of unknown words from corpus. *Computational Proceedings of Chinese and Oriental Languages*, 8:131–145.

Nianwen Xue. 2003. Chinese word segmentation as character tagging. *Computational Linguistics and Chinese Language Processing*, 8(1):29–48.

Suxiang Zhang, Ying Qin, Juan Wen, and Xiaojie Wang. 2006. Word segmentation and named entity recognition for SIGHAN Bakeoff3. In *SIGHAN-5*, pages 158–161, Sydney, Australia, July 22-23.

Hai Zhao and Chunyu Kit. 2007. Incorporating global information into supervised learning for Chinese word segmentation. In *PACLING-2007*, pages 66–74, Melbourne, Australia, September 19-21.

Hai Zhao, Chang-Ning Huang, and Mu Li. 2006a. An improved Chinese word segmentation system with conditional random field. In *SIGHAN-5*, pages 162–165, Sydney, Australia, July 22-23.

Hai Zhao, Chang-Ning Huang, Mu Li, and Bao-Liang Lu. 2006b. Effective tag set selection in Chinese word segmentation via conditional random field modeling. In *PACLIC-20*, pages 87–94, Wuhan, China, November 1-3.

An Agent-Based Approach to Chinese Word Segmentation

Samuel W.K. Chan
Dept. of Decision Sciences
The Chinese University of Hong Kong
Hong Kong, China
swkchan@cuhk.edu.hk

Mickey W.C. Chong
Dept. of Decision Sciences
The Chinese University of Hong Kong
Hong Kong, China
mickey@baf.msmail.cuhk.edu.hk

Abstract

This paper presents the results of our system that has participated in the word segmentation task in the Fourth SIGHAN Bakeoff. Our system consists of several basic components which include the pre-processing, token identification and the post-processing. An agent-based approach is introduced to identify the weak segmentation points. Our system has participated in two open and five closed tracks in five major corpora. Our results have attained top five in most of the tracks in the bakeoff. In particular, it is ranked first in the open track of the corpus from Academia Sinica, second in the closed track of the corpus from City University of Hong Kong, third in two closed tracks of the corpora from State Language Commission of P.R.C. and Academia Sinica.

1 Introduction

Our word segmentation system consists of three major components, namely, the pre-processing, token identification and the post-processing. In this paper, an overview of our system is briefly introduced and the structure of the paper is as follows. Section 2 presents the system description. An agent based approach is introduced in the system. Associated to each agent in the system, a vote is cast to indicate the certainty by each agent in the system. In Section 3, we describe the experimental results of our system, followed by the conclusion.

2 System Description

2.1 Preprocessing

In the preprocessing, the traditional Chinese characters, punctuation marks and other symbols are first identified. Instead of training all these symbols with the traditional Chinese characters in an agent-based system, an initial, but rough, segmentation points (SP_r) are first inserted to distinguish the symbols and Chinese characters. For example, for the input sentence shown in Figure 1, segmentation points are first assumed in the sentence as shown in the Figure 2, where '/' indicates the presence of a segmentation point. This roughly segmented sentence is then subject to an agent-based learning algorithm to have the token identification.

昨日 6 時 05 分終於成功發射了第一顆自行研製的探月衛星「嫦娥一號」。

Figure 1: Original sentence for the process

昨日/ 6/ 時/ 05/ 分終於成功發射了第一顆自行研製的探月衛星/「/ 嫦娥一號/ 」/ 。

Figure 2: Rough segmented sentence from preprocessing

2.2 Token Identification

In this stage, a learning algorithm is first devised and implemented. The algorithm is based on an agent based model which is a computational model for simulating the actions and interactions of an orchestra of autonomous agents in the determination of the possible segmentation points (SP_l) (Weiss, 1999; Wooldridge, 2002). Each agent will make its own decision, i.e., either true or false, for the insertion of "/" between the two characters. Moreover, associated with each decision, there is a vote that reflects the certainty of the decision. For each training corpus, we have trained more than 200 intelligent agents, each of which exhibits certain aspects of segmentation experience and language behaviors. In making the final verdict, the system will consult all the related agents by summing up their votes. For example, as shown in Table 1, the vote that supports there is a segmentation point between the characters 昨 and 日 is zero while 57.33 votes recommend that there should have no break point. All these votes are logged for the further post-processing.

C_1	C_2	*Vote(T)*	*Vote(F)*	*ND*	*Outcome*
昨	日	0	57.33	1.000	false
分	終	44.52	6.54	0.744	true
終	於	0	57.74	1.000	false
於	成	64.61	0	1.000	true
成	功	0	60.23	1.000	false
功	發	56.29	0.99	0.965	true
發	射	0.58	58.22	0.980	false
射	了	58.21	0	1.000	true
了	第	57.80	0	1.000	true
第	一	0	51.34	1.000	false
一	顆	48.70	0	1.000	true
顆	自	60.04	0	1.000	true
自	行	0	53.97	1.000	false
行	研	46.19	2.00	0.917	true
研	製	0	58.32	1.000	false
製	的	62.44	0	1.000	true
的	探	59.16	0	1.000	true
探	月	4.89	40.81	0.786	false
月	衛	45.83	3.41	0.862	true
衛	星	0	60.91	1.000	false
嫦	娥	0	59.39	1.000	false
娥	一	54.44	0.48	0.983	true
一	號	11.98	27.94	0.400	false

Table 1: Votes from agents and the ND of the corresponding segment point.

昨日/ 6 / 時/ 05 / 分/ 終於/ 成功/ 發射/ 了 / 第一/ 顆/ 自行/ 研製/ 的/ 探月/ 衛星/ 「/ 嫦娥/ 一號/ 」/ 。

Figure 3: Segmented sentence based on the votes from all agents.

2.3 Post-processing

In our experience, our system is most likely to generate over-segmented sentences. Several techniques have implemented in our post-processing to merge several tokens into ones. As shown in the previous steps, we have introduced two main types of segmentation points, SP_r and SP_l. In the type SP_r, segmentation points are pre-inserted between symbol and Chinese characters. For example, the token 6 時 will become 6/ 時 in the early beginning. Obviously, this kind of errors should be identified and the segmentation points should be removed. Similarly, in SP_l, segmentation points are decided by the votes. Our post-processing is to identify the weak segmentation points which are having tie-break votes. A normalized difference (*ND*) is defined for the certainty of the segmentation.

$$ND = \frac{\left|Vote_{true} - Vote_{false}\right|}{Vote_{true} + Vote_{false}} \qquad \text{Eqn.(1)}$$

The smaller the value of the *ND*, the lesser the certainty of the segmentation point. We define the segmentation point as weak if the value of *ND* is smaller than a threshold. For a weak segmentation point, the system will consult a dictionary and search for the presence of the token in the dictionary. The segmentation point will be removed if found. Otherwise, the system will leave as it is. As shown in the Table 1, almost all segmentation points with the ND value equal to 1. This shows that all the votes from the agents support the same decision. However, it seems that not all agents have the same decision to the last characters pair "一號", with *ND* equal to 0.4. If the threshold is set to be 0.4, the segmentation point will be re-examined in our post-processing.

Our dictionary is constructed by tokens from the training corpus and the local context of the text that is being segmented. That is to say, besides the corpus, the tokens from the previous segmented text will also contribute to the construction of the dictionary. On the other hand, Chinese idiom should be in one token as found in most dictionaries. However, idiom sometimes would be identified as a short phrase and segmented into several pieces. In this case, we tend to merge these small fragments into one long token. On the other hand, different training sources may produce different segmentation rules and, thus, produce different segmentation results. In the open tracks, some handlers are tailor-made for different testing data. These include handlers for English characters, date, time, organization.

昨日/ 6 時/ 05 分/ 終於/ 成功/ 發射/ 了/ 第一/ 顆/ 自行/ 研製/ 的/ 探月/ 衛星/ 「/ 嫦娥/ 一號/ 」/ 。

Figure 4: Final result of the segmentation

3 Experiments and Results

We have participated in five closed tracks and two open tracks in the bakeoff. While we have built a dictionary from each training data set for the closed tracks, a dictionary of more than 150,000 entries is maintained for the open tracks. Table 2 shows the size of the training data sets.

Source of training data	Size
Academia Sinica (CKIP)	721,551
City University of Hong Kong (CityU)	1,092,687
University of Colorado (CTB)	642,246
State Language Commission of P.R.C. (NCC)	917,255
Shanxi University (SXU)	528,238

Table 2: Size of the training data in the bakeoff.

Tables 3 and 4 show the recall (R), precision (P), F-score (F) and our ranking in the bakeoff. All the rankings are produced based on the best run of the participating teams in the tracks.

	R	*P*	*F*	*Rank*
CityU	0.9513	0.9430	0.9471	*2nd*
CKIP	0.9455	0.9371	0.9413	*3rd*
NCC	0.9365	0.9365	0.9365	*3rd*
SXU	0.9558	0.9552	0.9555	*5th*

Table 3: Performance of our system in the closed tracks of word segmentation task in the bakeoff.

	R	*P*	*F*	*Rank*
CKIP	0.9586	0.9541	0.9563	*1st*
NCC	0.9440	0.9517	0.9478	*4th*

Table 4: Performance of our system in the open tracks of word segmentation task in the bakeoff.

From the above tables, we have the following observations:

- First, our system is performing well if it is a sufficient large set of training data. This is evidenced by the results found in the training data from CKIP, CityU and NCC.
- Second, the dictionaries play an important role in our open tracks. While we have maintained a dictionary with 150,000 traditional Chinese words, no such a device is for our simplified characters corpora. Certainly, there is a room for our further improvement.

4 Conclusion

In this paper, we have presented the general overview of our segmentation system. Even though, it is our first time to participate the bakeoff, the approach is promising. Further exploration is needed to enhance the system.

Acknowledgement

The work described in this paper was partially supported by the grants from the Research Grants Council of the Hong Kong Special Administrative Region, China (Project Nos. CUHK4438/04H and CUHK4706/05H).

References

Weiss, G. (1999) *Multiagent Systems, A Modern Approach to Distributed Artificial Intelligence*, MIT Press.

Wooldridge, M. (2002). *An Introduction to MultiAgent Systems*, John Wiley.

Nanjing Normal University Segmenter for the Fourth SIGHAN Bakeoff

Xiaohe CHEN, Bin LI, Junzhi LU, Hongdong NIAN, Xuri TANG
Nanjing Normal University,
122, Ninghai Road, Nanjing, P. R. China, 210097
chenxiaohe5209@msn.com, gothere@126.com,
lujunzhi@gmail.com, nianhong-dong@hotmail.com,
tangxuriyz@hotmail.com

Abstract

This paper expounds a Chinese word segmentation system built for the Fourth SIGHAN Bakeoff. The system participates in six tracks, namely the CityU Closed, CKIP Closed, CTB Closed, CTB Open, SXU Closed and SXU Open tracks. The model of Conditional Random Field is used as a basic approach in the system, with attention focused on the construction of feature templates and Chinese character categorization. The system is also augmented with some post-processing approaches such as the Extended Word String, model integration and others. The system performs fairly well on the 5 tracks of the Bakeoff.

1 Introduction

The Nanjing Normal University (NJNU) team participated in CityU Closed, CKIP Closed, CTB Closed, CTB Open, SXU Closed, SXU Open tracks in the WS bakeoff. The system employed in the Bakeoff is based mainly on the model of CRF, optimized with some pre-processing and post-processing methods. The team has focused its attention on the construction of feature templates, Chinese character categorization, the use of Extended Word String and the integration of different segmentation models in the hope of achieving better performance in both IVs（In Vocabulary words） and OOVs (Out Of Vocabulary words). Due to time limitations, some of these methods are still not fully explored. However, the Bakeoff results show that the performance of the overall system is fairly satisfactory.

The paper is organized as follows: section 2 gives a brief description of the system; section 3 and 4 are devoted to the discussion of the results of closed test and open test; a conclusion is given to comment on the overall performance of the system.

2 System Description

Conditonal Ramdom Field (CRF) has been widely used by participants in the basic tasks of NLP since Peng(2004). In both SIGHAN 2005 and 2006 Bakeoffs CRF-based segmenters prove to have a better performance over other models. We have also chosen CRF as the basic model for the task of segmentation and uses the package CRF++ developed by Taku Kudo[1]. Some post-processing optimizations are also employed to improve the overall segmentation performance. The general description of the system is illustrated in Figure 1. The basic segmenter and post-processing are explained in the next two sections.

2.1 Basic Segmenter

As in many other segmentation models, our system also treats word segmentation as a task of classification problem. During the experiment of the model, two aspects are taken into consideration, namely tag set and feature template. The 6-tag (Table 1) set proposed in Zhao(2006) is employed to mark various character position status in a Chinese word. The feature template (Table 2) consid-

[1] Package CRF++, version 0.49, available at http://crfpp.sourceforge.net.

ers three templates of character features and three templates of character type features. The introduction of character type (Table 3) is based on the observation that many segmentation errors are caused by different segmentation standards among different corpora, especially between Traditional Chinese corpora and Simplified Chinese Corpora.

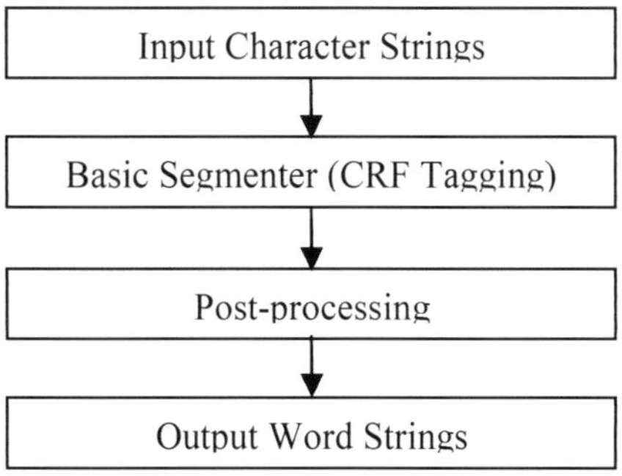

Figure 1: Flow Chat

Status	Tag
begin	B
2nd	B2
3rd	B3
middle	M
end	E
single	S

Table 1:6-tag Set

Type	Feature	Function
Char Unigram	C_n, n=-2, -1, 0, 1, 2	Character in position n to the current character
Char Bigram	C_nC_{n+1}, n=-1,0	Previous(next) character and current character
Char Jump	C_{-1} C_1	Previous character and next character
CharType Unigram	T_n, n=-1, 0, 1	Type of previous (current, next) character
CharType Bigram	T_nT_{n+1}, n=-1,0	Type of previous character and next character
CharType Jump	T_{-1} T_1	Type of previous character and next character

Table 2: Feature Templates in Close Test

Character Type	Example
Chinese Character	我 人
Serial Number	1.⑴ ①㈠
Roman Number	Ⅰ Ⅱ ⅷ
Aribic Number	12１２
Chinese Number	零〇百壹
Ganzhi	甲乙子丑
Foreign Character	A Δ は
National Pronunciation Letters	ㄅㄉ ˇ
Sentence Punctuation	；！。？
Hard Punctuation	\t\r\n
Punctuation	：…‥_¨"
Dun	、 、
Dot1	‥
Dot2	.·
Di	第
At	@
Other Character	⊙∽

Table 3:Character Type

2.2 Post-Processing

Two methods are used in post-processing to optimize the results obtained from basic segmenter. The first is the binding of digits and English Characters. The second is the use of extended word string to solve segmentation ambiguity.

2.2.1 Binding Digits and Roman Letters

Digits (ranging from "0" to "9") are always bound as a word in Chinese corpora, while roman letters are treated differently in different corpora, some adding a full-length blank between the letters, some not. The system employs rule-based approach to bind both digits and roman letters. We also submitted two segmentation results for the Bakeoff, please refer to section 3.2 for discussion of these results.

2.2.2 Extended Word String (EWS) Approach

The CRF model performs well in segmenting IV word strings in general, but not in all contexts. Our system thus uses a memory based method, which is named as Extended Word String approach, to prevent CRF from making such error. All the Chinese word strings, which are of character length from 2 to 10 and appear more than two times, are stored in a hash table, together with information of their segmentation forms. An example of EWS is given in Table 5. If the same character string appears in the test data, the system can easily re-segment them by querying the hash table. If the query finds that the character string has only one segmentation form and checking shows that the string has no overlapping ambiguity with its left or right word, the segmentation of the string is then modified according to the stored segmentation type. Our experiment shows that the approach can promote the F-measure by 0.2% to 1% on different tracks.

EWS	Seg Form	Freq
就我们	/就/我们/	4

Table 5: Example of EWS

3 Evaluation Results on Closed Test

3.1 CKIP Closed Test

In CKIP Closed Test, another kind of post processing is used for OOVs. Examination on the output from basic segmenter shows that some OOVs identified by CRFs are not OOV errors, but IV errors. Sometimes it can not always segment the same OOV correctly in different context. For example, the person name "陳子江" appears three times in the test, but it is only correctly detected twice, and for once it is wrongly detected. Our approach is to re-segment the OOVs string (with its left and right word) twice. Firstly the string is segmented using the training data wordlist, followed by a second segmentation using the OOV wordlist recognized by the Basic Segmenter. The result with the minimum number of words is accepted.

```
Example:
Basic Seg Output: /的/陳子/江本/
OOV Adjusting:    /的/陳子江/本/
Basic Seg Output: /血永/不融/和/
OOV Adjusting:    /血/永不/融和/
```

With the OOV Adjusting Approach mentioned above, we got the third place in the track (Table 6). But when we use it on other corpora, the method does not promote the performance. Rather, it lowers the performance score. The reason is still not clear.

System（rank）	F	F_{oov}	F_{iv}
Best(1/21)	0.9510	0.7698	0.9667
Njnu(3/21)	0.9454	0.7475	0.9637

Table 6: CityU Closed Test

3.2 CKIP and CTB Closed Test

In CKIP Closed Test, only the basic segmenter introduced in section 2 is used. Two segmentation results, namely ***a*** and ***b*** (Table 7 and 8) are submitted for the Bakeoff. Result ***a*** binds the roman letters as a word, while result ***b*** does not. The scores of the two results show that the approach is not stable in terms of score. We suggest that corpora submitted for evaluation purposes should pay more attention to non-Chinese word tagging and comply with the request of Bakeoff organizers.

System（rank）	F	F_{oov}	F_{iv}
Best(1/19)	0.9470	0.7524	0.9623
Njnu a(6/19)	0.9378	0.6948	0.9580
Njnu b(9/19)	0.9204	0.6341	0.9452

Table 7: CKIP Closed Test

System（rank）	F	F_{oov}	F_{iv}
Best(1/26)	0.9589	0.7745	0.9697
Njnu a(9/26)	0.9498	0.7152	0.9645
Njnu b(7/26)	0.9499	0.7142	0.9647

Table 8: CTB Closed Test

3.3 SXU Closed Test

Four results (***a***, ***b***, ***c*** and ***d***) are submitted for this track (Table 9). Results ***a*** and ***b*** are dealt in the same way as described in section 3.2. Result ***c*** is obtained by incorporating results from a memory-based segmenter. The memory-based segmenter is mainly based on memory-based learning proposed by Daelemans(2005). We tested it on the training data with 90% as training data and 10% as testing data. The result shows that performance is improved. However, when the method is applied on the Bakeoff test data, the performance is lowered. The reason is not identified yet.

Result ***d*** was based on result ***c***. It incorporates OOV words recognized by the system introduced in (Li & Chen, 2007) in the post-processing stage. Based on suffix arrays, Chinese character strings with mutual information value above 8.0 are automatically extracted as words without any manual operation. We can see from table 9 that the F-measure of result ***d*** improved and F_{oov} of ***d*** got 2rd place in the test. And it is likely to get higher score if we combine it with result ***a***.

System（rank）	F	F_{oov}	F_{iv}
Best(1/29)	0.9623	0.7292	0.9752
Njnu a(9/29)	0.9539	0.6789	0.9702
Njnu b(10/29)	0.9538	0.6778	0.9701
Njnu c(15/29)	0.9526	0.6793	0.9688
Njnu d(14/29)	0.9532	0.6817	0.9694

Table 9: Sxu Closed Test

4 Evaluation Results on Open Test

4.1 Methods

More features and resources are used in open test, mainly applied in the modification of feature templates. Besides the features used in the close test, we add to feature templates more information about Chinese characters, such as the Chinese radicals ("扌口"), tones (5 tones), and another 6 Boolean values for each Chinese character. The 6 Boolean values indicate respectively whether the character is of Chinese surnames ("张王"), or of Chinese names ("琴林"), or of characters used for western person name translation ("尼克"), or of character used for English location name translation("纽约"), or of affixes ("老-","-者"), or of single character words ("了他"). The feature templates constructed in this way is given in Table 10.

Type	Feature	Function
Char Unigram	C_n, n=-1,0,1	The prevoius (current, next) character
Char Bigram	$C_n C_{n+1}$, n=-1,0	The previous(next) character and current character
Char Jump	$C_{-1} C_1$	The previous character and next character
CharType Unigram	T_0	The type of the current, next character
CharType Trigram	$T_{-1} T_0 T_1$	The type of the previous, current and next character
Char Information Unigram	T_0^n, n=1,…,6	The 6 information of the current, next character
Char Information Trigram	$T_{-1}^n T_0^n T_1^n$, n=1,…,6	The 6 information of the previous, current and next character

Table10: Feature Templates for Open Test

In the post-processing stage, we also add a Chinese idiom dictionary (about 27000 items) to help increase the OOV word recall.

4.2 Results

In SXU open test, we submitted 3 results (***a***, ***b*** and ***c***), but only ***a*** achieves the 4th rank in F-measure (Table 11). Features and resources added to the system turns out not to be of much use in the task, compared with our score on the closed test.

Result ***b***, ***c*** and all the results in CTB open test submitted have errors due to our pre-processing stage with CRF. Thus, the scores of them are very low, and some are even lower than our scores in closed test (see table 12).

System（rank）	F	F_{oov}	F_{iv}
Best(1/9)	0.9735	0.8109	0.9820
Njnu a(4/12)	0.9559	0.6925	0.9714

Table 11: SXU Open Test

System（rank）	F	F_{oov}	F_{iv}
Best(1/12)	0.9920	0.9654	0.9936
Njnu a(9/12)	0.9346	0.6341	0.9528

Table 12: CTB Open Test

5 Conclusions and Future Work

This is the first time that the NJNU team takes part in SIGHAN WS Bakeoff. In the construction of the system, we conducted experiments on the CRF-based segmenter with different feature templates. We also employs different post-processing approaches, including Extended Word String approach, digit and western roman letter combination, and OOV detection. An initial attempt is also made on the integration of different segmentation models. Time constraint has prevented the team from fuller exploration of the methods used in the system. Future efforts will be directed towards more complicated segmentation models, the examination of the function of different features in the task, the integration of different models, and more efficient utility of other relevant resources.

References

Bin Li, Xiaohe Chen. 2007. A Human-Computer Interaction Word Segmentation Method Adapting to Chinese Unknown Texts, *Journal of Chinese Information Processing*, 21(3):92-98.

Daelemans, W. and Van den Bosch. 2005. *Memory-Based Language Processing*. Cambridge University Press, Cambridge, UK.

Fuchun Peng, et al. 2004. Chinese Segmentation and New Word Detection Using Conditional Random Fields, *COLING2004*, 562-568, 23-27 August, Geneva, Switzerland.

Gina-Anne Levow. 2006. The Third International Chinese Language Processing Bakeoff: Word Segmentation and Named Entity Recognition, *Proceedings of the Fifth SIGHAN Workshop on Chinese Language Processing*, 108-117, 22-23 July, Sydney, Australia.

Hai Zhao, et al. 2006. An Improved Chinese Word Segmentation System with Conditional Random Field, *Proceedings of the Fifth SIGHAN Workshop on Chinese Language Processing,* 162-165, 22-23 July, Sydney, Australia.

Richard Sproat and Thomas Emerson. 2003. The First International Chinese Word Segmentation Bakeoff, *The Second SIGHAN Workshop on Chinese Language Procesing*, 133-143, Aspporo, Japan.

Thomas Emerson. 2005. The Second International Chinese Word Segmentation Bakeoff, *Proceedings of the Fourth SIGHAN Workshop on Chinese Language Processing*, 123-133, Jeju Island, Korea.

Two Step Chinese Named Entity Recognition Based on Conditional Random Fields Models

Yuanyong Feng* **Ruihong Huang*** **Le Sun†**

*Institute of Software, Graduate University
Chinese Academy of Sciences
Beijing, China, 100080
{comerfeng,ruihong2}@iscas.cn

†Institute of Software
Chinese Academy of Sciences
Beijing, China, 100080
sunle@iscas.cn

Abstract

This paper mainly describes a Chinese named entity recognition (NER) system NER@ISCAS, which integrates text, part-of-speech and a small-vocabulary-character-lists feature and heristic post-process rules for MSRA NER open track under the framework of Conditional Random Fields (CRFs) model.

1 Introduction

The system NER@ISCAS is designed under the Conditional Random Fields (CRFs. Lafferty et al., 2001) framework. It integrates multiple features based on single Chinese character or space separated ASCII words. The early designed system (Feng et al., 2006) is used for the MSRA NER open track this year. The output of an external part-of-speech tagging tool and some carefully collected small-scale-character-lists are used as open knowledge. Some post process steps are also applied to complement the local limitation in model's feature engineering.

The remaining of this paper is organized as follows. Section 2 introduces Conditional Random Fields model. Section 3 presents the details of our system on Chinese NER integrating multiple features. Section 4 describes the post-processings based on some heuristic rules. Section 5 gives the evaluation results. We end our paper with some conclusions and future works.

2 Conditional Random Fields Model

Conditional random fields are undirected graphical models for calculating the conditional probability for output vertices based on input ones. While sharing the same exponential form with maximum entropy models, they have more efficient procedures for complete, non-greedy finite-state inference and training.

Given an observation sequence o=<o_1, o_2, ..., o_T>, linear-chain CRFs model based on the assumption of first order Markov chains defines the corresponding state sequence s' probability as follows (Lafferty et al., 2001):

$$p_\Lambda(\mathbf{s}\mid\mathbf{o}) = \frac{1}{Z_\mathbf{o}}\exp(\sum_{t=1}^{T}\sum_{k}\lambda_k f_k(s_{t-1}, s_t, \mathbf{o}, t)) \quad (1)$$

Where Λ is the model parameter set, Z_o is the normalization factor over all state sequences, f_k is an arbitrary feature function, and λ_k is the learned feature weight. A feature function defines its value to be 0 in most cases, and to be 1 in some designated cases. For example, the value of a feature named "MAYBE-SURNAME" is 1 if and only if s_{t-1} is OTHER, s_t is PER, and the t-th character in $\boldsymbol{o}$ is a common-surname.

The inference and training procedures of CRFs can be derived directly from those equivalences in HMM. For instance, the forward variable $\alpha_t(s_i)$ defines the probability that state at time t being s_i at time t given the observation sequence $\boldsymbol{o}$. Assumed that we know the probabilities of each possible value s_i for the beginning state $\alpha_0(s_i)$, then we have

$$\alpha_{t+1}(s_i) = \sum_{s'}\alpha_t(s')\exp(\sum_{k}\lambda_k f_k(s', s_i, \mathbf{o}, t) \quad (2)$$

In similar ways, we can obtain the backward variables and Baum-Welch algorithm.

3 Chinese NER Using CRFs Model Integrating Multiple Features

Besides the text feature(TXT), simplified part-of-speech (POS) feature, and small-vocabulary-character-lists (SVCL) feature, which use in the early system (Feng et al., 2006), some new features such as word boundary, adjoining state bigram – observation and early NE output are also combined under the unified CRFs framework.

The text feature includes single Chinese character, some continuous digits or letters.

POS feature is an important feature which carries some syntactic information. Unlike those in the earyly system, the POS tag set are merged into 9 categories from the criterion of modern Chinese corpora construction (Yu, 1999), which contains 39 tags.

The third type of features are derived from the small-vocabulary-character lists which are essentially same as the ones used in last year except with some additional items. Some examples of this list are given in Table 1.

Value	Description	Examples
digit	Arabic digit(s)	1,2,3
letter	Letter(s)	A,B,C,...,a, b, c
Continuous digits and/or letters (The sequence is regarded as a single token)		
chseq	Chinese order 1	㈠, ⑴, ①, Ⅰ
chdigit	Chinese digit	1 , 壹, 一
tianseq	Chinese order 2	甲, 乙, 丙, 丁
chsurn	Surname	李, 吴, 郑, 王
notname	Not name	将, 对, 那, 的, 是, 说
loctch	LOC tail character	区, 国, 岛, 海, 台, 庄, 冲
orgtch	ORG tail character	府, 团, 校, 协, 局, 办, 军
other	Other case	情, 规, 息, ！，。

Table 1. Some Examples of SVCL Feature

The fourth type of feature is word boundary. We use the B, I, E, U, and O to indicate Begining, Inner, Ending, and Uniq part of, or outside of a word given a word segmentation. The O case occurs when a token, for example the charactor "&", is ignored by the segmentator. We do not combine the boundary information with other features because we argue it is very limited and may cause errors.

The last type of features is bigram state combined with observations. We argue that observatoin (mainly is of named entity derived by early system or character text itself) and state transition are not conditionally independent and entails dedicate considerings.

Each token is presented by its feature vector, which is combined by these features we just discussed. Once all token feature (Maybe including context features) values are determined, an observation sequence is feed into the model.

Each token state is a combination of the type of the named entity it belongs to and the boundary type it locates within. The entity types are person name (PER), location name (LOC), organization name (ORG), date expression (DAT), time expression (TIM), numeric expression (NUM), and not named entity (OTH). The boundary types are simply Beginning, Inside, and Outside (BIO).

All above types of features are extracted from a varying length window. The main criteria is that wider window with smaller feature space and narrow window when the observation features are in a large range.

The main feature set is shown the following.

Character Texts(TXT): TXT_{-2}, TXT_{-1}, TXT_0, TXT_1, TXT_2, $TXT_{-1}TXT_0$, TXT_1TXT_0, TXT_1TXT_2
simplified part-of-speech (POS): unigram: $POS_{-4} \sim POS_4$

small-vocabulary-character-lists (SVCL): unigram: $SVCL_{-2} \sim SVCL_7$ bigram: $SVCL_0SVCL_1$, $SVCL_1SVCL_2$
Word Boundary (WB): WB_{-1}, WB_0, WB_1
Named Entity (NE): unigram: $NE_{-4} \sim NE_4$ bigram: $NE_{-2}NE_{-1}$, $NE_{-1}NE_0$, NE_0NE_1, NE_1NE_2
State Bigram (B) – Observation: B, B-TXT_0, B-NE_{-1}, B-NE_0, B-NE_1

Table 2. The Main Feature Set

4 Post Processing on Heuristic Rules

Observing from the evaluation, our model has worse performance on ORG and PER than LOC. Furthermore, the analysis of the errors tells us that they are hard to be tackled with the improvement of the model itself. Therefore, we decided to do some post-process to correct certain types of tagging errors of the unified model mainly concerning the two kinds of entities, ORG and PER.

At the training phrase, we compare the tagging output of the model with the correct tags and collect the falsely tagged instances. To identify the rules used in the post-process, we categorize the errors into several types, discriminate the types and encode them into the rules according to two principles:

1) the rules are applied on the tagged sequences output by the unified model.
2) The rules applied shouldn't introduce more other errors.

As a result, we have extracted eight rules, seven for ORG, one for PER. Generally, the rules work only on the local context of the examined tags, they correct some type of error by changing some tags when seeing certain pattern of context before or after the current tags in a limited distance. We want to give one rule as one example to explain the way they function.

Example: {<LOC>}+<ORG> ==> <ORG>,

After this rule is applied, one or more locations followed by a organization name will be tagged ORG. This is the case where there are a location name in a organization name. Besides, we can see since the location and latter part of the organization name are tagged separately in the unified model, we may only resort to the post-process to get the right government boundary.

5 Evaluation

5.1 Results

The evaluations in training phrase tell us the post-process can improve the performance by one percent. We are satisfied since we just applied eight rules.

The formal eveluation results of our system are shown in Table 3.

	R	P	F
Overall	86.74	90.03	88.36
PER	90.83	92.16	91.49
LOC	89.89	91.66	90.77
ORG	77.99	85.16	81.41

Table 3. Formal Results on MSRA NER Open

5.2 Errors from NER Track

The NER errors in our system are mainly of as follows:

- Abbreviations

Abbreviations are very common among the errors. Among them, a significant part of abbreviations are mentioned before their corresponding full names. Some common abbreviations has no corresponding full names appeared in document. Here are some examples:

R[1]: 总后[嫩江基地 LOC]的先进事迹

K: [总后嫩江基地 LOC]的先进事迹

R: [中 丹 LOC]兩國

K: [中 LOC][丹 LOC]兩國

In current system, the recognition is fully depended on the linear-chain CRFs model, which is heavily based on local window observation features; no abbreviation list or special abbreviation

[1] R stands for system response, K for key.

recognition involved. Because lack of constraint checking on distant entity mentions, the system fails to catch the interaction among similar text fragments cross sentences.

- Concatenated Names

For many reasons, Chinese names in titles and some sentences, especially in news, are not separated. The system often fails to judge the right boundaries and the reasonable type classification. For example:

R:将[瓦西里斯 LOC]与[奥纳西斯 PER]比较

K:将[瓦西里斯 PER]与[奥纳西斯 PER]比较

- Hints

Though it helps to recognize an entity at most cases, the small-vocabulary-list hint feature may recommend a wrong decision sometimes. For instance, common surname character "王" in the following sentence is wrongly labeled when no word segmentation information given:

R:[希腊 LOC]船[王 康斯坦塔科普洛斯 PER]

K:[希腊 LOC]船 王[康斯坦塔科普洛斯 PER]

Other errors of this type may result from failing to identify verbs and prepositions, such as:

R:全国保护明天行动组委会 举行表彰会

K:[全国保护明天行动组委会 ORG]举行表彰会

6 Conclusions and Future Work

We mainly described a Chinese named entity recognition system NER@ISCAS, which integrates text, part-of-speech and a small-vocabulary-character-lists feature for MSRA NER open track under the framework of Conditional Random Fields (CRFs) model. Although it provides a unified framework to integrate multiple flexible features, and to achieve global optimization on input text sequence, the popular linear chained Conditional Random Fields model often fails to catch semantic relations among reoccurred mentions and adjoining entities in a catenation structure.

The situations containing exact reoccurrence and shortened occurrence enlighten us to take more effort on feature engineering or post processing on abbreviations / recurrence recognition.

Another effort may be poured on the common patterns, such as paraphrase, counting, and constraints on Chinese person name lengths.

From current point of view, enriching the hint lists is also desirable.

Acknowledgements

This work is partially supported by National Natural Science Foundation of China under grant #60773027, #60736044 and by "863" Key Projects #2006AA010108.

References

Chinese 863 program. 2005. Results on Named Entity Recognition. *The 2004HTRDP Chinese Information Processing and Intelligent Human-Machine Interface Technology Evaluation.*

Yuanyong Feng, Le Sun, Yuanhua Lv. 2006. Chinese Word Segmentation and Named Entity Recognition Based on Conditional Random Fields Models. *Proceedings of SIGHAN-2006, Fifth SIGHAN Workshop on Chinese Language Processing,* Sydney, Australia,.

John Lafferty, Andrew McCallum, and Fernando Pereira. 2001. Conditional Random Fields: Probabilistic Models for Segmenting and Labeling Sequence Data. *ICML.*

Shiwen Yu. 1999. Manual on Modern Chinese Corpora Construction. Institute of Computational Language, Peking Unversity. Beijing.

A Morpheme-based Part-of-Speech Tagger for Chinese

Guohong Fu
School of Computer Science and Technology
Heilongjiang University
Harbin 150080, P.R. China
ghfu@hotmail.com

Jonathan J. Webster
Department of Chinese, Translation and Linguistics
City University of Hong Kong
83 Tat Chee Avenue, Hong Kong, P.R. China
ctjjw@cityu.edu.hk

Abstract

This paper presents a morpheme-based part-of-speech tagger for Chinese. It consists of two main components, namely a morpheme segmenter to segment each word in a sentence into a sequence of morphemes, based on forward maximum matching, and a lexical tagger to label each morpheme with a proper tag indicating its position pattern in forming a word of a specific class, based on lexicalized hidden Markov models. This system have participated four closed tracks for POS tagging at the Fourth International Chinese Language Processing Bakeoff sponsored by the ACL-SIGHAN.

1 Introduction

Part-of-speech (POS) tagging aims to assign each word in a sentence with a proper tag indicating its POS category. While a number of successful POS tagging systems have been available for English and many other languages, it is still a challenge to develop a practical POS tagger for Chinese due to its language-specific issues. Firstly, Chinese words do not have a strict one-to-one correspondence between their POS categories and functions in a sentence. Secondly, an ambiguous Chinese word can act as different POS categories in different contexts without changing its form. Thirdly, there are many out-of-vocabulary (OOV) words in real Chinese text whose POS categories are not defined in the dictionary used. All these factors make it much more difficult to achieve a high-performance POS tagger for Chinese.

Recent studies in Chinese POS tagging focus on statistical or machine learning approaches with either characters or words as basic units for tagging (Ng and Low, 2004; Fu and Luke, 2006). Very little research has been devoted to resolving Chinese POS tagging problems based on morphemes. In our system, we prefer morphemes to characters or words as tagging units for three reasons. First, words are made of morphemes instead of characters (Wu and Tseng, 1995; Packard, 2000). Second, most morphemes are productive in word formation (Baayen, 1989; Sproat and Shih, 2002; Nishimoto, 2003), particularly in the formation of morphologically-derived words (MDWs) and proper nouns, which are the major source of OOV words in Chinese texts. Third, Packard (2000) indicates that Chinese do have morphology. Moreover, morphology proves to be a very informative cue for predicting POS categories of Chinese OOV words (Tseng *et al*, 2005). Therefore, we believe that a morpheme-based framework would be more effective than the character- or word-based ones in capturing both word-internal morphological features and word-external contextual information for Chinese POS disambiguation and unknown word guessing (UWG) as well.

Thus we present a morpheme-based POS tagger for Chinese in this paper. It consists of two main components, namely a morpheme segmentation component for segmenting each word in a sentence into a sequence of morphemes, based on the forward maximum matching (FMM) technique, and a lexical tagging component for labeling each segmented morpheme with a proper tag indicating its position pattern in forming a word of a specific type, based on lexicalized hidden Markov models (HMMs). Lack of a large morphological knowledge base is a major obstacle to Chinese morphological analysis (Tseng and Chen, 2002). To overcome this problem and to facilitate morpheme-based POS tagging as well, we have also developed a statistically-based technique for automatically extracting morphemes from POS-tagged corpora. We participated in four closed tracks for POS tagging at the Fourth International Chinese Language Processing Bakeoff sponsored by the ACL-SIGHAN and tested our system on different testing corpora. In this paper, we also made a summary of this work and give some brief analysis on the results.

The rest of this paper is organized as follows: Section 2 is a brief description of our system. Section 3 details the settings of our system for different testing tracks and presents the scored results of our system at this bakeoff. Finally, we give our conclusions in Section 4.

2 System Description

2.1 Chinese Morphemes

In brief, Chinese morphemes can be classified into free morphemes and bound morphemes. A free morpheme can stand by itself as a word (viz. a basic word), whereas a bound morpheme can show up if and only if being attached to other morphemes to form a word. Free morphemes can be subdivided into true free morphemes and pseudo free morphemes. A pseudo free morpheme such as 然而 ran2-er2 'however' can only stand alone, while a true free morpheme like 生产 SHENG-CHAN 'produce' can stand alone by itself as a word or occur as parts of other words. Chinese affixes include prefixes (e.g. 非 fei1 'non-', 伪 wei3 'pseudo'), infixes (e.g. 分之 fei1-zhi1) or suffixes (e.g. 性 xing4 '-ity', 主义 zhu3-yi4 '-ism'), in terms of their positions within a word.

2.2 Formulation

To perform morpheme-based Chinese POS tagging, we represent a POS-tagged word in a Chinese sentence as a sequence of lexical chunks with the aid of an extended IOB2 tag set (Fu and Luke 2005). A lexical chunk consists of a sequence of constituent morphemes associated with their corresponding lexical chunk tags. A lexical chunk tag follows the format T1-T2, indicating the POS category *T2* of a word and the position pattern *T1* of a constituent morpheme within the word. As shown in Table 1, four position patterns are involved in our system, namely *O* for a single morpheme as a word by itself, *I* for a morpheme inside a word, *B* for a morpheme at the beginning of a word and *E* for a morpheme at the end of a word.

Tag	Definition	Corresponding morpheme types
O	A morpheme as a word by itself	Free morphemes
I	A morpheme inside a word	Free morphemes and infixes
B	A word-initial morpheme	Free morphemes and prefixes
E	A word-final morpheme	Free morphemes and suffixes

Table 1. Extended IOB2 tag set

2.3 Affix Extraction

Due to the increasing involvement of affixation in Chinese word formation, affixes play a more and more important role in Chinese POS tagging. In morpheme extraction, affixes are very useful in determining whether a given word is derived by affixation. To extract affixes from corpora, we consider three statistics, i.e. morpheme-position frequency $Count(m,T1)$, morpheme-position probability $MPP(m,T1) = Count(m,T1)/Count(m)$ and morphological productivity. Following the proposal in (Baayen, 1989), the morphological productivity of a morpheme m with a position pattern $T1$, denoted as $MP(m,T1)$, can be defined as

$$MP(m,T1) = \frac{n1(m,T1)}{Count(m,T1)} \quad (1)$$

where $n1(m,T1)$ is the number of word types that occur only once in the training corpus and at the same time, are formed by the morpheme m with the position pattern $T1$.

To estimate the above statistics for affix extraction, we only take into account the three position patterns B, I and E, for prefixes, infixes and suffixes, respectively. Thus we can extract affixes from training data with the following three conditions: $Count(m,T1) \geq TH_{MPF}$, $MPP(m,T1) \geq TH_{MPP}$ and $MP(m,T1) \geq TH_{MP}$, where TH_{MPF}, TH_{MPP} and TH_{MP} are three empirically-determined thresholds.

2.4 Morpheme Extraction

The goal of morpheme extraction is to identify MDWs and proper nouns in training corpora and prevent them from getting into the morpheme dictionary for POS tagging. In the present system, the following criteria are applied to determine whether a word in training data should enter the morpheme dictionary.

Completeness. With a view to the completeness of the morpheme dictionary, all characters in training data will be collected as morphemes.

Word length. In general, shorter morphemes are more productive than longer ones in word formation. As such, the length of a morpheme should not exceed four characters.

Word frequency. By this criterion, a word is selected as a morpheme if its frequency of occurrences in training data is higher than a given threshold.

MDWs. By this criterion, words formed by morphological patterns such as affixation, compounding, reduplication and abbreviation will be excluded from the morpheme dictionary.

Proper nouns. In some training corpora like the PKU corpus, some special tags are specified for proper nouns. In this case, they will be used to filter proper nouns during morpheme extraction.

2.5 Lexicalized HMM Tagger

As shown in Figure 1, our system works in three main steps as follows.

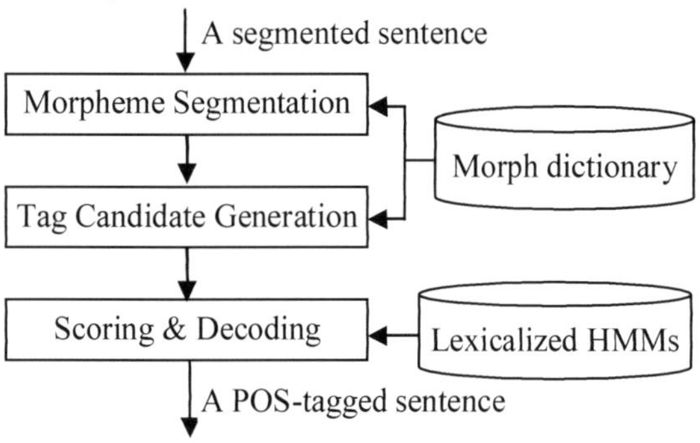

Figure 1. Overall architecture of our system

Morpheme segmentation. In this step, the FMM technique is employed to segment each word in a sentence to a sequence of morphemes associated with their position tags within the word.

Tag candidate generation. In this step, all possible POS candidates are generated for each word in the sentence by consulting the morpheme dictionary with its constitute morphemes and their related position patterns. All these candidates are stored in a lattice.

Scoring and Decoding. In this step, the lexicalized HMMs are first employed to score each candidate in the lattice and the Viterbi decoding algorithm is further used to search an optimal sequence of POS tags for the sentence. The details of lexicalized HMMs can be seen in (Lee *et al*, 200) and (Fu and Luke, 2005).

3 Evaluation Results

3.1 System Settings for Different Tracks

The POS tagging task at the fourth ACL-SIGHAN bakeoff consists of five closed tracks. We participated four of them, namely CKIP, CTB, NCC and PKU. Therefore our system is trained only using the relevant training corpora provided for the bakeoff. Furthermore, the morpheme dictionaries for these tracks are also extracted automatically from the relevant training data with the method presented in Sections 2.3 and 2.4. Table 2 illustrated the number of morphemes extracted from different training data.

Source	Training data (tokens/word types)	Number of morphemes
CKIP	721551 / 48045	30757
CTB	642246 / 42133	26330
NCC	535023 / 45108	28432
PKU	1116754 / 55178	30085

Table 2. Number of morphemes extracted from the training data for SIGHAN POS tagging bakeoff

3.2 Evaluation Results

Track	Total-A	IV-R	OOV-R	MT-R
CKIP-O	0.9124	0.9549	0.4756	0.8953
CTB-O	0.9234	0.9507	0.52	0.9051
NCC-O	0.9395	0.969	0.4086	0.9059
PKU-C	0.9266	0.9574	0.4386	0.9079

Table 3. Scores of our system for different tracks

Table 3 presents the scores of our system for different tracks. It should be noted that four measures are employed in the 4th ACL-SIGHAN bakeoff to score the performance of a POS tagging system, namely the overall accuracy (Total-A) and the recall with respect to in-vocabulary words (IV-R), OOV words (OOV-R) or multi-POS words (MT-R).

Although our system has achieved a promising performance, there is still much to be done to improve it. First, the quality of the morpheme dictionary is of particular importance to morpheme-based POS tagger. Although the present study proposed a statistical technique to extract morphemes from tagged corpora, further exploration is still needed on the optimization of this technique to acquire a more desirable morpheme dictionary for Chinese POS tagging. Second, morphological patterns prove to be informative cues for Chinese POS disambiguation and OOV word prediction. However, such a knowledge base is not publicly available for Chinese. As such, in the present study we only made use of certain surface morphological features, namely the position patterns of morphemes in word formation. Future research might usefully extend the present method to explore systematically more precise morphological features, including morpheme POS categories and morpho-syntactic rules for Chinese POS tagging.

4 Conclusion

In this paper we have presented a morpheme-based POS tagger for Chinese. We participated in four closed tracks at the fourth SIGHAN bakeoff. The scored results show that our system can achieve an overall accuracy of 0.9124-0.9395 for different corpora. However, the present system is still under development, especially in morphological knowledge acquisition. For future work, we hope to improve our system with a higher quality morpheme dictionary and more deep morphological knowledge such as morpheme POS categories and morpho-syntactic rules.

Acknowledgments

This study was supported in part by CityU Strategic Research Grant for fundable CERG (No. 7001879 & 7002037).

References

E. Nishimoto. 2003. Measuring and comparing the productivity of Mandarin Chinese suffixes. Computational Linguistics and Chinese Language Processing, 8(1): 49-76.

G. Fu and K.-K. Luke. 2005. Chinese named entity recognition using lexicalized HMMs. ACM SIGKDD Explorations Newsletter, 7(1): 19-25.

G. Fu and K.-K. Luke. 2006. Chinese POS disambiguation and unknown word guessing with lexicalized HMMs. International Journal of Technology and Human Interaction, 2(1): 39-50.

H. Tseng and K.-J. Chen. 2002. Design of Chinese morphological analyzer. In: Proceedings of the 1st SIGHAN Workshop on Chinese Language Processing, 1-7.

H. Tseng, D. Jurafsky, and C. Manning. 2005. Morphological features help POS tagging of unknown words across language varieties. In: Proceedings of the Fourth SIGHAN Workshop on Chinese Language Processing.

H.T. Ng and J.K. Low. 2004. Chinese part-of-speech tagging: One-at-a-time or all-at-once? Word-based or character-based?. In: Proceedings of the 2004 Conference on Empirical Methods in Natural Language Processing (EMNLP 2004), Barcelona, Spain, 277-284.

J. Packard. 2000. Morphology of Chinese: A linguistic and cognitive approach. Cambridge University Press, Cambridge, UK.

R. Sproat and C. Shih. 2002. Corpus-based methods in Chinese morphology. In: Proceedings of the 19th International Conference on Computational Linguistics (COLING 2002), Taipei, Taiwan.

R.H. Baayen. 1989. A corpus-based study of morphological productivity: Statistical analysis and psychological interpretation. Ph.D. thesis, Free University, Amsterdam.

S.-Z. Lee, T.-J. Tsujii, and H.-C. Rim. 2000. Lexicalized hidden Markov models for part-of-speech tagging. In: Proceedings of the 18th International Conference on Computational Linguistics (COLING 2000), Saarbruken, Germany, 481-487.

Z. Wu, G. Tseng. 1995. ACTS: An automatic Chinese text segmentation systems for full text retrieval. Journal of the American Society for Information Science, 46(2): 83-96.

Chinese Named Entity Recognition and Word Segmentation Based on Character

He Jingzhou, Wang Houfeng
Institution of Computational Linguistics
School of Electronics Engineering and Computer Science,
Peking University, China, 100871
{hejingzhou, wanghf}@pku.edu.cn

Abstract

Chinese word segmentation and named entity recognition (NER) are both important tasks in Chinese information processing. This paper presents a character-based Conditional Random Fields (CRFs) model for such two tasks. In The SIGHAN Bakeoff 2007, this model participated in all closed tracks for both Chinese NER and word segmentation tasks, and turns out to perform well. Our system ranks 2nd in the closed track on NER of MSRA, and 4th in the closed track on word segmentation of SXU.

1 Introduction

Chinese word segmentation and NER are two of the most fundamental problems in Chinese information processing and have attracted more and more attentions. Many methods have been presented, of which, machine learning methods have obviously competitive advantage in such problems. Maximum Entropy (Ng and Low, 2005) and CRFs (Hai Zhao et al. 2006, Zhou Junsheng et al. 2006) come to good performance in the former SIGHAN Bakeoff.

We consider both tasks as sequence labeling problem, and a character-based Conditional Random Fields (CRFs) model is applied in this Bakeoff. Our system used CRF++ package Version 0.49 implemented by Taku Kudo from sourceforge[1].

2 System Description

The system is mainly based on CRFs, while different strategies are introduced in word segmentation task and NER task.

2.1 CRFs

CRFs are undirected graphical models which are particularly well suited to sequence labeling tasks, such as NER & word segmentation. In these cases, CRFs are often referred to as linear chain CRFs.

CRFs are criminative models, which allow a richer feature representation and provide more natural modeling.

[1] http://www.sourceforge.net/

CRFs define the conditional probability of a state sequence given an input sequence as

$$p(\mathbf{s}|\mathbf{o}) = \frac{1}{Z(\mathbf{o})} \exp\left(\sum_k \lambda_k F_k(\mathbf{s}, \mathbf{o})\right)$$

Where F is a feature function set over its arguments, λk is a learned weight for each feature function, and Z is the partition function, which ensures that p is appropriately normalized.

2.2 Word Segmentation Task

Similar to (Ng and Low, 2005), a Chinese character comes into four different tags, as in Table 1.

Tag	Meaning
S	Character that occurs as a single-character word
B	Character that begins a multi-character word
I	Character that continues a multi-character word
E	Character that ends a multi-character word

Table 1. Word segmentation tag set

(Ng and Low, 2005) presented feature templates as:

(a) Cn(n = −2,−1, 0, 1, 2)
(b) CnCn+1(n = −2,−1, 0, 1)
(c) C−1C1
(d) Pu(C0)
(e) T(C−2)T(C−1)T(C0)T(C1)T(C2)

In order to find the effect of different features on the result, some experiments are conducted on these templates, with 90% of the training data provided by The SIGHAN Bakeoff 2007 for training, leaving 10% for testing. Based on our results, some templates are adjusted as follows.

First, the character-window is reduced to (-1, 0, 1) in (a).

Second, feature template (d) is not used. Instead, original sentences are split into clauses ended with punctuations "，", "。", "：", "？", "；" and "！". There are two advantages of this processing: (1) the template is simplified but little performance is lost; (2) shorter sentences make CRFs training quicker.

Third, template (e) is separate it to three items: T(C-1), T(C0) and T(C1), in which five types of the characters are considered: N stands for numbers, D for dates, E for English letters, S for punctuations and C for other characters. Besides, this feature template does not always contribute to the segmentation result in our experiments, so it will be a tradeoff whether to use it or not according to experiments.

Finally, we use the following feature templates:

(a) Cn(n = −1, 0, 1)
(b) CnCn+1(n = −1, 0)
(c) C−1C1
(d) T(Cn) (n = −1, 0, 1)

We only took part in word segmentation closed track, so no additional corpora, dictionary or linguistic resources are introduced.

1.1 NER Task

Many Chinese NER researches are based on word segmentation and even Part-Of-Speech (POS) tagging. In fact these steps are not necessary. The relationship of them is described in Figure 1.

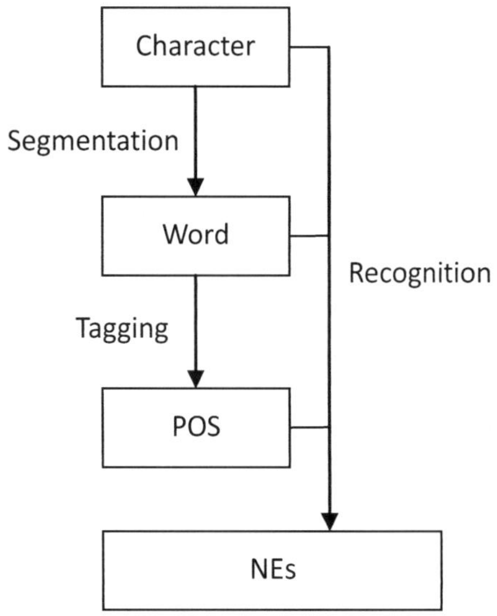

Figure 1. NER model achitecture

In closed track of both MSRA and CITYU, a character-based CRFs model is used in our system. There two reasons as follows:

First, no word-level information is provided in training data of NER tasks in closed track, so it's hard to perform word segmentation with good accuracy.

Second, we had done some experiments on Chinese NER, and found that character-based method outperformed word segmentation and word segmentation + POS, if only character sequence is given. Table 2 shows the comparison results.

Feature Level	Integrated F-measure
Character	0.8760
Word	0.8538
POS	0.8635

Table 2. Comparison result among different NER models[3]

[3] Train with Annotation Corpora of People's Daily 199801 and test with 199806

In our NER system, a Chinese character can be labeled as one of four different tags, as in Table 3.

Tag	Meaning
B	First character of a NE
I	Character in a NE but neither the first nor the last one
E	Last character of a NE except a single-character one
O	Character not in a NE

Table 3. NER tag set

It's similar to the standard of The SIGHAN Bakeoff 2007 NER track except for an additional tag "E". Unlike the tag set used in word segmentation task, there is no "S" tag for single-character NEs. This kind of entities is usually surname of a Chinese person. In this case, the tag "B" will handle it as well.

There are actually 3 types of NEs in MSRA and CITYU corpora: PER, LOC and ORG, so the tag set is further divided into 10 sub tags: B-PER, I-PER, E-PER, B-LOC, I-LOC, E-LOC, B-ORG, I-ORG, E-ORG and O.

The feature template is similar to the one used in word segmentation task except that here a character-window of (-2,-1, 0, 1,2) is applied:

(a) Cn(n = −2,−1, 0, 1, 2)

(b) CnCn+1(n = −2,−1, 0, 1)

(c) C−1C1

(d) T(Cn) (n = −1, 0, 1)

For CRFs, the precision is usually high while recall is low. To solve this problem, a set of feature templates (only differ in window size, or punctuations) are used to train several different models, and finally achieve a group of results. Merge them as in Table 4 (for the same Chinese character string in result A and B).

A	B	Result
Is a NE	Isn't a NE	Refer to A
Isn't a NE	Is a NE	Refer to B
Isn't a NE	Isn't a NE	Refer to A or B
Is a NE	Is the same NE type as A	Refer to A or B
Is a NE	Is a NE but not the same type as A	Choose A or B according to predefined rules

Table 4. Merge strategy of results

With a slight loss of precision, an improvement is achieved on recall rate.

In open track of MSRA, an additional segmentation system is used on the corpora and some NEs are retrieved based on several predefined rules. It was merged with closed track result to form open track result.

3 Evaluation Results

Our word segmentation system is evaluated in closed track on all 5 corpora of CITYU, CKIP, CTB, NCC and SXU. Table 5 shows our results on the best RunID. Columns R, P, and F show the recall, precision, and F measure, respectively. Column BEST shows best F-measure of all participants in the track.

Our NER system is evaluated in closed track on both MSRA and CITYU corpora, and open track on MSRA corpora only. Table 6 shows our official results on best RunID. Columns R, P, and F show the recall, precision, and F measure, respectively. Column BEST shows best F-measure of all participants in the track.

Track (all closed)	R	P	F	BEST
CITYU	0.9421	0.9339	0.938	0.951
CKIP	0.9369	0.927	0.9319	0.947
CTB	0.9487	0.9514	0.95	0.9589
NCC	0.9278	0.925	0.9264	0.9405
SXU	0.9543	0.9568	0.9556	0.9623

Table 5. Evaluation results on word segmentation

Track	R	P	F	BEST
CITYU closed	0.7608	0.8751	0.814	0.8499
MSRA closed	0.8862	0.9304	0.9078	0.9281
MSRA open	0.9135	0.9321	0.9227	0.9988

Table 6. Evaluation results on NER

4 Conclusion

In this paper, a character-based CRFs model is introduced on both word segmentation and NER. Experiments are done to form our feature templates, and approaches are used to further improve its performance on NER. The evaluation results show its competitive performance in The SIGHAN Bakeoff 2007. We'll launch more research and experiments on feature picking-up methods and combination between character-based model and other models in the future.

References

Hai Zhao, Chang-Ning Huang and Mu Li. An Improved Chinese Word Segmentation System with Conditional Random Field. 2006. *Proceedings of the Fifth SIGHAN Workshop on Chinese Language Processing.*

Jin Kiat Low, Hwee Tou Ng and Wenyuan Guo. A maximum Entropy Approach to Chinese Word Segmentation. 2005. *Proceedings of the Fourth SIGHAN Workshop on Chinese Language Processing.*

Wang Xinhao, Lin Xiaojun, Yu Dianhai, Tian Hao,Wu Xihong. Chinese Word Segmentation with Maximum Entropy and N-gram Language Model. 2006. *Proceedings of the Fifth SIGHAN Workshop on Chinese Language Processing.*

Zhou Junsheng, Dai Xinyu, He Liang, Chen Jiajun. Chinese Named Entity Recognition with a Multi-Phase Model. 2006. *Proceedings of the Fifth SIGHAN Workshop on Chinese Language Processing.*

Acknowledgement

This paper is supported by National Natural Science Foundation of China (No. 60675035), National Social Science Foundation of China (No. 05BYY043) and Beijing Natural Science Foundation (No. 4072012).

HMM and CRF Based Hybrid Model for Chinese Lexical Analysis

Degen Huang, Xiao Sun, Shidou Jiao, Lishuang Li, Zhuoye Ding, Ru Wan
Dept. of Computer Science and Engineering, Dalian University of Technology.
Dalian, Liaoning, 116023
huangdg@dlut.edu.cn, suntian@gmail.com, jiaoshidou@gmail.com,
computer@dlut.edu.cn, dingzhuoye@sina.com, wanrulove@sina.com

Abstract

This paper presents the Chinese lexical analysis systems developed by Natural Language Processing Laboratory at Dalian University of Technology, which were evaluated in the 4th International Chinese Language Processing Bakeoff. The HMM and CRF hybrid model, which combines character-based model with word-based model in a directed graph, is adopted in system developing. Both the closed and open tracks regarding to Chinese word segmentation, POS tagging and Chinese Named Entity Recognition are involved in our systems' evaluation, and good performance are achieved. Especially, in the open track of Chinese word segmentation on SXU, our system ranks 1st.

1 Introduction

Chinese presents a significant challenge since it is typically written without separations between words. Word segmentation has thus long been the focus of significant research because of its role as a necessary pre-processing phase for the tasks above. Meanwhile, the POS tagging and Chinese Named Entity Recognition are also the basic steps in Chinese lexical analysis. Several promising methods are proposed by previous researchers. In tradition, the Chinese word segmentation technologies can be categorized into three types, rule-based, machine learning, and hybrid. Among them, the machine learning-based techniques showed excellent performance in many research studies (Peng et al., 2004; Zhou et al., 2005; Gao et al., 2004). This method treats the word segmentation problem as a sequence of word classification. The classifier online assigns either "boundary" or "non-boundary" label to each word by learning from the large annotated corpora. Machine learning-based word segmentation method is adopted in the word sequence inference techniques, such as part-of-speech (POS) tagging, phrases chunking (Wu et al., 2006a) and named entity recognition (Wu et al., 2006b). But there are some cost problems in such machine learning problems, and sometimes choose between word-based and character based is also a dilemma.

In our system, we present a hybrid model for Chinese word segmentation, POS tagging and named entity recognition based on HMM and CRF model. The core of the model is a directed segmentation graph based on the maximum matching and second-maximum matching model. In the directed graph, the HMM model and CRF model are combined, the HMM model is used to process the known words (words in system dictionary); CRF model is adopted to process the unknown word, the cost problem can be solved. Meanwhile, for the CRF model, the character-based CRF model and word-based model are integrated under the framework of the directed segmentation graph, so the integrative CRF model can be more flexible to recognize both the simple and complex Chinese Named Entity with high precision. With the directed segmentation graph, Chinese word segmentation, POS tagging and Chinese Named Entity recognition can be accomplished simultaneously.

2 System Description

With the maximum matching and second-maximum matching (MMSM) model, CRF model, and several post processing strategies, our systems are established. First the MMSM model is applied, based on the system dictionary the original directed segmentation graph is set up. The directed graph is composed by the known words from the system dictionary, which are regarded as the candidate word of the segmentation result. Then some candidate Chinese Named Entity Recognition automata search the directed graph, and find out the candidate Chinese Named Entities into the directed graph based on some generation rules. Then the CRF is applied to the candidate Chinese Named Entities to determine if they are real Chinese Named Entities that should be added into the directed graph. During this procedure, the character-based CRF and word-based CRF are respectively applied to the simple and complex Chinese Named Entities recognition.

In the following section, the Chinese word segmentation, POS tagging and Chinese named entity recognition in open track will be mainly discussed.

2.1 The maximum matching and second-maximum matching model

The maximum matching and second-maximum matching(MMSM) model, which is a segmentation method that keeps the maximum and second-maximum segmentation result from a certain position in a sentence, and store the candidate segmentation results in a directed graph, then some decoding algorithm is adopted to find the best path in the directed graph. With the MMSM model, almost all the possible segmentation paths and most lexical information can be reserved for further use; little space cost is guaranteed by using the directed graph to store the segmentation paths; the context spaces are extended from single-dimension to multi-dimension.

2.2 Conditional Random Fields

Conditional random field (CRF) was an extension of both Maximum Entropy Model (MEMs) and Hidden Markov Models (HMMs) that was firstly introduced by (Lafferty *et al*., 2001). CRF defined conditional probability distribution *P(Y|X)* of given sequence given input sentence where *Y* is the "class label" sequence and *X* denotes as the observation word sequence.

A CRF on *(X,Y)* is specified by a feature vector *F* of local context and the corresponding feature weight λ. The *F* can be treated as the combination of state transition and observation value in conventional HMM. To determine the optimal label sequence, the CRF uses the following equation to estimate the most probability.

Conditional random fields (CRFs) are undirected graphical models trained to maximize a conditional probability (Lafferty et al., 2001). A linear-chain CRF with parameters $\Lambda = \{\lambda_1, \lambda_2, \cdots\}$ defines a conditional probability for a state sequence $y = y_1 \ldots y_T$, given that and input sequence $x = x_1 \ldots x_T$ is

$$P_\Lambda(y \mid x) = \frac{1}{Z_x} \exp\left(\sum_{t=1}^{T} \sum_{k} \lambda_k f_k(y_{t-1}, y_t, x, t) \right)$$

Where Z_x is the normalization factor that makes the probability of all state sequences sum to one; $f_k(y_{t-1}, y_t, x, t)$ is ofen a binary-valued feature function and λ_k is its weight. The feature functions can measure any aspect of a state transition, $y_{t-1} \rightarrow y_t$, and the entire observation sequence, x, centered at the current time step, *t*. For example, one feature function might have the value 1 when y_{t-1} is the state *B*, y_t is the state *I*, and x_t is some Chinese character.

2.3 Chinese Named Entity Recognition

First, we will introduce our Chinese Named Entity Recognition part for the Open track. Several NER automata are adopted to find out all the candidate NEs in the directed graph, then the CRF model is applied to filter the candidate NEs to check if the specified NE should be added into the graph. To use the CRF, first, we generate some lists from the training corpus.

PSur: the surname of Person Name.

PC: the frequency information of a character in Person Name

PPre: the prefix of Person Name

PSuf: the suffix of Person Name

LF: the frequency information of a character in Local Name

LC: the centre character of Local Name

LPre: the prefix of Local Name

LSuf: the suffix of Local Name

OF: the frequency information of a character in ORG Name

OC: the centre character of ORG Name

OPre: the prefix of ORG Name

OSuf: the suffix of ORG Name

We define the template as follows:

PER: PSur(n)PC(n) PPre(n)PSuf(n), (n = -2, -1, 0, +1, +2)

LOC: LF(n)LC(n)LPre(n)LSuf(n), (n = -2, -1, 0, +1, +2)

ORG: OF(n)OC(n)OPre(n)OSuf(n), (n = -2, -1, 0, +1, +2)

With the CRF we filter the candidate NEs. The candidate NEs are filtered and added into the directed segmentation graph as new nodes with new edges. The NEs includes personal name(PRE), location name(LOC) and organization name(ORG).

The "PER","LOC" in open track is the same as in the close track except some external resources. The external resources include external lexicon, name list for word segmentation, and generating the features.

In the "ORG" part, a different method is proposed. We adopt an automatic recognition method of Chinese organization name with the combination of SVM and Maximum Entropy. SVM model is used to decide the latter boundary of a organization name, and then Maximum Entropy is used to confirm the former boundary.

First, a characteristic dictionary is collected from the training corpus. As for the words appeared in the characteristic dictionary, whether it is the characteristic word of an organization name should be decided. As a problem of two value categorization, SVM is applied to complete this task. If it is considered to be a characteristic word, then the former boundary of an organization name is detected. Maximum Entropy can combine different kinds of text information, and solve the problem of the recognition of the more complex former words of the Chinese organization name, so the Maximum Entropy is adopted to confirm the former boundary of ORG. During the NEs recognition and filtering the word and POS tag as main features and adopt a context window of five words.

Because of the complex construction of the Chinese Named Entity, one single statistical model can not solve simple and complex NER simultaneously, such as the character-based CRF model makes lower recognition accuracy for complex NERs, meanwhile, the word-based CRF model will lose many useful features in processing simple NERs. Integrating the character-based and word-based CRF model into one framework is the key to solve all the NERs simultaneously.

In this paper, an integrative model based on CRF is proposed. With the preliminary results of the segmentation and POS tagging, at the bottom of the system, character-based CRF is applied to recognized simple PERs, LOCs, and ORGs; The recognition result will be transformed to the top of the system together with the segmentation and POS tagging result. At the top of system, word-based CRF is used to recognize the nested LOCs and ORGs. The character-based model and word based model are integrated into one framework to recognition the NEs with different complexions simultaneously. The identification results of the bottom-level provide decision support for the high-level, the limitations of the separated character-based model and word-based model are avoided, and improves recognition accuracy of the system.

2.4 Result from the directed graph

After the recognition and filtering of the Chinese Named Entity, the original segmentation directed graph is now with the candidate Chinese Named Entity nodes. Some decoding algorithm is needed to find final path from the directed graph. Here, we revised the Dijkstra minimum cost path algorithm to find out the minimum cost path from the directed graph. The calculation of the cost of the nodes and edges in the directed graph can be found in our related work(Degen Huang and Xiao Sun, 2007). The final path from the directed graph is the result for the Chinese word segmentation, POS tagging and Chinese Named Entity recognition.

3 Evaluations and Experimental Results

3.1 Result of Chinese word segmentation

We evaluated our Chinese word segmentation model in the open track on all the simple Chinese corpus, such as University of Colorado, United States (CTB, 642246 tokens), State Language Commission of P.R.C.,Beijing(NCC, 917255 tokens) and Shanxi University, Taiyuan (SXU 528238 tokens). The OOV-rate is 0.0555, 0.0474 and 0.0512.

The CTB open track is shown in the following table 1. We get the third position in the CTB track by the F result.

Table 1. CTB open track result

CTB	R	P	F
Base	0.8864	0.8427	0.8640
Top	0.9710	0.9825	0.9767
Our	0.9766	0.9721	0.9743
	IV-R	IV-P	IV-F
Base	0.9369	0.8579	0.8956
Top	0.9698	0.9832	0.9764
Our	0.9805	0.9794	0.9800
	OOV-R	OOV-P	OOV-F
Base	0.9920	0.9707	0.9812
Top	0.0273	0.1858	0.0476
Our	0.9089	0.8553	0.8813

The NCC open track is shown in the following table 2. In the NCC open track, we get the third position track by the F result.

Table 2. NCC open track result

NCC	R	P	F
Base	0.9200	0.8716	0.8951
Top	0.9735	0.9817	0.9776
Our	0.9620	0.9496	0.9557
	IV-R	IV-P	IV-F
Base	0.9644	0.8761	0.9181
Top	0.9725	0.9850	0.9787
Our	0.9783	0.9569	0.9675
	OOV-R	OOV-P	OOV-F
Base	0.0273	0.1858	0.0476
Top	0.9933	0.9203	0.9554
Our	0.7109	0.7619	0.7355

The SXU open track is shown in the following table 3. In the SXU open track, we get the first two positions by the F result.

Table 3. NCC open track result

NCC	R	P	F
Base	0.9238	0.8679	0.8949
Top	0.9820	0.9867	0.9844
Our	0.9768	0.9703	0.9735
	IV-R	IV-P	IV-F
Base	0.9723	0.8789	0.9232
Top	0.9813	0.9890	0.9851
Our	0.9872	0.9767	0.9820
	OOV-R	OOV-P	OOV-F
Base	0.0251	0.0867	0.0389
Top	0.9942	0.9480	0.9705
Our	0.7825	0.8415	0.8109

We also participate in the close track in CTB, NCC and SXU corpus. The result is shown in the following table 4.

Table 4. Segmentation Result in close track

	R	P	F	Foov	Fiv
CTB	0.9505	0.9528	0.9517	0.7216	0.9659
NCC	0.9387	0.9301	0.9344	0.5643	0.9524
SXU	0.9594	0.9493	0.9543	0.6676	0.9697

3.2 Result of Chinese NER

We evaluated our named entity recognizer on the SIGHAN Microsoft Research Asia(MSRA) corpus in both closed and open track.

Table 5. NER in MSRA closed track:

Close	R	P	F
PER	90.29%	95.19%	92.68%
LOC	81.85%	92.78%	86.97%
ORG	70.16%	84.05%	76.48%
Overall	80.58%	91.07%	85.5%

Table 6. NER in MSRA open track:

Open	R	P	F
PER	92.06%	95.17%	93.59%
LOC	83.62%	94.24%	88.62%
ORG	74.04%	79.66%	75.65%
Overall	82.38%	90.38%	86.19%

3.3 Result of POS tagging

The POS tagging result of our system is shown in the following table 7.

Table 7. POS tagging in close track

Close	Total-A	IV-R	OOV-R	MT-R
CTB	0.9088	0.9374	0.4866	0.8805
NCC	0.9313	0.9604	0.4080	0.8809
PKU	0.9053	0.9451	0.2751	0.8758

Table 8. POS tagging in open track

Open	Total-A	IV-R	OOV-R	MT-R
CTB	91.2%	93.74%	53.61%	88.05%
NCC	93.26%	96.04%	43.36%	88.09%
PKU	93.29%	95.18%	63.32%	89.72%

4 Conclusions and Future Work

In this paper, the hybrid model in our system is described, An integrative lexical analysis system is implemented, which completes all the steps of the lexical analysis synchronously, by integrating the segmentation, ambiguous resolution, POS tagging, unknown words recognition into one theory framework. The integrative mechanism reduces the conflicts between the steps of the lexical analysis. The experimental results demonstrate that, the integrative model and its algorithm is effective. The system used the automata recognition and CRF-based hybrid model to process the Chinese Named Entity. The Chinese word segmentation, POS tagging and Chinese Named Entity recognition are integrated; the character-based CRF and word-based CRF are integrated, the HMM, CRF and other statistic model are integrated under the same segmentation framework. With this model we participated in the "The Fourth SIGHAN Bakeoff" and got good performance.

References

Degen, Huang and Xiao *An Integrative Approach to Chinese NamedEntity Recognition*, In Proceedings of the 6th International Conference on Advanced Language Processing and Web Information Technology.

Gao, J., Wu, A., Li, M., Huang, C. N., Li, H., Xia, X., and Qin, H. 2004. *Adaptive Chinese word segmentation*. In Proceedings the 41st Annual Meeting of the Association for Computational Linguistics, pp. 21-26.

Lafferty, J., McCallum, A., and Pereira, F. 2001. *Conditional Random Field: Probabilistic models for segmenting and labeling sequence data*. In Proceedings of the International Conference on Machine Learning.

Lance A. Ramshaw and Mitchell P. Marcus. 1995. *Text chunking using transformation-based learning*. In Proceedings of the 3rd Workshop on Very Large Corpora, pages 82-94. Nocedal, J., and Wright, S. 1999. Numerical optimization. Springer.

Peng, F., Feng, F., and McCallum, A. 2004. *Chinese segmentation and new word detection using conditional random fields*. In Porceedings of the Computational Linguistics, pp. 562-568.

Shi, W. 2005. *Chinese Word Segmentation Based On Direct Maximum Entropy Model*. In Proceedings of the Fourth SIGHAN Workshop on Chinese Language Processing.

Wu, Y. C., Chang, C. H. and Lee, Y. S. 2006a. *A general and multi-lingual phrase chunking model based on masking method*. Lecture Notes in Computer Science (LNCS): Computational Linguistics and Intelligent Text Processing, 3878: 144-155.

Wu, Y. C., Fan, T. K., Lee Y. S. and Yen, S. J. 2006b. *Extracting named entities using support vector machines*," Lecture Notes in Bioinformatics (LNBI): Knowledge Discovery in Life Science Literature, (3886): 91-103.

Wu, Y. C., Lee, Y. S., and Yang, J. C. 2006c. *The Exploration of Deterministic and Efficient Dependency Parsing*. In Proceedings of the 10th Conference on Natural Language Learning (CoNLL).

Chinese Tagging Based on Maximum Entropy Model

Ka Seng Leong
Faculty of Science and Technology of University of Macau
Av. Padre Tomás Pereira, Taipa, Macau, China
ma56538@umac.mo

Fai Wong
Faculty of Science and Technology of University of Macau, INESC Macau
Av. Padre Tomás Pereira, Taipa, Macau, China
derekfw@umac.mo

Yiping Li
Faculty of Science and Technology of University of Macau
Av. Padre Tomás Pereira, Taipa, Macau, China
ypli@umac.mo

Ming Chui Dong
Faculty of Science and Technology of University of Macau, INESC Macau
Av. Padre Tomás Pereira, Taipa, Macau, China
dmc@inesc-macau.org.mo

Abstract

In the Fourth SIGHAN Bakeoff, we took part in the closed tracks of the word segmentation, part of speech (POS) tagging and named entity recognition (NER) tasks. Particularly, we evaluated our word segmentation model on all the corpora, namely Academia Sinica (CKIP), City University of Hong Kong (CITYU), University of Colorado (CTB), State Language Commission of P.R.C. (NCC) and Shanxi University (SXU). For POS tagging and NER tasks, our models were evaluated on CITYU corpus only. Our models for the evaulation are based on the maximum entropy approach, we concentrated on the word segmentation task for the bakeoff and our best official results on all the corpora for this task are 0.9083 F-score on CITYU, 0.8985 on CKIP, 0.9077 on CTB, 0.8995 on NCC and 0.9146 on SXU.

1 Introduction

In the Fourth SIGHAN Bakeoff, besides providing the evaluation tasks for the word segmentation and NER, it also introduced another important evaluation task, POS tagging for Chinese language. In this bakeoff, our models built for the tasks are similar to that in the work of Ng and Low (2004). The models are based on a maximum entropy framework (Ratnaparkhi, 1996; Xue and Shen, 2003). They are trained on the corpora for the tasks from the bakeoff. To understand the model, the implementation of the models is wholly done ourselves. We used Visual Studio .NET 2003 and C++ as the implementation language. The Improved Iterative Scaling (IIS) (Pietra et al., 1997) is used as the parameter estimation algorithm for the models. We tried all the closed track tests of the word segmentation, the CITYU closed track tests for POS tagging and NER.

2 Maximum Entropy

In this bakeoff, our basic model is based on the framework described in the work of Ratnaparkhi (1996) which was applied for English POS tagging. The conditional probability model of the framework is called maximum entropy (Jaynes, 1957). Maximum entropy model is a feature-based, probability model which can include arbitrary number of features that other generative models like N-gram model, hidden Markov model (HMM) (Rabiner, 1989) cannot do. The probability model can be defined over $X \times Y$, where X is the set of possible histories and Y is the set of allowable futures or classes. The conditional probability of the model of a history x and a class y is defined as

$$p_\lambda(y \mid x) = \frac{\prod_i \lambda_i^{f_i(x,y)}}{Z_\lambda(x)} \quad (1)$$

$$Z_\lambda(x) = \sum_y \prod_i \lambda_i^{f_i(x,y)} \quad (2)$$

where λ is a parameter which acts as a weight for the feature in the particular history. The equation (1) states that the conditional probability of the class given the history is the product of the weightings of all features which are active under the consideration of (x, y) pair, normalized over the sum of the products of all the classes. The normalization constant is determined by the requirement that $\sum_y p_\lambda(y \mid x) = 1$ for all x.

To find the optimized parameters λ of the conditional probability is one of the important processes in building the model. This can be done through a training process. The parameter estimation algorithm used for training is Improved Iterative Scaling (IIS) (Pietra et al., 1997) in our case. In training the models for this bakeoff, the training data is given in the form of a sequence of characters (for the tasks of word segmentation and NER) or words (POS tagging) and their classes (tags), the parameters λ can be chosen to maximize the likelihood of the training data using p:

$$L(p) = \prod_{i=1}^{n} p_\lambda(x_i, y_i) = \prod_{i=1}^{n} \frac{1}{Z_\lambda(x)} \prod_{j=1}^{m} \lambda_j^{f_j(x_i,y_i)} \quad (3)$$

But of course, the success of the model depends heavily on the selection of features for a particular task. This will be described in Section 5.

3 Chinese Word Segmenter

We concentrated on the word segmentation task in this bakeoff. For the Chinese word segmenter, it is based on the work that treats Chinese word segmentation as tagging (Xue and Shen, 2003; Ng and Low, 2004). Given a Chinese sentence, it assigns a so-called boundary tag to each Chinese character in the sentence. There are four possible boundary tags: S for a character which is a single-character word, B for a character that is the first character of a multi-character word, E for a character that is the last character of a multi-character word and M for a character that is neither the first nor last of a multi-character word. With these boundary tags, the word segmentation becomes a tagging problem where each character in Chinese sentences is given one of the boundary tags which is the most probable one according to the conditional probability calculated by the model. And then sequences of characters are converted into sequences of words according to the tags.

4 POS Tagger and Named Entity Recognizer

For the POS tagging task, the tagger is built based on the work of Ratnaparkhi (1996) which was applied for English POS tagging. Because of the time limitation, we could only try to port our implemented maximum entropy model to this POS tagging task by using the similar feature set (discussed in Section 5) for a word-based POS tagger as in the work of Ng and Low (2004). By the way, besides porting the model to the POS tagging task, it was even tried in the NER task by using the same feature set (discussed in Section 5) as used for the word segmentation in order to test the performance of the implemented model.

The tagging algorithm for these two tasks is basically the same as used in word segmentation. Given a word or a character, the model will try to assign the most probable POS or NE tag for the word or character respectively.

5 Features

To achieve a successful model for any task by using the maximum entropy model, an important step is to select a set of useful features for the task. In the following, the feature sets used in the tasks of the bakeoff are discussed.

5.1 Word Segmentation Features

The feature set used in this task is discussed in our previous work (Leong et al., 2007) which is currently the best in our implemented model. They are the unigram features: C_{-2}, C_{-1}, C_0, C_1 and C_2, bigram features: $C_{-2}C_{-1}$, $C_{-1}C_0$, C_0C_1, C_1C_2 and $C_{-1}C_1$ where C_0 is the current character, C_n (C_{-n}) is the character at the nth position to the right (left) of the current character. For example, given the character sequence "維多利亞港" (Victoria Harbour), while taking the character "利" as C_0, then C_{-2} = "維", $C_{-1}C_1$ = "多亞", etc. The boundary tag (*S*, *B*, *M* or *E*) feature T_{-1} is also applied, i.e., the boundary tag assigned to the previous character of C_0. And the last feature WC_0: This feature captures the word context in which the current character is found. It has the format "W_C_0". For example, the character "利" is a character of the word "維多利亞港". Then this will give the feature WC_0 = "維多利亞港_利".

5.2 POS Tagging Features

For this task, because of the time limitation as mentioned in the previous section, we could only port our implemented model by using a part of the feature set which was used in the word-based tagger discussed in the work of Ng and Low (2004). The feature set includes: W_n (n = -2 to 2), W_nW_{n+1} (n = -2, -1, 0, 1), $W_{-1}W_1$, $POS(W_{-2})$, $POS(W_{-1})$, $POS(W_{-2})POS(W_{-1})$ where W refers to a word, POS refers to the POS assigned to the word and n refers to the position of the current word being considered. For example, while considering this sentence taken from the POS tagged corpus of CITYU: "香港/Ng 特別/Ac 行政區/Nc 正式/Dc 成立/Vt" (Hong Kong S.A.R. is established), taking "行政區" as W_0, then W_{-2} = "香港", $W_{-1}W_1$ = "特別 正式", $POS(W_{-2})$ = "Ng", $POS(W_{-2})POS(W_{-1})$ = "Ac Dc", etc.

5.3 Named Entity Recognition Features

For the NER task, we directly used the same feature set as for the word segmentation basically. However, because the original NE tagged corpus is presented in two-column format, where the first column consists of the character and the second is a tag, a transformation which is to transform the original corpus to a sentence per line format before collecting the features or other training data is needed. This transformation actually continues to read the lines from the original corpus, whenever a blank line is found, a sentence of characters with NE tags can be formed.

After that, the features collected are the unigram features: C_{-2}, C_{-1}, C_0, C_1 and C_2, bigram features: $C_{-2}C_{-1}$, $C_{-1}C_0$, C_0C_1, C_1C_2 and $C_{-1}C_1$, NE tag features: T_{-1}, WC_0 (this feature captures the NE context in which the current character is found) where T_{-1} refers to the NE tag assigned to the previous character of C_0, W refers to the named entity. So similar to the explanation of features of word segmentation, for example, given the sequence from the NER tagged corpus of CITYU: "一/N 個/N 中/B-LOC 國/I-LOC 人/N" (One Chinese), while taking the character "中" as C_0, then C_{-2} = "一", $C_{-1}C_1$ = "個國", WC_0 = "中國__中", etc.

For all the experiments conducted, training was done with a feature cutoff of 1.

6 Testing

For word segmentation task, during testing, given a character sequence $C_1 \dots C_n$, the trained model will try to assign a boundary tag to each character in the sequence based on the probability of the boundary tag calculated. Then the sequence of characters is converted into sequence of words according to the tag sequence $t_1 \dots t_n$. But if each character was just assigned the boundary tag with the highest probability, invalid boundary tag sequences would be produced and wrong word segmentation results would be obtained. In particular, known words that are in the dictionary of the training corpus are segmented wrongly because of these invalid tag sequences. In order to correct these, the invalid boundary tag sequences are collected, such as for two-character words, they are "B B", "B S", "M S", "E E", etc., for three-character words, they are "B E S", "B M S", etc., and for four-character words, they are "B M M S", "S M M E", etc. With these invalid boundary tag sequences, some post correction to the word segmentation result can be tried. That is after the model tagger has done the tagging for a Chinese sentence every time, the invalid boundary tag sequences will be searched within the preliminary result given by the tagger. When the invalid boundary tag sequence is found, the characters corresponding to that invalid boundary tag sequence will be obtained. After, the word formed by these characters is looked up to see if it is indeed a word in the dictionary, if it is, then the correction is carried out.

Another kind of post correction to the word segmentation result is to make some guessed correction for some invalid boundary tag sequences such as "B S", "S E", "B B", "E E", "B M S", etc. That is, whenever those tag sequences are met within the preliminary result given by the model tagger, they will be corrected no matter if there is word in the dictionary formed by the characters corresponding to the invalid boundary tag sequence.

We believe that similar post correction can be applied to the NER task. For example, if such NE tag sequences "B-PER N", "N I-PER N", etc. occur in the result, then the characters corresponding to the invalid NE tag sequence can be obtained again and looked up in the named entity dictionary to see if they really form a named entity. However, we did not have enough time to adapt this for the NER task finally. Therefore, no such post correction was applied for the NER task in this bakeoff finally.

7 Evaluation Results

We evaluated our models in the closed tracks of the word segmentation, part of speech (POS) tagging and named entity recognition (NER) tasks. Particularly, our word segmentation model was evaluated on all the corpora, namely Academia Sinica (CKIP), City University of Hong Kong (CITYU), University of Colorado (CTB), State Language Commission of P.R.C. (NCC) and Shanxi University (SXU). For POS tagging and NER tasks, our models were evaluated on the CITYU corpus only. Table 1 shows our official results for the word segmentation task in the bakeoff. The columns R, P and F show the recall, precision and F-score respectively.

Run_ID	R	P	F
cityu_a	0.9221	0.8947	0.9082
cityu_b	0.9219	0.8951	0.9083
ckip_a	0.9076	0.8896	0.8985
ckip_b	0.9074	0.8897	0.8985
ctb_a	0.9078	0.9073	0.9075
ctb_b	0.9077	0.9078	0.9077
ncc_a	0.8997	0.8992	0.8995
ncc_b	0.8995	0.8992	0.8994
sxu_a	0.9186	0.9106	0.9145
sxu_b	0.9185	0.9107	0.9146

Table 1. Official Results in the Closed Tracks of the Word Segmentation Task on all Corpora

We submitted a few runs for each of the tests of the corpora. Table 1 shows the best two runs for each of the tests of the corpora for discussion here. The run (a) applied only the post correction to the known words that are in the dictionary of the training corpus but are segmented wrongly because of the invalid boundary tag sequences. The run (b) applied also the guessed post correction for some invalid boundary tag sequences in the results as mentioned in Section 6. From the results above, it can be seen that the runs with the guessed post correction generally gave a little bit better performance than those that did not apply. This shows that the guess somehow made some good guesses for some unknown words that appear in the testing corpora.

Table 2 shows our official results for the POS tagging task. The columns A shows the accuracy. The columns IV-R, OOV-R and MT-R show the recall on in-vocabulary words, out-of-vocabulary words and multi-POS words (multi-POS words are the words in the training corpus and have more than one POS-tag in either the training corpus or testing corpus) respectively. The run (a) used the paramters set which was observed to be the optimal ones for the model in the training phase. The run (b) used the parameters set of the model in the last iteration of the training phase.

Run_ID	A	IV-R	OOV-R	MT-R
cityu_a	0.1890	0.2031	0.0550	0.1704
cityu_b	0.2793	0.2969	0.1051	0.2538

Table 2. Official Results in the Closed Track of the POS Tagging Task on the CITYU Corpus

It can be seen that our results were unexpectedly low in accuracy. After releasing the results, we found that the problem was due to the encoding problem of our submitted result files. The problem probably occurred after the conversion from our Big5 encoded results to the UTF-16 encoded results which are required by the bakeoff. Therefore, we did the evaluation ourselves by running our POS tagger again, using the official evaluation program and the truth test set. Finally, our best result was 0.7436 in terms of accuracy but this was still far lower than the baseline (0.8425) of the CITYU corpus. This shows that the direct porting of English word-based POS tagging to Chinese is not effective.

Table 3 shows our official results for the NER task. The columns R, P and F show the recall, precision and F-score respectively. Again, similar to the POS tagging task, the run (a) used the paramters set which was observed to be the optimal ones for the model in the training phase. The run (b) used the parameters set of the model in the last iteration of the training phase.

Run_ID	R	P	F
cityu_a	0.0874	0.1058	0.0957
cityu_b	0.0211	0.0326	0.0256

Table 3. Official Results in the Closed Track of the NER Task on the CITYU Corpus

It can be seen that our results were again unexpectedly low in accuracy. The cause of such low accuracy results was due to parts of the wrong format of the submitted result files compared with the correct format of the result file. So like the POS tagging task, we did the evaluation ourselves by running our NE recognizer again. Finally, our best result was 0.5198 in terms of F-score but this was again far lower than the baseline (0.5955) of the CITYU corpus. This shows that the similar feature set for the word segmentation task is not effective for the NER task.

8 Conclusion

This paper reports the use of maximum entropy approach for implementing models for the three tasks in the Fourth SIGHAN Bakeoff and our results in the bakeoff. From the results, we got good experience and knew the weaknesses of our models. These help to improve the performance of our models in the future.

Acknowledgements

The research work reported in this paper was partially supported by "Fundo para o Desenvolvimento das Ciências e da Tecnologia" under grant 041/2005/A.

References

Adwait Ratnaparkhi. 1996. A maximum entropy model for part-of-speech tagging, in *Proceedings of Conference on Empirical Methods in Natural Language Processing*, Philadelphia, USA, pages 133-142.

Edwin Thompson Jaynes. 1957. Information Theory and Statistical Mechanics, *The Physical Review*, 106(4): 620-630.

Hwee Tou Ng, and Jin Kiat Low. 2004. Chinese part-of-speech tagging: One-at-a-time or all-at-once? Word-based or character-based? In *Proceedings of the 2004 Conference on Empirical Methods in Natural Language Processing (EMNLP 2004)*, Barcelona, Spain, pages 277-284.

Ka Seng Leong, Fai Wong, Yiping Li, and Ming Chui Dong. 2007. Chinese word boundaries detection based on maximum entropy model, in *Proceedings of the 11th International Conference on Enhancement and Promotion of Computational Methods in Engineering and Science (EPMESC-XI)*, Kyoto, Japan.

Lawrence Rabiner. 1989. A tutorial on hidden Markov models and selected applications in speech recognition, *Proceedings of the IEEE*, 77(2): 257–286.

Nianwen Xue, and Libin Shen. 2003. Chinese word segmentation as LMR tagging, in *Proceedings of the 2nd SIGHAN Workshop on Chinese Language Processing*, Sapporo, Japan, pages 176-179.

Steven Della Pietra, Vincent Della Pietra, and John Lafferty. 1997. Inducing features of random fields. *IEEE transactions on pattern analysis and machine intelligence*, 19(4): 380–393.

Training a Perceptron with Global and Local Features for Chinese Word Segmentation

Dong Song and **Anoop Sarkar**
School of Computing Science, Simon Fraser University
Burnaby, BC, Canada V5A1S6
{dsong,anoop}@cs.sfu.ca

Abstract

This paper proposes the use of global features for Chinese word segmentation. These global features are combined with local features using the averaged perceptron algorithm over N-best candidate word segmentations. The N-best candidates are produced using a conditional random field (CRF) character-based tagger for word segmentation. Our experiments show that by adding global features, performance is significantly improved compared to the character-based CRF tagger. Performance is also improved compared to using only local features. Our system obtains an F-score of 0.9355 on the CityU corpus, 0.9263 on the CKIP corpus, 0.9512 on the SXU corpus, 0.9296 on the NCC corpus and 0.9501 on the CTB corpus. All results are for the closed track in the fourth SIGHAN Chinese Word Segmentation Bakeoff.

1 Introduction

Most natural language processing tasks require that the input be tokenized into individual words. For some languages, including Chinese, this is challenging since the sentence is typically written as a string of characters without spaces between words. Word segmentation is the task of recovering the most plausible grouping of characters into words. In this paper, we describe the system we developed for the fourth SIGHAN Chinese Word Segmentation Bakeoff[1]. We test our system in the closed track[2] for all five corpora: Academia Sinica (CKIP), City University of Hong Kong (CityU), National Chinese Corpus (NCC), University of Colorado (CTB), and Shanxi University (SXU).

[1]Further details at: www.china-language.gov.cn/bakeoff08/bakeoff-08_basic.html

[2]We do not use any extra annotation, especially for punctuation, dates, numbers or English letters.

2 System Description

The architecture of our system is shown in Figure 1. For each of the training corpora in the bakeoff, we produce a 10-fold split: in each fold, 90% of the corpus is used for training and 10% is used to produce an N-best list of candidates. The N-best list is produced using a character-based conditional random field (CRF) (Lafferty et al., 2001; Kudo et al., 2004) tagger. The true segmentation can now be compared with the N-best list in order to train an averaged perceptron algorithm (Collins, 2002a). This system is then used to predict the best word segmentation from an N-best list for each sentence in the test data.

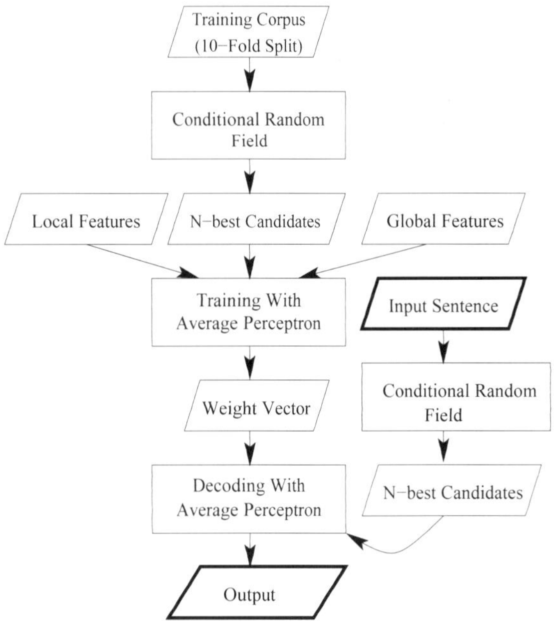

Figure 1: Outline of the segmentation process

2.1 Learning Algorithm

Given an unsegmented sentence x, the word segmentation problem can be defined as finding the most probable segmentation $F(x)$ from a set of possible segmentations of x.

$$F(x) = \underset{y \in GEN(x)}{\operatorname{argmax}} \Phi(x, y) \cdot \overline{w} \quad (1)$$

The set of possible segmentations is given by $GEN(x)$ and the naïve method is to first generate all possible segmented candidates. For a long sentence, generating those candidates and picking the one with the highest score is time consuming.

In our approach, N-best candidates for each training example are produced with the *CRF++* software (Kudo et al., 2004). The CRF is used as a tagger that tags each character with the following tags: for each multi-character word, its first character is given a **B** (Beginning) tag , its last character is assigned an **E** (End) tag, while each of its remaining characters is provided an **M** (Middle) tag. In addition, for a single-character word, **S** (Single) is used as its tag[3]. Let c_0 be the current character, c_{-1}, c_{-2} are the two preceding characters, and c_1, c_2 are the two characters to the right . Using this notation, the features used in our CRF models are: c_0, c_{-1}, c_1, c_{-2}, c_2, $c_{-1}c_0$, c_0c_1, $c_{-1}c_1$, $c_{-2}c_{-1}$ and c_0c_2.

We use the now standard method for producing N-best candidates in order to train our re-ranker which uses global and local features: 10-folds of training data are used to train the tagger on 90% of the data and then produce N-best lists for the remaining 10%. This process gives us an N-best candidate list for each sentence and the candidate that is most similar to the true segmentation, called y^b. We map a segmentation y to *features* associated with the segmentation using the mapping $\Phi(\cdot)$. The score of a segmentation y is provided by the dot-product $\Phi(y) \cdot \overline{w}$. The perceptron algorithm (Fig. 2) finds the weight parameter vector $\overline{w}$ using online updates. The predicted segmentation $y_i^{'}$ based on the current weight vector is compared to the the best candidate y^b, and whenever there is a mismatch, the algorithm updates the parameter vector by incrementing the parameter value for features in y^b, and by decrementing the value for features in $y_i^{'}$.

The voted perceptron (Freund and Schapire, 1999) has considerable advantages over the standard

[3]Note that performance of the CRF tagger could be improved with the use of other tagsets. However, this does not affect our comparative experiments in this paper.

Inputs: Training Data $\langle (x_1, y_1), \ldots, (x_m, y_m) \rangle$
Initialization: Set $\overline{w} = 0$
Algorithm:
  for $t = 1, \ldots, T$ **do**
    for $i = 1, \ldots, m$ **do**
      Calculate $y_i^{'}$, where
      $y_i^{'} = \underset{y \in N\text{-best Candidates}}{\operatorname{argmax}} \Phi(y) \cdot \overline{w}$
      if $y_i^{'} \neq y^b$ **then**
        $\overline{w} = \overline{w} + \Phi(y^b) - \Phi(y_i^{'})$
      end if
    end for
  end for

Figure 2: Training using a perceptron algorithm over N-best candidates.

perceptron. However, due to the computational issues with the voted perceptron, the averaged perceptron algorithm (Collins, 2002a) is used instead. Rather than using $\overline{w}$, we use the averaged weight parameter $\overline{\gamma}$ over the m training examples for future predictions on unseen data:

$$\overline{\gamma} = \frac{1}{mT} \sum_{i=1..m, t=1..T} \overline{w}^{i,t}$$

In calculating $\overline{\gamma}$, an accumulating parameter vector $\overline{\sigma}^{i,t}$ is maintained and updated using $\overline{w}$ for each training example; therefore, $\overline{\sigma}^{i,t} = \sum \overline{w}^{i,t}$. After the last iteration, $\overline{\sigma}^{i,t}/mT$ produces the final parameter vector $\overline{\gamma}$.

When the number of features is large, it is time consuming to calculate the total parameter $\overline{\sigma}^{i,t}$ for each training example. To reduce the time complexity, we adapted the lazy update proposed in (Collins, 2002b), which was also used in (Zhang and Clark, 2007). After processing each training sentence, not all dimensions of $\overline{\sigma}^{i,t}$ are updated. Instead, an update vector $\overline{\tau}$ is used to store the exact location (i, t) where each dimension of the averaged parameter vector was last updated, and only those dimensions corresponding to features appearing in the current sentence are updated. While for the last example in the last iteration, each dimension of $\overline{\tau}$ is updated, no matter whether the candidate output is correct.

2.2 Feature Templates

The feature templates used in our system include both local features and global features. For local features, we consider two major categories: word-based features and character-based features. Five specific types of features from (Zhang and Clark, 2007) that are shown in Table 1 were used in our system. In our initial experiments, the other features used in (Zhang and Clark, 2007) did not improve performance and so we do not include them in our system.

1	word w
2	word bigram $w_1 w_2$
3	single character word w
4	space-separated characters c_1 and c_2
5	character bi-gram $c_1 c_2$ in any word

Table 1: local feature templates. Rows 1, 2 and 3 are word-based and rows 4 and 5 are character-based features

In our system, we also used two types of global features per sentence (see Table 2). By global, we mean features over the entire segmented sentence.[4]

6	sentence confidence score
7	sentence language model score

Table 2: global feature template

The sentence confidence score is calculated by *CRF++* during the production of the N-best candidate list, and it measures how confident each candidate is close to the true segmentation.

The sentence language model score for each segmentation candidate is produced using the SRILM toolkit (Stolcke, 2002) normalized using the formula $P^{1/L}$, where P is the probability-based language model score and L is the length of the sentence in words (not in characters). For global features, the feature weights are not learned using the perceptron algorithm but are determined using a development set.

3 Experiments and Analysis

Our system is tested on all five corpora provided in the fourth SIGHAN Bakeoff, in the closed track.

3.1 Parameter Pruning

First, the value of the parameter N, which is the maximum number of N-best candidates, was determined. An oracle procedure proceeds as follows: 80% of the training corpus is used to train the CRF model, and produce N-best outputs for each sentence on the remaining 20% of the data. Then these N candidates are compared with the true segmentation, and for each training sentence, the candidate closest to the truth is chosen as the final output. Testing on different values of N, we chose N to be 20 in all our experiments since that provided the best tradeoff between accuracy and speed.

Next, the weight for sentence confidence score S_{crf} and that for language model score S_{lm} are determined. To simplify the process, we assume that the weights for both S_{crf} and S_{lm} are equal. In this step, each training corpus is separated into a training set (80% of the whole corpus) and a held-out set (20% of the corpus). Then, the perceptron algorithm is applied on the training set with different S_{crf} and S_{lm} values, and for various number of iterations. The weight values we test include 2, 4, 6, 8, 10, 20, 30, 40, 50, 100 and 200. From the experiments, the weights are chosen to be 100 for CKIP corpus, 10 for CityU corpus, 30 for NCC corpus, 20 for CTB corpus, and 10 for SXU corpus.

While determining the weights for global features, the number of training iterations can be determined as well. Experiments show that, as the number of iterations increases, the accuracy stabilizes in most cases, reflecting the convergence of the learning algorithm. Analyzing the learning curves, we fix the number of training iterations to be 5 for CKIP corpus, 9 for NCC corpus, and 8 for the CityU, CTB and SXU corpora.

3.2 Results on the Fourth SIGHAN Bakeoff

In each experiment, F-score (F) is used to evaluate the segmentation accuracy. Table 3 shows the F-score on the fourth SIGHAN Bakeoff corpora. In this table, we record the performance of our system, the score from the character-based CRF method and the score from the averaged perceptron using only local features.

Our system outperforms the baseline character-based CRF tagger. In addition, the use of global features in the re-ranker produces better results than only using local features.

The only data set on which the performance of our system is lower than the character-based CRF method is CKIP corpus. For this data set during the parameter pruning step, the weight for S_{crf} and S_{lm}

[4]It is important to distinguish this kind of global feature from another type of 'global' feature that either enforces consistency or examines the use of a feature in the entire training or testing corpus.

	CKIP	NCC	CityU	CTB	SXU
Character-based CRF method	0.9332	0.9248	0.9320	0.9468	0.9473
Averaged Perceptron with only local features	0.9180	0.9125	0.9273	0.9450	0.9387
Our System	0.9263	**0.9296**	**0.9355**	**0.9501**	**0.9512**
Our System (With modified weight for global features)	**0.9354**	–	–	–	–
Significance (p-value)	$\leq$ 1.19e-12	$\leq$ 4.43e-69	$\leq$ 3.55e-88	$\leq$ 2.17e-18	$\leq$ 2.18e-38

Table 3: F-scores on the Fourth SIGHAN Bakeoff Corpora

was too large. By lowering the weight from 100 to 4, we obtains an F-score of 0.9354, which is significantly better than the baseline CRF tagger.

The significance values in Table 3 were produced using the McNemar's Test (Gillick, 1989)[5]. All our results are significantly better.

4 Related Work

Re-ranking over N-best lists has been applied to so many tasks in natural language that it is not possible to list them all here. Closest to our approach is the work in (Kazama and Torisawa, 2007). They proposed a margin perceptron approach for named entity recognition with non-local features on an N-best list. In contrast to their approach, in our system, global features examine the entire sentence instead of partial phrases. For word segmentation, (Wang and Shi, 2006) implemented a re-ranking method with POS tagging features. In their approach, character-based CRF model produces the N-best list for each test sentence. The Penn Chinese TreeBank is used to train a POS tagger, which is used in re-ranking. However the POS tags are used as local and not global features. Note that we would not use POS tags in the closed track.

5 Conclusion

We have participated in the closed track of the fourth SIGHAN Chinese word segmentation bakeoff, and we provide results on all five corpora. We have shown that by combining global and local features, we can improve accuracy over simply using local features, and we also show improved accuracy over the baseline CRF character-based tagger for word segmentation.

[5]www.fon.hum.uva.nl/Service/Statistics/McNemars_test.html

References

M. Collins. 2002. Discriminative Training Methods for Hidden Markov Models: Theory and Experiments with Perceptron Algorithms. In *Proc. of the Empirical Methods in Natural Language Processing (EMNLP). MACL, 2002*, 1–8, 2000.

M. Collins. 2002. Ranking Algorithms for Named-Entity Extractions: Boosting and the Voted Perceptron. In *Proc. of ACL 2002*.

Y. Freund and R. Schapire. 1999. Large Margin Classification using the Perceptron Algorithm. In *Machine Learning*, 37(3): 277–296.

L. Gillick and S. Cox. 1989. Some Statistical Issues in the Comparison of Speech Recognition Algorithms. In *Proc. of IEEE Conf. on Acoustics, Speech and Sig. Proc., Glasgow, 1989*, 532–535.

J. Kazama and K. Torisawa. 2007. A New Perceptron Algorithm for Sequence Labeling with Non-local Features. In *Proc. of EMNLP-CoNLL 2007* , pages 315–324.

T. Kudo, K. Yamamoto, and Y. Matsumoto. 2004. Appliying Conditional Random Fields to Japanese Morphological Analysis. In *Proc. of EMNLP 2004*.

J. Lafferty, A. McCallum, and F. Pereira. 2001. Conditional Random Fields: Probabilistic Models for Segmenting and Labeling Sequence Data. In *Proc. of ICML-2001*, pages 591–598.

A. Ratnaparkhi. 1996. A Maximum Entropy Model for Part-of-Speech Tagging. In *Proc. of EMNLP 1996*.

A. Stolcke. 2002. SRILM - An Extensible Language Modeling Toolkit. In *Proc. Intl. Conf. Spoken Language Processing, Denver, Colorado, September 2002*.

M. Wang and Y. Shi. 2006. A Maximum Entropy Model for Part-of-Speech Tagging. In *Proc. of the Fifth SIGHAN Workshop on Chinese Language Processing, Sydney, 2006*, pages 205–208.

Y. Zhang and S. Clark. 2007. Chinese Segmentation with a Word-based Perceptron Algorithm. In *Proc. of ACL 2007*.

A Study of Chinese Lexical Analysis Based on Discriminative Models

Guang-Lu Sun Cheng-Jie Sun Ke Sun and Xiao-Long Wang
Intelligent Technology & Natural Language Processing Laboratory, School of Computer Science and Technology, Harbin Institute of Technology, 150001, Harbin, China
{glsun, cjsun, ksun, wangxl}@insun.hit.edu.cn

Abstract

This paper briefly describes our system in The Fourth SIGHAN Bakeoff. Discriminative models including maximum entropy model and conditional random fields are utilized in Chinese word segmentation and named entity recognition with different tag sets and features. Transformation-based learning model is used in part-of-speech tagging. Evaluation shows that our system achieves the F-scores: 92.64% and 92.73% in NCC Word Segmentation close and open tests, 89.11% in MSRA name entity recognition open test, 91.13% and 91.97% in PKU part-of-speech tagging close and open tests. All the results get medium performances on the bakeoff tracks.

1 Introduction

Lexical analysis is the basic step in natural language processing. It is prerequisite to many further applications, such as question answer system, information retrieval and machine translation. Chinese lexical analysis chiefly consists of word segmentation (WS), name entity recognition (NER) and part-of-speech (POS) tagging. Because Chinese does not have explicit word delimiters to mark word boundaries like English, WS is essential process for Chinese. POS tagging and NER are just like those of English.

Our system participated in The Fourth SIGHAN Bakeoff which held in 2007. Different approaches are applied to solve all the three tasks which are integrated into a unified system (ITNLP-IsLex). For WS task, conditional random fields (CRF) are used. For NER, maximum entropy model (MEM) is applied. And transformation-based learning (TBL) algorithm is utilized to solve POS tagging problem. The reasons using different models are listed in the rest sections of this paper. We give a brief introduction to our system sequentially. Section 2 describes WS. Section 3 and section 4 introduce NER and POS tagging respectively. We give some experimental results in section 5. Finally we draw some conclusions.

2 Chinese word segmentation

For WS task, NCC corpus is chosen both in close test and open test.

2.1 Conditional random fields

Conditional random fields are undirected graphical models defined by Lafferty (2001). There are two advantages of CRF. One is their great flexibility to incorporate various types of arbitrary, non-independent features of the input, the other is their ability to overcome the label bias problem.

Given the observation sequence *X*, on the basis of CRF, the conditional probability of the state sequence Y is:

$$p(Y/X)=\frac{1}{Z(X)}exp\left\{\sum_k l_k f_k(y_{i-1},y_i,X,i)\right\} \quad (1)$$

$$Z(X)=\sum_{y\in Y}exp\left\{\sum_k l_k f_k(y_{i-1},y_i,X,i)\right\} \quad (2)$$

Z(x) is the normalization factor. $f_k(y_{i-1},y_i,X,i)$ is the universal definition of features in CRF.

2.2 Word segmentation based on CRF

Inspired by Zhao (2006), the Chinese WS task is considered as a sequential labeling problem, i.e., assigning a label to each character in a sentence given its contexts. CRF model is adopted to do labeling.

6 tags are utilized in this work: B, B1, B2, I, E, S. The meaning of each tag is listed in Table 1. The

raw training file format from NCC can be easily to convert to this 6 tags format.

An example: 向/S 广/B 东/B1 省/B2 高/I 级/I 人/I 民/I 法/I 院/E 提/B 出/E 上/B 诉/E 。/S.

Table 1 Tags of character-based labeling

Tag	Meaning
B	The 1st character of a multi-character word
B1	The 2nd character of a multi-character word
B2	The 3rd character of a multi-character word
I	Other than B, B1, B2 and last character in a multi-character word
E	The last character of a multi-character word
S	Single character word

The contexts window size for each character is 5: C_{-2}, C_{-1}, C_0, C_1, and C_2. There are 10 feature templates used to generate features for CRF model including uni-gram, bi-gram and tri-gram: C_{-2}, C_{-1}, C_0, C_1, C_2, $C_{-1}C_0$, C_0C_1, $C_{-2}C_{-1}C_0$, $C_{-1}C_0C_1$, and $C_0C_1C_2$.

For the parameters in CRF model, we only do work to choose cut-off value for features. Our experiments show that the best performance can be achieved when cut-off value is set to 2.

Maximum likelihood estimation and L-BFGS algorithm is used to estimate the weight of parameters in the training module. Baum-Welch algorithm is used to search the best sequence of test data.

For close test, we only used CRF to do segmentation, no more post-processing, such as time and date finding, was done. So the performance could be further improved.

For open test, we just use our NER system to tag the output of our close segmentation result, no more other resources were involved.

3 Chinese name entity recognition

For NER task, MSRA is chosen in open test. Chinese name dictionary, foreign name dictionary, Chinese place dictionary and organization dictionary are used in the model.

3.1 Maximum entropy model

Maximum entropy model is an exponential model that offers the flexibility of integrating multiple sources of knowledge into a model (Berger, 1996). It focuses on the modeling of tagging sequence, replacing the modeling of observation sequence.

Given the observations sequence *X*, on the basis of MEM, the conditional probability of the state sequence Y is:

$$p(Y \mid X) = \frac{1}{Z(X)} \exp\left(\sum_j \lambda_j f_j(Y, X)\right) \quad (3)$$

$$Z(X) = \sum_Y \exp\left(\sum_j \lambda_j f_j(Y, X)\right) \quad (4)$$

Table 2 Feature templates of NER

Feature template	Description	
C_i	The word tokens in the window i =-2, -1, 0, 1, 2	
T_i	The NE tags i = -1	
C_iC_{i-1}	The bigram of C_i i = -1, 1	
P_i	The POS tags of word tokens i = -1, 0, 1	
$P_{-1}P_1$	The combination of POS tags	
$T_{-1}C_0$	The previous tag and the current word token	
$W(C_i)$	B	C_i is Chinese family name
	C	C_i is part of Chinese first name
	W	C_i is Chinese whole name
	F	C_i is foreign name
	S	C_i is Chinese first name
	O	other
$W(C_{i-1})W(C_i)$	The bigram of W(Ci) i = -1, 1	
IsInOrgDict(C_0)	The current word token is in organization dictionary	
IsInPlaceDict(C_0)	The current word token is in place dictionary	

Being Similar to the definition of CRF, Z(x) is the normalization factor. $f_j(Y,X)$ is the universal definition of features.

3.2 Name entity recognition based on MEM

Firstly, we use a segmentation tool to split both training and test corpus into word-token-based texts. Characters that are not in the dictionary are scattered in the texts. NE tags using in the model follow the tags in training corpus. Other word tokens that do not belong to NE are tagged as *O*. Based on the segmented text, the context window is also set as 5. Inspired by Zhang's (2006) work, there are 10 types of feature templates for generating features for NER model in Table 2.

When training our ME Model, the best performance can be achieved when cut-off value is set to 1.

Maximum likelihood estimation and GIS algorithm is used to estimate the weight of parameters in the model. The iteration time is 500.

4 Chinese part-of-speech tagging

For POS tagging task, NCC corpus and PKU corpus are chosen both in the close test and open test.

4.1 Transformation-based learning

The formalism of Transformation-based learning is first introduced in 1992. It starts with the correctly tagged training corpus. A baseline heuristic for initial tag and a set of rule templates that specify the transformation rules match the context of a word. By transformating the error initial tags to the correct ones, a set of candidate rules are built to be the conditional pattern based on which the transformation is applied. Then, the candidate rule which has the best transformation effect is selected and stored as the first transformation rules in the TBL model. The training process is repeated until no more candidate rule has the positive effect. The selected rules are stored in the learned rule sequence in turn for the purpose of template correction learning.

4.2 Part-of-speech tagging based on TBL

POS tagging is a standard sequential labeling problem. CRF has some advantages to solve it. Because both corpora have relative many POS tags, our computational ability can not afford the CRF model in condition of these tags. TBL model is utilized to replace with CRF.

We compute the max probability of current word's POS tag in training corpus. The POS tag which has max occurrence probability for each word is used to tag its word token. By this method, we got the initial POS tag for each word.

The rule templates which are formed from conjunctions of words match to particular combinations in the histories of the current position. 40 types of rule templates are built using the patterns. The cut-off value of the transformation rules is set to 3 (Sun, 2007).

For open test, our NER system is used to tag the output of our POS tagging result. Parts of NE tags are corrected.

5 Evaluation

Following the measurement approach adopted in SIGHAN, we measure the performance of the three tasks in terms of the precision (P), recall (R), and F-score (F).

5.1 Word segmentation results

Table 3 Word segmentation results on NCC corpus

NCC	close test	open test
R	.9268	.9268
C_r	.00133447	.00133458
P	.926	.928
C_p	.00134119	.00132534
F	.9264	.9273
R_{oov}	.6094	.6265
P_{oov}	.4948	.5032
F_{oov}	.5462	.5581
R_{iv}	.9426	.9417
P_{iv}	.9527	.9546
F_{iv}	.9476	9481

The WS results are listed on the Table 3. Some errors could be caused by the annotation differences between the training data and test data. For example, "阿珍" (A Zhen) was considered as a whole word in training data, while "阿兰" (A Lan) was annotated as two separate word "阿" (A) and "兰" (Lan) in the test data. Some post-processing rules for English words, money unit and morphology can improve the performance further, Following are such errors in our results: "vid eo",

"日 元" (Japan yen), "不 三 不 四" (not three not four).

For open test, we hoped to use NER module to increase the OOV recall. But the NER module didn't prompt the performance very much because it was trained by the MSRA NER data in Bakeoff3. The difference between two corpora may depress the NER modules effect. Also, the open test was done on the output of close test and all the errors were passed.

5.2 Name entity recognition results

The official results of our NER system on MSRA corpus for open track are showed in Table 4. As it shows, our system achieves a relatively high score on both PER and LOC task, but the performance of ORG is not so good, and the Avg1 performance is decreased by it. The reasons are: (1) The ORG sequences are often very long and our system is unable to deal with the long term, a MEMM or CRF model may perform better. (2) The resource for LOC and ORG are much smaller than that of PER. More sophisticated features such like "W(C_i)" may provide more useful information for the system.

Table 4 NER results on MSRA corpus

MSRA	P	R	F
PER	.9498	.9549	.9524
LOC	.9129	.9194	.9161
ORG	.8408	.7469	.7911
Avg1	.9035	.8791	**.8911**

5.3 Part-of-speech tagging results

We evaluate our POS tagging model on the PKU corpus for close and open track and NCC corpus for close track based on TBL. Table 5 is the official result of our system. In PKU open test, NER is used to recognize name entity of text, so its result is better than that of close test. The IV-R result is relative good, but the OOV-R is not so good, which drops the total performance. The reasons lie in: (1) TBL model is not good at tagging out of vocabulary words. CRF model may be a better selection if our computer can meet its huge memory requirements. (2) Our NER system is trained by MSRA corpus. It does not fit the PKU and NCC corpus.

Table 5 POS results on PKU and NCC corpus

Corpus	Total-A	IV-R	OOV-R	MT-R
PKU close test	.9113	.9518	.2708	.8958
PKU open test	.9197	.9512	.4222	.899
NCC close test	.9277	.9664	.2329	.9

6 Conclusions

Chinese lexical analysis system is built for the SIGHAN tracks which consists of Chinese word segmentation, name entity recognition and part-of-speech tagging. Conditional random fields, maximum entropy model and transformation-based learning model are utilized respectively. Our system achieves the medium results in all the three tasks.

References

A. Berger, S. A. Della Pietra and V. J. Della Pietra. A Maximum Entropy Approach to Natural Language Processing. *Computational Linguistics*, 1996. 22(1), pages 39-71.

G. Sun, Y. Guan and X. Wang. A Maximum Entropy Chunking Model With N-fold Template Correction. *Journal of Electronics*, 2007. 24(5), pages 690-695.

J. Lafferty, A. McCallum and F. Pereira. Conditional random fields: Probabilistic models for segmenting and labeling sequence data. *In Proceedings of ICML-2001*, Williams College, Massachusetts, USA. 2001. pages 282-289.

S. Zhang, Y. Qin, J. Wen, X. Wang. Word Segmentation and Named Entity Recognition for SIGHAN Bakeoff3. In *Proceedings of the Fifth SIGHAN Workshop on Chinese Language Processing*. Sydney, Australia. 2006. pages 158–161.

H. Zhao, C. Huang, and M. Li. An improved Chinese word segmentation system with conditional random field. In *Proceedings of the Fifth SIGHAN Workshop on Chinese Language Processing*, Sydney, Australia. 2006. pages 162–165.

Word Boundary Token Model for the SIGHAN Bakeoff 2007

Tsai Jia-Lin
Department of Information Management
Tungnan University
Taipei 222, Taiwan
tsaijl@mail.tnu.edu.tw

Abstract

This paper describes a Chinese word segmentation system based on word boundary token model and triple template matching model for extracting unknown words; and word support model for resolving segmentation ambiguity.

1 Introduction

In the SIGHAN bakeoff 2007, we participated in the CKIP and the CityU closed tasks. Our Chinese word segmentation system is based on three models: (a) word boundary token (WBT) model and (b) triple context matching model for unknown word extraction, and (c) word support model for segmentation disambiguation. Since the word support model and triple context matching model have been proposed in our previous work (Tsai, 2005, 2006a and 2006b) at the SIGHAN bakeoff 2005 (Thomas, 2005) and 2006 (Levow, 2006), the major descriptions of this paper is on the WBT model.

The remainder of this paper is arranged as follows. In Section 2, we present the WBT model for extracting words from each Chinese sentence. Scored results and analyses of our CWS system are presented in Section 3. Finally, in Section 4, we present our conclusion and discuss the direction of future research.

2 Word Boundary Token Model

To develop the WBT model, first, we define word boundary token. Second, we give definition and computation of the WBT probability and the WBT frequency for a given corpus. Finally, algorithm of our WBT model for word extraction is given.

2.1 Types of Word Boundary Token

We classify WBT into three types: left, right and bi-direction. The left and right word boundary (WB) tokens are the immediately preceding word and the following word of a word in a Chinese sentence, respectively. Suppose $W_1W_2W_3$ is a Chinese sentence comprised of three Chinese words W_1, W_2 and W_3. To this case, W_1 and W_3 are the left and the right WB tokens of W_2, respectively. On the other hand, those words that can simultaneously be left and right WB tokens of a word in corpus are defined as bi-direction WB tokens. Suppose $W_4W_2W_1$ is a Chinese sentence comprised of three Chinese words W_4, W_2 and W_1. Following the above cases, W_1 can be a bi-direction WB token for W_2. Table 1 is the Top 5 left, right and bi-direction WB tokens derived by the Academia Sinica (AS) corpus (CKIP, 1995 and 1996). From Table 1, the Top 1 left , right and bi-direction WB tokens is "的(of)."

	Left	Right	Bi-Direction
Top1	的(of)	的(of)	的(of)
Top2	是(is)	是(is)	是(is)
Top3	在(at)	了(already)	在(at)
Top4	個(a)	在(at)	了(already)
Top5	有(has)	一(one)	與(and)

Table 1. Top 5 left, right and bi-direction WB tokens derived from the AS corpus

2.2 WBT Frequency and WBT Probability

We first give the computation of WBT frequency, then, the computation of WBT probability.

(1) **WBT frequency**: we use WBT_F(*string*, *WBT*, *L*/*R*) as the function of WBT frequency, where *string* is a n-char string containing n Chinese characters, *WBT* is a word boundary token, and *L*/*R* indicates to compute left or right WBT frequency. Now, take WBT_F("我們(we)", "的(of)", *L*) as example. First, we submit the query "的我們" to system corpus. Second, set the number of sentences including this query is the WBT_F("我們(we)", "的(of), L).

(2) **WBT Probability**: we use WBT_P(*string1*, *string2*, *WBT, L*/*R*) as the function of WBT probability, where *string1* and *string2* are two n-char strings, *WBT* is a word boundary token, and *L*/*R* indicates to compute left or right WBT probability. The equations of left and the right WBT probability are:

WBT_P(*string1*, *string2*, *WBT, L*) =
WBT_F(*string1*, *WBT*, *L*) /
(WBT_F(*string1*, *WBT*, *L*)+WBT_F(*string2*, *WBT*, *L*)) (1)

WBT_P(*string1*, *string2*, *WBT, R*) =
WBT_F(*string1*, *WBT*, *R*) /
(WBT_F(*string1*, *WBT*, *R*)+WBT_F(*string2*, *WBT*, *R*)) (2)

2.3 Algorithm of WBT Model

We use WBTM(*n*, *WBT*, *threshold_p*, *threshold_f*) as the function of the WBT model, where *n* is the window size, *threshold_p* is the threshold value of WBT probability and *threshold_f* is the threshold value of WBT frequency. The algorithm of our WBT model applied to extract words from a given Chinese sentence is as follows:

Step 1. INPUT:
  n, *WBT*, *threshold_p* and *threshold_f*;
Step 2. IF sentence length is less or equal to *n* THEN GOTO Step 4;
Step 3.
SET loopCount to one
REPEAT
  COMBINE the characters of sentence between loopCount_{th} and $(\text{loopCount} + n - 1)_{th}$ to be a *string_a*
  COMBINE the characters of sentence between $(\text{loopCount}+1)_{th}$ and $(\text{loopCount} + n)_{th}$ to be a *string_b*
  IF WBT_P(*string_a*, *string_b*, *WBT*, *L*) ≥ *threshold_p* AND
    WBT_P(*string_a*, *string_b*, *WBT*, *R*) ≥ *threshold_p* AND
    WBT_F(*string_a*, *WBT*, *L*) ≥ *threshold_f* AND
    WBT_F(*string_a*, *WBT*, *R*) ≥ *threshold_f*
    THEN SET *string_a* is as word
  ENDIF
  IF WBT_P(*string_b*, *string_a*, *WBT*, *L*) ≥ *threshold_p* AND
    WBT_P(*string_b*, *string_a*, *WBT*, *R*) ≥ *threshold_p* AND
    WBT_F(*string_b*, *WBT*, *L*) ≥ *threshold_f* AND
    WBT_F(*string_b*, *WBT*, *R*) ≥ *threshold_f*
    THEN SET *string_b* to a word
  ENDIF
  INCREMENT loopCount
UNTIL loopCount > sentence length − *n*
Step 4. END.

loopCount is 1
  string_a = 廣義; *string_b* = 義地
  WBT_F(*string_a*, "的", L) = 0
  WBT_F(*string_a*, "的", R) = 7
  WBT_F(*string_b*, "的", L) = 0
  WBT_F(*string_b*, "的", R) = 0
  WBT_P(*string_a*, *string_b*, "的", *L*) = 0
  WBT_P(*string_a*, *string_b*, "的", *R*) = 1
  WBT_P(*string_b*, *string_a*, "的", *L*) = 0
  WBT_P(*string_b*, *string_a*, "的", *R*) = 0
  SET 廣義 to a word

loopCount is 2
  string_a = 義地; *string_b* = 地說
  WBT_F(*string_a*, "的", L) = 0
  WBT_F(*string_a*, "的", R) = 0
  WBT_F(*string_b*, "的", L) = 0
  WBT_F(*string_b*, "的", R) = 0
  WBT_P(*string_a*, *string_b*, "的", *L*) = 0
  WBT_P(*string_a*, *string_b*, "的", *R*) = 0
  WBT_P(*string_b*, *string_a*, "的", *L*) = 0
  WBT_P(*string_b*, *string_a*, "的", *R*) = 0

Table 2. An example of applying WBTM(2, "的", 0.95, 1) to extract word "廣義" from the Chinese sentence "廣義地說"

Table 2 is an example of applying WBTM(2, "的", 0.95, 1) to extract words from the Chinese sentence "廣義地說" by the AS corpus

3 Evaluation

In the SIGHAN Bakeoff 2007, there are five training corpus for word segmentation (WS) task: AS (Academia Sinica), CityU (City University of Hong Kong) are traditional Chinese corpus; CTB (University of Colorado, United States), NCC (State Language Commission of P.R.C., Beijing) and SXU (Shanxi University, Taiyuan) are simplified Chinese corpus. For each corpus, there are closed and open tasks. In this Bakeoff, we attend the AS (Academia Sinica) and CityU (City University of Hong Kong) closed WS tasks. Tables 3 and 4 show the details of CKIP and CityU tasks. From Table 3, it indicates that the CKIP should be a 10-folds design. From Table 4, it indicates that the CityU should be a 5-folds design.

	Training	Testing
Sentence	95,303	10,834
Wordlist	48,114	14,662

Table 3. The details of CKIP WS task

	Training	Testing
Sentence	36,227	8,093
Wordlist	43,639	23,303

Table 4. The details of CityU WS task

3.1 Our CWS System

The major steps of our CWS system with word boundary token model, triple context matching model and word support model are as below:

Step 0. Combine training corpus and testing corpus as system corpus;

Step 1. Generate the BMM segmentation for the given Chinese sentence by system dictionary;

Step 2. Use WBT model with system corpus to extract 2-char, 3-char and 4-char words from the given Chinese sentence, where *WBT* is set to "的," "是," "在," "了," "與," *threshold_p* is set to 0.95 and *threshold_f* is set to 1;

Step 3. Use TCT (triple context template) matching model to extract 2-char, 3-char and 4-char words from the segmented Chinese sentence of Step 1. The details of TCT matching model can be found in (Tsai, 2005);

Step 4. Add the found words of Steps 2 and 3 into system dictionary;

Step 5. Generate the BMM segmentation for the given Chinese sentence by system dictionary;

Step 6. Use word support model to resolve **Overlap Ambiguity (**OA) and **Combination Ambiguity (**CA) problems for the BMM segmentation of Step 5.

3.2 Bakeoff Scored Results

Table 5 is the comparison of scored results between our CWS and the SIGHAN Bakeoff 2007 baseline system for the CKIP closed WS task by the SIGHAN Bakeoff 2007. Table 6 is the comparison between our CWS and the SIGHAN Bakeoff 2007 baseline system for the CityU closed WS task by the SIGHAN Bakeoff 2007.

	Baseline	Our CWS	Increase
R	0.8978	0.915	0.0172
P	0.8232	0.9001	0.0769
F	0.8589	0.9075	0.0486

Table 5. The comparison of scored results between our CWS system and the SIGHAN Bakeoff 2007 baseline system for the CKIP closed WS task

	Baseline	Our CWS	Increase
R	0.9006	0.9191	0.0185
P	0.8225	0.9014	0.0789
F	0.8598	0.9102	0.0504

Table 6. The comparison of scored results between our CWS system and the SIGHAN Bakeoff 2007 baseline system for the CityU closed WS task

From Tables 5 and 6, it shows the major improvement of our CWS for the baseline system is on the precision of word segmentation. That is to say, the major target system for improving our CWS system is the unknown word extraction system, i.e. the word boundary model and the triple context template matching model.

3.3 Analysis

Table 7 is the coverage of 2-char, 3-char, 4-char and great than 4-char error words extracting by our CWS for the CKIP and the CityU closed WS tasks.

	Coverage (%)			
	2-char	3-char	4-char	> 4-char
CKIP	68%	24%	4%	4%
CityU	78%	19%	2%	1%
Total	75%	21%	3%	1%

Table 7. The coverage of 2-char, 3-char, 4-char and great than 4-char error words extracting by our CWS for the CKIP and the CityU closed WS tasks

From Table 7, it shows the major n-char unknown word extraction for improving our CWS system is on 2-char unknown word extraction. It is because that the total coverage of 2-char word errors extraction of our CWS system for the CKIP and the CityU WS tasks is 75%.

4 Conclusions

In this paper, we describes a Chinese word segmentation system based on word boundary token model and triple context matching model (Tsai, 2005) for extracting unknown words; and word support model (Tsai, 2006a and 2006b) for resolving segmentation ambiguity. To develop the word boundary model, we define WBT and classify WBT into three types of left, right and bi-direction. As per three types of WBT, we define WBT probability and WBT frequency.

In the SIGHAN Bakeoff 2007, we take part in the CKIP and the CityU closed word segmentation tasks. The scored results show that our CWS can increase the Bakeoff baseline system with 4.86% and 5.04% F-measures for the CKIP and the CityU word segmentation tasks, respectively. On the other hand, we show that the major room for improving our CWS system is the 2-char unknown word extraction of the word boundary model and triple context matching model. The performance of word support model is great and supports our previous work (Tsai, 2006a and 2006b).

We believe one major advantage of the WBT model is to use it with web as live corpus to minimum the corpus sparseness effect. Therefore, in the future, we shall investigate the WBT model with the web corpus, such as the searching results of GOOGLE and Yahoo!, etc.

References

CKIP (Chinese Knowledge Information Processing Group). 1995. *Technical Report no. 95-02, the content and illustration of Sinica corpus of Academia Sinica.* Institute of Information Science, Academia Sinica.

CKIP (Chinese Knowledge Information Processing Group). 1996. *A study of Chinese Word Boundaries and Segmentation Standard for Information processing* (in Chinese). Technical Report, Taiwan, Taipei, Academia Sinica.

Levow, Gina-Anne. 2006. The Third International Chinese Language Processing Bakeoff: Word Segmentation and Named Entity Recognition, In *Proceedings of SIGHAN5 the 3rd International Chinese Language Processing Bakeoff at Coling/ACL 2006*, July, Sydney, Australia, 108-117.

Thomas, Emerson. 2005. The Second International Chinese Word Segmentation Bakeoff, In *Proceedings of The 2nd International Chinese Word Segmentation Bakeoff at SIGHAN-4*, October, Jeju Island, Korea, 123-133.

Tsai, Jia-Lin. 2005. Report to BMM-based Chinese Word Segmentor with Context-based Unknown Word Identifier for the Second International Chinese Word Segmentation Bakeoff, In *Proceedings of The 2nd International Chinese Word Segmentation Bakeoff at SIGHAN-4*, October, Jeju Island, Korea, 142-145.

Tsai, Jia-Lin. 2006. Using Word Support Model to Improve Chinese Input System, In *Proceedings of Coling/ACL 2006*, July, Sydney, Australia, 842-849.

Tsai, Jia-Lin. 2006. BMM-based Chinese Word Segmentor with Word Support Model for the SIGHAN Bakeoff 2006, In *Proceedings of SIGHAN5 the 3rd International Chinese Language Processing Bakeoff at Coling/ACL 2006*, July, Sydney, Australia, 130-133.

An Improved CRF based Chinese Language Processing System for SIGHAN Bakeoff 2007

Xihong Wu, Xiaojun Lin, Xinhao Wang, Chunyao Wu, Yaozhong Zhang and **Dianhai Yu**
Speech and Hearing Research Center
State Key Laboratory of Machine Perception,
Peking University, China, 100871
{wxh,linxj,wangxh,wucy,zhangyaoz,yudh}@cis.pku.edu.cn

Abstract

This paper describes three systems: the Chinese word segmentation (WS) system, the named entity recognition (NER) system and the Part-of-Speech tagging (POS) system, which are submitted to the Fourth International Chinese Language Processing Bakeoff. Here, Conditional Random Fields (CRFs) are employed as the primary models. For the WS and NER tracks, the n-gram language model is incorporated in our CRFs based systems in order to take into account the higher level language information. Furthermore, to improve the performances of our submitted systems, a transformation-based learning (TBL) technique is adopted for post-processing.

1 Introduction

Among 24 closed and open tracks in this bakeoff, we participated in 23 tracks, except the open NER track of MSRA. Our systems are ranked 1st in 6 tracks, and get close to the top level in several other tracks.

Recently, Maximum Entropy model(ME) and CRFs (Low et al., 2005)(Tseng et al., 2005) (Hai Zhao et al., 2006) turned out to be promising in natural language processing tracks, and obtain excellent performances on most of the test corpora of Bakeoff 2005 and Bakeoff 2006. Compared to the generative models, like HMM, the primary advantage of CRFs is that it relaxes the independence assumptions, which makes it able to handle multiple interacting features between observation elements (Wallach et al., 2004).

However, the ME and CRFs emphasize the relation of the basic units of sequence, like the Chinese characters in these tracks. While, the higher level information, like the relationship of the words is ignored. From this point of view, the n-gram language model is incorporated in our CRFs based systems in order to cover the word level language information.

Based on several pilot-experimental results, we found that the tagging errors always follow some patterns. In order to find those error patterns and correct the similar errors, we integrated the TBL post-processor in our systems. In addition, extra training data, which is transformed from People Daily Corpus (Shiwen Yu et al., 2000) with some auto-extracted transition rules, is used in each corpus for the open tracks of WS.

The remainder of this paper is organized as follows. The scheme of our three developed systems are described in section 2, 3 and 4, respectively. In section 5, evaluation results based on these systems are enumerated and discussed. Finally some conclusions are drawn in section 6.

2 Word Segmentation

The WS system mainly consists of three components, CRFs, n-gram language model and post-processing strategies.

2.1 Conditional Random Fields

Conditional Random Fields, as the statistical sequence labeling models, achieve great success in natural language processing, such as chunking (Fei Sha et al., 2003) and word segmentation (Hai Zhao et al., 2006). Different from traditional generative model, CRFs relax the constraint of the independence assumptions, and therefore turn out to be more suitable for natural language tasks.

CRFs model the conditional distribution $p(Y|X)$ of the labels Y given the observations X directly with the formulation:

$$P_\lambda(Y|X) = \frac{1}{Z(X)} exp\{\sum_{c \in C} \sum_k \lambda_k f_k(Y_c, X, c)\} \quad (1)$$

Y is the label sequence, X is the observation sequence, $Z(X)$ is a normalization term, f_k is a feature function, and c is the set of cliques in Graphic.

In our tasks, $C = \{(y_{i-1}, y_i)\}$, X is the Chinese character sequence of a sentence.

To label a Chinese character, we need to define the label tags. Here we have six types of tags according to character position in a word (Hai Zhao et al., 2006):

$$tag = \{B_1, B_2, B_3, I, E, S\}$$

"B_1, B_2, B_3, I, E" represent the first, second, third, continue, and end character positions in a multi-character word, and "S" is the single-character word tag.

The unigram feature templates used here are:

$$C_n \ (n = -2, -1, 0, 1, 2)$$
$$C_n C_{n+1} \ (n = -2, -1, 0)$$
$$C_n C_{n+1} C_{n+2} \ (n = -1)$$

Where C_0 refers to the current character and $C_{-n}(C_n)$ is the *n*th character to the left(right) of the current character. We also use the basic bigram feature template which denotes the dependency on the previous tag and current tag.

2.2 Multi-Model Integration

In order to integrate multi-model information, we use a log-linear model(Och et al., 2002) to compute the posterior probability:

$$\begin{aligned} Pr \ (W|C) &= p_{\alpha_1^M}(W|C) \\ &= \frac{exp[\sum_{m=1}^M \alpha_m h_m(W, C)]}{\sum_{W'} exp[\sum_{m=1}^M \alpha_m h_m(W', C)]} \end{aligned} \quad (2)$$

Where W is the word sequence, and C is the character sequence. The decision rule here is:

$$\begin{aligned} W_0 &= argmax_W \{Pr(W|C)\} \\ &= argmax_W \{\sum_{m=1}^M \alpha_m h_m(W, C)\} \end{aligned} \quad (3)$$

The parameters α_1^M of this model can be optimized by standard approaches, such as the Minimum Error Rate Training used in machine translation (Och, 2003). In fact, the CRFs approach is a special case of this framework when we define $M = 1$ and use the following feature function:

$$h_1(W, C) = log P_\lambda(Y|X) \quad (4)$$

In our approach, the logarithms of the scores generated by the two kinds of models are used as feature functions:

$$\begin{aligned} h_1(W, C) &= log P_{crf}(W, C) \\ &= log \prod_{w_i} P_\lambda(w_i|C) \end{aligned} \quad (5)$$

$$h_2(W, C) = log P_{lm}(W) \quad (6)$$

The first feature function(Eq.5) comes from CRFs. Instead of computing the score of the whole label sequence Y with character sequence X through $P_\lambda(Y|X)$ directly, we try to get the posterior probability of a sub-sequence to be tagged as one whole word $P_\lambda(w_i|C)$. Then we combine all the score of words together. The second feature function(Eq.6) comes from n-gram language model, which aims to catch the words information.

The log-linear model with the feature functions described above allows the dynamic programming search algorithm for efficient decoding. The system generates the word lattice with posterior probability $P_\lambda(w_i|C)$. Then the best word sequence is searched on the word lattice with the decision rule(Eq.3).

Since arbitrary sub-sequence can be viewed as a candidate word in word lattice, we need to deal with the problem of OOV words. The unigram of an OOV word is estimated as:

$$Unigram(OOV \ Word) = p^l \quad (7)$$

where p is the minimal value of unigram scores in the language model; l is the length of the OOV word, which is used as a punishment factor to avoid overemphasizing the long OOV words (Xinhao Wang et al., 2006).

2.3 Post-Processing Strategies

The division and combination rule, which has been proved to be useful in our system of Bakeoff 2006 (Xinhao Wang et al., 2006), is adopted for the post-processing in the system.

2.4 Training Data Transition

For the WS open tracks, the unique difference from closed tracks is that the additional training data is supplemented for model refinement.

For the Simplified Chinese tracks, the additional training data are collected from People Daily Corpus with a set of auto-extracted transition rules. This process is performed in a heuristic strategy and contains five steps as follows:
(1) Segment the raw People Daily texts with the corresponding system for the closed track of each corpus.
(2) Compare the result of step 1 with People Daily Corpus to get the conflict pairs. For example,

{pair1: 江泽民 vs. 江泽 民}
(Zhemin Jiang)
{pair2: 两手抓 vs. 两 手 抓}
(catch with two hands)

In each pair, the left phrase follows the People Daily Corpus segmentation guideline, while the right one is the phrase obtained from step 1.
(3) Divide the pairs into two sets: **the first set** contains the pairs with right phrase appearing in the target training data; the other pairs are in **the second set**.
(4) Select sentences which contain the left phrase of the pairs in **the second set** from People Daily Corpus.
(5) Transform these selected sentences by replacing their phrase in the left side of the pair in **the first set** to the right one. This is used as our transition rules.

3 Named Entity Recognition

The named entity recognition track is viewed as a character sequence tagging problem in our NER system and the log-linear model mentioned above is employed again to integrate multi-model information. To find the error patterns and correct them, a TBL strategy is then used in the post-processing module.

3.1 Model Description

In this NER track, we employe the log-linear model and use the logarithms of the scores generated by the two types of models as feature functions. Besides CRFs, another model is the class-based n-gram language model:

$$\begin{aligned} h_1(Y,X) &= logP_{crf}(Y,X) \\ &= logP_{\lambda}(Y|X) \qquad (8) \\ h_2(Y,X) &= logP_{clm}(Y,X) \qquad (9) \end{aligned}$$

Y is the label sequence and X is the character sequence.

CRFs are used to generate the N-best tagging results with the scores of whole label sequence Y on character sequence X by $P_{\lambda}(Y|X)$. And then, the log-linear model is used to reorder the N-best tagging results by integrating the CRFs score and the class-based n-gram language model score together.

CRFs

In this track, one Chinese character is labeled by a tag of ten classes, which denoting the beginning, continue, ending character of a specified named entity or a non-entity character. There are three types of named entities in these tracks, including person name, location name and organization name.

In CRFs, the basic features used here are:

$$C_n \ (n=-2,-1,0,1,2)$$
$$C_nC_{n+1} \ (n=-2,-1,0,1)$$
$$C_nC_{n+2} \ (n=-1)$$

Besides basic unigram features, the bigram transition features considering the previous tag is adopted with template C_n $(n=-2,-1,0,1,2)$.

Class-Based N-gram Language Model

For the class-based n-gram language model, we define that each character is a single class, while each type of named entity is viewed as a single class. With the character sequence and label sequence, the class sequence can be generated. Take this sentence for instance:

但伊卜拉依莫夫并不满足
(But Ibrahimov is not satisfied)

Table 1 shows its class sequence. Class-based n-gram language model can be trained with class sequence.

3.2 TBL

Since the analysis on our experiments shows that the tagging errors always follow some patterns in NER track, TBL strategy is adopted in our system to find these patterns and correct the similar errors.

character sequence	但	伊	卜	拉	依	莫	夫	并	不	满	足
label sequence	N	Per-B	Per-C	Per-C	Per-C	Per-C	Per-E	N	N	N	N
class sequence	但	*PERSON*						并	不	满	足

Table 1: A class sequence example

Transformation-based learning is a symbolic machine learning method, introduced by (Eric Brill, 1995). The main idea in TBL is to generate a set of transformation rules that can correct tagging errors produced by the initial process.

There are four main procedures in our TBL framework: An initial state assignment which is operated by the system we described above; a set of allowable templates for rules, ranging from words in a 3 positions windows and name entity information in a 3-word window with their combinations considered, and rules which are learned according to the tagging differences between training data and results generated by our system, at last, those rules are introduced to correct similar errors.

4 POS Tagging

The POS tagging track is to assign the part-of-speech sequence for the correctly segmented word sequence. In our system, for the CTB corpus, the CRFs are adopted; however for the other four corpora, considering the limitations of resources and time, the ME model is adopted. To improve the performance of ME model, the POS tag of the previous word is taken as a feature and the dynamic programming strategy is used in decoding.

In the closed track, the features include the basic features and their combined features. Firstly the previous and next words of the current word are taken as the basic features. Secondly, based on the analysis of the OOV words, the first and last characters of the current word, as well as the length of the current word are proven to be effective features for the OOV POS. Furthermore since the long distance constraint word may impact the POS of current word (Yan Zhao et al., 2006), in the open track, a Chinese parser is imported and the word depended on the current word is extracted as feature.

5 Experiments and Results

We have participated in 23 tracks, except the open NER track of MSRA. CRFs, ME model and n-gram language model are adopted in these systems. Our implementation uses the CRF++ package[1] provided by Taku Kudo, the Maximum Entropy Toolkit[2] provided by Zhang Le, and the SRILM Toolkit provided by Andreas Stolcke (Andreas Stolcke et al., 2002).

5.1 Chinese Word Segmentation

In the closed tracks, CRFs and bigram language model are trained on the given training data for each corpus. In order to integrate these two models, it is necessary to train the corresponding parameter α_1^M with Minimum Error Rate Training approache based on a development data. Since the development data is not provided in this bakeoff, a ten-fold cross validation approach is employed to implement the parameter training. A set of parameters can be trained independently, and then the mean value is calculated as the estimation of each parameter.

Table 2 gives the results of our WS system for closed tracks.

	baseline	+LM	+LM+Post
CTB	94.7	94.7	94.8
NCC	92.6	92.4	92.9
SXU	94.7	95.7	95.8
CITYU	92.9	93.7	93.9
CKIP	93.2	93.7	93.7

Table 2: Word segmentation performance on F-value with different approach for the closed tracks

In the open tracks, as we do not have enough time to finish the parameter estimation on the new data, our system adopt the same parameters α_1^M used in closed tracks. The unique difference from closed

[1] http://chasen.org/taku/software/CRF++

[2] http://homepages.inf.ed.ac.uk/s0450736/maxent toolkit.html

tracks is that extra training data is added for each corpus to improve the performance. For the Simplified Chinese tracks, additional data comes from People Daily Corpus which is transformed by our transition strategy. At the same time, for the Traditional Chinese tracks, additional data comes from the training and testing data used in the early Bakeoff. However, we implement two systems for the CTB open track. The system (a) takes the training and testing data used in the early Bakeoff as additional data, and System (b) takes the translated People Daily Corpus as additional data. Table 3 gives the results of our open WS system.

	baseline	+LM	+LM+Post
CTB(a)	99.2	99.2	99.3
CTB(b)	95.6	95.1	97.0
NCC	93.7	93.0	92.9
SXU	96.4	87.0	95.8
CITYU	95.8	90.6	91.0
CKIP	94.5	94.8	95.1

Table 3: Word segmentation performance on F-value with different approach for the open tracks

The result shows that the system performance is sensitive to the parameters α_1^M. Although we train the useful parameter for closed tracks, it plays a bad role in open tracks as we do not adapt it for the additional training data.

5.2 Named Entity Recognition

In the closed NER tracks, CRFs and class-based trigram language model are trained on the given training data for each corpus. The same approach employed in the WS tracks is adopted to train the corresponding parameter α_1^M in our NER systems. Meanwhile, the TBL rules trained via five-fold cross validation approach are also used in post-processing procedure. Table 4 reports the results of our closed NER system.

5.3 POS Tagging

The experiments show that the CRFs/ME method is superior to the TBL method, and the concurrent errors for these two methods are less than 60%. Therefore we adopted TBL to correct the output results of CRFs/ME: If the output tags of CRFs/ME and TBL are not consistent and the output probability of CRFs/ME is below a certain threshold, the TBL results are fixed. Here the 90% of the training set is taken as the training data and remained 10% is separated as the development data to get the threshold, which is 0.60 for the CRFs, and 0.90 for the ME. In addition, the POS tagged corpus of the Chinese Treebank 5.0 from LDC is added to the training data for CTB open track. In our system, the Berkeley Parser (Slav Petrov et al., 2006) is adopted to obtain the long distance constraint words. The performance achieved by the methods described above on each corpus are reported in Table 5.

	baseline	+LM	+LM+Post
MSRA	89.3	89.7	89.9
CITYU	79.3	80.6	80.5

Table 4: Named entity recognition F-value through different approaches for the closed tracks

	CRFs/ME	TBL	CRFs/ME +TBL	CRFs/ME +TBL +Syntax
CTIYU	88.7	87.7	89.1	89.0
CKIP	91.8	91.4	92.2	92.1
CTB	94.0	92.7	94.3	96.5
NCC	94.6	94.3	94.9	95.0
PKU	93.5	93.2	94.0	94.1

Table 5: POS tagging performance on total-accuracy with different approach

6 Conclusion

In this paper, we have briefly described our systems participating in the Bakeoff 2007. In the WS and NER systems, the log-linear model is adopted to integrate CRFs and language model, which improves the system performances effectively. At the same time, system integration approach used in the POS system also proves its validity. In addition, a heuristic strategy is imported to generate additional training data for the open WS tracks. Finally, several post-processing strategies are used to further improve our systems.

References

Jin Kiat Low, Hwee Tou Ng and Wenyuan Guo. 2005. A Maximum Entropy Approach to Chinese Word Segmentation. *Proceedings of the Fourth SIGHAN Workshop on Chinese Language Processing.* pp. 161-164. Jeju Island, Korea.

Huihsin Tseng, Pichuan Chang, Galen Andrew, Daniel Jurafsky, Christopher Manning. 2005. A Conditional Random Field Word Segmenter for Sighan Bakeoff 2005. *Proceedings of the Fourth SIGHAN Workshop on Chinese Language Processing.* pp. 168-171. Jeju Island, Korea.

Hai Zhao, Chang-Ning Huang and Mu Li. 2006. An Improved Chinese Word Segmentation System with Conditional Random Field. *Proceedings of the Fifth SIGHAN Workshop on Chinese Language Processing.* pp. 162-165. Sydney, Australia.

Hanna M. Wallach. 2004. Conditional Random Fields: An Introduction. *Technical Report, UPenn CIS TR MS-CIS-04-21.*

Shiwen Yu, Xuefeng Zhu and Huiming Duan. 2000. Specification of large-scale modern Chinese corpus. *Proceedings of ICMLP'2001.* pp. 18-24. Urumqi, China.

Fei Sha and Fernando Pereira. 2003. Shallow Parsing with Conditional Random Fields. *Proceedings of Human Language Technology/NAACL.* pp. 213-220. Edmonton, Canada.

Franz Josef Och and Hermann Ney. 2002. Discriminative training and maximum entropy models for statistical machine translation. *Proceedings of the 40th Annual Meeting of the Association for Computational Linguistics (ACL).* pp. 295-302. Philadelphia, PA.

Franz Josef Och. 2003. Minimum Error Rate Training in Statistical Machine Translation. *Proceedings of the 41th Annual Meeting of the Association for Computational Linguistics (ACL).* pp. 160-167. Sapporo, Japan.

Xinhao Wang, Xiaojun Lin, Dianhai Yu, Hao Tian, Xihong Wu. 2006. Chinese Word Segmentation with Maximum Entropy and N-gram Language Model. *the Fifth SIGHAN Workshop on Chinese Language Processing.* pp. 138-141. Sydney, Australia.

Eric Brill. 1995. Transformation-based error-driven learning and natural language processing: a case study in Part-of-Speech tagging. *Computational Lingusitics.* 21(4).

Yan Zhao, Xiaolong Wang, Bingquan Liu, and Yi Guan. 2006. Fusion of Clustering Trigger-Pair Features for POS Tagging Based on Maximum Entropy Model. *Journal of Computer Research and Development.* 43(2). pp. 268-274.

Andreas Stolcke. 2002. SRILM - An Extensible Language Modeling Toolkit. *Proceedings of International Conference on Spoken Language Processing.* pp. 901-904. Denver, Colorado.

Slav Petrov, Leon Barrett, Romain Thibaux and Dan Klein. 2006. Learning Accurate, Compact, and Interpretable Tree Annotation. *Proceedings of the 21st International Conference on Computational Linguistics and the 44th annual meeting of the ACL.* pp. 433-440. Sydney, Australia.

Description of the NCU Chinese Word Segmentation and Part-of-Speech Tagging for SIGHAN Bakeoff 2007

Yu-Chieh Wu
Dept. of Computer Science and Information Engineering
National Central University
Taoyuan, Taiwan
bcbb@db.csie.ncu.edu.tw

Jie-Chi Yang
Graduate Institute of Network Learning Technology
National Central University
Taoyuan, Taiwan
yang@cl.ncu.edu.tw

Yue-Shi Lee
Dept. of Computer Science and Information Engineering
Ming Chuan University
Taoyuan, Taiwan
leeys@mcu.edu.tw

Abstract

In Chinese, most of the language processing starts from word segmentation and part-of-speech (POS) tagging. These two steps tokenize the word from a sequence of characters and predict the syntactic labels for each segmented word. In this paper, we present two distinct sequential tagging models for the above two tasks. The first word segmentation model was basically similar to previous work which made use of conditional random fields (CRF) and set of predefined dictionaries to recognize word boundaries. Second, we revise and modify support vector machine-based chunking model to label the POS tag in the tagging task. Our method in the WS task achieves moderately rank among all participants, while in the POS tagging task, it reaches very competitive results.

1 Introduction

With the rapid expansion of online text articles such as blog, web news, and research/technical reports, there is an increasing demand for text mining and management. Different from western-like languages, handling oriented languages is far more difficult since there is no explicit boundary symbol to indicate what a word is in the text. However the most important preliminary step for natural language processing is to tokenize words and separate them from the word sequence. In Chinese, the word tokenization is also known as word segmentation or Chinese word tokenization. The problem of the Chinese word segmentation is very critical for most Chinese linguistics because the error segmented words deeply affects the downstream purpose, like POS tagging and parsing. In addition tokenizing the unknown words is also an unavoidable problem.

To support the above targets, it is necessary to detect the boundaries between words in a given sentence. In tradition, the Chinese word segmentation technologies can be categorized into three types, (heuristic) rule-based, machine learning, and hybrid. Among them, the machine learning-based techniques showed excellent performance in many recent research studies (Peng et al., 2004; Zhou et al., 2005; Gao et al., 2004). This method treats the word segmentation problem as a sequence of word classification. The classifier online assigns either "boundary" or "non-boundary" label to each word by learning from the large annotated corpora. Machine learning-based word segmentation method is quite similar to the word sequence inference techniques, such as part-of-speech (POS) tagging (Clark et al., 2003; Gimenez and Marquez, 2003), phrase chunking (Lee and Wu, 2007) and word dependency parsing (Wu et al., 2006, 2007).

In this paper, we present two prototype systems for Chinese word segmentation and POS tagging tasks. The former was basically an extension of previous literatures (Ng and Low, 2004; Zhou et al., 2006), while the latter incorporates the unknown word and known word tagging into one step. The two frameworks were designed based on two variant machine learning algorithms, namely CRF and SVM. In our pilot study, the SVM showed better performance than CRF in the POS tagging task. To identify unknown words, we also encode the suffix and prefix features to represent the training example. The strategy was showed very effective for improving both known and unknown word chunking on both Chinese and English phrase chunking (Lee and Wu, 2007). In this year, the presented word segmentation method achieved moderate rank among all participants. Meanwhile, the proposed SVM-based POS tagging model reached very competitive accuracy in most POS tasks. For example, our method yields second best result on the CTB POS tagging track.

The rest of this paper is organized as follows. Section 2 describes employed machine learning algorithms, CRF and SVM. In section 3, we present the proposed word segmentation and POS tagging framework which used for the SIGHAN-bake-off this year. Experimental result and evaluations are reported in section 4. Finally, in section 5, we draw conclusion and future remarks.

2 Classification Algorithms

2.1 Conditional Random Fields

Conditional random field (CRF) was an extension of both Maximum Entropy Model (MEMs) and Hidden Markov Models (HMMs) that was firstly introduced by (Lafferty et al., 2001). CRF defined conditional probability distribution P(*Y*|*X*) of given sequence given input sentence where *Y* is the "class label" sequence and *X* denotes as the observation word sequence.

A CRF on (*X*,*Y*) is specified by a feature vector *F* of local context and the corresponding feature weight λ. The *F* can be treated as the combination of state transition and observation value in conventional HMM. To determine the optimal label sequence, the CRF uses the following equation to estimate the most probability.

$$y = \arg\max_y P(y \mid x, \lambda) = \arg\max_y \lambda F(y, x)$$

The most probable label sequence y can be efficiently extracted via the Viterbi algorithm. However, training a CRF is equivalent to estimate the parameter set λ for the feature set. In this paper, we directly use CRF++ (Kudo and Matsumoto, 2003) which included the quasi-Newton L-BFGS [1] method (Nocedal and Wright, 1999) to iterative update the parameters.

2.2 Support Vector Machines

Assume we have a set of training examples,

$$(x_1, y_1), (x_2, y_2), \ldots, (x_n, y_n),\ x_i \in \Re^D,\ y_i \in \{+1, -1\}$$

where x_i is a feature vector in *D*-dimension space of the *i*-th example, and y_i is the label of x_i either positive or negative. The training of SVMs involves minimizing the following object function (primal form, soft-margin (Vapnik, 1995)):

$$\text{minimize}: W(\alpha) = \frac{1}{2}\vec{W}\cdot\vec{W} + C\sum_{i=1}^{n} Loss(\vec{W}\cdot x_i, y_i) \quad (1)$$

The loss function indicates the loss of misclassification risk. Usually, the hinge-loss is used (Vapnik, 1995; Keerthi and DeCoste, 2005). The factor *C* in (1) is a parameter that allows one to trade off training error and margin size. To classify a given testing example *X*, the decision rule takes the following form:

$$y(X) = sign\left(\left(\sum_{x_i \in SVs} \alpha_i y_i K(X, x_i)\right) + b\right) \quad (2)$$

α_i represents the weight of training example x_i which lies on the hyperplane, and *b* denotes as a bias threshold. *SVs* means the support vectors and obviously has the non-zero weights of α_i. $K(X, x_i) = \phi(X)\cdot\phi(x_i)$ is a pre-defined kernel function that might transform the original feature space from $\Re^D$ to $\Re^{D'}$ (usually *D*<<*D*'). In the linear kernel form, the $K(X, x_i)$ simply compute the dot products of the two variables. By introducing of the polynomial kernel, we re-write the decision function of (1) as:

[1] http://www-unix.mcs.anl.gov/tao/

$$y(X) = sign((\sum_{x_i \in SVs} \alpha_i y_i K(X, x_i)) + b) \\ = sign((\sum_{x_i \in SVs} \alpha_i y_i (1 + dot(X, x_i)^d) + b) \quad (3)$$

where

$$K(X, x_i) = (1 + dot(X, x_i))^d \quad (4)$$

and d is the polynomial kernel degree.

In many NLP problems, the training and testing examples are represented as bits of binary vectors. In this section, we focus on this case. Later, we present a general form without considering this constraint.

3 System Description

In this section, we first describe the problem settings for the word segmentation problems. In section 3.2, the proposed POS tagging framework is then presented.

3.1 Word Sequence Classification

Similar to English text chunking (Ramshaw and Marcus, 1995; Lee and Wu, 2007), the word sequence classification model aims to classify each word via encoding its context features.

By encoding with BIES (LMR tagging scheme) or IOB2 style, both WS and NER problems can be viewed as a sequence of word classification. During testing, we seek to find the optimal word type for each Chinese character. These types strongly reflect the actual word boundaries for Chinese words or named entity phrases.

As reported by (Zhou et al., 2006), the use of richer tag set can effectively enhance the performance. They extend the tag of "Begin of word" into "second-begin" and "third-begin" to capture more character types. However, there are some ambiguous problem to the 3-character Chinese words and 4-character Chinese words. For example, to encode "素還真" with his extended tag set, the first character can be encoded as "B" tag. But for the second character, we can use "second-begin" or "I" tag to represent the middle of word.

In order to make the extension clearer, in this paper, we explicitly extend the B tag and E tag with "after begin" (BI), and "before end" (IE) tags. Table 1 lists the difference between the traditional BIES and the proposed E-BIES encodings methods. Table 2 illustrates an example of how the BIES and E-BIES encode with different number of characters.

Table 1: BIES and E-BIES encoding strategies

	BIES	E-BIES
Begin of a word	B	B
After begin of a word	-	BI
Middle of a word	I	I
Before end of a word	-	IE
End of a word	E	E
Single word	S	S

Table 2: An example of the BIES and E-BIES encoding strategies

N-character word	BIES	E-BIES
看	S	S
中原	B,E	B,E
素還真	B,I,E	B,BI,E
玄子神功	B,I,I,E	B,BI,IE,E
一氣化三千	B,I,I,I,E	B,BI,I,IE,E

To effect classify each character, in this paper, we adopted most feature types to train the CRF (Kudo and Matsumoto, 2004). Table 3 lists the adopted feature templates. The dictionary flag is very similar to previous literature (Ng and Low, 2004) while we adding up English full-character into our dictionary.

Table 3: Feature template used for Chinese word segmentation task

Feature Type	Context Position	Description
Unigram	C_{-2},C_{-1},C_0,C_1,C_2	Chinese character fe ature
Nearing Bi-gram	(C_{-2},C_{-1})(C_{-1},C_0) (C_1,C_0)(C_1,C_2)	Bi-character feature
Jump Bigram	(C_{-1},C_1)	Non-continuous char acter feature
Dictionary Flag	C_0	Date, Digital, Englis h letter or punctuatio n
Dictionary Flag *N*-gram	(C_{-1},C_0,C_1)	*N*-gram of the dictio nary flags

3.2 Feature Codification for Chinese POS Tagging

As reported by (Ng, and Low, 2004; Clark et al., 2003), the pure POS tagging performance is no more than 92% in the CTB data and no more than

96.8% in English WSJ. The learner used in his literature is maximum entropy model. However the main limitation of his POS tagging strategy is that the unknown word classification problem was not resolved.

To circumvent this vita, we simply extend the idea of SVM-based chunker (Lee and Wu, 2007) and develop our own SVM-based POS tagger. Although CRF showed excellent performance in word segmentation task, in English POS tagging, the SVM is more effective than CRF. Also in our closed experiment, we had tried transformation-based error-driven learner (TBL), CRF, and SVM classifiers. The pilot experiment showed that the SVM outperformed the other two learners and achieved almost 94% accuracy in the CTB data. Meanwhile TBL reached the worst result than the other two classifiers (~88%).

Handling unknown word is very important to POS tagging problem. As pointed out by (Lee and Wu, 2007; Gimenez, and Marquez, 2003), the introduction of suffix features can effectively help to guess the unknown words for tagging and chunking. Different from (Gimenez and Marquez, 2003), we did not derive data for unknown word guessing. Instead, we directly encode all suffix- and prefix-features for each training instance. In training phase, the rich feature types are able to disambiguate not only the unknown word guessing, but also improve the known word classification. As reported by (Lee and Wu, 2007), the strategy did improve the English and Chinese chunking performance for both known and unknown words.

Table 4: Feature patterns used for Chinese POS tagging task

Feature Type	Context Position	Description
Unigram	$W_{-2},W_{-1},W_0,W_1,W_2$	Chinese word feat ure
Nearing Bigram	$(W_{-2},W_{-1})(W_{-1},W_0)$ $(W_1,W_0)(W_1,W_2)$	Bi-word feature
Jump Bi-gram	$(W_{-2},W_0)(W_{-1},W_1)$ $(W_2,W_0)(W_1,W_3)$	Non-continuous c haracter feature
Possible tags	W_0	Possible POS tag i n the training data
Prefix 3/2/1 characters	W_{-1},W_0,W_1	Pre-characters of word
Suffix 3/2/1 characters	W_{-1},W_0,W_1	Post-characters of word

The used feature set of our POS tagger is listed in Table 4. In this paper, we did not conduct the feature selection experiment for each tagging corpus, instead a unified feature set was used due to the time line. We trust our POS tagger could be further improved by removing or adding new feature set.

The learner used in this paper (SVM) is mainly developed by our own (Wu et al., 2007). The cost factor C is simply set as 0.15 for all languages. Furthermore, to remove rare words, we eliminate the words which appear no more than twice in the training data.

4 Evaluations and Experimental Result

4.1 Dataset and Evaluations

In this year, we mainly focus on the close track for WS and POS tagging tracks. The CTB, SXU, and NCC corpora were used for evaluated the presented word segmentation method, while all the released POS tagging data were tested by our SVM-based tagger, included CityU, CKIP, CTB, NCC, and PKU. Both settings of the two models were set as previously noted. The evaluation of the two tasks was mainly measured by the three metrics, namely, recall, precision, and f-measure. However, the evaluation process for the POS tagging track is somewhat different from WS. In WS, participant should reform the testing data into sentence level whereas in the POS tagging track the word had been correctly segmented. Thus the measurement of the POS tagging track is mainly accuracy-based (correct or incorrect).

4.2 Experimental Result on Word Segmentation Task

In this year, we only select the following three data to perform our method for the word segmentation task. They are CTB, NCC, and SXU where the NCC and SXU are fresh in this year. Table5 shows the experimental results of our model in the close WS track with except for CKIP and CityU corpora.

Table 5: Official results on the word segmentation task (closed-task)

	Recall	Precision	F-measure
CTB	0.9471	0.9500	0.9486
NCC	0.9236	0.9269	0.9252
SXU	0.9505	0.9515	0.9510

As shown above, our method in the CTB data showed 10th best out of 26 submissions. In the NCC and SXU datasets, our method achieved 19/26 and 18/30 rank. In overall, the presented extend-BIES scheme seems to work well on the CTB data and results in middle rank in comparison to the other participants.

4.3 Experimental Result on Part-of-Speech Tagging Task

In the second experiment, we focus on the designed POS tagging model. To measure the effectiveness, we apply our method to all the released dataset, i.e., CityU, CKIP, CTB, NCC, and PKU. Table 6 lists the experimental result of our method in this task.

Similar to WS task, our method is still very effective to CTB dataset. It turns out our method achieved second best in the CTB, while for the other corpora, it achieved 4th best among all the participants. We also found that our method was very close to the top 1 score about 1.3% (CKIP) to 0.09%. For the NCC, and PKU, our method was worse than the best system in 0.8% in overall accuracy. We conclude that by selecting suitable features and cost factor C to SVM, our method can be further improved. We left the work as future direction.

Table 6: Official results on the part-of-speech tagging task (closed-task)

	Riv	Roov	Rmt	Accuracy
CityU	0.9326	0.4322	0.8707	0.8865
CKIP	0.9504	0.5631	0.9065	0.9160
CTB	0.9554	0.7135	0.9183	0.9401
NCC	0.9658	0.5822	0.9116	0.9456
PKU	0.9591	0.5832	0.9173	0.9368

5 Conclusions and Future Work

Chinese word segmentation is the most important infrastructure for many Chinese linguistic technologies such as text categorization and information retrieval. In this paper, we present simple Chinese word segmentation and part-of-speech tagging models based on the conventional sequence classification technique. We treat the two tasks as two different learning framework and applying CRF and SVM as separated learners. Without any prior knowledge and rules, such a simple technique shows satisfactory results on both word segmentation and part-of-speech tagging tasks. In POS tagging task, our model shows very competitive results which merely spend few hours to train. To reach state-of-the-art, our method still needs to further select features and parameter tunings. In the future, one of the main directions is to extend this model toward full unsupervised learning from large un-annotated text. Mining from large unlabeled data have been showed benefits to improve the original accuracy. Thus, not only the stochastic feature analysis, but also adjust the learner from unlabeled data are important future remarks.

References

Clark, S., Curran, J. R., and Osborne, M. 2003. Bootstrapping POS Taggers Using Unlabeled data. In Proceedings of the 7th Conference on Natural Language Learning (CoNLL), pages 49-55.

Gao, J., Wu, A., Li, M., Huang, C. N., Li, H., Xia, X., and Qin, H. 2004. Adaptive Chinese word segmentation. In Proceedings the 41st Annual Meeting of the Association for Computational Linguistics, pp. 21-26.

Giménez, J., and Márquez, L. 2003. Fast and accurate Part-of-Speech tagging: the SVM approach revisited. In Proceedings of the International Conference on Recent Advances in Natural Language Processing, pages 158-165.

Keerthi, S., and DeCoste, D. 2005. A Modified Finite Newton Method for Fast Solution of Large Scale Linear SVMs. Journal of Machine Learning Research, 6: 341-361.

Kudo, T., and Matsumoto, Y. 2004. Appliying Conditional Random Fields to Japanese Morphological Analysis. In Proceedings of the Empirical. Methods in Natural Language Processing (EMNLP), pages 230-237.

Lafferty, J., McCallum, A., and Pereira, F. 2001. Conditional Random Field: Probabilistic models for segmenting and labeling sequence data. In Proceedings of the International Conference on Machine Learning.

Ramshaw, L. A., and Marcus, M. P. 1995. Text Chunking Using Transformation-based Learning.

In Proceedings of the 3rd Workshop on Very Large Corpora, pages 82-94.

Lee, Y. S. and Wu, Y. C. 2007. A Robust Multilingual Portable Phrase Chunking System. Expert Systems with Applications, 33(3): 1-26.

Ng, H. T., and Low, J. K. 2004. Chinese Part-of-Speech Tagging: One-at-a-time or All-at-once? Word-based or Character-based? In Proceedings of the Empirical. Methods in Natural Language Processing (EMNLP).

Nocedal, J., and Wright, S. 1999. Numerical optimization. Springer.

Peng, F., Feng, F., and McCallum, A. 2004. Chinese segmentation and new word detection using conditional random fields. In Porceedings of the Computational Linguistics, pp. 562-568.

Shi, W. 2005. Chinese Word Segmentation Based On Direct Maximum Entropy Model. In Proceedings of the Fourth SIGHAN Workshop on Chinese Language Processing.

Vapnik, V. N. 1995. The Nature of Statistical Learning Theory. Springer.

Wu, Y. C., Yang, J. C., and Lee, Y. S. 2007. An Approximate Approach for Training Polynomial Kernel SVMs in Linear Time. In Proceedings of the Annual Meeting of the Association for Computational Linguistics, pages 65-68.

Wu, Y. C., Lee, Y. S., and Yang, J. C. 2007. Multilingual Deterministic Dependency Parsing Framework using Modified Finite Newton Method Support Vector Machines. In Proceedings of the Joint Conferences on Empirical Methods on Natural Language Processing and Conference on Natural Language Learning (EMNLP-CoNLL), pages 1175-1181.

Wu, Y. C., Lee, Y. S., and Yang, J. C. 2006. The Exploration of Deterministic and Efficient Dependency Parsing. In Proceedings of the 10th Conference on Natural Language Learning (CoNLL).

Zhou, H., Huang, C. N., and Li, M. 2006. An Improved Word Segmentation System with Conditional Random Fields. In Proceedings of the SIGHAN Workshop on Chinese Language Processing Workshop, pages 162-165.

Zhou, J., Dai, X., Ni, R., Chen, J. 2005. .A Hybrid Approach to Chinese Word Segmentation around CRFs. In Proceedings of the Fourth SIGHAN Workshop on Chinese Language Processing.

CRF-based Hybrid Model for Word Segmentation, NER and even POS Tagging

Zhiting Xu, Xian Qian, Yuejie Zhang, Yaqian Zhou
Department of Computer Science & Engineering,
Shanghai Key Laboratory of Intelligent Information Processing,
Fudan University, Shanghai 200433, P. R. China
{zhiting, qianxian, yjzhang, zhouyaqian}@fudan.edu.cn

Abstract

This paper presents systems submitted to the close track of Fourth SIGHAN Bakeoff. We built up three systems based on Conditional Random Field for Chinese Word Segmentation, Named Entity Recognition and Part-Of-Speech Tagging respectively. Our systems employed basic features as well as a large number of linguistic features. For segmentation task, we adjusted the BIO tags according to confidence of each character. Our final system achieve a F-score of 94.18 at CTB, 92.86 at NCC, 94.59 at SXU on Segmentation, 85.26 at MSRA on Named Entity Recognition, and 90.65 at PKU on Part-Of-Speech Tagging.

1 Introduction

Fourth SIGHAN Bakeoff includes three tasks, that is, Word Segmentation, Named Entity Recognition (NER) and Part-Of-Speech (POS) Tagging. In the POS Tagging task, the testing corpora are pre-segmented. Word Segmentation, NER and POS Tagging could be viewed as classification problems. In a Segmentation task, each character should be classified into three classes, B, I, O, indicating whether this character is the Beginning of a word, In a word or Out of a word. For NER, each character is assigned a tag indicating what kind of Named Entity (NE) this character is (Beginning of a Person Name (PN), In a PN, Beginning of a Location Name (LN), In a LN, Beginning of an Organization Name (ON), In an ON or not-a-NE). In POS tagging task defined by Fourth SIGHAN Bakeoff, we only need to give a POS tag for each given word in a context.

We attended the close track of CTB, NCC, SXU on Segmentation, MSRA on NER and PKU on POS Tagging. In the close track, we cannot use any external resource, and thus we extracted several word lists from training corpora to form multiple features beside basic features. Then we trained CRF models based on these feature sets. In CRF models, a margin of each character can be gotten, and the margin could be considered as the confidence of that character. For the Segmentation task, we performed the Maximum Probability Segmentation first, through which each character is assigned a BIO tag (B represents the Beginning of a word, I represents In a word and O represents Out of a word). If the confidence of a character is lower than the threshold, the tag of that character will be adjusted to the tag assigned by the Maximum Probability Segmentation (R. Zhang et al., 2006).

2 Conditional Random Fields

Conditional Random Fields (CRFs) are a class of undirected graphical models with exponent distribution (Lafferty et al., 2001). A common used special case of CRFs is linear chain, which has a distribution of:

$$P_\Lambda(\vec{y} \mid \vec{x}) = \frac{1}{Z_{\vec{x}}} \exp\left(\sum_{t=1}^{T} \sum_{k} \lambda_k f_k(y_{t-1}, y_t, \vec{x}, t)\right) \quad (1)$$

where $f_k(y_{t-1}, y_t \vec{x}, t)$ is a function which is usually an indicator function; λ_k is the learned weight of feature f_k; and $Z_{\vec{x}}$ is the normalization factor. The feature function actually consists of two kinds of features, that is, the feature of single state and the feature of transferring between states. Features will be discussed in section 3.

Several methods (e.g. GIS, IIS, L-BFGS) could be used to estimate λ_k, and L-BFGS has been showed to converge faster than GIS and IIS. To build up our system, we used Pocket CRF[1].

3 Feature Representation

We used three feature sets for three tasks respectively, and will describe them respectively.

3.1 Word Segmentation

We mainly adopted features from (H. T. Ng et al., 2004, Y. Shi et al., 2007), as following:

a) $C_n(n=-2, -1, 0, 1, 2)$
b) $C_nC_{n+1}(n=-2,-1,0,1)$
c) $C_{-1}C_1$
d) $C_nC_{n+1}C_{n+2}$ (n=-1, 0, 1)
e) *Pu*(C_0)
f) $T(C_{-2})T(C_{-1})T(C_0)T(C_1)T(C_2)$
g) $L_{Begin}(C_0)$, $L_{end}(C_0)$
h) *Single*(C_0)

where C_0 represents the current character and C_n represents the n^{st} character from the current character. *Pu*(C_0) indicates whether current word is a punctuation. this feature template helps to indicate the end of a sentence. T(C) represents the type of character C. There are four types we used: (1) Chinese Number ("一/one", "二/two", "十/ten"); (2) Chinese Dates ("日/day", "月/month", "年/year"); (3) English letters; and (4) other characters. The (f) feature template is used to recognize the Chinese dates for the construction of Chinese dates may cause the sparseness problem. $L_{Begin}(C_0)$ represents the maximum length of the word beginning with the character C_0, and $L_{end}(C_0)$ presents the maximum length of the word ending with the character C_0. The (g) feature template is used to decide the boundary of a word. *Single*(C_0) shows whether current character can form a word solely.

3.2 Named Entity Recognition

Most features described in (Y. Wu et al., 2005) are used in our systems. Specifically, the following is the feature templates we used:

a) *Surname*(C_0): Whether current character is in a Surname List, which includes all first characters of PNs in the training corpora.
b) *PersonName*($C_0C_1C_2$, C_0C_1): Whether $C_0C_1C_2$, C_0C_1 is in the Person Name List, which contains all PNs in the training corpora.
c) *PersonTitle*($C_{-2}C_{-1}$): Whether $C_{-2}C_{-1}$ is in the Person Title List, which is extracted from the previous two characters of each PN in the training corpora.
d) *LocationName*(C_0C_1,$C_0C_1C_2$,$C_0C_1C_2C_3$): Whether C_0C_1,$C_0C_1C_2$,$C_0C_1C_2C_3$ is in the Location Name List, which includes all LNs in the training corpora.
e) *LocationSuffix*(C_0): Whether current character is in the Location Suffix List, which is constructed using the last character of each LN in the training corpora.
f) *OrgSuffix*(C_0): Whether current character is in the Organization Suffix List, which contains the last-two-character of each ON in the training corpora.

3.3 Part-Of-Speech Tagging

We employed part of feature templates described in (H. T. Ng et al., 2004, Y. Shi et al., 2007). Since we are in the close track, we cannot use morphological features from external resources such as HowNet, and we used features that are available just from the training corpora.

a) W_n, (n=-2,-1,0,1,2)
b) W_nW_{n+1}, (n=-2,-1,0,1)
c) $W_{-1}W_1$
d) $W_{n-1}W_nW_{n+1}$ (n=-1, 1)
e) $C_n(W_0)$ (n=0,1,2,3)
f) *Length*(W_0)

where C_n represents the nth character of the current word, and *Length*(W_0) indicates the length of the current word.

4 Reliability Evaluation

In the task of Word Segmentation, the label of each character is adjusted according to their reliability. For each sentence, we perform Maximum Probability Segmentation first, through which we can get a BIO tagging for each character in the sentence.

After that, the features are extracted according to the feature templates, and the weight of each feature has already been estimated in the step of training. Then marginal probability for each character can be computed as follows:

[1] http://sourceforge.net/project/showfiles.php?group_id=201943

$$p(y \mid \vec{x}) = \frac{1}{Z(x)} \exp(\lambda_i f_i(\vec{x}, y)) \quad (2)$$

The value of $p(y \mid \vec{x})$ becomes the original reliability value of BIO label y for the current character under the current contexts. If the probability of y with the largest probability is lower than 0.75, which is decided according to the experiment results, the tag given by Maximum Probability Segmentation will be used instead of tag given by CRF. The motivation of this method is to use the Maximum Probability method to enhance the F-measure of In-Vocabulary (IV) Words. According to the results reported in (R. Zhang et al., 2006), CRF performs relatively better on Out-of-Vocabulary (OOV) words while Maximum Probability performs well on IV words, so a model combining the advantages of these two methods is appealing. One simplest way to combine them is the method we described. Besides, there are some complex methods, such as estimation using Support Vector Machine (SVM) for CRF, CRF combining boosting and combining Margin Infused Relaxed Algorithm (MIRA) with CRF, that might perform better. However, we did not have enough time to implement these methods, and we will compare them detailedly in the future work.

5 Experiments

5.1 Results on Fourth SIGHAN Bakeoff

We participated in the close track on Word Segmentation on CTB, NCC and SXU corpora, NER on MSRA corpora and POS Tagging on PKU corpora.

For Word Segmentation and NER, our memory was enough to use all features. However, for POS tagging, we did not have enough memory to use all features, and we set a frequency cutoff of 10; that is, we could only estimate variables for those features that occurred more than ten times.

Our results of Segmentation are listed in the Tabel 1, the results of NER are listed in the Tabel 2, and the results of POS Tagging are listed in the Tabel 3.

	R	P	F	R_{oov}	R_{iv}
CTB	0.9459	0.9418	0.9439	0.6589	0.9628
NCC	0.9396	0.9286	0.9341	0.5007	0.9614
SXU	0.9554	0.9459	0.9507	0.6206	0.9735

Tabel 1. Results of Word Segmentation

MSRA	P	R	F
PER	0.8084	0.8557	0.8314
LOC	0.9138	0.8576	0.8848
ORG	0.8666	0.773	0.8171
Overall	0.873	0.8331	0.8526

Tabel 2. Results of NER

	Total-A	IV-R	OOV-R	MT-R
PKU	0.9065	0.9259	0.5836	0.8903

Tabel 3. Results of POS Tagging

5.2 Errors Analysis

Observing our results of Word Segmentation and POS Tagging, we found that the recall of OOV is relatively low, this may be improved through introducing features aiming to enhance the performance of OOV.

On NER task, we noticed that precision of PN recognition is relative low, and we found that our system may classify some ONs as PNs, such as "吉尼斯(Guinness)/ORG" and "世界记录(World Record)/)". Besides, the bound of PN is sometimes confusing and may cause problems. For example, "胡绳/PER 曾/ 有/ 题词" may be segmented as "胡绳曾/PER 有/ 题词". Further, some words beginning with Chinese surname, such as "丁丑盛夏", may be classified as PN.

For List may not be the real suffix. For example, "玉峰山麓" should be a LN, but it is very likely that "玉峰山" is recognized as a LN for its suffix "山". Another problem involves the characters in the Location Name list may not a LN all the time. In the context "华裔/ 作家/", for example, "华" means Chinese rather than China.

For ONs, the correlative dictionary also exists. Consider sequence "人大代表", which should be a single word, "人大" is in the Organization Name List and thus it is recognized as an ON in our system. Another involves the subsequence of a word. For example, the sequence "湖北钟祥市工业局长", which should be a person title, but "湖北钟祥市工业局" is an ON. Besides, our recall of ON is low for the length of an ON could be very long.

6 Conclusions and Future Works

We built up our systems based on the CRF model and employed multiple linguistics features based on the knowledge extracted from training corpora.

We found that these features could greatly improve the performance of all tasks. Besides, we adjusted the tag of segmentation result according to the reliability of each character, which also helped to enhance the performance of segmentation.

As many other NLP applications, feature plays a very important role in sequential labeling tasks. In our POS tagging task, we could only use features with high frequency, but some low-frequency features may also play a vital role in the task; good non-redundant features could greatly improve classification performance while save memory requirement of classifiers. In our further research, we will focus on feature selection on CRFs.

Acknowledgement

This research was sponsored by National Natural Science Foundation of China (No. 60773124, No. 60503070).

References

O. Bender, F. J. Och, and H. Ney. 2003. Maximum Entropy Models for Named Entity Recognition. *Proceeding of CoNLL-2003.*

A. L. Berger, S. A. Della Pietra, and V. J. Della Pietra. 1996. A Maximum Entropy Approach to Natural Language Processing. *Computational Linguistics, 22(1).*

H. L. Chieu, H. T. Ng. 2002. Named Entity Recognition: A Maximum Entropy Approach Using Global Information. *International Conference on Computational Linguistics (COLING).*

J. N. Darroch and D. Ratcliff. 1972. Generalized Iterative Scaling for Log-Linear Models. *The Annals of Mathematical Statistics, 43(5).*

J. Lafferty, A McCallum, and F. Pereira..2001. Conditional Random Fields: Probabilistic Models for Segmenting and Labeling Sequence Data. In *Proceedings of the 18th International Conf. on Machine Learning (ICML).*

R. Li, J. Wang, X. Chen, X. Tao, and Y. Hu. 2004. Using Maximum Entropy Model for Chinese Text Categorization. *Computer Research and Development, 41(4).*

H. T. Ng and J. K. Low. 2004. Chinese Part-Of-Speech Tagging: One-at-a-Time or All-at-Once? Word-Base or Character-Based? *Proceedings of Conference on Empirical Methods in Natural Language Processing (EMNLP).*

A. Ratnaparkhi. 1997. A Simple Introduction to Maximum Entropy Models for Natural Language Processing. *Institute for Research in Cognitive Science Report, 97(8).*

F. Sha and F.Pereira. 2003. Shallow parsing with conditional random fields. In *Proceedings of HLT-NAACL.*

Y. Shi and M. Wang. 2007. A Dual-Layer CRFs Based Joint Decoding Method for Cascaded Segmentation and Labeling Tasks. In *International Joint Conferences on Artificial Intelligence (IJCAI).*

C. A. Sutton, K. Rohanimanesh, A. McCallum. 2004. Dynamic conditional random fields: factorized probabilistic models for labeling and segmenting sequence data. In *International Conference on Machine Learning (ICML).*

M. Volk, and S. Clematide. 2001. Learn - Filter - Apply -- Forget Mixed Approaches to Named Entity Recognition. *Proceeding of the 6th International Workshop on Applications of Natural Language for Information Systems.*

Y. Wu, J. Zhao, B. Xu and H. Yu. 2005. Chinese Named Entity Recognition Based on Multiple Features. *Proceedings of Human Language Technology Conference and Conference on Empirical Methods in Natural Language Processing (HLT/EMNLP).*

H. Zhang, Q. Liu, H. Zhang, and X. Cheng. 2002. Automatic Recognition of Chinese Unknown Words Based on Roles Tagging. *Proceeding of the 19th International Conference on Computational Linguistics.*

R. Zhang, G. Kikui and E. Sumita. 2006. Subword-based tagging by conditional random fields for Chineseword segmentation. Companion volume to theproceedings of the North American chapter of the Association for Computational Linguistics (NAACL).

Y. Zhou, Y. Guo, X. Huang, and L. Wu. 2003. Chinese and English BaseNP Recognition Based on a Maximum Entropy Model. *Journal of Computer Research and Development, 40(3).*

CRFs-Based Named Entity Recognition Incorporated with Heuristic Entity List Searching

Fan Yang
National Laboratory of Pattern Recognition
Institute of Automation, Chinese Academy of Sciences
fyang@nlpr.ia.ac.cn

Jun Zhao
National Laboratory of Pattern Recognition
Institute of Automation, Chinese Academy of Sciences
jzhao@nlpr.ia.ac.cn

Bo Zou
National Laboratory of Pattern Recognition
Institute of Automation, Chinese Academy of Sciences
bzou@nlpr.ia.ac.cn

Abstract

Chinese Named entity recognition is one of the most important tasks in NLP. Two kinds of Challenges we confront are how to improve the performance in one corpus and keep its performance in another different corpus. We use a combination of statistical models, i.e. a language model to recognize person names and two CRFs models to recognize Location names and Organization names respectively. We also incorporate an efficient heuristic named entity list searching process into the framework of statistical model in order to improve both the performance and the adaptability of the statistical NER system. We participate in the NER tests on open tracks of MSRA. The testing results show that our system can performs well.

1 Introduction

Named Entity Recognition (NER) is one of the most important tasks in NLP, and acts as a critical role in some language processing applications, such as Information Extraction and Integration, Text Classification etc. Many efforts have been paid to improve the performance of NER.

NER task in Chinese has some differences from in English as follows. 1) There is no space between Chinese characters, which make boundary recognition more difficult. 2) In English, a capitalized letter at the beginning position of a word implies that the word is a part of a named entity. However, this kind of characteristic does not exist in Chinese.

In the paper, we will focus on two kinds of problems. 1) How to improve the performance of Chinese NER in one corpus, which contains boosting precision rate, recall rate and F-measure rate. 2) How to enhance the adaptability of a Chinese NER system, which means that a system can get a good performance on a testing set which has many differences from the training set. To solve the first problem, we should select a good model and adjust parameters carefully. But there is no framework that can solve the second problem completely.

Our goal is to find a way to solve these two problems. We select a language model to recognize Person names, and two CRFs models are used to recognize Location and Organization separately. We also try to incorporate a large-scale named entity list into the statistical model, where a heuristic searching method is developed to match the entities in the list quickly and efficiently.

2 Framework of NER System

The Input of the system is a raw text. We will apply some pre-processing such as code transformation. Then the heuristic searching will be executed to find the appearance of the entities in the named entity list. After that, two CRFs that have been trained before will be used to recognize Location and Organization based on the result of word segmentation, and a language model will be used to find Person names. All the results will be integrated at last.

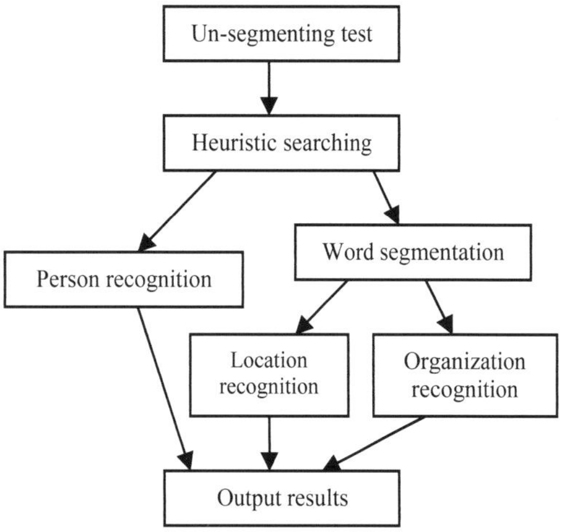

Figure 1. System Frameworks

3 System Details

3.1 Using heuristic method to search entity list

NER task meets many difficulties which come from the complexity of the construction of named entities. Named entities have flexible internal styles and external environments. Building a good model to describe the condition precisely will have many troubles. The statistical models we commonly used have some shortcomings, especially when they are adapted to a corpus of new domains or styles. We try to use an improved searching method to make up the relatively poor adaptability of the statistical models. The heuristic searching method is more flexible especially in the following two aspects. 1) Abbreviation can be matched. 2) Suffix in location and organization is universal, but it should not be taken in count when we search named entities.

The framework of the algorithm can be briefly described as follows:

1)	Building an inverse index using Chinese characters as key term;
2)	Using the text as a query to search for entities;
3)	When comes terminal condition, a heuristic function is invoked to determine whether the character sequence is an entity;
4)	When comes creation condition, a heuristic function is invoked to judge whether a new entity is created;
5)	The labeled sequence is output.

Table 1. Heuristic Searching Method

One advantage of heuristic searching method is that the heuristic function can be set to fit a special corpus. The heuristic searching method we used in Bakeoff-4 is as follows:

- Ignoring the suffix key word in Location and Organization names. For example "同方/Tongfang 公司/Corporation" and "同方/Tongfang" will get same score under this heuristic rule.
- Ignoring the Location name as a prefix in an Organization name. For example, "美国/American 通用/General Motors " and "通用/General Motors" will get same score under this heuristic rule
- Taking Abbreviation rules in consideration. For example"北京/Peking 大学/University" can be abbreviated as "北/Bei 大/Da" rather than "北京/Peking" or "大学/University"

Heuristic searching method also has such advantages as follows:

It is easy to be expanded to a corpus of new domain or style. We only need to add the entities in the new domain into list

Searching method will improve the recall performance remarkably

But the precision will be reduced for the ambiguities, i.e. whether a sequence that matches an entity in the list really constructs an entity in the text. We will disambiguate it using statistical models.

3.2 Conditional Random Fields Model

Conditional Random Fields (CRFs) is an undirected graphical model that encodes a conditional probability distribution using a given set of features. Currently it is widely used as a discriminate model for sequence labeling:

$$P(Y \mid X) = \frac{1}{Z}\exp(\sum_{c \in C}\sum_{i=1}^{k}\lambda_i f_i(y_{c1}, y_{c2}, X)) \quad (1)$$

CRFs is considered to be a very effective model to resolve the issue of sequence labeling for the following characteristics:

Because it uses a non-greedy whole sentence joint labeling method, high accuracy rate can be guaranteed and bias labeling can be avoided.

Any types of features can be integrated in the model flexibly.

Over-fitting can be avoided to some extent by integrating a priori with training data.

As a discriminate model, CRFs inherits the advantages of both Hidden Markov Model (HMM) and Maximum Entropy Markov Model (MEMM) as well.

3.3 Person names recognize

We use language model to recognize Personal names. We use character-based rather than word-based model to avoid the word segmentation errors. We construct a context model and an entity model to respectively describe external and internal features of Personal names. The details of the model are as follows:

We use a tri-gram model as the context model:

$$P(WC) \approx \prod_{i=1}^{m} P\left(wc_i \mid wc_{i-2}\ wc_{i-1}\right) \qquad (2)$$

Entity model:

$$P\left(w_{wc_{i1}} \cdots w_{wc_{ik}} \mid wc_i\right) = P\left(w_{wc_{i1}} \cdots w_{wc_{ik}} \mid B_1 \overbrace{M_2 \cdots M_{k-1}}^{k-2} E_k\right) \qquad (3)$$

$$\cong P\left(w_{wc_{i1}} \mid B_1\right) \times \prod_{l=2}^{k-1} P\left(w_{wc_{il}} \mid M_l, w_{wc_{i(l-1)}}\right) \times P\left(w_{wc_{ik}} \mid E_k, w_{wc_{i(k-1)}}\right)$$

Where B means the beginning of the entity, M means middle, E means end.

Some expert knowledge is employed to assist the recognition process of language model.

- A Chinese family name list (476) and a Japanese family name list (9189) are used to restrict and select the generated candidates.
- A list of commonly used character in Russian and European name.
- Constrain of name length: A Chinese name cannot contain more than 8 characters.

3.4 Location names recognition

Location names have some composition characters. 1) There may be some key words as suffix, such as: "市/Shi, 镇/Zheng, 湖/Hu, 山/Shan" etc. 2) Other parts of Location names are always OOV words, such as "大岗村/Dagang Village, 夫子庙/Fuzi Temple". So the right boundary of Location can be determined easily. The mainly problem in Location recognition is on abbreviation, such as "晋冀鲁豫/JinJiLuYu" is the combination of four location abbreviations. In our system, CRFs model can be supported by the heuristic searching method because it can match the abbreviation of entity in list. Using the searching method can boost the recall rate of location recognition significantly. We construct the recognition model based on the word-segmented texts.

To construct a CRFs model, we select the following features:

- A list of key word suffix is used to trigger the recognition processing.
- Using a list of indication words to restrict the boundary.
- Heuristic searching method is used to assist Location recognition.

The features we used in CRFs model is followed:

W_0	Current Word
W_{-1}, W_{-2}, W_1, W_2	Two words before and behind
$W_{-1}W_0$, W_0W_1	Bi-gram Features
POS_0	POS tag
PRE_{-1}, PRE_0, PRE_1	Pre-Position reference words
SRE_{-1}, SRE_0, SRE_1	Suf-Position reference words
Key	Has Key suffix
DIC	In Dictionary

Table 2. Features used in Location recognition

Statement:

The indication words used in Location recognition include "for-indicate" and "back-indicate" words, where "for-indicate" denotes the indicating words that occur as the left neighbor of the candidate Location named entity, while "back-indicate" denotes the indicating words that occur as the right neighbor. "for-indicate" and "back-indicate" words are got from the training corpus. We calculate the mutual information between neighbor words and location entity, and get the top N words as indication words.

$$MI(x,y) = p(x,y)\log\frac{p(x,y)}{p(x)p(y)} \qquad (4)$$

We select 1216 for-indicate words and 1227 back-indicate words. We also get 607 key words as location name suffix.

3.5 Organization names recognition

Organization name recognition is the most difficult part in NER task. The difficulties are as follows. 1) The composition of Organization name is very complex. For example: "大连/Dalian 实德/Shide 集团/Group", the first words in the entity is a location name. The second is a phonetic name which is also an OOV word and the last one is a key word as suffix.2) The boundary of organization name is hard to be classified, and the length of organization names is dynamitic. 3) Organization names are easily confused as Location names. We must use contextual information to determine its type. 4) To recognize the abbreviation of an organization is also a difficult task. So we choose the following features to solve the above problems.

- A list of key word suffix is used to trigger the recognition processing.
- Using indication words to define the boundary of organization.
- Heuristic searching method is used to assist Location recognition.

The features we used in the CRFs model are the same as used in Location model. We use the mutual information to select 513 for-indicate words and 1195 back-indicate words from training corpus. The number of key suffix words is 3129.

4 Experiments

We participate in the SigHAN Microsoft Research Asia (MSRA) corpus in open track. The table 3 is the official result of NER by our system.

	R	P	F
Person	0.9657	0.9574	0.9615
Location	0.9593	0.9769	0.968
Organization	0.8778	0.9338	0.9049
overall	0.9377	0.9603	0.9489

Table 3. SigHAN MSRA corpus test results

The training corpora we used comes from 1) 1998 People's Daily corpus; 2) the training corpus supplied by MSRA for SigHAN bakeoff 4. These two corpora have many difference and we focus on how to get a good performance both on training corpus and testing corpus. We select some general features and get assistance from the heuristic searching method. A good list is very important, which has been proved by the experimental data. We collect nearly 1 million personal names, 40 thousand location names and more than 300,000 organization names.

5 Conclusion

In the paper, we give a presentation to our Chinese Named Entity Recognition System. It uses a language mode to recognize personal names, and two CRFs models to find Location and organization separately. We also have a flexible heuristic searching method to match entity in named entity list with text characters sequence. Our system achieves a good result in the open NER track of MSRA corpus.

Acknowledgement

The work is supported by the National High Technology Development 863 Program of China under Grants no. 2006AA01Z144, the National Natural Science Foundation of China under Grants No. 60673042, the Natural Science Foundation of Beijing under Grants no. 4052027, 4073043.

References

J. Lafferty, A. McCallum, and F. Pereira. 2001. *Conditional random fields: Probabilistic models for segmenting and labeling sequence data,* In Proc. ICML 2001.

F. Sha, F. Pereira. *Shallow parsing with conditional random fields.* In Proc. NAACL 2003

HP Zhang, HK Yu, DY Xiong, Q Liu and Liu Qun. *HHMM-based Chinese Lexical Analyzer ICTCLAS.* In Proc. Second of SIGHAN Workshop on Chinese Language Processing 2003.

Youzheng Wu, Jun Zhao, Bo Xu. *Chinese Named Entity Recognition Model Based on Multiple Features.* In Proceedings of HLT/EMNLP 2005

Youzheng Wu, Jun Zhao, Bo Xu. *Chinese Named Entity Recognition Combining a Statistical Model with Human Knowledge.* In Proceedings of ACL2003 Workshop on Multilingual and Mixed-language Named Entity Recognition

A Chinese Word Segmentation System Based on Cascade Model

Zhang Jianfeng
School of Computer and Information Technology, Shanxi University
Zhangjianfeng83@163.com

Zheng Jiaheng
School of Computer and Information Technology, Shanxi University
jhzheng@sxu.edu.cn

Zhang Hu
School of Computer and Information Technology, Shanxi University
zhanghu@sxu.edu.cn

Tan Hongye
School of Computer and Information Technology, Shanxi University
Hytan_2006@126.com

Abstract

This paper introduces the system of Word Segmentation and analyzes its evaluation results in the Fourth SIGHAN Bakeoff[1]. A novel method has been used in the system, which main idea is: firstly, the main problems of WS have been classified, and then a cascaded model has been used to gradually optimize the system. The core of this WS system is the segmentation of ambiguous words and the internal information extraction of unknown words. The experiments show that the performance is satisfying, with the RIV-measure 96.8% in NCC open test in the SIGHAN bakeoff 2007.

1 Introduction

Chinese Word Segmentation is a fundamental task for some Chinese NLP tasks, such as ma chine translation, speech recognition and information retrieval etc. However, the current performance of WS is not satisfying. In WS the disambiguation processing and unknown words recognition are the two difficult problems. So, we aim at the solution of the both problem in our WS system. We participated the SIGHAN bakeoff 2007 evaluation, and a cascade model has been used in the process of word segmentation. In the WS system, the core modules are the segmentation of ambiguous words and the extraction of internal information of unknown words.

[1] This research was partially supported by the National Natural Science Foundation of China No. 60473139, the National Natural Science Foundation of China No. 60775041and the Natural Science Foundation of Shanxi Province No. 20051034.

2 System Description Introduction

Figure1 shows the workflow of our WS system. The system is made up of the following modules: small sentences segmentation, disambiguation, and unknown words recognition.

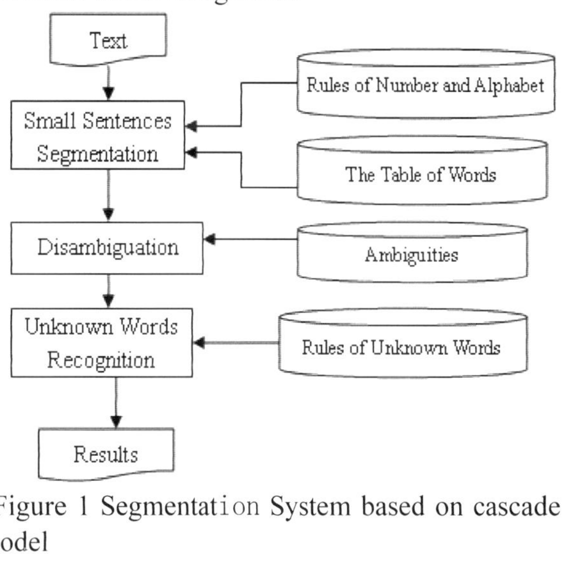

Figure 1 Segmentation System based on cascade model

In fact, ambiguities may appear between two lexical words or between a lexical word and an unknown word. Based on the observation, the disambiguation processing is prior to the unknown word recognition in the system.

2.1 Disambiguation

We classify the ambiguities into two categories: one is true-ambiguity, the other is pseudo-ambiguity. And the process of the true-ambiguity is the disambiguation emphasis.

According to the NCC training corpus, we build pseudo-ambiguity database. For pseudo-ambiguity, disambiguation can be realized through matching against the database.

We get all ambiguities from the training corpus. Pseudo-ambiguity can be solved by finding the database of pseudo-ambiguities which built on the base of the analyses of NCC corpus.

For true-ambiguities, we also build a database and use a statistical model to disambiguate.

Based on the examination of the database of ambiguities, we find that true-ambiguities appear in the two cases: (1) both frequencies of two segmentations of ambiguities are low, or the gap between the two frequencies is too large; (2) both frequencies of two segmentations of ambiguities are high. For the former case, the segmentation form corresponding to the lower frequency is saved in the database. For the latter case, both segmentations and their context are saved in the database. And the system will choose the appropriate segmentation according to the statistic model.

The statistic model can be represented as the following formulas:

$$y = \arg\max_{y} p(y \mid x)$$

$$p(y \mid x) = \sum_{i=0}^{3} bi \sum_{j} f_{ij}(x,y) p(x,y)$$

$$p(x,y) = \frac{freq(x,y)}{\sum_{x \in X, y \in Y} freq(x,y)}$$

Among the formulas, x is the context, and y is the segmentation form, fi(x,y) is the feature functions, p(x,y) is the empirical probability, and bi is the impact factor of the feature function, whose value is determined according to the Tongyici Cilin [2]. Here, (x,y) can considers not only the neighboring words but also the semantic information of the neighboring words.

The impact factor bi is defined as follows:

Let $p \in pre(S), t \in next(S)$, so

$$bi = \begin{cases} 2, & p \in pre(S) \wedge n \in next(S) \quad i=0 \\ 1, & p \in pre(S) \otimes n \in next(S) \quad i=1 \\ 0.5, & \text{e is the synonym of p, or t is the synonym of n} \quad i=2 \\ 0.25, & \text{p only has one same character with e, or n only has one same character with t} \quad i=3 \end{cases}$$

Where pre(S) is the set of the ambiguity *S*'s environment which is consist of former word; *next(S)* is the set of the ambiguity *S*'s environment which is consist of latter word; *p* is the former word of the current ambiguity, *n* is the latter word of the current ambiguity.

In the model the synonym is defined as:

Let s1 and s2 are both words. If the first three bits of s1's code in Tongyici Cilin are same with the first three bits of s2's code in Tongyici Cilin, s1 is the synonym of s2, or s2 is the synonym of s1.

2.2 Unknown Words Recognition

In the process of unknown words recognition, we consider not only the inner information of unknown words, but also the environment of unknown words.

(1) Related definition (productivity): Productivity is the weight which measures the single character's location in the whole word.

If Ai is a single character, ti is the tag of Ai's location, let ti∈{B, M, S}, $P_{Ai}(t_i)$ is the productivity of the single character Ai in the location ti, which we can write as follows:

$$P_{A_i}(t_i) = \frac{count(A_i, t_i)}{\sum_{t_i \in T} count(A_i, t_i)}$$

(2)The inner information of unknown words mainly refer to the frequent of each character as word's begin, middle and end, as show in Table 1.

Word	Tag	Freq
A1	B/M/E	447/26/3
A2	B/M/E	2/0/0
A3	B/M/E	979/76/206
. . .	. . .	. . .

Table1 inner information of unknown words [3]

[2] HIT IR-Lab Tongyici Cilin (Extended)

[3] A1, A2, A3 represent the single character of Chinese. B, M, E represent respectively current character as the word's head, middle and end.

In the process of abstracting the exterior information, we have analyzed the tagged corpus and found that feature words have an important effect on the unknown words recognition, such as: predicate, post, specific behavior verb, etc.

For example:

Post: chairman, prime minister, etc.

Job： reporter, singer, writer, etc.

Appellation： comrade, sir, miss, etc.

Specific behavior verb： say, think, nominate, investigate, etc.

The process of unknown words recognition: "A1 A2 A3A4 A5A6….." is the disambiguation results, if single character of A2 has $P_{A2}(B)>0.35$ and $P_{A2}(M)>0.35$ or $P_{A2}(E)>0.35$, A1 A2 have the possibility to be an unknown words. After that, we filter it using the exterior information in order to improve R_{oov}.

3 Performance and analysis

The performance of our system in the SIGHAN bakeoff 2007 is presented in table 2.

OPEN	R	P	F	P_{OOV}	R_{IV}
NCC	94.5	92.6	93.5	71.6	96.9

Table 2 NCC test in SIGHAN bakeoff 2007 (%)

Our system has better performance in terms of Riv measure which attributed to the module of disambiguation. However, because the unsuitable threshold choice leads lots words combined incorrectly, the Roov measure is lower.

4 Conclusions

In this paper we use a cascade model to finish WS task and the system achieves a good performance on R_{iv} measure. It indicates that this method is feasible and effective. However, the shortcoming of the system is that the method of unknown words recognition hasn't got ideal performance which will be our future research focus.

References

Maosong Sun, Jiayan Zou, etc. 1999 .*The Role of High Frequent Maximal Crossing Ambiguities in Chinese Word Segmentation*. Journal of Chinese of Information Processing, 13(1):27-37

Kaiying Liu. 2000. *Automatic Chinese Word Segmentation and POS Tagging*. Business Publishing House. Beijing.

Luo Zhiyong, Song Rou. 2006. *Disambiguation in a Modern Chinese General-Purpose Word Segmentation System*. Journal of Computer Research and Development, 6:1122-1128.

Huang Changning, Zhao Hai. 2006. *Character-Based Tagging: A New Method for Chinese Word Segmentation*. Frontiers of Chinese Information Processing: 53-63.

Linxin, NetEase. 2006. *Automatic Chinese Word Segmentation*. Proceedings of the Fifth SIGHAN Workshop on Chinese Language Processing, Sydney: 193–196.

Wu Liu, Heng Li. 2006. *France Telecom R&D Beijing Word Segmenter for Sighan Ba*keoff2006. Proceedings of the Fifth SIGHAN Workshop on Chinese Language Processing, Sydney: 193–196.

Achilles: NiCT/ATR Chinese Morphological Analyzer for the Fourth Sighan Bakeoff

Ruiqiang Zhang[1,2] and **Eiichiro Sumita**[1,2]
[1]National Institute of Information and Communications Technology
[2]ATR Spoken Language Communication Research Laboratories
2-2-2 Hikaridai, Seiika-cho, Soraku-gun, Kyoto, 619-0288, Japan
{ruiqiang.zhang,eiichiro.sumita}@atr.jp

Abstract

We created a new Chinese morphological analyzer, Achilles, by integrating rule-based, dictionary-based, and statistical machine learning method, conditional random fields (CRF). The rule-based method is used to recognize regular expressions: numbers, time and alphabets. The dictionary-based method is used to find in-vocabulary (IV) words while out-of-vocabulary (OOV) words are detected by the CRFs. At last, confidence measure based approach is used to weigh all the results and output the best ones. Achilles was used and evaluated in the bakeoff. We participated the closed tracks of word segmentation and part-of-speech tagging for all the provided corpus. In spite of an unexpected file encoding errors, the system exhibited a top level performance. A higher word segmentation accuracy for the corpus ckip and ncc were achieved. We are ranked at the fifth and eighth position out of all 19 and 26 submissions respectively for the two corpus. Achilles uses a feature combined approach for part-of-speech tagging. Our post-evaluation results prove the effectiveness of this approach for POS tagging.

1 Introduction

Many approaches have been proposed in Chinese word segmentation in the past decades. Segmentation performance has been improved significantly, from the earliest maximal match (dictionary-based) approaches to HMM-based (Zhang et al., 2003) approaches and recent state-of-the-art machine learning approaches such as maximum entropy (MaxEnt) (Xue and Shen, 2003), support vector machine (SVM) (Kudo and Matsumoto, 2001), conditional random fields (CRF) (Peng and McCallum, 2004), and minimum error rate training (Gao et al., 2004). After analyzing the results presented in the first and second Bakeoffs, (Sproat and Emerson, 2003) and (Emerson, 2005), we created a new Chinese word segmentation system named as "Achilles" that consists of four modules mainly: Regular expression extractor, dictionary-based Ngram segmentation, CRF-based subword tagging (Zhang et al., 2006), and confidence-based segmentation. Of the four modules, the subword-based tagging, differing from the existing character-based tagging, was proposed in our work recently. We will give a detail description to this approach in the following sections.

In the followings, we illustrate our word segmentation process in Section 2, where the subword-based tagging is implemented by the CRFs method. Section 3 illustrates our feature-based part-of-speech tagging approach. Section 4 presents our experimental results. Section 5 describes current state-of-the-art methods for Chinese word segmentation. Section 6 provides the concluding remarks.

2 Introduction of main modules in Achilles

The process of Achilles is illustrated in Fig. 1, where three modules of Achilles are shown: a dictionary-

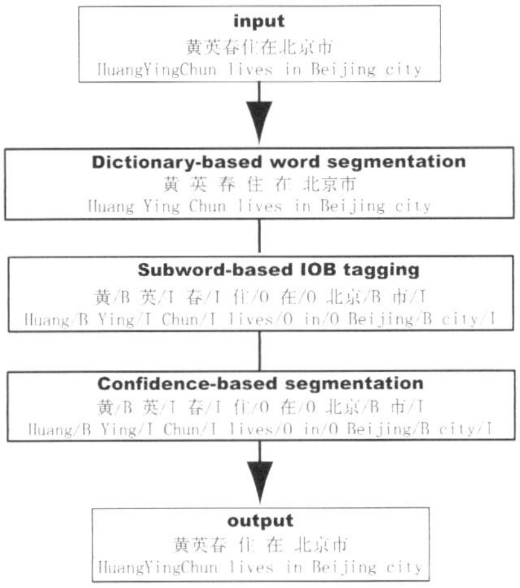

Figure 1: Outline of word segmentation process

based N-gram word segmentation for segmenting IV words, a subword-based tagging by the CRF for recognizing OOVs, and a confidence-dependent word segmentation used for merging the results of both the dictionary-based and the IOB tagging. An example exhibiting each step's results is also given in the figure.

The rule-based regular expression is not shown in the figure because this module interweaves with the other modules. This module can be called if needed at any time. The function of this module is to recognize numerical, temporal expression and others like product number, telephone number, credit number or alphabets. For example, "三万五千(35,000)", "八月(August)", "0774731301", "George Bush".

2.1 Dictionary-based N-gram word segmentation

Dictionary-based N-gram word segmentation is an important module for Achilles. This module can achieve a very high R-iv, but no OOV detection. We combined with it the N-gram language model (LM) to solve segmentation ambiguities. For a given Chinese character sequence, $C = c_0 c_1 c_2 \dots c_N$, the problem of word segmentation can be formalized as finding a word sequence, $W = w_{t_0} w_{t_1} w_{t_2} \dots w_{t_M}$, which satisfies

$$
\begin{aligned}
&w_{t_0} = c_0 \dots c_{t_0}, \quad w_{t_1} = c_{t_0+1} \dots c_{t_1} \\
&w_{t_i} = c_{t_{i-1}+1} \dots c_{t_i}, \quad w_{t_M} = c_{t_{M-1}+1} \dots c_{t_M} \\
&t_i > t_{i-1}, \quad 0 \le t_i \le N, \quad 0 \le i \le M
\end{aligned}
$$

such that

$$
\begin{aligned}
W &= \arg\max_W P(W|C) = \arg\max_W P(W)P(C|W) \\
&= \arg\max_W P(w_{t_0} w_{t_1} \dots w_{t_M}) \delta(c_0 \dots c_{t_0}, w_{t_0}) \\
&\quad \delta(c_{t_0+1} \dots c_{t_1}, w_{t_1}) \dots \delta(c_{t_{M-1}+1} \dots c_M, w_{t_M})
\end{aligned} \tag{1}
$$

We applied Bayes' law in the above derivation. Because the word sequence must keep consistent with the character sequence, $P(C|W)$ is expanded to be a multiplication of a Kronecker delta function series, $\delta(u, v)$, equal to 1 if both arguments are the same and 0 otherwise.

Equation 1 indicates the process of dictionary-based word segmentation. We looked up the lexicon to find all the IVs, and evaluated the word sequences with the LMs.

2.2 Subword-based IOB tagging using CRFs

If dictionary-based module recognizes IVs successfully, the subword-based IOB tagging can recognize OOVs. Before the subword-based tagging, the character-based "IOB" tagging approach has been widely used in Chinese word segmentation recently (Xue and Shen, 2003; Peng and McCallum, 2004; Tseng et al., 2005). Under the scheme, each character of a word is labeled as 'B' if it is the first character of a multiple-character word, or 'O' if the character functions as an independent word, or 'I' otherwise." For example, "全(whole) 北京市(Beijing city)" is labeled as "全(whole)/O 北(north)/B 京(capital)/I 市(city)/I".

We proposed the subword-based tagging (Zhang et al., 2006) to improve the existing character-based tagging. The subword-based IOB tagging assigns tags to a pre-defined lexicon subset consisting of the most frequent multiple-character words in addition to single Chinese characters. If only Chinese characters are used, the subword-based IOB tagging is downgraded into a character-based one. Taking the same example mentioned above, "全(whole) 北京市(Beijing city)" is labeled as "全(whole)/O 北京(Beijing)/B 市(city)/I" in the subword-based tagging, where "北京(Beijing)/B" is labeled as one unit.

We used the CRFs approach to train the IOB tagger (Lafferty et al., 2001) on the training data. We downloaded and used the package "CRF++" from the site "http://www.chasen.org/~taku/software." According to the CRFs, the probability of an IOB tag sequence, $T = t_0 t_1 \cdots t_M$, given the word sequence, $W = w_0 w_1 \cdots w_M$, is defined by

$$p(T|W) =$$
$$\exp\left(\sum_{i=1}^{M}\left(\sum_{k}\lambda_k f_k(t_{i-1}, t_i, W) + \sum_{k}\mu_k g_k(t_i, W)\right)\right)/Z,$$
$$Z = \sum_{T=t_0 t_1 \cdots t_M} p(T|W) \quad (2)$$

where we call $f_k(t_{i-1}, t_i, W)$ bigram feature functions because the features trigger the previous observation t_{i-1} and current observation t_i simultaneously; $g_k(t_i, W)$, the unigram feature functions because they trigger only current observation t_i. λ_k and μ_k are the model parameters corresponding to feature functions f_k and g_k respectively.

The model parameters were trained by maximizing the log-likelihood of the training data using L-BFGS gradient descent optimization method. In order to overcome overfitting, a gaussian prior was imposed in the training.

The types of unigram features used in our experiments included the following types:

$w_0, w_{-1}, w_1, w_{-2}, w_2, w_0 w_{-1}, w_0 w_1, w_{-1} w_1, w_{-2} w_{-1}, w_2 w_0$

where w stands for word. The subscripts are position indicators. 0 means the current word; $-1, -2$, the first or second word to the left; $1, 2$, the first or second word to the right.

For the bigram features, we only used the previous and the current observations, $t_{-1} t_0$.

As to feature selection, we simply used absolute counts for each feature in the training data. We defined a cutoff value for each feature type and selected the features with occurrence counts over the cutoff.

A forward-backward algorithm was used in the training and viterbi algorithm was used in the decoding.

2.3 Confidence-dependent word segmentation

Before moving to this step in Figure 1, we produced two segmentation results: the one by the dictionary-based approach and the one by the IOB tagging. However, neither was perfect. The dictionary-based segmentation produced results with higher R-ivs but lower R-oovs while the IOB tagging yielded the contrary results. In this section we introduce a confidence measure approach to combine the two results. We define a confidence measure, $CM(t_{iob}|w)$, to measure the confidence of the results produced by the IOB tagging by using the results from the dictionary-based segmentation. The confidence measure comes from two sources: IOB tagging and dictionary-based word segmentation. Its calculation is defined as:

$$CM(t_{iob}|w) = \alpha CM_{iob}(t_{iob}|w) + (1-\alpha)\delta(t_w, t_{iob})_{ng} \quad (3)$$

where t_{iob} is the word w's IOB tag assigned by the IOB tagging; t_w, a prior IOB tag determined by the results of the dictionary-based segmentation. After the dictionary-based word segmentation, the words are re-segmented into subwords by FMM before being fed to IOB tagging. Each subword is given a prior IOB tag, t_w. $CM_{iob}(t|w)$, a confidence probability derived in the process of IOB tagging, is defined as

$$CM_{iob}(t|w_i) = \frac{\sum_{T=t_0 t_1 \cdots t_M, t_i=t} P(T|W, w_i)}{\sum_{T=t_0 t_1 \cdots t_M} P(T|W)}$$

where the numerator is a sum of all the observation sequences with word w_i labeled as t.

$\delta(t_w, t_{iob})_{ng}$ denotes the contribution of the dictionary-based segmentation. It is a Kronecker delta function defined as

$$\delta(t_w, t_{iob})_{ng} = \begin{cases} 1 & \texttt{if } t_w = t_{iob} \\ 0 & \texttt{otherwise} \end{cases}$$

In Eq. 3, α is a weighting between the IOB tagging and the dictionary-based word segmentation. We found the value 0.7 for α, empirically.

By Eq. 3 the results of IOB tagging were re-evaluated. A confidence measure threshold, t, was defined for making a decision based on the value. If the value was lower than t, the IOB tag was rejected and the dictionary-based segmentation was used; otherwise, the IOB tagging segmentation was used. A new OOV was thus created. For the two extreme cases, $t = 0$ is the case of the IOB tagging while $t = 1$ is that of the dictionary-based approach. In a real application, a satisfactory tradeoff between

R-ivs and R-oovs could find through tuning the confidence threshold.

3 Part-of-speech Tagging

Our POS tagging is a traditional maximum entropy tagging (A.Ratnaparkhi, 1996) as follows,

$$p(t|h) = \frac{1}{Z(h)} exp(\sum_{i=1}^{M} \lambda_i f_i(h,t)) \quad (4)$$

where $Z(h)$ is a normalizing factor determined by requirement $\Sigma_t p(t|h) = 1$ over all t:

$$Z(h) = \sum_{t} exp(\sum_{i=1}^{M} \lambda_i f_i(h,t)) \quad (5)$$

In the evaluation, 17 categories of triggers were used, which include:

(w,t) , $(w_{-2}w_{-1}w,t)$, $(w_{-1}ww_1,t)$, (ww_1w_2,t) , $(w_{-1}w,t)$, (ww_1,t) , (t_{-1},t) , $(t_{-2}t_{-1},t)$, $(t_{-1}w_1,t)$, $(t_{-1}ww_1,t)$, $(w_{-1}w_1,t)$, (w_{-1},t) , (w_1,t) , $(t_{-1}w,t)$, $(t_{-2}t_{-1}w,t)$, $(w_{-2}w_{-1},t)$, (w_1w_2,t)

where:

w is the word whose tag we are predicting; t is the tag we are predicting; t_{-1} is the tag to the left of tag t; t_{-2} is the tag to the left of tag t_{-1}; w_{-1} is the word to the left of word w; w_{-2} is the word to the left of word w_{-1}; w_1 is the word to the right of word w; w_2 is the word to the right of word w_1 ;

In addition to the ME based POS tagging approach, we also combined a N-gram based POS tagging.

N-gram tagger is the most widely used tagger in part-of-speech tagging methods. The basic idea is to maximize a posterior probability $p(T|W)$ given a word sequence in order to find its tag sequence. By using Bayes rule, this can be transformed as to maximize $p(T) * p(W|T)$. Prior probability $p(T)$ is a N-gram language model of tag sequence. $p(W|T)$ is thought as an unigram model. In this experiment we used trigram to model $p(T)$.

Differing from the interpolation smoothing algorithm used in(Merialdo, 1994), both $p(T)$ and $p(W|T)$ were smoothed by back-off methods(Katz, 1987). Because a N-gram backoff model $P(T)$ is well-known, a backoff implementation of $p(W|T)$ was given here only. It is of the following equation.

	R	P	F	R-oov	R-iv
CKIP	0.938	0.931	0.935	0.640	0.966
CITYU	0.943	0.933	0.938	0.686	0.965
CTB	0.941	0.943	0.942	0.663	0.961
NCC	0.931	0.933	0.932	0.592	0.950
SXU	0.932	0.929	0.930	0.487	0.971

Table 1: Post evaluation of word segmentation.

$$p(w|t) = \begin{cases} \bar{p}(w|t) & \text{if } \bar{p}(w|t) \neq 0 \\ \beta(t)\bar{p}(w) & \text{otherwise} \end{cases} \quad (6)$$

where:

- $\bar{p}(w|t)$ and $\bar{p}(w)$ are discounting relative frequencies of $p(w|t)$ and $p(w)$, calculated by back-off discounting algorithm. The discount thresholds of $\bar{p}(w|t)$ and $\bar{p}(w)$ in present experiment were 12 and 1 respectively. A new word 'UNK' was added to the vocabulary, whose probability $\bar{p}(w)$ represents that of all the unseen words.
- $\beta(t)$ is a normalizing value to ensure $\Sigma_w p(w|t) = 1$.

4 Experiments

We participated all the closed evaluation of word segmentation and part-of-speech tagging. Our scores should have achieved better than the official numbers if we had submitted the results in the right format. Achilles outputs results in GBK/BIG5 format. However, the format determined by bakeoff organizers is Unicode-16. We made a lethal error when we converted the files from GBK/BIG5 to Unicode-16. Hence, the official results display wrong scores for our system's results.

We evaluated our results again in the post-evaluation. The results for word segmentation is shown in Table 1. The results for POS tagging is shown in Table 2.

Table 1 and Table 2 represent the real performance of Achilles in this evaluation. The official data do not.

5 Discussion

Achilles achieved good word segmentation results as shown in Table 1. Achilles was designed through

	Acc.	R-oov	R-iv
CKIP	0.913	0.530	0.946
CITYU	0.881	0.470	0.914
CTB	0.934	0.709	0.947
NCC	0.945	0.575	0.963
PKU	0.937	0.646	0.952

Table 2: Post evaluation of part-of-speech tagging.

three perspectives: IV recognition, OOV recognition and regular expression recognition. IV recognition can be solved at higher accuracy by dictionary-based approach. OOV recognition can be solved by IOB tagging. However, the flexible numerical and temporal expression cannot be solved by the above two methods. Hence, we used regular expression. Finally, the inconsistency of the above methods are resolved by confidence measure approach. These features causes higher performance achieved by Achilles.

6 Conclusions

This paper described systematically the main features of our Chinese morphological analyzer, Achilles. Because of its delicate design and state-of-the-art technological integration, Achilles achieved better or comparable segmentation results when it was compared with the world best segmenter.

You can get Achilles from the site "http://www.slc.atr.jp/~rzhang/Achilles.html".

References

A.Ratnaparkhi. 1996. A maximum entropy part-of-speech tagger. In *Proceedings of the Empirical Methods in Natural Language Processing Conference*.

Thomas Emerson. 2005. The second international chinese word segmentation bakeoff. In *Proceedings of the Fourth SIGHAN Workshop on Chinese Language Processing*, Jeju, Korea.

Jianfeng Gao, Andi Wu, Mu Li, Chang-Ning Huang, Hongqiao Li, Xinsong Xia, and Haowei Qin. 2004. Adaptive chinese word segmentation. In *ACL-2004*, Barcelona, July.

S. Katz. 1987. Estimation of probabilities for sparse data for the language model component of a speech recognizer. *IEEE Transactions on Acoustics Speech and Signal Processing*, 35:400–401.

Taku Kudo and Yuji Matsumoto. 2001. Chunking with support vector machine. In *Proc. of NAACL-2001*, pages 192–199.

John Lafferty, Andrew McCallum, and Fernando Pereira. 2001. Conditional random fields: probabilistic models for segmenting and labeling sequence data. In *Proc. of ICML-2001*, pages 591–598.

B. Merialdo. 1994. Tagging english text with a probabilistic model. *Computational Linguistics*, 20(2):155–172.

Fuchun Peng and Andrew McCallum. 2004. Chinese segmentation and new word detection using conditional random fields. In *Proc. of Coling-2004*, pages 562–568, Geneva, Switzerland.

Richard Sproat and Tom Emerson. 2003. The first international chinese word segmentation bakeoff. In *Proceedings of the Second SIGHAN Workshop on Chinese Language Processing*, Sapporo, Japan, July.

Huihsin Tseng, Pichuan Chang, Galen Andrew, Daniel Jurafsky, and Christopher Manning. 2005. A conditional random field word segmenter for Sighan bakeoff 2005. In *Proceedings of the Fourth SIGHAN Workshop on Chinese Language Processing*, Jeju, Korea.

Nianwen Xue and Libin Shen. 2003. Chinese word segmentation as LMR tagging. In *Proceedings of the Second SIGHAN Workshop on Chinese Language Processing*.

Huaping Zhang, HongKui Yu, Deyi xiong, and Qun Liu. 2003. HHMM-based Chinese lexical analyzer ICTCLAS. In *Proceedings of the Second SIGHAN Workshop on Chinese Language Processing*, pages 184–187.

Ruiqiang Zhang, Genichiro Kikui, and Eiichiro Sumita. 2006. Subword-based tagging by conditional random fields for chinese word segmentation. In *Proc. of HLT-NAACL*.

Author Index

Association for Computational Linguistics
209 N. Eighth Street
Stroudsburg, Pennsylvania 18360